MANAGERIAL ECONOMICS

MANAGERIAL ECONOMICS

Anand Kumar Sharma

ANMOL PUBLICATIONS PVT. LTD.
NEW DELHI - 110 002 (INDIA)

ANMOL PUBLICATIONS PVT. LTD.
H.O.: 4374/4B, Ansari Road, Darya Ganj,
New Delhi-110 002 (India)
Ph.: 23261597, 23278000

B.O.: No. 1015, Ist Main Road, BSK IIIrd Stage
IIIrd Phase, IIIrd Block,
Bangalore - 560 085 (India)
Visit us at: www.anmolpublications.com

Managerial Economics

First Published, 2006

ISBN 81-261-2687-6

PRINTED IN INDIA

Published by J.L. Kumar for Anmol Publications Pvt. Ltd., New Delhi - 110 002 and Printed at Mehra Offset Press, Delhi.

Preface

"Managerial Economics" as a paper is being taught at M.Com., M.B.A. and Other Management Courses at various universities and institutions. This book is designed as an introductory text to the above paper, encompassing vital information on all pertinent aspects. Thus the material presented here would be of interest as well as of great use to the students, teachers and professionals of Business Management. This book will provide complete knowledge of nature of business, managerial economics, theory of demand, demand forecast, production theory, cost cvurves, cost analysis, market structure, macro economics, theories of demand for money, monetary policy, fiscal policy, national income, consumption and investment function etc. to the students.

The major topics dealt in this book are—Nature of Business; Nature and Scope of Managerial Economics; Theory of Demand; Demand Forecasts; Classification of Demand or Demand Distinctions; Production Theory; Cost Curves; Cost Analysis; Market Structure; Macro Economics Concepts; Inflation; Balance of Payments; Money Supply; Theories of Demand for Money; Monetary Policy; Fiscal Policy; Measurement of National Income; Consumption Function; Investment Function etc.

It is hoped that all those will benefit from the contents of this book for whom it is meant. The author will feel amply rewarded, if motive is achieved.

Editor

Contents

1

Nature of Business

BUSINESS FIRM

In Managerial Economics we study the activities of a firm. Therefore, some people call it as a Economics of Firm. In traditional economic theory, a firm has been defined as an organisation of an individual or a group of individuals formed to obtain some economic ends or objectives. Economics of the firm deals with the theory of the firm *i.e.*, a body of economic principles selecting to the firm alone but we are mainly concerned with the application of the same principles to business. A business firm is a legal entity on the basis of ownership and contractual relationship organised for production and sale of goods and services. It may be a sole trader, partnership firm, joint-stock company or a public corporation. In modern times, the tendency is towards large scale operations. So, in the field of business also joint stock company, a form of business organisations, is more popular as management can raise as much capital as needed to run the business on a large scale.

Objectives of a Firm

A business firm exists for certain objectives or goals. The primary purpose of a business firm is to produce and distribute goods or services to the society. But a business firm can never have only one objective. To manage a business means to balance a variety of goals. Therefore, a firm may have a number of goals at a time. Here, we shall discuss different approaches to the objectives of a business firm:

1. Profit Maximisation Approach. Profit maximisation approach about the behaviour of the firm is one of the most fundamental assumptions of traditional new-classical economic theory. The attempt of the entreprenur to maximise profit is regarded as the rational behaviour of the entrepreneur. Just as the rational behaviour in the case of firms is profit maximisation, is basic to the philosophy of the free enterprise system. Adam Smith saw profit as the device which transforms the selfishness of mankind into channels of useful service.

2. Long-Term Survival. According to Rothschilf, main objective of a firm is to obtain the stage of long-run survival. A firm having this aim is always very cautious and its all decisions are safety-oriented. Such firms do not like to reap larger profits in short-run but prefer lower profits in the long run.

3. Financial Soundness. Banking concerns give preference to security to profitability. The success of any business firm also depends greatly on its business credit which in its turn depends on financial soundness. Financial soundness is the basic requirement on which the progress and success of any business firm rests in the long run.

4. Economic Self-Sufficiency. Economic self-sufficiency is a laudible aim for any business firm. Such firms do not depend on external resources for their expansion and diversification. They depend mostly on their own internal resources. Such firms plough back their profit for expansion and other programmes.

5. Sale Maximisation Objective. Prof Baumol has put forward sales of revenue maximisation as an alternative goal to profit maximisation. He offers serveral justifications of sales maximisation as a goal of the firm. Here, sales maximisation means, maximisation of the money value of sales. The objective of a firm is one of constrained maximisation where the firm maximises total revenue subject to a minimum profit constraints. According to Prof. Baumol it is the better evaluator of performance of the firm than the traditional profit maximisation model.

6. Growth Maximisation Marris Model of the Managerial Enterprise. Marris has developed a model of managerial discretion.

In Marris model the goal of the firm is the maximisation of the balanced rate of growth of the firm *i.e.* the maximisation of the rate of growth of demand for the products of the firm and of the growth of its capital supply.

The rationale for this goal is that by jointly maximising the rate of growth of demand and capital, the managers maximise their own utility as well as of the utility of the owners.

7. Satisfying Behaviour Theory. Prof Simon gave the behaviour theory of the firm which was subsequently elaborated by Cyest and March. Here the firm is not treated as a single goal, single decision unit, but as a multi-goal, multi-decision organisational coalition. The firm is regarded as a coalition of different groups which are concerned with its activity in vairous ways. The partners of this coalition are managers, workers, shareholders, customers, suppliers, bankers etc. Each group has its own set of goals. The firm tries to satisfy and not to maximise anything under the theory. In other words the firm wants to obtain a satisfactory over all performance. Thus, in the behaviour theory the firm is a satisfying organisation and not a maximising organisation. They exhibit satisfying behaviour, satisfactory profits and satisfactory sales etc. Their profits are for the purpose of expansion and other rationalization programmes.

8. Maximum Welfare of Employees. Some firms aim at providing maximum facilities to their employees. They spend huge sums for the welfare of their employees so that they might remain well contended and happy. In the long run it pays to the management in the form of increased production. Good conditions of work, fair wages, all kinds of facilities and conveniences etc. bring about favourable psychological effect on the minds of the employees and they keep away from anti production activities like go slow, strikes, mass leave etc.

9. Business Empire. Some big business houses aim at controlling the whole market. They desire to extend their sway by capturing the market. In order to achieve their object they even go to sell their products below cost price. Temporarily they forego their nominal profits in order to crush their rivals. They resort to dumping and offering incentives an reward first to capture the market and establish their business empire.

Whatever may be the aim of a business firm but the basic aim is always to earn maximum money profits. In the long run profits provide the chief measure of success.

ALTERNATE HYPOTHESIS ABOUT THE OBJECTIVES OF AN INDUSTRIAL FIRM

Objectives of a firm decide its optimum size. In economic terminology 'size' may be defined as 'scale' of production or of operation or of output.

If we look around, we notice that tailors, hair-dressers, medical practitioners, grocery-shops, hotels, departmental stores, cottage industrial establishments, a modern cotton textile factory, a sugar factory, iron and steel factory, etc., have different sizes of scales of operation or production.

Minimum Cost. It stands to reason that an industrial or commercial establishment or firm to be efficient should be such as would produce its output at minimum average cost per unit of production. The size of an industrial establishment must not be 'too small', nor 'too large', as both would have an adverse effect on its efficiency (*i.e.* on the average cost of production per unit). For example, imagine a huge vegetable shop or a hotel or a cycle repair shop at one end of the corner of a city employing hundreds of persons and with big capital investment, or imagine only one gigantic steel factory in the public sector in India employing thousands of workers and with vast amount of machinery established in some remote corner of the country. Common sense would tell that both would be inefficient which means in all the above cases, the average cost of production per unit will be very high.

Optimum Size. This would mean that in the case of different industries or different industrial establishments or units, there is an ideal size of 'optimum size' which ensures that the average cost of production per unit is the least possible and the margin of profit is the highest possible.

How does one measure the ideal or optimum size of an industrial unit? Several standards or measures are suggested, such as volume of output, value of output, total capital invested, amount of power consumed, number of workers employed, the extent of profit made, and so on.

To what extent each standard of measuring the ideal or optimum size of an industrial unit will be useful will depend upon two basic factors, namely, *(1)* nature of the industry under consideration, and *(2)* accuracy of data that become available.

The optimum size will depend upon factors such as changing conditions in techniques of production, changing state of know-how, improvement in transport and communications in marketing organization, on organising ability of entrepreneurs and so on. Thus, if there is a radical improvement in transport (as has happened at present when any part of the world can be reached in a day or messages can be instantaneously relayed to any part of the world), if raw materials can be obtained quickly from different parts of the world and products can be sold in different markets of the world quickly (as, for example, flowers and fruits are at present being sent to different countries of the world from India by aero plane), it will make a larger size than before the optimum size of a firm.

FACTORS TO DETERMINE OPTIMUM SIZE OF A FIRM

Prof. E.A.G. Robinson has grouped the forces that influence the optimum size of a firm under following heads:

(1) Technical forces which influence the optimum size from the technical point of view;

(2) Managerial forces providing 'optimum managerial unit;'

(3) Financial forces providing 'optimum financial unit;'

(4) Marketing forces providing 'optimum managerial unit'; and

(5) Factor of fluctuations and risk providing 'optimum survival unit or firm'.

It is possible that all the above five forces lead to the same 'optimum size of a firm' (that means what is 'optimum size of a firm' from the technical point of view is also the optimum size from managerial, financial, marketing point of view as also from the point of view of fluctuations and risk-taking).

But often occasions arise where the size of a firm that is optimum from the technical point of view may not be the optimum size from managerial point of view, and what is optimum size from the managerial point of view may not be optimum size from financial or marketing points of view.

In the case of such a conflict, attempts will have to be made to resolve the conflict by adopting different devices and forms of organization. As Prof. E.A.G. Robinson says. "The equilibrium may be similar either to that of tug of war of ropes, which is motionless because no one is yet pulling in either direction or to the tug-of-war which is motionless because the two teams are for the moment equally matched".

It would be instructive to discuss how the five factors or forces have their influence on the optimum size of a firm.

1. Technical Forces. Technical advances have been taking place and especially more rapidly during post-World War II period. Technological advance would generally favour increasingly larger size of an optimum firm.

Also a large-scale organization can reap advantages of division of labour and specialization. Greater the division of labour and specialization, greater the advantages due to, as pointed out by Adam Smith, increasing skill in every worker who will be specializing only in one process; saving in time which is lost in moving from one job to another (for example, from spinning to weaving and then to bleaching etc.) as different people will be specializing only in one or two processes; and thirdly, repeatedly doing the same work facilitates or results in inventions and increase in productivity and improvement in quality.

(a) Integration of Processes. Prof. Robinson also has drawn attention to the advantages of 'the integration of processes'. As sophisticated machinery begins to be used, it begins to perform a number of processes, thus reversing the above process of machinery leading to increasing division of labour or specialization and increase in quantity and improvement in quality. Thus, technological advance makes an increasingly larger size of a firm's 'optimum size'.

(b) Technological Optimum. Generally, a technologically optimum unit will be fairly large where the machinery is very large (*e.g.* railway engines, tractors, bulldozers, textile machinery, etc.) or in those industries where the product is very complex (as, for example, in the case of typewriters, watches, etc.).

On the other hand, where the product is simple and small and where personal tastes count for much, technological optimum unit will be fairly small as in the case of tailoring firms, jewellery works, bread-making, sweet meat shops, etc.

As the size of a unit grows because of advanced technology beyond a point, large size begins to have its disadvantages. For example, a double-decker bus may be more efficient than a single decker bus as it carries more passengers with only some additional use of petrol and wear and tear of tyres, etc. But though technologically possible, treble size decker bus may be uneconomical because it would mean raising the heights of bridges, raising telegraph and telephone wires to much higher heights and so on.

2. Managerial Factor. As the size of a firm becomes larger, managerial economies begin to accrue. For example, in a big firm, specialists with different abilities can be put in different but suitable types of work such as in the case of marketing specialists, accountants, purchase experts, labour welfare and industrial relations experts and so on. The high quality to their abilities can thus be fully exploited to make the firm more efficient and profitable. Experts may not be required to spend their valuable time and energy on works for which they have no aptitude and for which temperamentally they are unsuited.

(a) ***Wheels within Wheels.*** But as in the case of technological factor, in the case of management also, a stage is reached when expansion beyond that limit becomes either impossible or unprofitable. When for example, a firm becomes very large and various specialists and experts begin to take their own decisions in their specialized fields, the problem of coordinating all these decisions goes on becoming more and more difficult. With far too many experts, bureaucracy and red tape and delayed final decisions all begin to contribute to the inefficiency of the firm.

(b) ***Quick Decisions.*** On the other hand, in a small and manageable firm, decisions can be reached more or less quickly and appropriately. That is why in cases where quick decisions are necessary as in medical dispensaries, tailoring firms, hotels, petrol pumps, retail shops, etc., firms are generally small. It will be seen that even in the most highly developed and industrialized countries like the United States, Japan, France, England and Germany, small-sized firms are seen functioning quite smoothly, efficiently and prosperously amidst large-scale industrial establishments. In their cases, 'optimum size' of the firm is relatively small.

3. Financial Factor. The amount of funds a firm can raise and also borrow from banks has also great influence on the optimum size of a firm.

A large firm can take the form of a joint-stock company and raise funds by selling equity shares and is also in a better position to borrow funds from banks and through debentures from the public.

4. Selling Side. On the other hand, small firms or small industrial proprietary firms die because of limited funds at their disposal and the extremely limited funds they can raise from the money market and banks.

5. Marketing Factor. There are economies of large-scale buying and selling of products. This may make much difference to profits of a firm. In the case of large firm, there can be skilful buying which is economical as big firms have large bargaining power as against suppliers, especially small suppliers; the large firm can afford to appoint an expert purchase officer. In the case of large purchases, the quality of goods may be tested and therefore, the quality of the products will be better and therefore, can command higher prices.

On the selling side also, compared to small firms, a large firm can have a number of advantages such as appointing an advertising expert, establishing elaborate selling and servicing organisation and adopting large-scale advertisement through T.V. Advertisement is the heart of modern business and only a relatively large firm can afford effective advertisement, producing and distributing calendars, presenting diaries, using T.V. and prominent newspapers as advertisement media and so on. All these are bound to push up sales, generating higher profits.

6. Forces of Fluctuations and Risks. In every business, there is bound to be a certain amount of uncertainty and risk element. For example, the fluctuations in demand may occur because of permanent changes in tastes of people; the change in demand may be seasonal or cyclical or even erratic. Also, there may come about changes in the method of production, because highly sophisticated machinery is available in place of less efficient machinery (for example, Xerox machinery for copying in place of traditional typewriters, or automatic composing in place of hand or manual composing of types in a printing press).

(a) ***Adjustment.*** If the size of the firm is large with a considerable amount of costly machinery installed in suitable structures, specially erected for the purpose, such a firm will find it difficult to adjust itself with speed to the changing demand for its product or changing to new process of production of appearance of a new product as a substitute for what the firm is producing. In a sense, therefore, larger the size of a firm, greater will be the inflexibility and inability to adjust itself with speed to changing conditions which are taking place in all spheres like demand, supply, production techniques, appearance of new products, etc. Large-sized firm cannot easily dispose of its costly machinery which is in perfect working condition, not quickly changing its building structure to suit new machinery, nor be in a position to train its vast manpower in new skills.

(b) ***Staying Power.*** But large-sized firms have greater staying power and can wait for the wave of change to pass over or wait for a boom after a depression or seasonal conditions to change in their favour. They have the capacity to wait and absorb whatever temporary changes like seasonal changes or cyclical changes may cause, resulting in losses. From that point of view, small firms with little staying power may come to grief soon, if the depression does not lift soon or if seasonal changes continue to be adverse for long.

(c) ***Conflicts.*** Since there is the possibility of a large number of possible conflicts arising among different optima, it is just not possible to provide solutions to all possible conflicts that might arise. Here attempt will, therefore, be made only to provide illustrations as to how important conflicts might be resolved in this field.

Suppose the optimum size of a firm is not identical from technical and managerial points of view, and that technically, the optimum size is bigger than the optimum size from managerial point of view.

(d) ***Resolution.*** This conflict might be resolved by breaking the firm into several departments, each department put in charge of an expert and the work of coordination being done at the central bureau or office by a small body of experts. The second solution is to require the large-sized optimum firm from technical point of view to specialize in the production of certain items only of production and thus enable reduction in its size so that it roughly corresponds to the optimum size from the managerial point of view.

If the optimum size from the managerial point of view is larger than the optimum size from the technical point of view, the conflict can be resolved by setting up another unit under the same management to bring technical optimum firm in line with the optimum size from managerial point of view or another possibility is that the firm may expand vertically undertaking different processes of production or even trying to produce a product-mix.

(e) ***Marketing Point of View.*** If the optimum size of a firm from marketing point of view is bigger than the optimum size from technical point of view, the firm may specialize in the production of only a few items or parts on a large-scale and take advantage of marketing.

But if the optimum size from the marketing point of view is smaller than that from the technical point of view, the firm may engage a number of selling organizations to market its products.

(f) ***Technical Point of View.*** It is possible that when a firm has reached an optimum size from one point of view (say, technical), depending upon the nature of the industry, it is possible that the same size is also the optimum size from all the other factors like marketing, finance, risk and so on.

But it is also possible that in the case of a firm while the technical optimum is at the level of 50,000 units of production per year, the managerial optimum size is at the level of 40,000 units of production per year, and the marketing optimum size is only 20,000 units per year.

PROFIT MAXIMISATION ALWAYS THE AIM OF FIRM

For over a century the basic assumption of economic theory has been as much money profit as they can. Profit is basic to the philosophy of the free enterprising system. *i.e.*, private sector, Adam Smith saw profits as the device which transforms the selfishness of making into channels of useful service. "It is not from the benevolence of the butcher, the brewer or the banker that we expect our dinner" wrote Adam Smith, "but from their regard to their self interst."

The assumption of profit maximisation has served Economics well for many years, it has become clear that it now needs supplementing, though perhaps not replacing by other assumptions. Economics is perhaps too slow to alter its assumption to enable it to continue anlysisng a changing world with success. It is true that every enterpreneur enters a business or an industry primarily with a view to earn maximum profit. It is also true that the success of a firm is measured by the amount of profits it makes annually. But gradually changes are noticeable in the outlook of the firms, Now most of the firms have come to realise that earning reasonable and limited profits pays in the long run. For this change in outlook the following causes can be mentioned:

1. Forestalling Potential Competiton. If a particular firm or an industry continues to earn abnormal profits over along time, it attracts other enterpreneurs to enter in that particular business or industry. These new entrants might succeed in capturing the market. The new producers, sometimes imitate the patents and designs of popular brand and sell them comparatively at cheaper rate in the market. They may go even to persuade their faithful and talented employees to leave their old employers and join them on higher remuneration. Similarly they might also exploit the source of raw materials in their favour. To escape all these possibilities the old firms would like to be contented with only reasonable amount of profits.

2. Preventing Government Intervention. Earning excess profit by any firm smacks monopolistic condition and exploitation of consumers. Sooner or later there is an agitation against it and the attention of the Government is drawn towards nationalisation in the interest of the society or Government intervention is sought in the control of the pricing and distribution policies of the firm. In order to prevent Government intervention of any kind the business firm curtails its profit and remains content with reasonable profits.

3. Maintaining Consumer Goodwill. One of the objectives of earning rasonable profit is also to win the goodwill of the consumer. In modern times this factors has come to be realised as very important. We often come across with such advertisements in which an attempt is made to assure the consumer that only marginal profits are being earned and that the firm exists to serve the interests of the people. Some firms do not enhance the price of their products even the cost of production goes up slighly and when they are obliged to raise the price they take pains to explain apologetically under what circumstances they have been forced to increase the price.

4. Attainment of Industry Leadership. Sometimes an aspiring firm tries to attain the leadership in a particular industry. This is possible only by capturing the market or increasing the market share for its products. This is possible only if the firm manufacturing quality goods and secondly charges reasonable prices by curtailing its profits to the minimum level.

5. Accent on the Liquidity of the Firm. A good firm regards financial soundness more important than earning abnormal profits. One of the causes of this trend is that more and more resources are always needed by the firm for expansion and to enter new areas where the possibilities of making high profits are greater and this is possible only when the firm commands heavy financial resources. Therefore there is increasing an accent on liquidity rather than earning excess profits.

6. Restraining the Demand for Wage Increase. The labour unions are always on the look-out to get the rates of wages increased and they get this opportunity when they see that the firm is making abnormal profits. The usual argument is making huge profits at the cost of employees get strained. In order to avoid such situations mostly the firms prefer to make only reasonable profits.

7. Avoiding Risk. A business firms has to carry on its economy activities under conditions of uncertainties. Every decision involves risk. This fact of uncertainty makes the function of decision making and forward planning all the more complicated. Decision making has to be done through an uncertain future involving risk at every step. As far as possible management tries to avoid risk. Therefore, most of the firms remain contented with marginal profits only.

It is clear from the above analysis that profit maximisation is not always the objective of a firm. Goodwill of the firm, prevention of government intervention, attainment of leadership in a particular industry, good relations between the employers and employees, moral obligation to the society etc. are some of the other considerations which the firm keeps in view and accordingly limits its profits.

MANAGERIAL THEORY OF FIRM

For over a century the basic assumption of economic theory has been that businessmen have one aim only; to make as much money profit as they can. Economic theory has also assumed that every firm is a one man firm run by its owner who is described in economic theory as 'the entrepreneur.' These two basic assumptions do not hold good under present circumstances. Firstly, the firms do not continually seek maximum profit, though clearly profit is important. Secondly, most large firms that account for a large percentage of industrial and commercial activity in all developed countries are run by salaried managers whose interests may, and often do differ from those of shareholders. The typical modern firm is run by a group of managers, not by one-man entrepreneur. The basic points of the theory of firm are as follows:

1. Maximising Long Run Profits. Profit is a very significant functional institution of a capitalistic or a private enterprise economy. It would simply be unthinkable to have a private enterprise economy function without entrepreneurs getting profit. The main objective of a firm is to maximise long run profits. All its decision and policies are directed to achieve this objective. Profit is the difference of total revenue and total cost. Therefore, the firm always tries to increase its revenue and reduce its costs. A firm is able to earn the maximum profit at a point where the Marginal Revenue (MR) and the Marginal Cost (MC) coincide.Therefore a study of revenue and cost and analysis of average marginal revenue and cost become essential.

2. Rational Behaviour of the Firm. In the presence of several alternatives the business firm is expected to choose one which will likely to bring it the maximum profits.

3. Firm as Transformation Unit. Scarcity in relation to the aggregate demands of the people shall always be an important feature of the economic world. Human wants are unlimited and the productive resources are limited. They have to be used most economically avoiding all kinds of waste. The business executive is expected to have a complete knowledge of input-output relationship and minimum cost mix.

4. Firm Decision. A firm's decision in regard to production and pricing policies is influenced by the market conditions, the number of competitive firms in the field, the quality of their productive resources and their cost etc. As such the firm should have brought knowledge of these matters before important decisions in regard to production and prices.

OBJECTIVES AND BRANCHES OF ECONOMIC THEORY

Professor Boulding states that there are four types of economic activities which people generally perform: production, consumption, utilization and exchange. In his view tranformation of raw materials and labour into products or transportation of goods to places where they are wanted is production. Likwise, use of goods and services for the satisfaction of human wants is generally defined as consumption. Commodities are utilised as well as consumed; the satisfication, we gain from using clothes, houses, furniture etc., is not concerned with the fact that they are being worn out gradually. Finally, exchange consists of activities related to the purchase of goods, services of labour, capital and other factors of production. When labour of an individual is exchanged for money, or a house is rented, such activity is also considered as exchange.

The activities related to production, consumption, utilization and exhcange may be performed by individuals, firms and government. It is also likely that the acts of exchange may be performed between individuals or firms located in different countries. Nevertheless, whether economic activities are performed within a country or between countries a common features present in them is the use of money as a unit of account as well as a medium of exchange.

As mentioned above, economics or economic analysis provides a description of these activities. It also lists certain principles or laws which are followed by a vast majority of individuals or firms while performing their economic activities. Since the description of such activities and the principle related to them is not generally backed by empirical evidence and since these principles are based on certain assumptions, economic analysis is also described as economic theory.

PURPOSES OR GENERAL OBJECTIVES OF ECONOMIC THEORY

A theory generally attempts to answer the question "why"? As mentioned above, some sequence of events, some regularity between two or more things is observed in the real world, and a legitimate question may be asked by some one: Why this should be so? Whatever may be the answer to this question, one of the main purposes of a theory is that it enables us to predict as yet unobserved events. For example, national income theory predicts that a government budget deficit would reduce the amount of unemployment. As we shall see later, the simple theory of market behaviour predicts that under certain specific conditions the imposition of sales tax or excise duty will raise the price of the product concerned, and that the increase in price will be less than the amount of tax.

Boulding contends that economic analysis is generally undertaken with four objectives. In the first place, economic analysis enables us to study the economic phenomenan. It studies the conditions in which resources are optionally used in consumption, and in which resources are optionally distributed among various factors of production. Secondly, the economist analyses economic quantities, *i.e.*, data related to consumption production, exchange and distribution of the various goods, resources and services placed at the disposal of an individual, a firm or the entire economy. Thirdly, economic analysis is a study of the economic institutions with direct economic activity, who produces, who consumes, who exchanges? Such acts are performed by individuals on behalf of some organisations. A housewife buys grocery for a family, a manager deposits or lends funds for a bank, a producer buys raw mateirals or hires labour for his firm or a government official borrows for a government. These organizations or institutions on whose behalf economic activities of consumption, prodcution or exchange are performed, are economic organisms. Finally, economic analysis selects from economic activities such facts that are significant. Boulding argues, "Theories wihtout facts may be barren, but facts wihtout theoreis may be meaningless." Economic analysis provides theories which are helpful in interpreting the facts. Economic analysis presents certain theories—a body of economic principles—in the absence of which one might obtain a wide range of complex and contradictory interpretation of facts. For example, for exchange one may need three relevant facts, namely Px, Dx and Sx (price, demand and supply). Economic theory would enable us to identify only the relevant facts and ignore the ones which have nothing to do with the economic problems under review.

Describing the signifiance of economic theories, richard D. Ripsey contends that they really help us in putting our observations in a well defined order. He argues: "Without theories we would have only a shape of meaningless observations" what appears to be an obvious link between an event and the changes in the behaviour of certain economic units, can be explained only with the help of a theory.

Leftwich maintains that economic theories, and hence economic analysis, generally have the following purposes:

(i) they are used as a means of understanding how the economy of a country operates, and whether or not it operates efficiently,

(ii) they are used for predictions, or help in predicting the impact of various changes in the economic variables on a consumer a firm or on the entire economic situation and

(iii) they are used as a basis for prescribing policy measures.

Briefly stated, economic analysis describes the mode of which an individual consumer, producer or resource-owner ought to behave. The implicit assumption of all economic theories is that every micro-economic unit of an economy bahaves rationally. That is, subject to the availability of resources at his every indivdiual attempts to reach the optimum; a consumer makes an attempt to get maximum satisfaction from his given level of income whereas a firm tries to maximize its profit. Likewise, a producer tries to secure an optimum combination of resources so as to minimize the per unit cost of production. To quote Robbins, economics or economic analysis explain how scarce resources are used by an individual or by a society for the satisfaction of unlimited ends (wants). It provides theories or principles which depict the rational behaviour of an individual unit, and/or helps in identifying the optimum levels of gross national product and employment of human and natural resources.

However, economic theories may depict the behaviour of an individual of the entire economic system. Thus, principles or theories governing the optimizing behaviour of a consumer may be significantly different from those portraying the equilibrium level of employment or national income. J. Hadar explains that economic theory consists of three levels which may be thought of as forming a payramid. At the bottom of this pyramid are the theories related to individual decision-making units. They include theories of the firm and theories of consumer behaviour.

The second level consists of market theories for which the theories of individual bahaviour serve as building stocks. These theories are generally concerned with the impact of the decisions of individual traders on the market price and on quantities exchanged. Thus market theories deal with the allocation of resources and the distribution of goods among various economic units. Lastly, on the top of the pyramid, we have the theory of general equilibrium in which all markets of the economy are integrated into a whole for the purpose of studying the workings of the entire system.

Yet, the theoretical approach does not give a true picture of the real world. This is particularly true of the theories related to micro-economic behaviour of individual and firms. A micro-economic theory is abstract because it does not and cannot encompass all the economic data of the real world. Consequently, we single out what appear to be the most relevant data and from these we build up an overall theory of how the price system operates. Thus, in order to give a specific prediction on the basis of a theory, an economist has to specify those conditions in which only such predictions would come true. In other words, predictions given by an economist are usually conditional. For example, he would say : If there is a partial failure of wheat crop, and also, if the demand for wheat remains unchanged, then the price of wheat would go up. The prediction says that price will go up whenever a partial crop failure occurs. We may argue that the theory is unbounded both in time and space. Yet, for proving that predictions given by theory are always true, we must make unlimited observations.

Referring to the purposes of micro-economic theory Bilas also contends that it (micro-economic theory) uses abstract model in an attempt to see how product prices are established and how resources are allocated to various uses. Yet, he adds, the use of theory should enable the possessor to determine which of many factors are particularly relevant to the problem being studied. Bilas emphasizes that economic theory is related only to economic problems, *i.e.*, the problems which involve utilization of scarce resources for the satisfaction of unlimited ends. Further, economic theory also suggests the manner in which resources are used most efficiently at the micro as well as at the macro levels. Finally, economic theory can be used as the basis for prediction.

Though theoretical approach to an economic problem may not give a true picture of the real world, and though the predictions given by economic theory are generally conditional, yet a theory is useful like a road map which does not depict every bump in the road or every bend. Further all economic theories present an abstraction from reality. If we do not abstract, we would merely be duplicating the world and would add nothing to our understanding. Economic theory has the capacity to predict the implications of an event or a policy under certain assumptions. A theory or an underlying assmption can be tested empirically. What is, howover, important is to gather adequate facts which are relevant to the problems being studied.

BRANCHES OF ECONOMIC THEORY

It was stated above that an economic theory deals with an economic problem. An economic problem arises when a decision-making individual, society or a planning agency confronts a problem of choice, *i.e.*, a problem of using scarce means for satisfying the unending human wants. There are two main branches of economic theory. They are commonly called macro-economic theory and micro-economic theory. Economic theory is also classified into static and dynamic analysis. Finally, economic theory is classified into positive versus normative analysis. On the basis of methodology followed by an economist, economics may be identified as a deductive or inductive analysis.

Macro and Micro Economics. Micro-economics relates to individual decision-making units such as a consumer, a firm or an owner of the factorless of production. A micro-economic theory explains how an individual optimizes the use of available resources for the attainment of his objective. Thus, micro-economics explains how would a consumer maximize his satisfaction within the given income constraint, or how would a firm maximize its level of output (or profit) within the given resources at its disposal. Likewise, micro-economics may also explain the bahaviour of an individual resource owner whose general objectives would be to attain maximum income (or level of satisfaction) for the land, labour of capital placed under his command.

The term "micro" comes from the Greek mikros which means small. This implies that micro-economic theory analyses the behaviour of a single economic unit—a consumer, a firm or a resource owner. The implicit assumption in micro-economic analysis is that all consumers, all firms and all resource owners behave identically. In other words, we study the behaviour of a representative consumer, a representative firm or a representative resource owner.

Micro-economic theory is also known as price theory, as it is primarily concerned with the flow of goods and services from business firms to households, the flow of productive services from households to business firms, the composition of these flows, and the pricing of goods and productive services. It is believed that prices of productive services serve as a major guide in the allocation of productive services (resources or factors) among a set of goods to be produced. Conversely, prices of goods help in determining the level of output in respect of each commodity and the level of satisfaction to be attained by every consumer in the society. For example, if the price of a good, X, is raised while that of Y remains unchanged, more productive resources will flow into the production of X and the output of X will increase in relation to Y. By the same token it may be argued that if wage rates fall while the rate of interest remains unchanged, more units of labour will be used in the production of different goods and services.

Thus, micro-economic or price theory may also be a theory of demand and/or supply in respect of goods and productive services. It may explain how does an individual consumer or a firm attains equilibrium if the product and factor prices are determined exogenously by the aggregate demand and supply in the product and the input markets.

On the other hand, macro-economic theory studies aggregates of individual decision-making units. Thus, aggregtate consumption, investment, employment and gross national product (GNP) comes under the domain of macro-economic theories. Likewise, general price level or interest rate determination would constitute an integral part of macro-economics. Briefly stated, macro-economics simplifies the task of analysing the overall working of a price mechanism. Micro-economics explains the particular flows of expenditure on different capital goods that go from firm (and households) to other firms; and those on different factors that go from firms to households. However, macro-economics aggregates the particular flows of expenditure.

Micro vis-a-vis Macro-Economic Equilibrium. Anything is in equilibirum when the forces acting on it are such that it has no tendency to change its conditions. A ball is in equilibrium in relation to its surrounding if it is at rest on round. Conversely, a ball rolling on the ground or falling through the air is not in equilibrium; the forces acting upon it do not balance, and therefore it changes position. By the same token it may be said that any quantity—say a price—is in equilibrium if there are not net forces acting upon it, on balance; tending to change it one way or another.

A micro-economic equilibrium is attained when a consumer or a producer has no incentive to change his existing position. Assuming that the objective functions of a consumer is to maximize his satisfaction within the given budget (income) constraint, he will be in equilibrium when the marginal utility of every good is equal to its price; or when the ratios of marginal utilities and prices in respect of all goods are equal. Similarly a firm is in equilibrium when it obtains maximum profit by equating the marginal revenue of its product with its marginal cost. A resource owner can be said to be in equilibrium when his incremental income (or the satisfaction received from it) is equal to the marginal disutility of parting with the factor (s) in his command. To sum up, micro-economic equilibrium exists when *(i)* a consumer has attained maximum satisfaction, *(ii)* a firm has maximized its profit, or *(iii)* a resource owner has obtained maximum income. Other things remaining the same, no individual producer or consumer will have tendency to change his position once equilibrium is arrived at.

Macro-economic equilibrium also involves a balance between the market demand and market supply in respect of a product or a factor of a product. Such a balance between demand and supply yields the equilibrium or the market price for the good or the factor in questions. It may be noted that while analysing the behaviour of an individual economic unit, the market prices of goods and productive services are generally assumed to be exogenously given. In other words, it is generally assumed that an individual consumer or a single firm has no capacity to influence the market price. However, a monopolist or a monoponist can certainly influence the equilibrium (market) price and in that situation his own price is deemed as the equilibrium (market) price.

Quite different from micro-economic equilibrium is the macro-economic equilibrium. As stated above, macro-economic deals with the aggregate values, *i.e.*, aggregate consumption (C), aggregate investment (I), foreign trade etc., or else it deals with the level of employment and general price level.

Macro-economic equilibrium therefore exists, if *(i)* aggregate spending (C+I) is equal to aggregate income (Y), *(ii)* aggregate supply of labour is equal to aggregate demand for labour, *(iii)* total savings are equal to total investment. Generally it is argued that for macro-economic equilibrium wages are flexible such that there is no involuntary unemployment in the economy; where prices are flexible, there is no excess demand or supply. In other words, full employment is ensured if only prices and wages are perfectly flexible. However, J.M. Keynes had dissented from this classical line of economic thought and argued that due to strong trade unionism wages in the modern age are inflexible downward. For this reason, Keynes contemplated the attainment of a 'less than full employment equilibrium.'

If any one of more forces act upon the dependent variable, it may attain a new equilibrium. Thus, a change in price would shift the equilibrium of the consumer or the firm. Likewise, a change in consumer's income will also shift his equilibrium position. In the macro-economic world, any change in money supply, rate of interest or wage rate is likely to reflect in a change in the aggregate level of income and employment.

Interdependence of Micro and Macro-Economics. Micro-economics deals with the behaviour of an individual consumer of firm, whereas macro-economics is concerned with the aggregates of individual decision-making units. Apparently, they appear independent of each other. As noted above, the size of an individual unit is assumed to be so atomistic that generally it is assumed to have no bearing on the aggregate demand, supply or prices. An individual may become richer, or economically weaker; or he may win a lottery ticket. In either case, the increase in individual's wealth has no macro-economic implications, albeit for his own welfare it has. On the other hand, the GNP of a country may increase or the level of employment may rise, yet it has no bearing on an individual.

However, despite their sharp differences, the two analyses are not mutually exclusive. Generally, micro-economic units do exert a direct influence on the macro-economic variables and vice versa. This is more so because generally micro-economic analysis is based on the assumption that we are studying the behaviour of a representative is maximized if only each micro units optimizes the use of resources at its disposal. Conversely, from macro-economic point of view welfare is maximized if only the nation is capable of producing at the full employment level. When the GNP (and implicitly the level of employment) increases, nation's economic welfare is said to have increased. At the same time it is also assumed that the distribution of GNP among different micro-economic (individual) unit has remained unchanged, and therefore, increase in GNP is assumed to have increased the welfare of individual units as well.

Yet, in reality macro-economic variables are distinctly apart from macro-economic variables. GNP may rise, yet a larger fraction of such increased output may be appropriated by a few individuals, thus rendering others poorer and denying them the benefits of increased GNP. Likewise, an individual may optimize the use of his resources, yet the economy may not be operating at the full employment level. Black marketeers increase their wealth by exploiting the poor, yet the nation's GNP may remain unchanged. These are only few facts of life which explain the diversion of micro-economic welfare from its macro-economic counterpart.

ROLE OF A MANAGERIAL ECONOMIST

One of the principal objectives of any management in its decision-making process is to determine the key factors which will influence the business over the period ahead. In general, these factors can be divided into two categories : *(i)* external, and *(ii)* internal. The external factors lie outside the control of management because they are external to the firm and are said to constitute business environment. The internal factors lie within the internal scope and operations of a firm and hence within the control of management, they are known as business operations.

To illustrate, a business firm is free to take decisions about what to invest, where to invest, how much labour to employ and what to pay for it, how to price its products, and so on. But all these decisions are taken within the framework of a particular business environment, and the firm's degree of freedom depends on such factors as the government's economic policy, the actions of its competitors and the like.

Environmental Studies. An analysis and forecast of external factors constituting general business conditions, *e.g.*, prices, national income and output, volume of trade, etc., are of great significance since every business firm is affected by them. Certain important relevant questions in this connection are as follows:

(1) What is the outlook for the national economy? What are the most important local, regional or world-wide economic trends? What phase of the business cycle lies immediately ahead?

(2) What about population shifts and the resultant ups and downs in regional purchasing power?

(3) What are the demand prospects in new as well as established markets? Will changes in social behaviour and fashions tends to expand or limit the sales of a compnay's products, or possibly make the products obsolete?

(4) Will the availability and cost of credit tend to increase or decrease buying? Are money or credit conditions ahead likely to be easy or tight?

(5) What are prices of raw materials and finished products are likely to be?

(6) Where are the market and customer opportunities likely to expand or contract most rapidly?

(7) Will overseas markets expand on contract, and how will new foreign government legislations effect operation of the overseas plants?

(8) Is competition likely to increase or decrease?

(9) Will Reserve Bank's decisions stimulate or depress industrial production and consumer spending? How will these decisions affect the company's cost, credit, sales and profits?

(10) What is the outlook regarding government's economic policies and regulations? What about changes in defence expenditures, tax rates, tariffs and import restrictions?

Reasonably accurate answers to these and similar questions can enable managements to chalk out more wisely the scope and direction of their own business plans and to determine the timing of their specific actions. And it is these questions which present some of the areas where a managerial economist can make effective contribution.

Business Operations. A managerial economist can also be helpful to the management in making decisions relating to the internal operation of a firm in respect of such problems a price, rate of operation, investment, expansion or contraction. Certain relevant questions in this context would be as follows :

(1) What will be a reasonable sales and profit budget for the next year?

(2) What will be the most appropriate production schedules and inventory policies for the next six months?

(3) What changes in wage and price policies should be made now?

(4) How much cash will be available next month and how should it be invested?

Specific Functions. A further idea of the role managerial economists can play can be had from the following specific function performed by them as revealed by a survey pertaining to Britain conducted by K.J.W. Alexander and Alexander G. Kemp :

(1) Sales forecasting.

(2) Industrial market research.

(3) Economic analysis of competing companies.

(4) Pricing problems of industry.

(5) Capital projects.

(6) Production programmes.

(7) Advice on foreign exchange.

(8) Economic analysis of agriculture.

(9) Analysis of underdeveloped economies.

(10) Security/investment analysis and forecasts.

(11) Advice on trade and public relations.

(12) Advice on primary commodities.

(13) Environmental forecasting.

It is thus clear that in practice managerial economists perform many and varied functions. However, of these, marketing function, *i.e.*, sales forecasting and industrial market research, has been the most important. For the purpose, they may compile statistical records of the sales performance of their own business and those relating to their rivals, carry out analysis of these records and report on trends in demand, their market shares, and the relative efficiency of their retail outlets. There are, of course, differences in the relative importance of the various functions performed from firm to firm and in the degree of sophistication of the methods used in carrying them out.

Economic Intelligence. Besides these functions involving sophisticated analysis, managerial economist may also provide general intelligence service supplying management which economic information of general interest such as competitors' prices and products, tax rates, tariff rates, etc. In fact, a good deal of published material is already available and it would be useful for a firm to have some one who understands it. The managerial economist can do the job with competence.

❒

2

Nature and Scope of Managerial Economics

FUNDAMENTAL ECONOMIC CONCEPTS OF MANAGERIAL ECONOMICS

Economics offers a number of concepts and analytical tools which can be used and are generally used by modern business organisations in business decision making process. Following are the five main concepts:

1. Opportunity Cost. Opportunity cost of a decision is the sacrifice of alternative courses of action for that decision. Opportunity cost may be defined as the revenue foregone or opportunity lost by not using the resources in second best alternative use. In other words opportunity cost refers to the amount of revenue sacrificed by not using the resources in the best alternative. These are also called imputed costs. Opportunity cost requires measurement of sacrifice. If measures the sacrifice made for making (taking) dicision. For example, a farmer has chosen to produce cotton with same inputs instead of paddy. Therefore opportunity cost of a quintal cotton is the amount of output of paddy given up.

It is said rightly too that opportunity cost are the only relevant costs to take business decisions. It determines the soundness of decision. The concept is subject to the following limitations:

(a) In many cases a specific factor has no opportunity cost

(b) The foregone alternative cannot be quantitavely measured. We cannot know in advance how much a farmer would lose by not producing wheat instead of rice.

(c) Immobility of factors of production makes this concept a limited concept

(d) The concept is based on perfect competition which is unreal.

2. Incremental Principle. Incremental concept is closely related with the marginal cost and marignal revenue concepts of economic theory. Marginal cost is the cost of producing an additional unit of a commodity. Whereas marginal revenue is the revenue from the sale of an additional unit of the commodity. But M.C. and M.R. cannot be calculated in all situations because some units are indivisible. Therefore, incremental principle is used in business in place of marginal concepts in situations where input is changed in sufficient quantity.

Incremental concept means impact of alternative decision on cost and revenue. In other words, incremental principle involves estimating the impact of alternative decision on cost and revenue resulting from change in the level or nature of activity, change in price, new products, procedure, design, investment etc. There are two components of incremental concept:

(a) Incremental Cost. Incremental costs are added costs of a change in the level or nature of activity or any kind of change. Incremental cost may be defined as change in total cost consequent upon a decision. It measures the difference between old cost and new cost. In symbols:

$$IC = C_2 - C_1 - \Delta C$$

where IC = incremental cost

C_2 = denotes new total cost

C_1 = denotes old total cost

MC can also be computed:

$$MC = \frac{C_2 - C_1}{Q_2 - Q_1} - \frac{\Delta C}{\Delta C}$$

Incremental cost appears to be more relevant in decision-making at firm level.

(b) Incremental Revenue. Incremental revenue can be defined as the change in total revenue resulting from a decision In symbols:

$$IR = R_2 - R_1 = \Delta R$$

where IR = indicates incremental revenue

R_2 = indicates new total revenue

R_2 = indicates old total revenue

ΔR = Change in revenue

$$MR = \frac{R_2 - R_1}{Q_2 - Q_1} - \frac{\Delta R}{\Delta Q} = \frac{\delta R}{\delta R}$$

A decision is profitable if :

(i) It increases revenue more than cost or it reduces cost more than revenue.

(ii) It increases some revenue more than it decreases some other revenue.

(iii) It decreases some cost more than it increases some other cost.

BUSINESS IMPLICATION OF INCREMENTAL CONCEPT

Generally businessmen are of the view that to make an overall profit they must make profit on every job (activity). Consequently, they often refuse orders that do not cover full cost. But incremental princple shows that such a policy or action is inconsistent with profit maximization in short run. It can be illustrated with an example.

Suppose a firm gets a new order (for purchase of goods) which will give income equal to Rs. 6000/- (additional revenue). The full cost computed by accountant is more than Rs. 6000/-. Estimated cost to execute the order is

Labour Cost	Rs. 1600
Material Cost	Rs. 2500
Overhead Cost	Rs. 1900
Selling and Admi. Expenses	Rs. 800
Full Cost	Rs. 6800

The order appears to be unprofitable. But now suppose there is idle productive capacity which can be utilised to execute the order. Suppose due to idle capacity the order add to overhead cost only Rs. 1000 and it incurs additional labour cost only Rs. 1000/-. Then the incremental cost of executing the order will be as under :

Add about cost	1000
Material Cost	2500
Add Overhead Cost	1000
Incremental Cost	4500
Profit	1500

Incremental reasoning does not mean that the firm should accept all orders at price which covers their incremental cost. The acceptance of the order depends on existence of spare productive capacity and idle labour that would go unutilised in the absense of more profitable opportunity. Earley's study of "excellently managed" large firm suggests that progressive corporation do not make formal use of incremental analysis but observed behaviour being variable, thus no generalisation. Observed behaviour is different.

This principle should be wisely applied.

3. Time Perspective. Time element is of crucial importance in business decisions. Business decisions have both short-run and long-run impact on costs and revenue. The crucial problem in decision-making is to maintain right balance between the short-run and long-run business perspectives. In other words while taking decision management should take long range view of effect on cost and revenue rather than merely a short-run view. A decision may be made on the basis of short-run consideration but as time passes, have long run repercussion which makes it more or less profitable that at first sight (seemed).

Suppose there is excess productive capacity in a firm. An order of 2000 units comes to management notice. The customer is willing to pay Rs. 5/- per unit or Rs. 1000/- for the whole lot but no more. Suppose the short-run incremental cost (ignoring FC) is Rs. 4/-. Therefore contribution to overhead and profit is Re. 1/- per unit (Rs. 2000). But there may be long-run repercussions and these must be kept in mind.

(a) Series of Orders. If the management commits itself to a series of repeated orders at this rate (Rs. 5), in tie fixed cost may become variable. For example, it will eventually become necessary to replace the machinery. Moreover, accumulation of orders may require addition to productive capacity with consequent added depreciation and cost of supervision.

(b) Discrimination. If other customers come to know about the low price, they would demand to supply the goods at low price. Such customers may complain of unfair treatment and discrimination. They may opt to patronise other firm. The reduction of prices under condition of excess capacity may adversely affect the goodwill of the firm.

It is, therefore, important to give due considertion to the time perspective. The principle of time perspective may be stated as, "decision should take into account both short-run and long-run effect on cost and revenue and maintain a right balance between the long-run and short-run perspectives.

4. Discounting Principle. The principle has its genesis in valuing the money received at different points of time. It is used to compute the present value of money which is received to be in future. Many transactions in value making or receiving cash payments at various future data. It is a technique to know the present value of money to be received or paid at future date.

The value of Rs. 100/- one year hence is not equal to Rs. 100 today, but less than that. But then how much money today is equal to Rs. 100 of one years hence. To find out this we will have to take into account the relevance of interest. Then we will discount Rs. 100 at that rate of interest to ascertain the value of 100 rupees one year hence or two years hence.

This discounting principle is:

$$PV = FV\left[\frac{1}{(1+r)^n}\right]$$

$$PV = \frac{1000}{(1+r)^n} = \frac{1000}{1+1} 909/90$$

$$FV_n = S\,(1+r)^n$$

Here : FV_n is future value in n years

S is the present amount

Example :

$$FV = 1000\,(1+r)^5$$

$$= 1000\,(1.1)^5 = 1610.51 \text{ Rupees}$$

The process of reducing future value to their present value is often referred to a discounting. The interest rate is (in the present problem) use a discount rate. This concept is highly useful in making investment decisions.

5. The Equimarginal Principle. The Equi-marginal principle states that a factor (input) should be allocated in different uses in such a way that the value added by the last unit is the same in all use.

Suppose a firm is involved in three activities viz., A, B and C Activity. All these activities require services of labour. The firm should allocate the available labour in these activities in such a manner that the value of marginal product of labour is equal in all the three activities. In symbols:

$$VMP_{La} = VMP_{Lb} = VMPl_{LC}$$

Here L indicates labour and a, b, c represent activities. If the firm finds that value of Marginal Productivity is greater in A use than in B or C use, then optimum use of labour is not achieved. This means that it will be profitable to shift labour from the low marginal value activity to a high marginal value activity.

If $VMP_{La} = 60$ and $VMP_{Lb} = 40$

It must be noted that :

1. Value of marginal productivity are not of incremental cost.
2. If the revenue resulting from the addition of labour is to be received in future, the revenue should be discounted before comparison in alternative activites is made.
3. The measurement of VMP may have to be corrected if the expansion of an activity requires a reduction in the price of the output.
4. If any VMP belongs to future then it should be discounted before comparison.

NATURE OF MANAGERIAL ECONOMICS

The main function of management of a business organisation is decision-making and forward planning. Decision-making and forward planning go hand in hand with each other. Decision-making is a process selecting a course of action out of alternative course of actions available to a firm to realise its ojectives. Forward planning, on the other hand, refers to formulating plans for the future to implement of decisions taken. The firm is to choose a course of action out of alternative course of actions because resources of the firm are limited. The management has to take a number of decisions such as financial dcision, production decisions, marketing decision, decision to purchase raw material, inventory control, etc. These decisions should not contradict each other, but should be in consonance with the overall objectives of the firm. Therefore, the management has to co-ordinate its different decisions.

The function of decision-making and forward planning is very complex because the modern business world is full of risks and uncertainties. Risk is involved because future is uncertain and no one can predict the future accurately. Before taking any decision management has to consider past records, current informations and future predictions. As plans are implemented overtime, more facts come into light and decisions or plans are revised in the light of such new facts and a different course of action may be adopted. Management, thus, is engaged in a continuous process of decision-making.

The above discussion reveals that all managerial decisions involve some degree of choice and they are, therefore, essentially economic in nature. Different economic theory and logic aided by certain other disciplines, like accountancy, statistics and mathematics may solve or at least throw some light on the problems confronted by business management. Thus management economics applies economic theory and logic to help the management in making business policies.

Thus, we can say that:

1. Managerial Economics is both a Science and Art. As science, it establishes cause and effect relationship by collecting, classifying and analysing the facts on the basis of certain principles. For example, it coordinates production and distribution by analysing internal and external factors concerning the firm. Such analysis is based on certain principles of economics, accounting and statistics. Managerial economics is positive science because it answers the questions what are present business conditions and problems and what changes in business condition are expected in times to come. It is also normative science because it tells what goals a firm should

pursue and what business policies and programmes it should adopt to achieve these objectives.

Managerial economics is also an art. Art offers the mode of doing a particular thing. Managerial economics applies economic theory and other disciplines to analyse the business problems faced by an organisation. In the process of decision-making management chooses a course of action out of alternative course of actions by applying managerial economics.

SCOPE OF MANAGERIAL ECONOMICS

Managerial economics is the application of economic theories in the process of decision-making and formulation of future plans for performing the above two functions. The management will have to analyse the business problems that are faced by the firm. Business problems involving decision- making and forward planning may be divided into two main categories :

(a) Operational or internal problems.

(b) External or environmental problems.

Therefore, the scope of managerial economics includes all those economic theories and concepts which can be used to analyse the operational and environmental problems to take appropriate business decision and to formulate future plans. Thus, the principles relating to following topics constitute the scope of subject matter of managerial economics:

1. Demand Analysis. A business firm is an economic organisation which is engaged in transforming productive resources into goods that are to be sold in the market. A major part of managerial decision-making depends on accurate estimates of demand. A forecast of future sales serves as a guide to management for preparing production schedules and employing resources. It will help management to maintain or strengthen its market position and profit-base. Demand analysis also identifies a number of other factors influencing the demand for a product.

2. Cost Analysis. Cost estimates are most useful for management decision. The different factors that cause variations in cost estimates should be given due considertion for planning purpose. There is the element of uncertainty of cost as other factors influencing cost are either uncontrollable or not always known. If one is able to measure cost it is very important for more sound profit planning, cost control and often for sound pricing practices.

3. Profit Management. The chief purpose of a business firm is to earn the maximum profit. There is always an element of uncetainty about profits because of variation in costs and revenues. If knowledge about the future were perfect, profit analysis would have been very easy task. But in this world of uncertainty expectations are not always realised. Hence profit planning and its measurement constitute the most difficult part of Managerial Economics. Under profit management we study nature and management of profit, profit policies and techniques of profit planning like Break Even Analysis.

4. Pricing Practices and Policies. As price gives income to the firm, it constitutes as the most important field of Managrial Economics. The success of a business firm depends very much on the correctness of the price decisions taken by it. The various aspects that are dealt under it cover the price determination in various market forms, pricing policies, pricing method, differential pricing, productive and price forecasting.

5. Capital Management. The problems realting to firm's capital investments are perhaps the most complex and troublesome. Capital management implies planning and control of capital expenditure because it involves a large sum and moreover the problems in disposing the capital assets are so complex that they require considerable time and labour. The main topics dealt with under capital management are cost of capital, rate of return and selection of projects.

The topics discussed under headings from 1 to 5 are related with operational issues of a firm.

6. Analysis of Business Environment. The environmental factors influence the working and performance of a business undertaking. Therefore the managers will have to consider the environment factors in the process of decisions-making. Decisions taken in isolation of environmental factors would prove harmful to the firm. Therefore, the management must be fully aware of economic environment, particularly those economic factors which constitute the business climate. Nevertheless, the management must have an idea of social and political trends. Also the main factors that affect the business climate are; general trend in national income and consumption expendiure, general prices, trends, trading relations with other countries, trends in world market, economic and business policies of the government, industrial relations etc.

Certain macro-economic theories such as income and employment theory. monetary theory etc. help in analysing business climate. Analysis of monetary policy, fiscal policy, industrial policy, foreign trade policy and other direct controls also help in forecasting business climate. Therefore macro-economic theory and government policies are also included in the scope of managerial economics.

7. Allied Disciplines. The concepts that help the management in taking business decisions are quantitative in nature. Therefore, mathematical tools are widely used in determining relationships between economic variables. The linear programming techniques, which is mathematical, is used by firms to maximise or minimise their objective functions. Similarly statistical and accounting principles are used for taking business decision. Therefore, mathematical tools, statistical technique and accounting principles that are used in analysing business problems also come under the scope of Managerial Economics.

DIFFERENCE BETWEEN MANAGERIAL ECONOMICS AND TRADITIONAL ECONOMICS

Managerial Economics has been described as economics applied to decision-making. It may be viewed as a special branch of Economics. However, the main points of differences are the following:

(1) The Traditional Economics has both micro and macro aspects whereas Managerial Economics is essentially micro in character.

(2) Traditional Economics is both positive and normative science but the Managerial Economics is essentially normative in nature.

(3) Traditional Economics deals mainly with the theoretial aspect only whereas Managerial Economics deals with the practical aspect.

(4) Under Traditional Economics we study only the economic aspect of the problems but under Managerial Economics we have to study both the economic and non-economic aspects of the problems.

(5) Traditional Economics studies human bahaviour on the basis of certain assumptions but these assumptions sometimes do not hold good in Managerial Economics as it concerns mainly with practical problems.

(6) Managerial Economics studies activities of an individual firm or unit. Its analysis of problems is micro in nature, whereas Traditional Economics analyses problems both form micro and macro points of views.

(7) The scope of Managerial Economics is limited and not so wide as that of Traditional Economics.

(8) Traditional Economics studies principles underlying rent, wages, interest and profits but in Managerial Economics we study mainly the principles of profit only.

(9) Sound decision-making in Managerial Economics is considered to be the most important task for the improvement of efficiency of the business firm; but in Traditional Economics it is not so.

Thus, it is obvious that Managerial Economics is very closly related to economics but its scope is narrow as compared to Traditional Economics.

Managerial Economics is also closely related to the subjects, *viz.*, Statistics, Mathematics and Accounting. A trained managerial economist integrates concepts and methods from all those disciplines bringing them to bear on business problems of a firm.

BASIC PRINCIPLES MANAGERIAL ECONOMICS

The most signficant contribution of economics to managerial economics lies in certain principles which are basic to the entire gamut of managerial economics. These basic principles may be identified as :

1. The Opportunity Cost Concept. By the opportunity cost of a decision is meant the sacrifice of alternatives required by that decision. This can best be understood with the help of a few illustrations:

(i) The opportunity cost of the funds employed in one's own business is the interest that could be earned on those funds had they been employed in other ventures;

(ii) The opportunity cost of using a machine to produce one product is the earnings forgone which would have been possible from other products;

(iii) The opportunity cost of the time an entrepreneur devotes to his own business is the salary he could earn in other occupations;

(iv) The opportunity cost of using a machine that is useless for any other purpose is zero, since its use requires no sacrifice of other opportunities.

Thus it should be clear that opportunity cost require ascertainment of sacrifices. If a decision involves no sacrifice, its opportunity cost is nil.

For decision-making, opportunity costs are the only relevant costs. The opportunity cost principle may be stated as : "The cost involved in any decision consists of the sacrifices of alternatives required by that decision. If there are no sacrifices, there is no cost."

2. Incremental Concept. Incremental concept is closely related to the marginal costs and marginal revenues of economic theory. Incremental concept involves estimating the impact of decision alternatives on costs and revenues, emphasizing the changes in total cost and total revenue resulting from changes in prices, products, procedures, investments or whatever may be at stake in the decisions. The two basic components of incremental reasoning are: incremental cost and incremental revenue. Incremental cost may be defined as the change in total cost resulting from a decision. Incremental revenue is the changes in total revenue resulting from a decision.

A decision is obviously a profitable one if:

(i) it increases revenue more than costs;

(ii) it decreases some costs to a greater extent than it increases others;

(iii) it increases some revenue more than it decreases others; and

(iv) it reduces cost more than revenue.

Some businessmen take the view that to make an overall profit, they must make a profit on every job. The result is that they refuse orders that do not cover full cost (labour, materials and overhead) plus a provision for profit. Incremental resoning indicates that this rule may be inconsistent with profit maximization in the short run. A refusal to accept business below full cost may mean rejection of a possibility of adding more to revenue than to cost. The relevant cost is not the full cost but rather the incremental cost.

3. Concept of Time Perspective. The economic concepts of the long run and short run have become part of everyday language. Managerial Economists are also concerned with the short-run and long-run effects of decisions on revenues as well as costs. The really important problem in decision-making is to maintain the right balance between the long-run and short-run considerations. A decision may be made on the basis of short-run considerations, but may as time elapses, have long-run repercussions which make it more or less profitable than it at first appeared.

4. The Discounting Principle. One of the fundamental ideas in economics is that a rupee tomorrow is worth less than a rupee today.

This seems similar to saying that a bird in hand is worth two in the bush. A simple example would make this point clear. Suppose a person is offered a choice to make between a gift of Rs. 100 today or Rs. 100 next year. Naturally he will choose the Rs. 100 today. This is true for two reasons. First, the future is uncretain and there may be uncertainty in getting Rs. 100 if the present opportunity is not availed of. Secondly, even if he is sure to receive the gift in future, today's Rs. 100 can be invested so as to earn interest say, at 8 per cent so that one year after the Rs. 100 of today will become Rs. 108 whereas if he does not accept Rs. 100 today he will get Rs. 100 only one year hence. Naturally he would prefer the first alternative because he is likely to gain by Rs. 8 in future. Another way of saying the same thing is that Rs. 100 one year hence is not equal to Rs 100 of today but less than that. But then how much money today is equal to Rs. 100 of the year hence? To find it out, we shall have to find out the relevent rate of interest which one would earn if one decides to invest the money. Suppose the rate of interest is 8 per cent. Then we shall have to discount Rs. 100 at 8 per cent in order to ascertain how much money today will become Rs. 100 one year after. The formula is:

$$V = \frac{\text{Rs.}100}{1+i}$$

where

V = present value

i = rate of interest

Now, applying the formula, we get

$$V = \frac{\text{Rs.}100}{1+i}$$

$$= \frac{100}{1.08} = \text{Rs. } 92.59$$

As a crosscheck, if we multiply Rs. 92.59 by 1.08, we shall get the money which will accumulate at 8% after one year:

$$92.59 \times 1.08 = 99.9972$$

$$= \text{Rs. } 100$$

The same reasoning applies to longer periods. A sum of Rs. 100 two years from now is worth

$$V = \frac{\text{Rs.}100}{(1+i)^2} = \frac{\text{Rs.}100}{(1.08)^2} = \frac{\text{Rs.}100}{1.1664}$$

Rs. 85.73

Again, we can check by computing how much the cumulative interest will be after two years.

The principle involved in the foregoing discussion can be called the discounting principle and may be stated as under: "If a decision affects costs and revenues at future dates, it is necessary to discount those costs and revenues to present values before a valid comparison of alternatives is possible."

5. The Equi-marginal Principle. One of the widest known principles of economics is the proposition that an input should be so allocated that the value added by the last unit is the same in all cases. This generalization is called the equimarginal principle.

Suppose a firm has 100 units of labour at its disposal. The firm is engaged in four activities which need labour services, viz., A, B, C and D. It can enhance any one of these activities by adding more labour but only at the cost of other activities.

It should be clear that if the value of the marginal product is higher in one activity than another, and optimum allocation has not been attained. It would therefore be profitable to shift labour from low marginal value activity to high marginal value activity, thus increasing the total value of all products together. To take an example, if in activity A, the value of marginal product of labour is Rs. 20 while that in activity B, it is Rs. 30, it is profitable to shift labour from activity A to activity B thereby expanding activity B and reducing activity A. The optimum will be reached when the value of the marginal product is equal in all the four activities or symbolically expressed, when

$$VMP_{LA} = VMP_{LB} = VMP_{LC} = VMP_{LD}$$

whereby the subscripts indicate labour in respective activities.

Certain aspects of the equi-marginal principle need clarification. First the values of marginal products are net of incremental costs. In activity B we may add one unit of labour with an increase in physical output of 1000 units. Each unit is worth 50 paise so that the 100 units will sell for Rs 50. But the increased output consumes raw materials, fuel and other inputs so that variable costs in Activity B (not counting the labour cost) are higher. Let us say that the incremental costs are Rs. 30 leaving a net addition of Rs. 20. The value of the marginal product relevant for our purpose is thus Rs. 20.

Secondly, if the revenues resulting from the addition of labour are to occur in future, these revenues ought to be discounted before comparison in the alternative activities are possible. Activity A may produce revenue immediately, but activities B, C and D may take 4 and 5 years respectively. Here the discounting of these revenues will render them comparable.

Thirdly, the measurement of the value of the marginal product may have to be corrected if the expansion of an activity requires a reduction in the price of the output. If activity B represents the production of radios and it is not possible to sell more radios without a reduction in price, it is necessary to make adjustment for the fall in price.

Fourthly, the equi-marginal principle may break under sociological pressures. For instance, due to inertia, activities are cotinued simply because they exsit. Again, motivated by empire building managers may keep on expanding activities to fulfill their ambition for power. Departments which are already overbudgeted often use some of their excess resources to build up propaganda machines (public relations offices) to win additional support. Governmental agencies are more prone to bureaucratic self-perpetuation and inertia.

❐

3

Theory of Demand

Demand implies a desire backed by ability and willingness to pay. Mere desire of a person to purchase a commodity is not his demand. He must possess adequate resources and must be willing to spend his resources to buy the commodity. Besides, the quantity demanded has always a reference to 'a price' and 'unity of time'. The demand for a commodity, therefore, always refers to the quantity of that commodity demanded at a certain price during any particular period of time, say, a week or a month. Thus, demand has no meaning without any reference to price. It must also be borne in mind that whenever demand is mentioned, it relates to a period of time. In other words demand is always measured as a flow, *i.e.*, so much per unit of time.

DETERMINANTS OF DEMAND FOR A COMMODITY

The amount of a commodity demanded by a household during any particular period depends on the following factors :

(i) Price of the goods under consideration,

(ii) Prices of othei goods,

(iii) Income of the household,

(iv) Tastes or scales of preferences of the household,

(v) Distribution of national income,

(vi) Population

(vii) Consumer-credit facility and

(viii) Demonstratio.ı effect.

This information can be expressed in the form of an equation known as the demand functions. Such a demand function may be expressed symbolically as follows :

$$D_x = F\,(P_x, P_1\text{--------}P_{x-1}, Y, T, Yd, P, C_R, D_F)$$

Where D_x stands for the demand for x; p_1------p_{x-1}, for the prices of other related goods, Y for consumer's income, T for tastes and preferences of households, Yd for distribution of national income, P for population, C_R for consumer credit facility and D for demonstration effect. Now we shall discuss these factors in detail:

(i) Price of the Commodity. The quantity demanded of a commodity is very greatly influenced by the price of that commodity. A rise in the price of the commodity will contract the demand of the commodity and vice versa. The price factor is, in fact, the most importamt factor determining the demand of the commodity.

(ii) Consumer's Income. An increase in consumer's income leads to an increase in the demand of various commodities, assuming that their prices remain unchanged. The demand for Giffen Goods may, however, decrease when consumers' income increases because they, then, take to their superior substitutes.

(iii) Consumer's Tastes and Preferences. If the consumers acquire taste for a particular commodity, its demand is bound to increase even though its price remains constant. For example, the synthetic fibres are becoming increasingly fashionable in India and hence the demand for them is constantly on the increase.

(iv) Prices of Complementary and Substitute Goods. Two types of related goods are substitutes and complements. For example, tea and coffee are good substitutes. A rise in the price of coffee, assuming the price of tea to be constant, will increase the demand for tea and vice versa. Two good are said to be complements when both are needed to satisfy the same want. Bread and butter, for example, are complements. A fall in the price of bread will increase the demand for butter and vice versa.

(v) Distribution of National Income. Apart from the levels of individual incomes, the distribution pattern of national income also affects the demand for a commodity. If national income is evenly distributed, market demand for normal goods will be the largest. The market demand on the other hand will be largest in case of uneven distribution of national income.

(vi) Demonstration Effect. When new commodities or new models of existing ones appear in the market, rich people buy them first. Some people buy them because they have genuine need for them while others buy because they want to exhibit their influence. The purchases by the latter group of buyers are the result of demonstration effect or the 'Band-wagon Effect'. These effects have a positive effect on the demand. On the contrary, when a commodity becomes the thing of common use, some people, mostly rich, decrease or give up the consumptions of such goods. This is knoun as 'Snob Effect.' It has a negative effect on the demand for the related goods.

(vii) Consumer-Credit Facility. Availability of the consumers from sellers, banks, relations and friends or from any other source encourages the consumers to buy more than what they could buy in the absence of credit facility. That is why the consumers who can borrow more can consume more than those who can borrow less. Credit facility affects mostly the demand for durable goods, particularly those which require bulk payment at the time of pruchase.

(viii) Miscellaneous Factors. Under this head, we can include the remaining factors, such as, population, state of business, anticipations about future prices etc. These miscellaneous factors also influence the state of demand of a commodity. For example, an increase of population in a country will increase the demand for foodgrains.

ELASTICITY OF DEMAND

Demand is a function of price. When price changes demand changes. But it seldom happens that price changes lead to uniform changes in demand. Sometimes demand varies much, at other times little, due even to the same change in price. There are certain goods like vegetable, ghee, salt, etc., whose demand does not contract much with the rise in their price. While there are goods like radios, cars, etc., whose demand changes due to a change in prices. The credit goes to Dr. Marshall who offered a solution by formulating the concept of price elasticity of demand in these words : "The elasticity (or responsiveness) of demand in a market is great or small according as the amount demanded increases much or little for a given fall in price, and diminishes much or little for a given rise in price." Modern economists define elasticity of demand in a mathematical manner, as in the words of Professor Lipsey : "Elasticity of demand may be defined as the ratio of the percentage change in demand to the percentage change in price." Mrs Robinson's definition is more clear : "The elasticity of demand at any price or at any output, is the proportional change of amount purchased in response to a small change in price, divided by the proportional change of price." Thus, price elasticity of demand is the ratio of percentage change in amount demanded to a percentage change in price. It may be written as

$$E_p = \frac{\%\text{ Change in amount demanded}}{\%\text{ Change in price}} = \frac{\Delta q / q}{\Delta p / p}$$

If the percentages for quantity and prices are known the value of the coefficient E can be calculated.

Price elasticity of demand may be unity, greater than unity, less than unity, zero or infinite. These five cases are explained with the aid of the following figures.

Price elasticity of demand is unity when the change in demand is exactly proprotionate to the change in price. For example, a 20% change in price causes 20% change in demand, In the $E_p = \frac{20\%}{20\%} = 1$. In the above figures Δp represents change in price, Δq change in demand, and DD the demand curve. Price elasticity on the first demand curve in Figure (A) is unity, for $\frac{\Delta q}{\Delta p} = 1$.

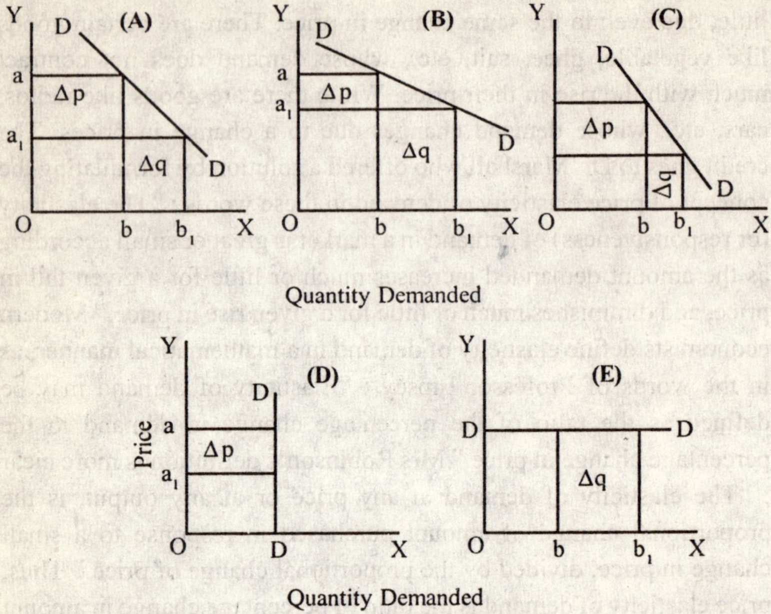

Figure

When the change in demand is more than proportionate to the change in price, price elasticity of demand is greater than unity. If the change in demand is 40% when price changes by 20% then $E_p = \frac{40\%}{20\%} = 2$, in Figure $\frac{\Delta q}{\Delta p} > 1$. It is also known as relatively elastic demand.

If, however, the change in demand is less than proportionate to the change in price, price elasticity of demand is less than unity. When a 20% change in price cuases 10% change in demand, then $E_p = \frac{10\%}{20\%} = \frac{1}{2} = < 1$, in Figure (C), $\frac{\Delta q}{\Delta p} > 1$. It is also known as relatively inelastic demand.

Zero elasticity of demand is one when whatever the change in price, there is absolutely no change in demand. Price elasticity of demand is perfectly inelastic in this case. A 20% rise or fall in price leads to no change in the amount demanded, $E_p = \frac{0}{20\%} = 0$, in Figure (D), $\frac{0}{\Delta p} = 0$. It is perfectrly inelastic demand.

Lastly, price elasticity of demand is infinite when an infinitesimal small change in price leads to an infinitely large change in the amount demanded. Visibly, no change in price causes an infinite change in demand, $E_p = \frac{\infty}{0} = \infty$, in Figure (E), at OD price, the quantity demanded continues to increase from Ob to Ob_1 .... n. It is perfectly elastic demand.

METHODS OF MEASURING ELASTICITY

There are four methods of measuring elasticity of demand. They are the percentage method, point method, arc method and expenditure method. They are discussed below:

(1) The Percentage Method. One of the most satisfactory methods of measurement is to regard elasticity as the ratio of the percentage change in the amount demanded to the percentage change in the price of the commodity.

$$E_p = \frac{\text{Percentage change in amount demanded}}{\text{Percentage change in price}}$$

$$= \frac{\dfrac{\text{Change in amount demanded}}{\text{Amount demanded before change}}}{\dfrac{\text{Change in price}}{\text{Price before change}}}$$

If we use (delta) Δ for a change, q for amount demanded and p for price, the algebraic equation from the four-storey formula is

$$E_p = \frac{\dfrac{\Delta q}{q}}{\dfrac{\Delta p}{p}} = \frac{\Delta p}{q} \times \frac{p}{-\Delta q} = -\frac{\Delta q}{\Delta p} \times \frac{p}{q}$$

The coefficient of price elasticity of demand is always negative because when price changes demand moves in the opposite direction. It is, however, customery to disregard the negative sign. Let us measure elasticity with aid of the formula.

Suppose 5 kg. of a commodity are demanded at Rs. 10. If price falls to Rs. 6 the amount demanded rises to 6 kg. Elasticity of demand in this case as per the above formula will be

$$E_p = \frac{\Delta p}{\Delta q} \times \frac{p}{q} = \frac{1}{4} \times \frac{10}{5} = \frac{1}{2} =< 1 \text{ (less elastic)}$$

The original amount of 5 kg. at the price of Rs. 10 being given, if price rises to Rs. 12, quantity demanded falls to 4 kg, then

$$E_p = \frac{1}{2} \times \frac{10}{5} = \frac{1}{2} = 1 \text{ (Unity)}$$

In the final case, if price rises from Rs. 10 to Rs. 11, and amount demanded falls from 5 kg to 4 kg.

$$E_p = \frac{1}{1} \times \frac{10}{5} = 2 => 1 \text{ (Elastic)}$$

This percentage method dispenses with the gradient method and is used to measure elasticity at a point on the demand curve.

(2) The Point Method. Prof. Marshall devised a geometrical method for measuring elasticity at a point on the demand curve. Let RS be a straight line demand curve. If the price falls from PB (=OA)

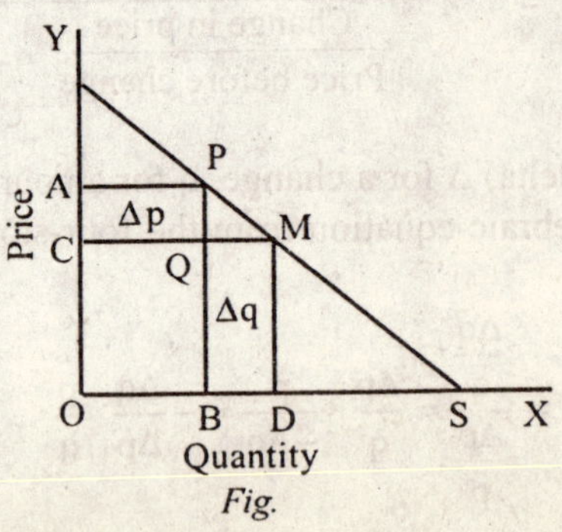

Fig.

to MD (=OC), the quantity demanded increase from OB to OD. Elasticity at point P on RS demand curve according to the formula is:

$$E_p = \frac{\Delta p}{\Delta q} \times \frac{p}{q}$$

where Δq represents changes in quantity demanded, Δp changes in price level while p and q are initial price and quantity levels.

From fig.

$$\Delta q = BD = QM$$

$$\Delta p = PQ$$

$$p = PB$$

$$q = OB$$

Substituting these values in the elasticity formula:

$$E_p = \frac{QM}{PQ} \times \frac{PB}{OB}$$

Moreover, $\frac{QM}{PQ} \times \frac{BS}{PB}$ [$\angle$ PQM = $\angle$PBS being right angles and PQM and PBS are similar Δs]

$$\therefore \frac{BS}{PB} \times \frac{PB}{OB} = \frac{BS}{OB}$$

Since ΔPBS and ROS are similar, price elasticity of demand at point

$$P = \frac{BS}{OB} = \frac{OA}{AR} = \frac{PS}{PR} = \frac{\text{Lower Segment}}{\text{Upper Segment}}$$

With the help of the point method it is easy to point out the elasticity at any point along a demand curve. Suppose that the straight line demand curve DC in Figure is 6 centimetres. Five points L, M, N, P and Q are taken on this demand curve. The elasticity of demand at each point N be in the middle of the demand curve. So elasticity of demand at point

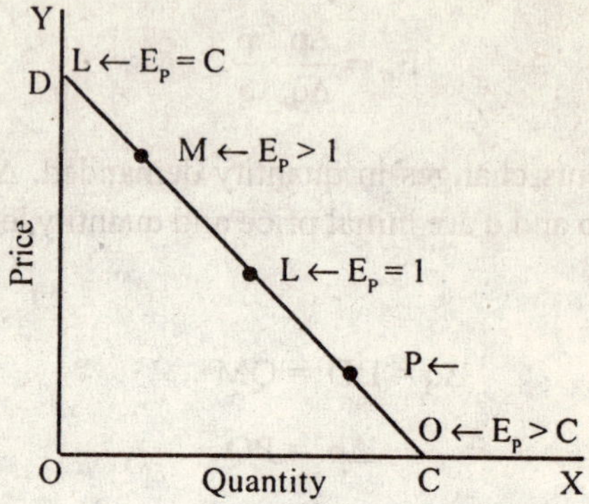

Fig.

$$N = \frac{CN\ (\text{Lower Segment})}{ND\ (\text{Upper Segment})}$$

$$= \frac{3}{3} = 1\ (\text{Unity}).$$

Elasticity of demand at point

$$M = \frac{CM}{MD} = \frac{5}{1} = 5\ (\text{Greater than Unity}).$$

Elasticity of demand at point

$$L = \frac{CL}{LD} = \frac{6}{0} = \infty\ (\text{Infinite}).$$

Elasticity of demand at point

$$P = \frac{CP}{PD} = \frac{1}{5} = (\text{Less than Unity}).$$

Elasticity of demand at point

$$Q = \frac{CQ}{QD} = \frac{0}{6} = 0\ (\text{Zero}).$$

We arrive at the conclusion that at the mid-point on the demand curve the elasticity of demand is unity. Moving up the demand curve from the mid-point, elasticity becomes greater. When the demand curve touches the Y-axis, elasticity is infinite. Ipso facto, any point below the mid-point towards the X-axis will show elastic demand. Elasticity becomes zero when the demand curve touches the X-axis. We may have some applications of the above method of measuring elasticity on demand curves of different shapes:

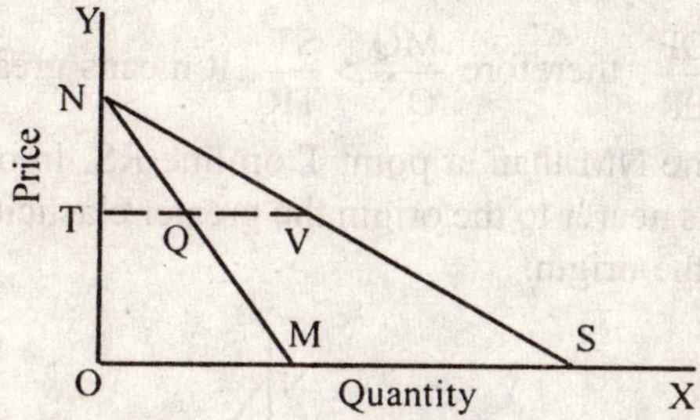

Fig.

(a) Two Straight Line Demand Curves Which are Neither Parallel Nor Intersecting. This method of measuring elasticity helps to compare the elasticity of demand curves, and shows the flexibility of the notion that elasticity depends upon the slope of a curve. In Fig. we have taken two siraight line demand curves NM and NS. If we draw a dotted line passing through these curves and touching the Y-axis at point T, The elasticity at point Q on the NM curve according to the point formula is :

$$\frac{MQ}{QN} = \frac{OT}{TN}, \text{ being sides of right angle } \Delta OBM.$$

Similarly, elasticity at point V on the NS curve is

$$\frac{SV}{VN} = \frac{OT}{TN}, \text{ being sides of right angle } \Delta ONS.$$

$$\therefore \frac{MQ}{QN} = \frac{SV}{VN} = \frac{OT}{TN}$$

Thus, elasticity is equal on both points Q and V.

(b) Two Parallel Strainght Lines Demand Curve. Let NM and RS be two parallel straight line demand curves and draw a line PT which passes through these straight lines at point Q and T. According to the point formula, elasticity at point Q on the NM curve is being $\frac{MQ}{QN} = \frac{OP}{PN}$ being sides of right angle ΔONM. Similarly, elasticity at point T on the RS curve, $\frac{ST}{TR} = \frac{OP}{PR}$, being sides of right angle ΔORS.

Since $\frac{OP}{PN} > \frac{OP}{PR}$, therefore $\frac{MQ}{QN} > \frac{ST}{TR}$. It means greater elasticity at point Q on line NM than at point T on line RS. In other words, the curve which is nearer to the origin the greater elasticity than which is farther from the origin.

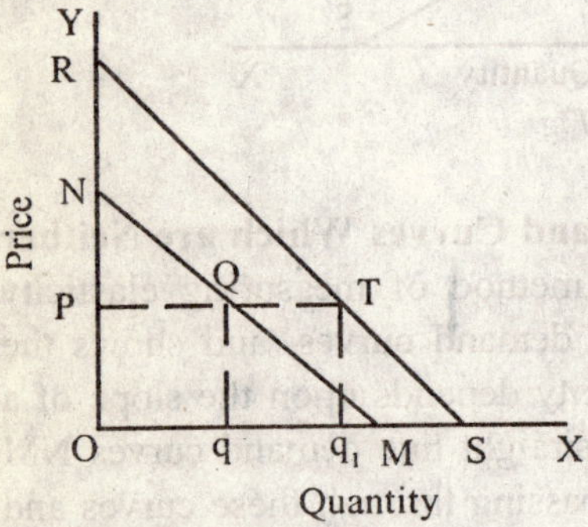

Fig.

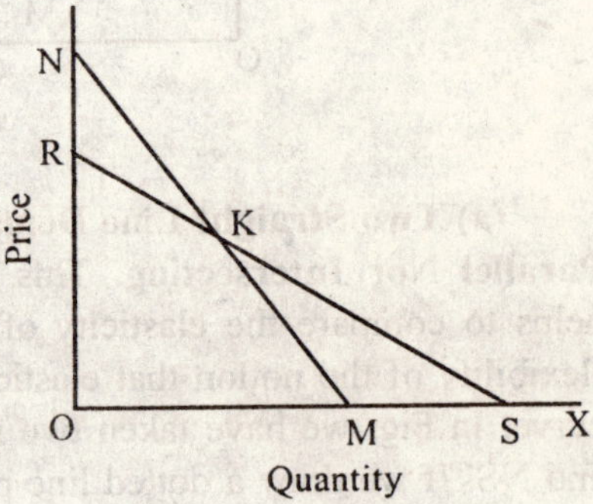

Fig.

(c) Two Intersecting Straight Line Demand Curves. Let NM and RS be two intersecting straight line demand curves. The slope of the RS curve shows that it is flatter whereas the curve NM is steeper. Figure shows that SK>MK and KR<KN. Therefore, $\frac{SK}{KR} > \frac{MK}{KN}$. Thus the flatter curves RS has greater elasticity than the steeper curve NM at point K.

(d) Two Point on the Same Demand Curve. Let us take points A and B on a curved demand curve D in Figure. Elasticity at point B is BM/BN, and at point A is AS/AR. Since AS/AR is greater than BM/BN, elasticity at point A is greater than unity and at point B it is less than unity.

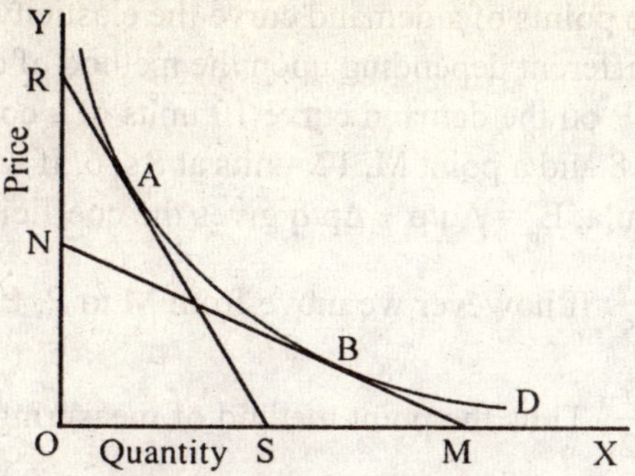

Fig.

But in Figure, the elasticity at point A on the demand curve D is equal to unity because A_1 lies at the middle of the line R_1S_1. Similarly elasticity at point B_1 on the same demand curve D_1 is unity, because this point also lies half way on the line N_1M_1. A demand curve which has unit elasticity (equal to 1) on all points is a rectangular hyperbola, as is the demand curve D in Figure.

(3) The Arc Method. We have studied the measurement of elasticity at a point on a demand curve. But when elasticity is measured between two points on the same demand curve, it is known as arc elasticity. In the words of Baumol, "Arc elasticity is a measure of the average responsiveness to price change exhibited by a demand curve over some finite stretch of the curve."

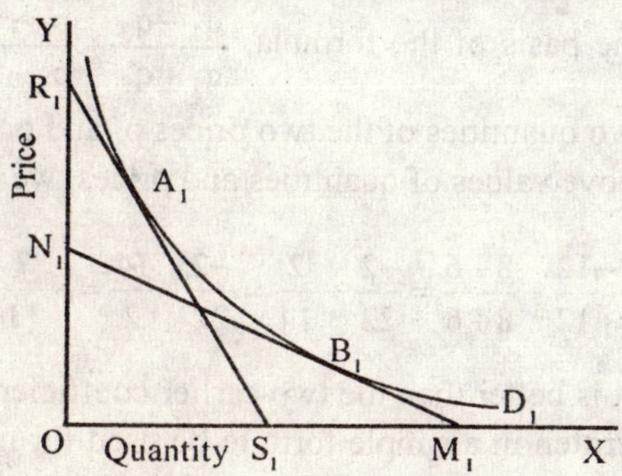

Fig.

Any two points on a demand curve make an arc. The area between P and M on the DD curve in figure is an arc which measures elasticity over a certain range of price and quantities.

On any two points of a demand curve the elasticity coefficients are likely to be different depending upon the method of computation. Suppose a point P on the demand curve 10 units of a commodity are demanded at Rs. 8 and a point M, 12, units at Rs. 6. If we move from P to M, the formula, $E_p = \Delta q/p \div \Delta p/q$ gives the coefficient 2/10 ÷ 2/

$8 = -\frac{2}{10} \times \frac{8}{2} = -\frac{4}{5}$. If however we move from M to P, E_p = 2/12 ÷ 2/

$6 = -\frac{2}{12} \times \frac{6}{2} = -\frac{1}{2}$. Thus the point method of measuring elasticity at two points on a demand curve gives different elasticity coefficients.

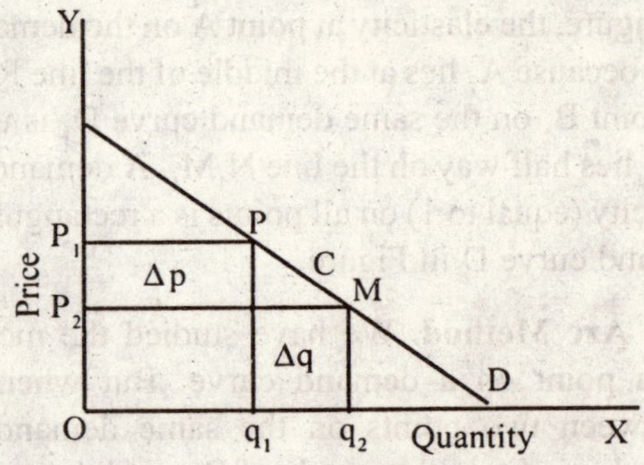

Fig.

To avoid this discrepancy, an average of the two values is calculated on the basis of the formula, $\frac{q_1 - q_2}{q_1 + q_2} \div \frac{p_1 - p_2}{p_1 + p_2}$ where q_1 and q_2 are the two quantities of the two prices p_1 and p_2 respectively. Applying the above values of quantities and prices, we have

$$\frac{10-12}{10+12} \div \frac{8-6}{8+6} = \frac{-2}{22} \div \frac{2}{14} = \frac{-2}{22} \times \frac{14}{2} = -\frac{7}{11}$$

This result is better than the two earlier coefficients arrived at. It can also be written in a simple form to be used for measuring arc elasticity on Figure where $\Delta q = q_1 - q_2$ and $\Delta p = p_1 - p_2$. Therefore the elasticity between points P and M is $\frac{\Delta q}{q_1 + q_2} \div \frac{\Delta p}{p_1 + p_2}$, or in plain language,

$$\frac{\text{Difference in q}}{\text{Sum of q}} \div \frac{\text{Difference in q}}{\text{Sum of p}}.$$

The closer the two points P and M are, the more accurate is the measure of elasticity on the basis of the formula. The arc elasticity is in fact the elasticity of the mid-point between P and M, on the demand curve, DD. If there is no difference between the two points and they merge into each other, arc 'elasticity' becomes point elasticity.

FACTORS AFFECTING THE ELASTICITY OF DEMAND

Alfred Marshall showed his awareness of the factors which generally influence the elasticity of demand for certain products. For example, he argues that the demand for necessaries has very little elasticity, and even though the price of a necessary article, say wheat; has fallen substantially, the consumption of bread will not increase much. Likewise, very low prices of certain products induce the consumer to ignore the overall expenditure on this product and its demand becomes inelastic. However, the elasticity increases in the range of higher prices.

Marshall also stated that very costly and luxurious goods are consumed by a very small section of rich people, and the demand for such products may be inelastic. He, however, conceded that the elasticity of demand also depends on the economic status of the consumer in the society. Finally, possibility of postponing the consumption also increases the magnitude of elasticity of demand.

However, Marshall obliviated the effect of substitutes on the elasticity of demand, as he had stressed the independence of demand for each product. In the modern micro-economic theory the elasticity of demand is assumed to depend on several forces, the prominent of which are listed below:

(i) **Availability of Substitutes.** If a large number of substitutes are available, demand for the product will be highly elastic.

(ii) **Nature of the Product.** Following the Marshallian line of reasoning, the demand for necessaries is inelastic (so is the demand for very costly products) while the demand for luxurious articles is elastic or highly elastic.

(iii) **Inter-dependence in Decision Making and Snob Effect.** Harvey Leibenstein explains in an article that if consumption decision by an individual draws largely from the decision of fellow inhabitants, the demand for a product is price-inelastic at the micro level. The snob effect refers to the behaviour of an individual whose behaviour runs contrary to the decisions of fellow citizens. The elasticities of demand for different products constituting his basket are, therefore, unpredictable.

(iv) **Possibility of Postponing the Consumption.** If consumption can be postponed, the demand for such a product will be more elastic as compared to another product for which no such possibility exists.

(v) **Uses of the Product.** Elasticity of demand increases with the number of uses to which a product can be put, and vice versa. Milk, water and electricity are those products which can be put to several uses, and have, therefore, highly elastic demand.

(vi) **Price of the Product and its Ratio to Total Budget.** Elasticity of demand varies directly with the product of total outlay on the product to total consumer budget.

(vii) **Length of the Period.** In the short run demand for most commodities will be inelastic, as the consumer cannot quickly change his habits, tastes or preferences in response to certain change in prices and/ or income.

Stable Equilibrium Between Demand and Supply

Before reviewing the stability of equilibrium between supply and demand it seems desriable to explain the meaning of supply. The supply of a product refers to different quantities that the producers or sellers are willing to offer at given levels of price. Supply curve generally slopes upward—explaining that unlike demand, the supply is positively related to price.

Figure (1) shows an equilibrium between demand and supply. While holding all other prices and consumer's income, the market will be in equilibrium at the price OP and equilibrium quantity,OQ. At any price other than OP, either there would be excess supply in the market, (such as the one existing at OP_1) or there would be excess demand (such as the one exisiting at OP_2). In either case, competition among sellers or buyers will tend to restore the equilibrium price-quantity relationship.

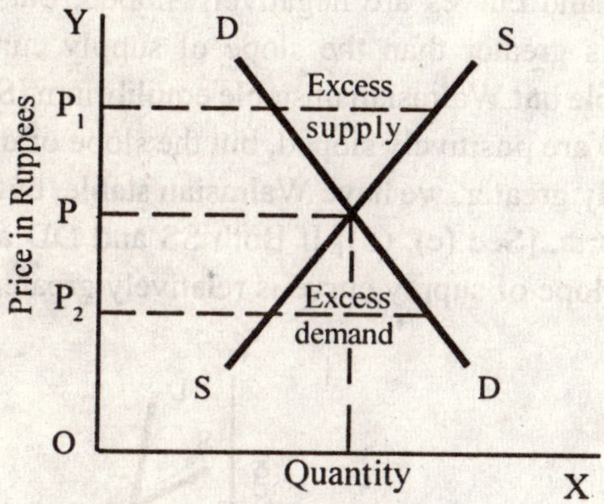

Fig. 1: Equilibrium between demand and supply.

Marshall argues that the market would always tend to restore equilibrium quantity (and thus price) and even if there is a deviation in the equilibrium quantity, correcting forces would move the price. In such a fashion that the market is back to equilibrium between demand and supply. This has been termed as Marshallian stable equilibrium by R.A. Bilas. On the other hand, if we move price away from equilibrium, correcting force would operate on demand and/or supply, thus restoring the equilibrium. This is known as Walrasian stable equilibrium. To put it differently, while Marshall takes price as the dependent variable, Walras takes it as an independent variable. If one takes a price and measures the discrepancy between supply and demand he would be following the Walrasian line. On the other hand, if one looks at certain quantity, move vertically so as to examine the discrepancy between the supply price and the demand price corresponding to this quantity, he is looking for the Marshallian equilibrium. Starting again at the equilibrium price and quantity relationship E, in Fig. (1), we may argue that the equilibrium will be restored, regardless of fact that quantity is moved away from E (Marshallian case) or price is moved away from this level (Walrasian case). Fig. (1) depicts the normal supply and demand funcitons.

If both the supply and demand curves are negatively sloped but the slope of the former exceeds that of the latter, we have Walrasian stable but Marshallian unstable equilibria. [See (a). (b)] If both the supply and demand curves are negatively sloped, but the slope of demand curve is greater than the slope of supply curve, we have Marshallian stable but Walrasian unstable equilibrium [See (b). (c)] If both SS and DD are positively sloped, but the slope of demand curve (DD) is relatively greater, we have Walrasian stable, but Marshallian unstable equilibria. [See (c). (d)] If Both SS and DD are positively sloped but the slope of supply curve is relatively greater.

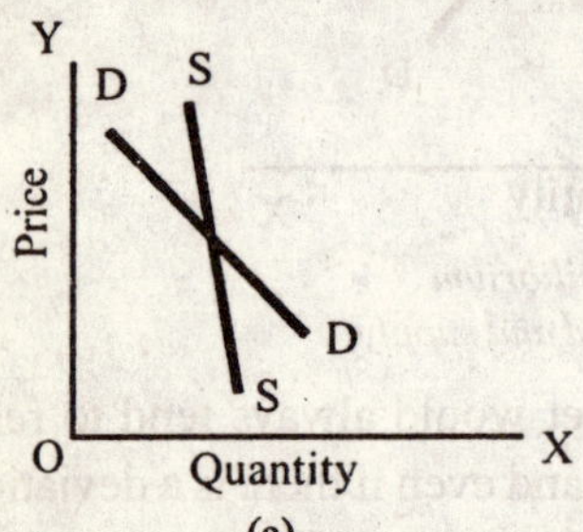

(a)

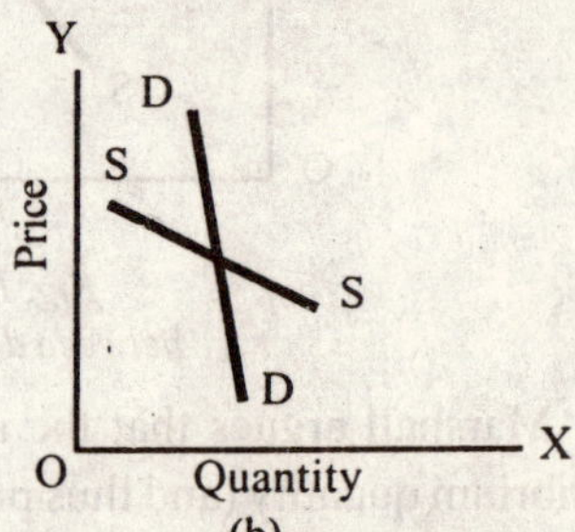

(b)

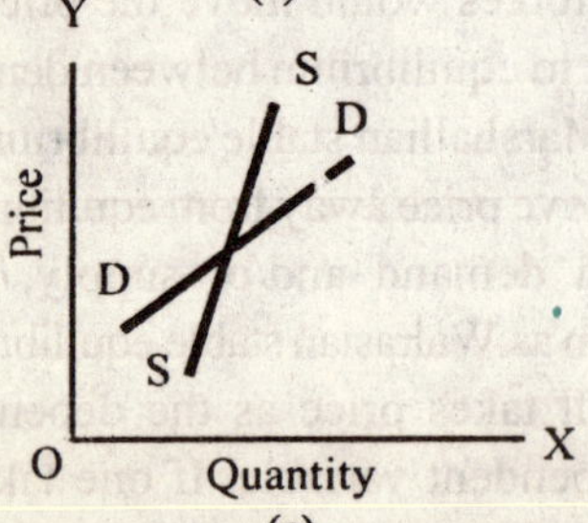

(c)

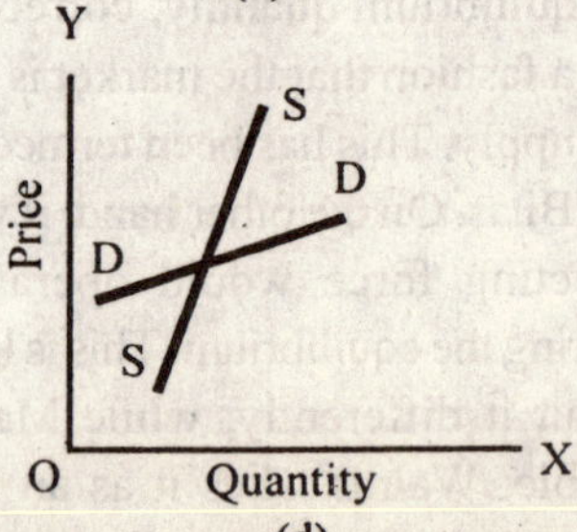

(d)

As has been argued above, a demand curve is drawn with an assumption of ceteris paribus. However, while defining a demand function. we had argued that the quantity demanded is generally a function of price, price of other goods (P_y), tastes (T) and the consumer's income (M). The demand curve presented in Fig. relates the quantity demanded to the price of a product, while holding P_yT and M constant. however, demand curve will shift upward or downward with a given change in any of these variables.

(i) Change in the Price (s) of Related Goods (or P_y). If two goods are related, say, they are substitutes, a change in the price of one will obviously bring about a shift in the demand for the other. Suppose X and Y are substitutes. If the price of Y falls (say from Rs. 10 to Rs. 8), the demand curve for X will shift downward. A rise in the price of Y will, however, bring about an upward shift in the demand for X. This fact has been illustrated in Fig. (2)

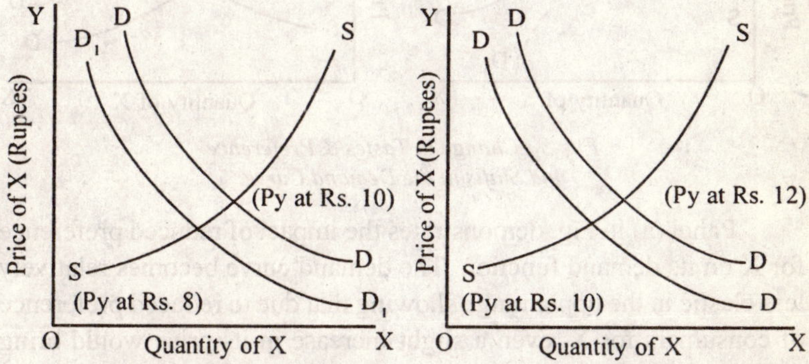

Panel (a) : Shift in demand for X when Py falls

Panel (b) : Shift in demand for X when Py rises

Fig. 2 : Shift in demand resulting from a change in the price of related goods.

Panel (a) in Fig. (2) depicts a downward shift in the demand curve for X following a fall in P_y. It should be noted here that in case X and Y are complementary goods, a fall in P_y would bring about an upward shift in the demand for X. On the other hand, a rise in Py from Rs. 10 to Rs. 12 causes the demand curve for X to shift from DD to D'D' (Panel B) showing that the consumers will increase the demand for X regardless of the fact that P_y remains unchanged.

However, if X and Y, happen to be complementary goods, a rise in P_y will bring about a downward shift in the demand curve for X.

(ii) Change in Tastes. It seems appropriate to argue that changes in the prices of related goods (substitues or complements) and/or consumers' income bring about only a parallel shift in the demand curve for a product. However, changes in taste over time will bring about significant changes in the slope of the prevailing demand curves. Fig. (3) depicts the effects of the change in consumers' tastes for X, though P_x, P_y and their money income are held unchanged.

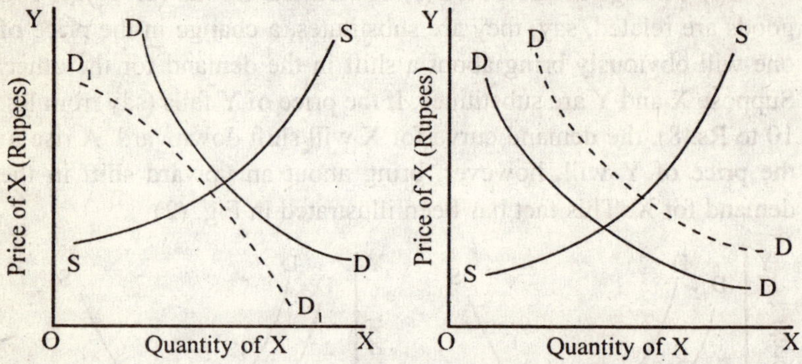

Fig. 3 : Change in Tastes & Preference and Shifts in the Demand Curve.

Panel (a) in Fig. demonstrates the impact of reduced preference for X on its demand function. The demand curve becomes relatively less elastic in the upper range showing that due to reduced preference of consumers for X, even a slight increase in its price would bring about a larger contraction in its demand than before (see the new demand curve D_1D_1 in Panel a). On the other hand, the lower range of this demand curve shows higher elasticity of demand for X than before. Panel (b) in Fig. (3) shows that due to higher preference for X, the demand curve not only shifts upward, (from DD to D'D') but rather becomes inelastic in the upper range of price while highly elastic in the lower range.

(iii) Change in Consumers' Income (M). Even if the price of related goods and consumers' preferences for X remained unchanged, a shift in its demand function may be brought about by a change in consumer's money income. An increase in income will shift the demand curve upward, showing that with higher money income, the consumer is willing to buy larger quantity of X despite the fact the P_y has not fallen. On the contrary, following a fall in money income, the consumer's demand curve will shift downward, implying that he would buy smaller quantity of X even though P_y has not risen.

Since X^1 is at least as expensive a combination of commodities as X^2, and since the consumer refuses to choose X^1, X^2 is "revealed" to be preferred to X^1. Consistency or transitivity implies that once X^2 is "revealed" preferred to X^1, the latter must never be revealed preferred to X^2.

Finally, revealed preference will alter only if the price is sufficiently lowered. In other words, X^1 can be revealed to be preferred to X^2 only when price situation has changed such that the consumer can also afford to buy X^1. In other words X^1 is revealed to be preferred if

$$P^2X^2 \leq P^1X^1$$

The theory of "revealed preference" is based on the axiom that (6.40) can never hold if (6.39) does. Further, it also states that if X^2 is revealed to be preferred to X^1, which is revealed to be preferred to X^o,....... which is revealed to be preferred to X^k, X^k must never be preferred to X^2. This axiom ensures the transitivity of revealed preferences, but is stronger than the usual transitivity condition.

The entire revealed preference analysis is based on a rather simple idea. A consumer will decide to buy some particular set of goods either because he likes them more than the other goods which are available to him, or because they happen to be cheap. If your combinations of goods A, B, C and D all are available to the consumer at the same price, yet he prefers A, we would infer that A has been revealed preferred to others (B, C and D) because the consumer likes A as compared to others.

CHANGES IN DEMAND

Demand is a function of price, income, prices of related goods and tastes and is expressed as D = f (p, y, pr, t). When income, prices of related goods and tastes are given, the demand function is D = f (p). It shows quantities of a commodity purchased at given prices. Demand is also related to a period of time. In the words of Prof. Benham: "The demand for anything, at a given prices, is the amount of it which will be bought per units of time at that price." An individual's demand for a commodity is shown on the demand schedule and on the demand curve. A demand schedule is a list of prices and quantities and its graphic representation is a demand curve.

Table : Demand Schedule

Price	*Quantity*
Rs. 0.60	10 units
0.50	20
0.40	30
0.30	40

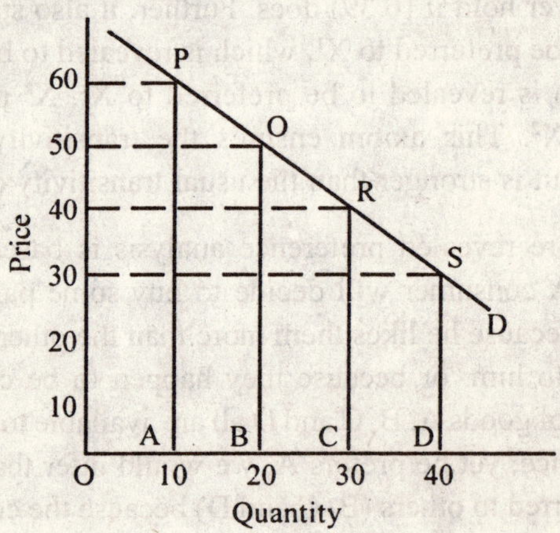

Fig. 4

The demand schedule reveals that when the price is 60 paise, quantity demanded is 10 units. If the price happens to be 50 paise, quantity demanded is 20- units, and so on. In Figure, D is the demand curve drawn on the basis of the above demand schedule. The dotted pointed P, Q, R, S, on the D curve, show the various price-quantity combinations. Marshall calls them "demand points". The first combination is represented by the first dot and the remaining price quantity combinations move to the right toward D. Viewed in an unconventional manner any point on an individual demand curve may be thought of as the highest price at which is given quantity of the commodity will be bought by the consumer.

The individual demand curve focuses our attention on the effects of a fall (rise) in the price of one commodity on the consumer's behaviour. They are the substitution and income effects.

(1) It results in a tendency for the consumer to buy more of the good since it has become cheaper and less of it when it becomes dearer. This is due to the substitution effect of the change in relative prices.

(2) A change in the price of the commodity affects the income of the consumer. With a fall in the price of the commodity, the consumer's real income increases and as a consequence of the income effect he buys more of the commodity. If the fall in price is moderate, the income effect will be very small, The income effect will also be negligible if the consumer spends very little on the commodity. Both the substitution and income effects are responsible for the negative slope of the demand curve. But the negative income effect may partly offset the positive substitution effect in the case of inferior goods. However, in the case of Giffen goods a strong negative income effect may completely offset the substitution effect and the demand curve may lose its usual negative slope.

The market demand is the summation of the individual consumers demands for a homogeneous commodity. If we sum up the different quantities of a commodity demanded by a number of individuals at various prices, we have a market demand schedule. If we depict their price-quantity relations on a figure, we have a market demand curve. Table represents four different A, B, C, D, who are shown to demand different units of the commodity at different

Table

Price Rs.	*Quantities Demanded in '000 units in '000 units*				*Total Demand in '000 units*
	A	*B*	*C*	*D*	
0.60	6	3	1	0	10
0.50	10	5	3	2	20
0.40	14	8	5	3	30
0.30	16	12	7	5	40

prices. Since the total quantity demanded by all the individuals is the same which we took in the case of the individual consumer as shown in Table, the curve D in the Figure express the market demanded on the X-axis in '000 units.

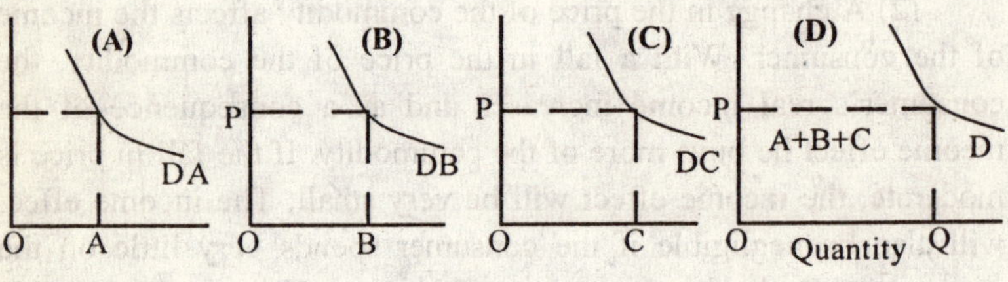

Fig. 5

But a better way of drawing a market demand curve is to add together sideways (lateral summation) of all the individual demand curves. In this case, the different quantities demanded by consumers at one price are represented on each individual demand curve and then a lateral summation is done as shown in Figure.

Suppose there are three individuals A, B and C in a market who buy OA, OB and OC quantities of the commodity at the price OP as shown in figure A, B, and C respectively. In the market QQ quantity will be bought which is made up by adding, together the quantities OA, OB and OC. The market demand curve D is obtained by the lateral summation of the individual demand curves D_A, D_B, D_C.

CHANGES IN DEMAND

Demand does not remain fixed. It, however, changes. If the change in demand is due to a rise or a fall in the price of a commodity alone, it is known as contraction or extension in demand. In the Figure, when price rises from QB to PA, demand contracts from OB to OA. The movement on the demand curve is to the left from Q to P. On the other hand, a fall in the price from RC to SD brings an extension in demand from OC to OD. It is a movement to the right on the demnad curve from R to S.

If the change in demand is due to a factor other than the price, it is known as increase or decrease in demand as the case may be, such changes in demand are shown by drawing a demand curve to the right or left of the original demand curve as shown in the following Figure.

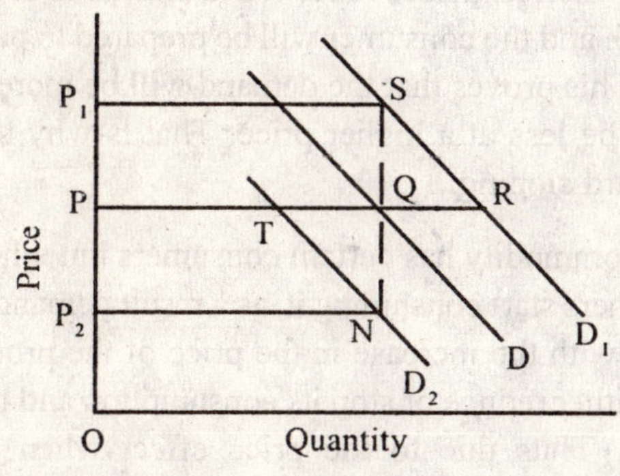

Fig. 6

Let D be the original demand curve where at price OP, quantity PQ is demanded. D_1 shows an increase in demand. An increase in demand can be in either of the two ways : larger quantity at the same price or, the same quantity at a higher price. When the demand increases to D_1, larger quantity PR is bought at the original price OP, or the same quantity P_1 S (=PQ) is bought at the higher price OP_1. On the contrary, a decrease in demand, the same quantity P_2N (=PQ) is bought at the lower price OP_2 or the smaller quantity PT is purchased at the same price OP. Demand curves are thus not stationary, rather they shift to the right or left due to a number of causes. There are changes in tastes, habits and customs of the consumer; changes in income expenditure; changes in the prices of substitutes and complements; expectations about future changes in prices and incomes, and changes in the age and composition of the population.

DOWNWARD SLOPING DEMAND CURVE

Why does a demand curve slopes downward from left to right? The reasons for this also clarify the working of the law of demand. The following are the main reasons for the downward sloping demand curve:

(1) The law of demand is based on the law of Diminishing Marginal Utility. According to this law, when a consumer buys more units of a commodity, the marginal utility of that commodity continues to decline. Therefore, the consumer will buy more units of that commodity only when its prices falls. When less units are available, utility will be high and the consumer will be prepared to pay more for the commodity. This proves that the demand will be more at a lower price and it will be less at a higher price. That is why the demand curve is downward sloping.

(2) Every commodity has certain consumers but when its price falls, new consumers start consuming it, as a result demand increases. On the contrary, with the increase in the price of the product, many consumers will either reduce or stop its consumption and the demand will be reduced. Thus due to the price effect when consumers consume more or less of the commodity, the demand curve slopes downward.

(3) When the price of a commodity falls, the real income of the consumer increase because he had to spend less in order to buy the same quantity. On the contrary, with the rise in the price of the commodity, the real income of the consumer falls. This is called the income effect. Under the influence of this effect with the fall in the price of the commodity the consumer buys more of it and also spends a portion of the increased income in buying other commodities. For instance, with the fall in the price of milk, he will buy more of it but at the same time, he will increase the demand for other commodities.

On the other hand, with the increase in the price of milk he will reduce its demand. The income effect of changes in the price of ordinary commodities being positive, the demand curve slopes downward.

(4) There are persons in different income groups in every society but the majority is in low income group. The downward sloping demand curve depends upon this group. Ordinary people buy more when price falls and less when price rises. The rich do not have any effect on the demand curve because they are capable of buying the same quantity even at a higher price.

(5) The other effect of change in the price of the commodity is the substitution effect. With the fall in the price of a commodity, the prices of its substitutes remaining the same, consumers will buy more of this commodity rather than the substitutes. As a result, its demand will increase. On the the contrary, with the rise in the price of the commodity (under consideration) its demand will fall, given the price of the substitutes.For instance, with the fall in the price of tea, the price of coffee being unchanged, the demand for tea will rise, and contrarywise, with the increase in the price of tea, its demand will fall.

(6) There are different uses of certain commodities and services that are responsible for the negative slope of the demand curve. With the increase in the price of such products, they will be used only for more important uses and their demand will fall. On the contrary, with the fall in price, they will be put to various uses and their demand will rise. For instance, with the increas in the electricity charges, power will be used primarily for domestic lighting, but if the charges are reduced, people will use power for cooking, fans, heaters, etc.

Exceptions of the Law of Demand

In certain cases the demand curve slopes up from left to right, *i.e.* it has a positive slope. Under certain circumstances, consumers buy more when the price of the commodity rises, and less when price falls, as is shown in Figure. Many causes are attributed to an upward sloping demand curve:

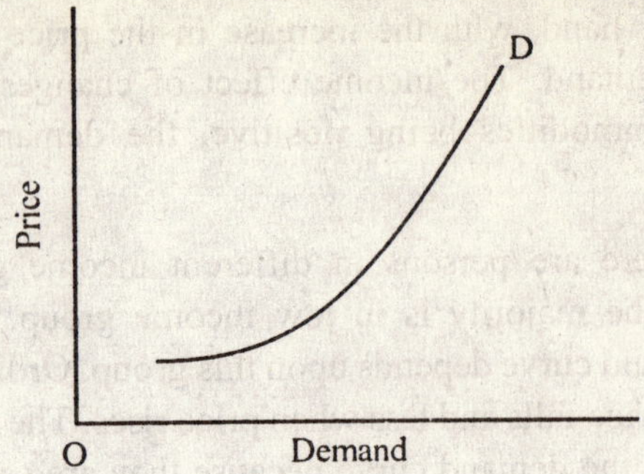

Fig. 7

(i) War. If a shortage is feared in anticipation of war, people may start buying for building stocks, for hoarding even when the price rises.

(ii) Depression. During a depression, the prices of commodities are very low and the demand for them is also less. This is because of the lack of purchasing power with consumers.

(iii) Giffen Paradox. If a commodity happens to be a necessity of life like wheat and its prices goes up, consumers are forced to curtail the consumption of more expensive foods like meat and fish, and wheat being still the cheapest they will consume more of it. The Marshallian example is applicable to developed economies. In the case of underdeveloped economy, with the fall in the price of an inferior commodity like maize, consumers will start consuming more of the superior commodity like wheat. As a result, the demand for maize will fall. This is what Marshall called Giffen Paradox which makes the demand curve to have a positive slope.

(iv) Ignorance Effect. Consumers buy more at a higher price under the influence of "ignorance effect," where a commodity may be mistaken for some other commodity, due to its price, deceptive packing, lable, etc.

(v) Demonstration Effect. If consumers are affected by the principle of conspicuous consumption of demonstration effect they will like to buy more such commodities which confer distinction on the possessor, when their prices rise. On the other hand, with the fall in the prices of such articles, their demand falls, as is the case with diamonds.

(vi) Speculation. Marshall mentions speculation as one of the important exceptions to the downward sloping demand curve. According to him : "The law of demand does not apply to the demand in a campaign between groups of speculators. A group, which desires to unload a great quantity of a thing on to the market, often begins by buying some of it openly. When it has thus raised the price of the thing, it arranges to sell a great quietly, and through unaccustomed channels."

Income Demand

We have so far studied price demand in its various aspects, keeping other things constant. Let us now study income demand which indicates the relationship between income and the quantity to commodity demanded. It relates to the various quantities of a commodity or service that will be bought by the consumer at various levels of incceme in a given period of time, other things being equal. Things that are assumed to remain equal are the price of the commodity in question, the prices of related commodities and the tastes, preference and habits of the consumer for it. The income-demand function for a commodity is written as D = f (y). The income-demand relationship is usually direct. The demand for the commodity increases with the

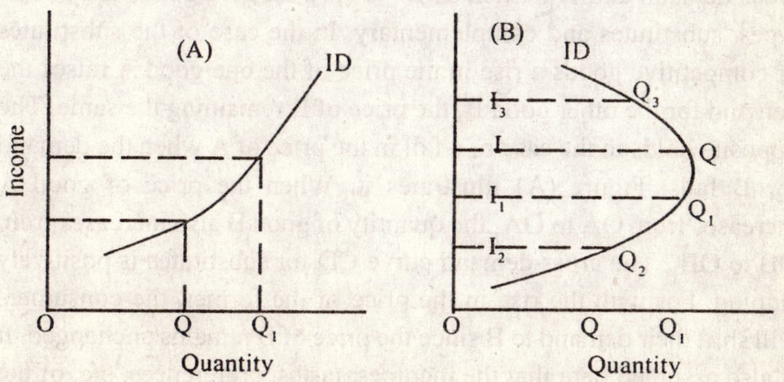

Fig. 8

rise in income and decreases with fall in income. as shown in Figure (A). When income is OI, the quantity demanded is OQ, and when income rises of OI_1, quantity demanded also increases to OQ_1. The reverse case can also be shown likewise. Thus, the income demand curve IP has a positive slope. But this slope in the case of the normal goods.

Let us take the case of a consumer who is in the habit of consuming an inferior good. So long as his income remains below a particular level of his minimum subsistence, he will continue to buy more of this inferior goods even when his income increases by small increments. But when his income starts rising above that level he reduces his demand for the inferior goods. In Figure (B), OI is the minimum subsistence level of income where he buys IQ of the commodity. Upto this level this commodity is a normal goods for him. So that he increases its consumption when his income rises gradually from OI_1 and OI_2, and so on. As his income rises above OI, he starts buying less of the commodity. For instance, at OI_2 income level, he buys I_3O_3. Thus, in the case of inferior goods, the income demand curve ID is backward sloping.

Cross Demand

Let us now take the cause of related goods and how the change in the price of one affects the demand of the other. This is known as cross demand and is wirtten as D = f (pr). Related goods are of two types, substitutes and complementary. In the case of the substitutes or competitive goods a rise in the price of the one good A raises the demand for the other good B, the price of B remaining the same. The opposite holds in the case of a fall in the price of A when the demand for B falls, Figure (A) illustrates it. When the price of good A increases from OA to OA_1 the quantity of good B also increases from OB to OB_1. The cross demand curve CD for substitutes is positively sloping. For with the rise in the price of the former, the consumers will shift their demand to B since the price of B remains unchanged. It is also assumed here that the incomes, tastes, preferences, etc. of the consumers do not change.

In case the two goods are complementary or jointly demanded, a rise in the price of one good A will bring a fall in the demand for good B. Conversely, a fall in the price of A will raise the demand for B. This is illustrated in Figure (B) where, when the price of A falls from OA_1 and OA, the demand for B increases from OB to OB_1. The cross demand curve in the case of complementary goods is negatively sloping like the ordinary demand curve.

If, however, the two goods are independent, a change in the price of A will have no effect on the demand for B. We seldom study the relation between two unrelated goods like wheat and chairs. Mostly as consumers, we are concerned with the price-demand relation of substitutes and complementary goods.

DEFECTS OF UTILITY ANALYSIS OF DEMAND

The Marshallian utility analysis has many defects and weaknesses which are discussed below:

(1) Utility cannot be Measured Cardinally. The entire Marshallian utility analysis is based on the hypothesis that utility is cardinally measured. According to the cardinal system, the utility of a commodity is measured in 'untils' or units and that utility can be added and substracted. For instance, when a consumer takes the first equivalent to 15 units; from the second and third chapati 10 and 5 units respectively and when he consumes the fourth chapati marginal utility becomes zero. If it is supposed that he has no desire after the fourth chapati, the utility from the fifth will be negative 5 units; if he takes this chapati. In this way, the total utility in each case will be 15, 25, 30 and 30, when from the fifth chapati the total utility will be 25 (30 – 5).

Besides, the utility analysis is based on this assumption that the consumer is aware of his preferences and is capable of comparing them. For example, if the utility of one apple is 10 units, of banana 20 units and of orange 40 units, it means that the consumer gives twice the preference to banana as against apple and four times to orange. It shows that utility is transitive. Hicks opines that the basis of the utility analysis, that it is measurable, is defective because utility is a subjective and psychological concept which cannot be measured cardinally. In reality, it can be measured ordinally.

(2) Single Commodity Model is Unrealistic. The utility analysis is a single commodity model in which the utility of one commodity is regarded independent of the other. Marshall considered substitutes and complementaries as one commodity, but it makes the utility analysis unrealistic. For instance, tea and coffee are substitute products. When there is change in the stock of any one product, there is change in the marginal utility of both the products. Suppose, there is increase in the stock of tea. There will not only be fall in the marginal utility of tea but also of coffee. Similarly, a change in the stock of coffee will bring a change in the marginal utility of both coffee and tea. The effect of one commodity on the other and vice versa, is called the cross effect. The utility analysis neglects the cross effects of substitutes, complementaries and unrelated goods. This makes the utility analysis unrealistic. To overcome it, Hicks constructed the two-commodity model in the indifference curve approach.

(3) Marginal Utility of Money is not Constant. The utility analysis assumes the marginal utility of money to be constant. Marshall supported this argument on the plea that a consumer spends only a small portion of his income on a commodity at a time so that there is insignificant reduction in the stock of the remaining amount of money. But the fact is that a consumer does not buy only one commodity but a number of commodities at a time. In this way when a major part of his income is spent on buying commodities, the marginal utility of the remaining stock of money increases. For instance, every consumer spends a major portion of his income in the first week of the month to meet his domestic requirements. After this, he spends the remaining amount of money wisely. It implies that the utility of the remaining sum of money has increased.

(4) Money is an Imperfect Measure of Utility. Marshall measures utility in terms of money, but money is an incorrect and imperfect measure of utility because the value of money often changes. If there is fall in the value of money, the consumer will not be getting the same utility from the homogeneous units of a commodity at different times. Fall in the value of money is a natural consequence of rise in prices. Again, if two consumers spend the same amount amount of money at a time, they will not be getting equal utilities because the amount of utility depends upon the intensity of desire of each consumer for the commodity. For inistance, consumer A may be getting more utility than B by spending the same amount of money if his intensity of desire for the commodity is greater. Thus, money is an imperfect and unreliable measuring rod of utility.

(5) Man is not Rational. The utility analysis is based on the assumption that the consumer is rational who prudently buys the commodity and has the capacity to calculate the disutilities and utilities of different commodities, and buys only those units which give him greater utility. This assumption is also unrealistic because no consumer compares the utility and disutility from each unit of a commodity while buying it. Rather he buys them under the influence of his desires, tastes or habits. Moreover, consumer's income and prices of commodities also influence his purchases. Thus the consumer does not buy commodities rationally. This makes the utility analysis unrealistic and impracticable.

(6) Utility Analysis Fails to Clarify the Study of Inferior and Giffen Goods. Marshall's utility analysis of demand does not clarify the fact as to why a fall in the price of inferior and Giffen goods leads to a decline in its demand. Marshall failed to explain this paradox because the utility analysis does not discuss the income and substitution effects of the price effect. This makes the Marshallian law of demand incomplete.

(7) Utility Analysis does not Study Income Effect, Susbtitution Effect and Price Effect. The greatest defect in the utility analysis is that it ignores the study of income effect, substitution effect and price effect. The utility analysis does not explain the effect of a rise or fall in the income of the consumer on the demand for the commodities. It thus neglects the income effect. Again when with the change in the price of one commodity there is a relative change in the price of the other commodity, the consumer substitutes one for the other. This is the substitution effect which the utility analysis fails to discuss, being based on one-commodity model. Besides, when the price of one commodity changes, there is change in its demand and in the demand for related goods. This is the price effect which is also ignored by the utility analysis. When say, the price of good X falls the utility analysis only tells us that its demand will increase. But it fails to analyse the income and substitution effects of a price fall via the increase in the real income of the consumer.

(8) This Analysis Fails to Explain the Demand for Indivisible Goods. As a corollary to the above, we may say that the utility analysis breaks down in the case of durable consumer goods like scooters, transistors, radios, etc. because they are indivisible. The consumer buys only one unit of such commodities at a time so that it is neither possible to calculate the marginal utility of one unit nor can the demand schedule and the demand curve for that goods be drawn. Hence the utility analysis is not applicable to indivisible goods.

These glaring defects in the utility analysis led economists like Hicks to explain the demand analysis of the consumer with the help of indifference curve approach.

LAW OF DEMAND AND DEMAND CURVE

This law is also known as the First Law of Purchase. It indicates the relationship between the price of a commodity and its quantity demanded in the market. The Law of Demand states that other things remaining the same, a houselold or an individual consumer will demand more of a good at a lower price than at a higher price. That is to say, the consumer will buy more of the goods than when its price is lower than when it is higher. The other things which are assumed to remain unchanged here are: *(i)* the price of all the other goods, *(ii)* the income of the consumer and *(iii)* his taste or scales of preferences as between different goods. There is also a fourth assumption which is implicit, *viz.*, that a rise or fall in the price of the goods the demand does not generate an expectation of a further change in the price in the same direction in the near future. If there is such an expectation, the law of demand may not hold true. Given these assumptions, the law of demand postulates an inverse relation between the amount demanded of a commodity and its price. The following numerical example illustrates this relationship:

Price of Rice per kg.	*Amount of Rice demanded by a household per month (in kg.)*
Rs. 6/-	2
Rs. 5/-	3
Rs. 4/-	4
Rs. 3/-	5
Rs. 2/-	6

This numerical example gives us what is called the demand schedule of rice on the part of a consumer, and is just a numerical illustration of the law of demand.

The law of demand can also be illustrated geometrically in a price-quantity diagram measuring price along the vertical axis and

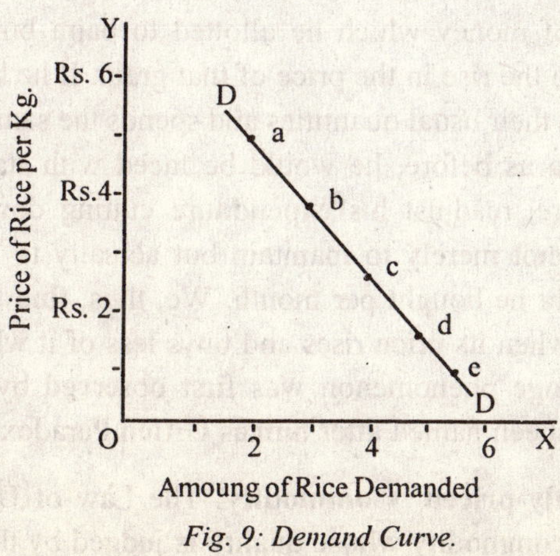

Fig. 9: Demand Curve.

quantity demanded along the horizontal axis. The information contained in the above table is plotted in the figure. Each of the points a, b, c, d, and e, shows the quanitity of rice demanded at a particular price. By joining all these points the demand curve DD is obtained, which is the geometrical representation of the demand schedule. This demand curve shows that more is demanded at a lower price than at a higher price, and is thus a geometrical illustration of the law of demand.

As pointed out above when the law of demand applies the demand curve normally, slopes downward from the left to the right. But there can be certain exceptional cases where the demand curve will slope upward from left to right *i.e.* law of demand does not hold true. There are four exceptions to the normal demand curve or law of demand, namely:

(1) 'Giffen' Paradox. The Giffen Good is often considered an exception to the normal demand curve. In other words, it is an exception to the Law of Demand : A fall in its price tends to reduce and a rise in its price tends to extend its demand. For example, take the case of a poor man who spends a major portion of his money income on an inferior commodity like bajra and is, therefore, able to spend only a small part of it on other commodities. Now suppose that the price of bajra rises but the prices of other commodities remain the same. His real income would have fallen. He would find that the monthly sum of money which he allotted to bajra buys less than before owing to the rise in the price of that grain. If he bought other commodities in their usual quantities and spends the same amount of money on bajra as before, he would be faced with starvation. He would, therefore, readjust his expenditure cutting down on other items in order not merely to maintain but actually to increase the quantity of bajra he bought per month. We, thus, find that he buys more of bajra when its price rises and buys less of it when its price falls. This strange phenomenon was first observed by Sir Robert Giffen and has been named after him as Giffen Paradox.

(2) 'Highly-priced' Commodity. The Law of Demand may not apply to a commodity whose quality is judged by the consumer by its high price. The producers of several luxury goods have discovered that their sales of these goods often go up when they increase their prices. The ignorant consumers consider those products superior which are sold at higher prices. As such, they buy more of these products at higher than at lower prices.

(3) 'Status Symbol' Commodity. A commodity is sometimes bought not because it has any intrinsic worth but because its possession confers a social distinction on the holder. For example, diamonds are bought largely by the richer class for the prestige they confer upon the possessor. If the price of diamonds were to fall, so that even the poorer classes could have them in plenty, they would not longer confer any social distinction and the richer classes may stop buying them altogehter.

(4) Speculation. If the price of a commodity is increasing and it is expected to increase still further, the consumers will buy more of the commodity at the higher price than they did at the lower price. Thus, an increase in price may not be accompanied by a contraction in demand, negating the Law of Demand itself.

INCREASE AND DECREASE OF DEMAND

In ordinany language, we do not observe any distinction between 'increase in demand' and 'extension of demand', and betwen 'decrease in demand' and 'contraction of demand.' But in economics, we do observe this distinction.

The law of demand states that consumers demand more of a good at a lower price than at a higher price, other things remaining the same. In other words, with a fall in price, the consumers buy more of a good. This represents a movement along the same demand curve and is technically called an expansion of demand. Increase in demand for a good is to be carefully distinguished from such expansion of demand. Increase of demand means that on account of changes in certain factors other than the price of the commodity, consumers now demand a larger quantity than before at the same price or the same quanitity at a higher price. This is illustrated diagramatically in the figure. The demand curve DD represents the initial state of demand. At the price OR (=PQ), OQ of a good is demanded. An increase in demand is represented by a rightward shift of the demand curve. D_1D_1 represents this new position of the demand curve. With the increase in demand, the same quantity OQ is demanded at the higher price P_2 Q, and at the old price OR_1 (= P_1 Q_1) a large quantity OQ_1 is demanded. Similarly, a decrease in demand is to be distinguished from contraction of demand. The latter relates to a smaller quantity being demanded by the consumers at a higher price, other things remaining the same, and is represented by a movement along the same demand curve. Decrease in demand, on the other hand, means that on account of a change in any of these other factors, such as, income, taste or prices of other goods, consumers demand the same quantity at a lower price or a smaller quantity at the same price as before. Diagramatically, this is represented by a leftward shift of the demand curve. This can also be illustrated by the figure, if D_1 is taken to represent the initial state of demand, and DD the position of the demand curve after the decrease in demand.

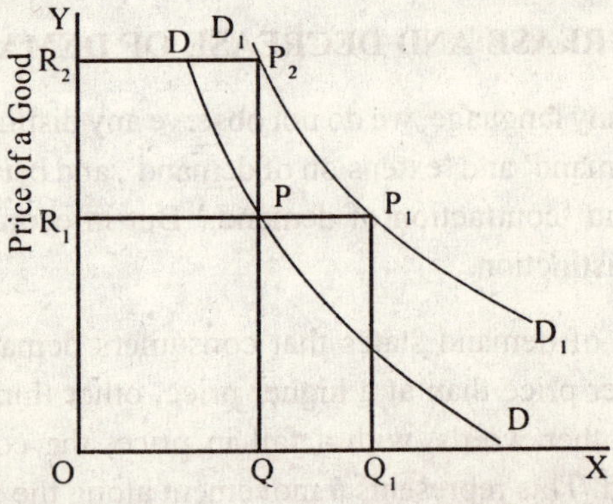

Fig. 10: Increase and Decrease and Expansion and contraction of Demand.

Thus, expansion and contraction of demand relate simply to the law of demand indicating the changes in the quantity of a good demanded with changes in its price, all other factors affecting the demand remaining unchanged. Increase and decrease in the demand for a good, on the other hand, relate to the effect of changes in any of these other factors on the quantity bought. The effect of a change in these other factors, therefore, is represented by a shift, rightward or leftward as the case may be, of the demand curve for the good under consideration.

PRICE ELASTICITY OF DEMAND

In terms of degree, price elasticity of demand is classified into five categories: *(i)* perfectly elastic demand, *(ii)* perfectly inelastic demand, *(iii)* unitary elasticity of demand, *(iv)* elastic demand, and *(v)* inelastic demand.

1. Perfectly Elastic Demand. If the demand for a commodity changes though there is no change in its price, it is a case of perfectly elastic demand. In other words, if the quantity demanded keeps on increasing or decreasing in spite of the fact that the price remains constant, elasticity of demand is said to be equal to infinite (e = ∞). The demand curve representing perfectly elastic demand is parallel to X-axis as shown in Figure (11). One would observe that at price OD there is no fixed quantity demanded. At this price the demand may be OQ or OQ_1 or even OQ_2. This implies that the quantity demanded changes in spite of price remaining unchanged. However, in practice a case of perfectly elastic demand does not exist.

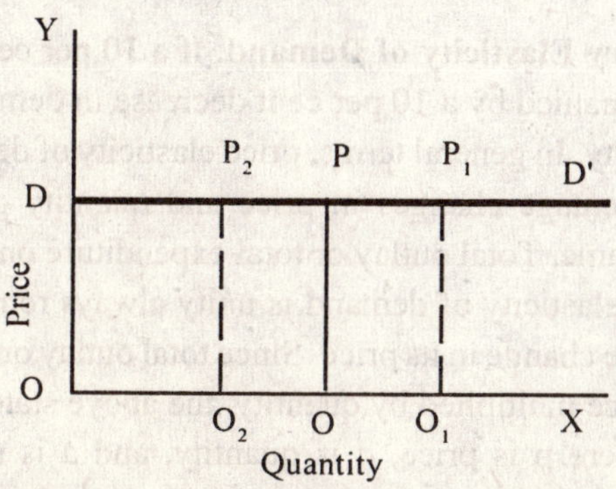

Fig. 11: Perfectly Elastic Demand Curve

2. Perfectly Inelastic Demand. If the demand for a commodity does not change in spite of an increase or decrease in its price, we have a case of perfectly inelastic demand. This implies a situation where demand is totally unresponsive to changes in the price of the commodity. Thus elasticity of demand is zero (e=0). Perfectly inelastic demand is also a hypothetical situation. In practice there is perhaps no commodity for which demand may be perfectly inelastic under any situation. Hence the concept of perfectly inelastic demand has little importance outside theoretical analysis. A demand curve showing perfectly inelastic demand is always parallel to Y-axis. Such a demand curve has been shown in Figure. As is clear from this figure, the demand for the commodity remains the same (=OD') whatever the price.

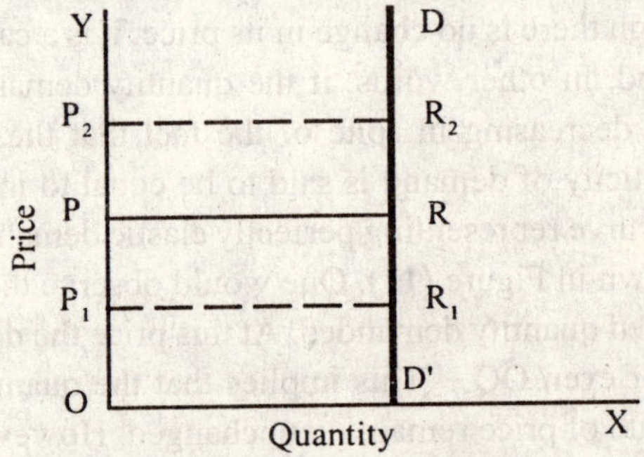

Fig. 12: Perfectly Inelastic Demand Curve

3. Unitary Elasticity of Demand. If a 10 per cent increase in price is accompanied by a 10 per cent decrease in demand, the price elasticity is unity. In general terms, price elasticity of demand is unity (E_d=1) if percentage changes in price and quantity demanded are precisely the same. Total outlay or total expenditure on a commodity for which the elasticity of demand is unity always remains constant whatever be the change in its price. Since total outlay on a commodity is given by price multiplied by quantity, the above statement implies that pq=a (where p is price, q is quantity, and a is some positive constant). In mathematics, such a curve is known as rectangular hyperbola. Therefore, the demand curve representing unitary elasticity of demand on each of its point assumes the shape of a rectangular hyperbola. Such a demand curve is shown in Figure.

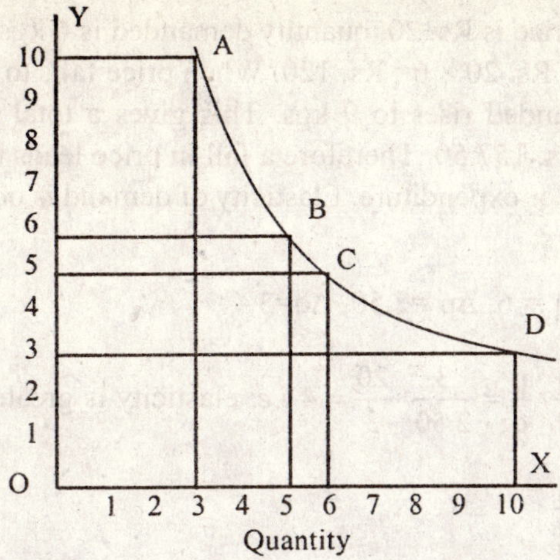

Fig. 13: Unitary Elastic Demand Curve

At all points A, B, C and D on the demand curve, total expenditure is Rs. 30. Therefore, the demand curve exhibits unitary elasticity of demand.

4. Elastic Demand. In certain cases the responsiveness of demand measured in terms of percentage change is far greater than the percentage change in the price of the commodity. This implies that if the price of a commodity rises by 10 per cent, then in response to it the demand falls by a higher percentage. This is known as elastic demand. Generally, the demand for luxury goods is elastic. It is often seen that the demand for these products increases considerably in response to small reduction in their price. Conversely, if the price of a luxury good rises, the quanity demanded decreases by a larger percentage. Numerically, elastic demand is greater than one but less than infinite ($1 < e < \infty$). A price rise in respect of a commodity for which demand is elastic results in a fall of total outlay on it. By the same logic a decrease in the price of such a commodity will result in an increase in total outlay on it. We may now consider the graphical represen-tation of elastic demand. If the demand curve is linear, sloping downward from left to right, and touches the two axes as in Figure, elasticity at all points between D (The point on the Y-axis) and K (the mid-point on the demand curve) will be greater than one but less than infinite.

When price is Rs. 20, quantity demanded is 6 kgs. This gives a total outlay of Rs. 20 × 6= Rs. 120. When price falls to Rs. 17.50 the quantity demanded rises to 9 kgs. This gives a total outlay of Rs. 17.50 × 9 = Rs. 157.50. Therefore a fall in price leads to an increase in total outlay or expenditure. Elasticity of demand is obtained in this case as follows:

$p = 20, q = 6, \Delta p = 2.50, \Delta q = 3$

$$E_d = \frac{\Delta q}{\Delta P} \times \frac{p}{q} = \frac{3}{2.50} \times \frac{20}{3} = 4 \text{ i.e. elasticity is greater than unity.}$$

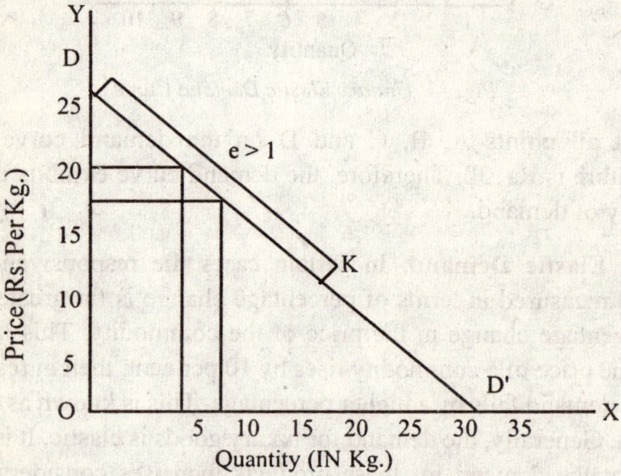

Fig. 14: Elastic Demand — elasticity is greater than one for all points between D and K

5. Inelastic Demand. If the demand is not much responsive to the price change, that is, a considerable increase or decrease in the price does not result in much change in quantity demanded, the demand is inelastic. To be more precise, if the quantity demanded changes by a smaller percentage than does price, we have the case of inelastic demand. Demand for commodities which fall in the category of necessities display such elasticity. Consumption of a necessary commodity cannot be reduced proportionately when its price rises. Conversely it is also true that the consumption of such a commodity does not increase considerably in response to even large reduction in the price of the product. For example, salt is a necessity and its demand does not change much in response to change in price. Therefore, it exhibits inelastic demand. Numerically elasticity of demand for necessities is greater than zero but less than unity ($0 < e < 1$). In case of a linear demand curve which touches the two axes as in figure (5), elasticty of demand at all points between the point D (on X-axis) and mid-point K will be greater than zero but less than unity.

When price is Rs. 7, the quantity demanded is 20.5 kgs. This gives a total outlay of Rs. 7 × 20.5= Rs. 143.50. When price falls to Rs. 5, the quantity demanded increases to 24 kgs. This gives a total outlay of Rs. 5 × 24= Rs. 120. Thus a fall in price leads to a fall in total revenue. Elasticity of demand in this case is obtained as follows:

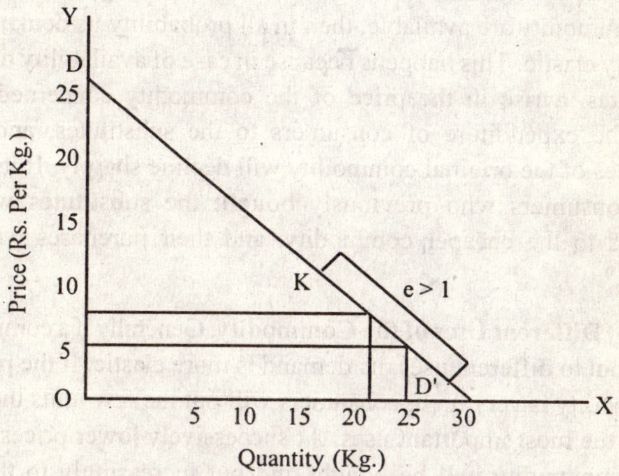

Fig. 15: Elastic Demand—elasticity is greater than one for all points between D and K

DETERMINANTS OF PRICE ELASTICITY OF DEMAND

Elasticity of demand for a product depends upon a number of factors operating simultaneously. We shall now consider the major determinants of price elasticity of demand for a commodity:

(1) Nature of the Commodity. Elasticity of demand for a commodity depends upon the nature of the commodity concerned.

Demand for necessities is invariably inelastic. This is so because consumers find it difficult to reduce their consumption of necessities like foodgrains, salt, cooking fuel etc., even if their prices increase. Therefore, whatever be the price rise, demand for necessities does not decline substantially. Conversely, in the case of a fall in price, the demand for a necessary good does not rise. Elasticity of demand for most of the goods falling in the category of comforts is generally unitary as the consumer's outlay on them is generally constant in spite of price changes. As pointed out earlier, the demand for most of the luxury goods is elastic.

(2) Availability of Substitutes. Boulding maintains that it is the availability of good substitutes which determines the elasticity of demand for a commodity in a decisive manner. If good substitutes for a commodity are available, then in all probability its demand will be highly elastic. This happens because in case of availability of good substitutes, a rise in the price of the commodity concerned "will divert the expenditure of consumers to the substitutes, and their purchases of the original commodity will decline sharply. If its price falls, consumers who previously bought the substitutes will be attracted to the cheaper commodity, and their purchases will rise sharply."

(3) Different Uses of the Commodity. Generally if a commodity can be put to different uses, its demand is more elastic. If the price of a commodity is very high, consumers will put the few units they buy only to the most important uses. At successively lower prices, more of the commodity will be bought and put increasingly to the less important uses. This can be illustrated from the case of petroleum. We all know that petroleum can be put to a variety of uses. It can be used for operating machines and means of transport, lighting, cooking etc. If the price of petroleum increases, it is possible that many households stop using it as a fuel for cooking purposes. If, on the other hand, its price declines it may be used for all possible purposes and in that case its demand may increase considerably.

(4) Importance of the Commodity in Consumer's Budget. If consumers spend a very small proportion of their income on a commodity, the price elasticity of the commodity is likely to be very low. For example, the demand for items like salt and matches is inelastic. The consumers spend such a low proportion of their income on these commodities that even a substantial hike in their price does not lead to a fall in their consumption. On the other hand, demand for goods on which consumers spend a relatively larger portion of their income is elastic. For example, let us suppose that a household has an income of Rs. 5,000 per month. Of this, Rs. 20 are spent on salt and Rs. 600 on transportation. Suppose that, the price of both, salt and transportation, goes up by 100 per cent. If the household continues to buy the same amount of salt, it will now have to spend Rs. 40 per month on it. Thus it will be required to reduce other expenditure by a mere Rs. 20 per month and this is only 0.4 per cent of its monthly expenditure of Rs. 5000. However, the transportation cost will now rise to Rs. 1,200 (if the household continues to demand the same amount of transportation services). This involves an additional expenditure of Rs. 600 *i.e.*, 12 per cent of total monthly expenditure. Therefore, expenditure on othe items will have to be drastically pruned. This shows that the reaction of the household to the doubling of prices under the two conditions would be different. The household would continue to buy the same amount of salt but will cut down on transportation expenses.

(5) Joint Demand. In the case of goods having joint demand, demand of one good varies alongwith the demand of the other good. In such a case the elasticity of demand of the good which is more important determines the elasticity of demand for the other good.

(6) Possibilities of Postponing the Consumption. There are certain commodities consumption of which cannot be postponed even for a short period. Foodgrains, salt, sugar, and medicines are a few commodities falling in this category. Their demand is generally inelastic because the consumer has no choice but to maintain his consumption level in spite of price rise. Purchase of commodities like woollen clothes, shoes, etc....., on the other hand, can be deferred for some time and thus their demand is relatively elastic.

(7) Time for Adjustment in Purchases. Demand for a commodity always exists in some specific period of time, say a day, a week, a month, a year *etc*. Elasticity of demand varies with the length of time. Generally, demand is more elastic longer the period of time under consideration. This is due to the reason that longer the period of time, the greater is the case of substitution for both consumers and producers. For example, consider a price decrease. If the price decrease persists for a sufficiently long time, the consumers will discover many new uses for the commodity. Moreover, a number of new users of the commodity in question will also arise.

(8) Fashion, Tastes and Preferences of Consumers. Elasticity of demand is also affected by the tastes and preferences of the consumers and the fashions in vogue. For example, a person accustomed to smoking Four Square King brand will not easily shift over to other brands even if the price of Four Square King cigarettes increases substantially. Thus, his demand for Four Square King cigarettes will be inelastic over a wide price-range. Similarly consumers have their own preferences for different brands of tea (Taster's Choice, Green Label Lipton tea, Brooke Bond tea, Taj Mahal tea etc.), different brands of soaps (Lux, Liril, Cinthol etc.), different brands of talcum powder (Ponds, Cinthol, Liril etc.) and do not easily switch over to other brands even if the prices of the brands they use increase considerably. Therefore, their demands for their particular brands are inelastic over a wide price-range. Fashion also affects elasticity. If a certain type of readymade garment is in vogue and its customers stick to it, a sharp increase in its price will not reduce its demand much. Therefore, demand for that garment would be relatively inelastic.

ROLE OF ELASTICITY OF DEAMND IN MANAGERIAL/BUSINESS DECISIONS

The concept of price elasticity of demand and income elasticity are of great importance in managerial decision making. Often a businessman has to consider whether a lowering of price will lead to an increase in the demand for his product and if so to what extent and whether his profits would increase as a result thereof. The concept of elasticity of demand becomes crucial in this aspect. In demand, if the increase in sale is more than proportionate to decline in price, the total scale proceeds or revenue will increase resulting into increase in profit. In case, profit declines due to change in price than the business manager has to reconsider the pricing of his product. The knowledge of the elasticity of demand will help a businessman to determine whether and to what extent the increase in cost could be passed on through price on the consumer. A monopolist would not be able to increase the price of his product the demand of his product is elastic.

The income elasticity of a product is also of great significance in production planning and management in the long run particularly the period of business cycles. The concept of income elasticity can be used in demand forecasting provided the rate of increase in income and income elasticity of demand for the products are known. The knowledge of income elasticity helps in avoiding over production or under production because both are harmful to the business and responsibility comes to the managerial part.

In practice an accurate estimate of the probable response of volume of sales to price changes is extremely difficult. The subjective judgement of certain managers also is based on their years of experience and happens to be more accurate than the estimated through statistical methods. It must be emphasized that an accurate knowledge of elasticity of demand of a commodity as well as the brand produced by the company is essential for the effective analysis of a wide range of a business problems, especially, pricing and marketing problems.

Application of Elasticity of Demand in Business

The elasticity of demand is widely used by the management in taking business decisions which is discussed as under :

(1) Elasticity of demand is of vital importance for the monopolist to adopt discriminatory price policy. He can charge higher price in that market where demand is less elastic and will charge comparatively low price where demand for the product is more elastic.

(2) It is also used in the decisions of joint supply of certain goods by the management such as the demand of wool and button used on the wool products.

(3) In case of public utilities, govt. adopt a pricing policy with the objective of social welfare. A higher price is charged from the rich people. This type of practice is being adopted by the Govt. in case of public utilities like supply of electricity, drinking water and railway services etc.

(4) In the modern business, super market and departmental stores where a number of products are sold by a single organisation. They are suppose to sell where products at slightly lower prices because a buyer comes to purchase one product, may also purchase another product due to display in the premises.

(5) The elasticity of demand is also helpful for factor pricing by the management. Those factors of production whose supply in less elastic like that of technocrates they are paid more and workers whose supply is elastic are paid less.

(6) The elasticity of demand is also used by the management in making a decision regarding the choice between labour and machine, brands of machine and substitutes of inputs.

(7) The elasticity of demand is also being used by the management in shifting the tax burden. If the demand for the product is perfectly elastic, tax burden cannot be shifted on the buyer. On the other hand if demand is perfectly inelastic the producer may be able to shift entire tax burden on the consumer. Practically, tax burden is shared by both buyers and sellers.

(8) The elasticity of demand also play indespensable role in determining international trade. The various methods of correcting adverse balance of payments like devaluation and exchange rate depreciation are also effected by the elasticity of demand of the products being exported and imported.

❐

4

Demand Forecasts

MEANING OF DEMAND FORECASTING

In literary sense forecasting mean prediction. Forecasting may be defined as a technique of translating past experience into production of things to come. It tries to evaluate the magnitude and significance of forces that will affect future operating conditions in an enterprise. Thus demand forecasting is an estimation of future demand.

Acccording to Marketing Association, "An estimate of sales in dollars or physical units for a specified future period under a proposed marketing plan or programme and under an assumed set of economic and other forces outside the unit for which the forecast is made. The forecast may be for a specified items of merchandise or for entire line." In the words of Philip Kotler, "The company sales forecast is the expected level of company sales based on a chosen marketing plan and assumed environmental conditions."

Thus, in simple words, sales forecasting is an estimate of future sales. From a company's or firm's point of view, sales forecasting mean deciding in advance its share in the total market demand. This estimate is made considering various factors—controllable and non-controllable, and present and anticipated market conditions.

Accurate demand forecasting is essential for a firm to enable it to produce the required quantities at the right time and arrange well in advance for the various factors of production, viz. raw materials, machines, accessories, labour buildings etc. Some firms produce to order but generally, firms produce in anticipation of future demand. Forecasting helps a firm to assess the probable demand for its products and plan its production accordingly.

The following are the main components of a demand forecasting system:

(i) Market Research Operation to get the relevant and reliable information about the trends in markets.

(ii) A data processing and analysing system to estimate and evaluate the sales performance in various markets.

(iii) Proper co-ordination of steps *(i)* and *(ii)* and then to place the findings before the top managements for making final decisions.

PURPOSE OR OBJECTIVES OF DEMAND FORECASTING

The objectives of demand forecasting differ according to types of forecasting. They can be divided in two categories namely (i) Short Term Objectives (ii) Long Term Objectives.

Short Term Objectives

(i) Formulation of a Suitable Production Policy. Sales forecasts help in formulating suitable production policy so that there may not be any gap between demand and supply of product. This can avoid the problem of over production and under-production.

(ii) Regular Supply of Material. By the determination of desired volume of production on the basis of sales forecasts, one can evaluate the necessary raw material requirements in future so as to ensure regular and continuous supply of the material as well as controlling the size of inventory at economic level. This helps the firm by reducing cost of purchasing raw material.

(iii) Maximum Utilisation of Machines. The operations can be so planned that the machines are utilised to its maximum capacity.

(iv) Price Policy Formulation. Sales forecasts enables the management to formulate some appropriate pricing machanism so that the level of price does not fluctuate too much in the periods of depression or inflation.

(v) Regular Availability of Labour. Skilled and unskilled workers can be properly arranged to meet the production schedule requirement.

(vi) Proper Control of Sales. Sales forecasts are calculated region-wise and then the sales targets for various territories are fixed accordingly. This later on becomes the basis to evaluate sales performance.

(vii) Arrangement of Finance. On the basis of sales forecast, one can determine the financial requirements of the enterprise for the production of desired output. This can lead to minimise the cost of procuring finance.

Long Term Objectives

If period of a forecast is more than a year then it is termed a long-term forecast. The following are the main objectives of such forecasts :

(i) To Decide about Production Capacity. The size of the plant should be such that the output conforms with sales requirements. Too small or too large size of the plant may not be in the economic interest of the enterprise.

(ii) Labour Requirements. Expenditure on labour is one of the most important components in cost of production. Reliable and accurate sales forecast can help the management to assess the appropriate labour requirements. This can ensure best labour facility and no hindrances in the production process.

(iii) Long Term. Production planning can help the managment to arrange for long-term finances on reasonable terms and conditions.

The analysis of long term sales is more signficant than short term sales. Long term sales forecast helps the management to take some policy decisions of great significance and any error committed in this may be very difficult or expensive to be rectified.

Thus the overall success of an enterpise mainly depends on the quality and reliability of sales forecasting machanism.

UTILITY OR IMPORTANCE OF DEMAND FORECASTING

(i) Balanced Policies. Sales forecast tries to maintain a balance between production and distribution policies of the enterprises. With decentralisation of function and increase in the size of the organisation, forecasting is of great value for proper control and co-ordination of various activities.

(ii) Helps in Suitable Decision. An efficient demand forecast helps the management to take suitable decisions regarding plant capacity, raw material requirement, space and building needs and availability of labour and capital. Production schedules can be prepared in conformity with demand requirements minimising inventory production and other related costs.

(iii) Helps Sales Department. Demand forecasting also helps in evaluating the performance of sales department.

(iv) An Effective Tool. Demand forecasting is a necessary and effective tool in the hands of the management of an enterprise to have finished goods of right quality and quantity at right time with minimum cost.

(v) Helps in Financial Requirements. Demand forecasting is also very useful for a firm in estimating its financial requirements. Cash requirements depend on sales level and production operations. Moreover, it also requires sometimes to get funds on reasonable term. Sales forecasts will, therefore, enable arrangement of sufficient funds on reasonable terms well in advance.

(vi) Helps Old and New Firms. Demand forecasting is essential for both the old and new firms in large-scale production and there is a long gestation period in the production process. In such circumstances, an idea about future demand is necessary to avoid under-production and over production.

(vii) Provides Guidelines. Demand forecast for a particular product also provides a guideline for demand forecast of related industries. For example, demand forecast for the automobile industry also helps the industry in estimating the demand for 2-wheelers, 3-wheelers and 4-wheelers.

(viii) Helps in the Determination of Import and Export. At macro level, demand forecasting is useful to the government also for determining the targets of imports and exports for different commodities and planning the international business.

NEED OF FORECASTING DEMAND

Business managers depending upon their functional areas need demand forecast so that supply, profit and other factors may be arranged to meet the requirement of demand. The significance of demand forecasting in business policy decisions can hardly be over-emphasised. Demand forecasting is closely connected with sales forecast which is needed for production planning, inventory planning, profit planning and so on. The survival and continuity of business totally depends upon accurate demand forecast.

In the short-period, the demand forecasting is essential and of primary importance due to the following reasons:

(1) The schedule appropriate production.

(2) To help in reducing cost of purchasing inputs like raw material.

(3) To determine the changes in technique of production.

(4) To adopt adequate price policy to control market.

(5) To adopt suitable advertising programmes.

(6) To forecast short-terms financial requirements.

(7) To set-up sales targets.

(8) To decide incentives to be given to the sellers.

The success of a product in the short-period encourages and inspires the producer to accurately forecast demand for the long-term. In the long period, producer's object is to control the market and check the rivals to enter into the market. Long-term forecasting is important for the following reasons:

(1) To plan the expansion of existing unit.

(2) To determine long-term financial requirements so that funds may be arranged accordingly.

(3) To determine the need and requirement of providing training to its staff.

(4) To estimate the necessity of change or innovation in the product.

Hence, demand forecasting is badly needed in both short-period and long-period for the success of a product in the market.

STEPS INVOLVED IN FORECASTING

Demand forecasting is a scientific exercise and requires following steps for efficient forecast :

1. Nature of Forecast. First of all, it must be determined, what type of demand is to be forcasted. Whether it is for short-period or long-period; whether for an individual firm or for the economy as a whole and so on. The nature must be clear before the forecasting process is undertaken.

2. Identification of Objective. It is necessary to clearly identify what does one want to get from the forecast. The purpose of the exercise like quantity, quality, composition of demand sale's planning, inventory control etc. must be well-known and clear.

3. Nature of Product. The next important consideration is determining the nature of product for which demand is to be forecasted. One has to examine carefully whether the product is perishable or durable, primary, intermediatery or final product. All these factors influence the demand forecasting. The nature of product will determine whether the demand is new demand or replacement demand. Time factor is very crucial determinant in demand forecasting because goods of perishable nature and of daily consumption requires quick adjustment in demand forecasting. Time element enters into demand forecasting through a product life cycle given below. The forecasting of demand must keep in mind the stage in which the product is passing through its cycle.

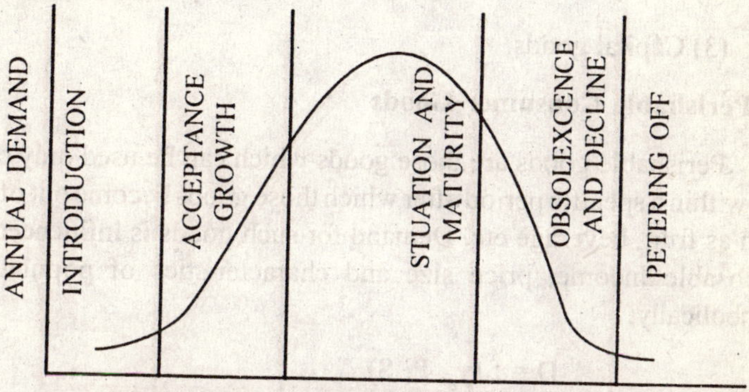

4. Selecting a Proper Method of Forecasting. There are various techniques of demand forecasting based on statistical and non-statistical methods. The selection of a suitable method of forecasting depends upon the objectives of forecasting, type of data available, period for which the forecast is to be made etc.

5. Interpretation of Results. The process of demand forecasting will be incomplete unless results are properly interpreted. Efficiency of forecasting depends to a large extent upon the efficiency in the interpretations of its results. The forecasting interpretation must be reasonably supported by the backward factors like govt. policy, general business environments, international economic and political practice.

6. Analysis of Factors. The analysis of trend which affect the demand function also require consideration in demand forecasting. Trend, seasonal variations, cyclical fluctuation and irregular fluctuations also effect forecasting and require adequate considerations and adjustments in forecasting. Analysis of factor is important depending upon whether it is the aggregate demand in the economy or the demand for a firm.

DETERMINANTS FOR DEMAND FORECASTING

The goods are generally classified into three categories:

(1) Perishable consumer goods.

(2) Durable consumer goods.

(3) Capital goods.

(1) Perishable Consumer Goods

Perishable goods are those goods which can be used only once and within a specific period after which those goods become out of use such as fruit, beverage etc. Demand for such goods is influenced by disposable income, price size and characteristics of population, Symbolically;

$$D = f(y_d, P, S)$$

where, D = demand

y_d = disposable income

P_d = Price

S = Size and characteristics of population.

(i) **Disposable Income.** Disposable income refers to that part of income of the consumer which is available with him to be spent on consumption. Disposable income determines the purchasing power of the consumer. Some Economists believe that it is most appropriate to use discretionary income instead of disposable income.

(ii) **Price.** Price has direct impact on the demand of a consumer. Price of substitutes and related goods also affects the demand. Moreover, the price elasticity and cross elasticity also effects demand of consumer for a product.

(iii) **Size and Characteristics of Population.** It is commonly known that population size, income groups, social status, age/sex composition, geographical characteristics, urban-rural ratio etc. influence the demand for perishable goods.

Durable Consumer Goods.

All consumer goods which can be used again and again and can be stored are known as durable consumer goods such as capital goods, machinery appliances etc. are durable goods. The major important consideration for forecasting demand for durable consumer goods are as under:

(i) Consumer has to make a choice between choosing the goods for longer period by repairing it or by disposing it and replacing with a new one. For example, we replace black and white T.V. into a coloured T.V.

(ii) These goods require special facilities for their use and require important variable for determining their demand.

(iii) As consumer durables like cycle are to be used by more than one person, the decision to purchase by family characteristics.

(iv) The nature upto which durable goods are used by household rather than individuals. The few consumer durable like electronic goods are expected by more than one person.

(v) Total demand consists of replacement demand and new demand. Once a person is accustomed to use a product, he is unlikely to give it up. This creates regular demand and predictable. The purchasing power, the number of families and some other factors depending upon the product concerned set-up upper limit to the maximum level.

(vi) Price and credit conditions. If the price is reasonable to the life time of the product, it will influence demand forecasting. The credit terms can also influence the demand forecasting. The development of higher purchase system helps in pushing demand for a product.

Thus, demand for a durable product is influenced by a number of factors. Moreover, this is not obligatory for any consumer to purchase a particular quantity of a product.

Capital Goods

Capital goods are defined as those goods which help in further production of goods. It includes building machinery, tools etc. The demand for capital goods is derived demand. As the demand for capital goods is derived demand, it depends upon profitability, ratio of production to capacity and level of wage rates. New demand as well as replacement demand will have to be considered. The data required for estimating the demand for capital goods are:

(i) The growth prospects of the user industries.

(ii) The norms of consumption.

The demand for capital goods is also influenced by the size of the market, availability of finance, growth of prospective customers and labour saving equipment.

Hence, the factors or determinants of demand forecasting depends upon the nature of a product and influenced by a number of economic and non-economic factors.

METHODS OF FORECASTING

Broadly speaking, there are two approaches of demand forecasting. One is to obtain information about the likely purchase behaviour of the buyer through collecting information by conducting interviews with the consumer. The second is based upon statistical analysis. There are various forecasting techniques, varying in the terms of accuracy and satisfaction. Though, statistical techniques are essential in clarifying relationship and providing techniques of analysis, they are not substitutes for judgement. In statistical tools, past experience is used as a guide and extrapolating past ends, future demand is estimated. The survey method is used in short-term forecasting.

(1) Simple Survey Methods. The simple survey methods are discussed below:

(A) Consumer Survey Method. In this method, investigators contact personally to the consumer to ask about their future plans.

Under this method, in a particular locality, all the consumer are contacted, information collected regarding the total consumption of the product and then a report is prepared. In consumer survey method; there are following three methods:

(i) Complete Enumeration Survey. Under this method, all the consumer are contacted one by one and the information so collected is used for demand forecasting. This method has the advantage of simplicity, accuracy and most authenticity but this method suffers from personal prejudice of the investigator, costly proposition and the hesitation of the informent. Moreover, consumer from which we collect information may not be in a position to show his future purchases.

(ii) Sample Survey Method. This method is also known as consumer clinic approach under which the probable demand expressed by each selected unit is summed up to get the total demand of a product in the forecast period. This is a method very commonly used in common demand forecasting. Under this method, it is presumed that all the consumers are alike. This method is less tedious and less costly as compared to complete survey method but this method is subjected to the limitations like : *(a)* Continued test, *(b)* Product must be produced in bulk, out of which is proportion is sold in test area, *(c)* Uniformity of consumers.

(iii) End Use Method. In this method, the sale of the product under consideration is projected on the bases of demand survey of the industries using this product as an intermediate product. In other words, demand for the final product is end use demand of the intermediate product used in the production of final product but the following points must be kept in mind:

(a) An intermediate product like steel may have many end uses like agriculture, industry machinery, transportation etc.

(b) Intermediate goods may have demand both in the national and international market. This method is also known as input-output method which shows one product is input as well as output. Except in the case of intermediate products, demand forecasting through end use method is neither desirable nor fisible.

(B) Sales Forces Opinion Method. Under this method, the salesmen who are close to the market are questioned regarding the demand and sales of a product and on the basis of response given by them, demand is forecasted. This method is cheap, easy and does not involve any statistical method of mathematical calculations but it has certain disadvantages like congenital optimism or pessimism of the salesman, there is a possibility of under estimation or overestimation of the salesman. The accuracy of this method depends upon the behaviour of salesman and their attitude towards the product.

(C) Delphi Method or Expert Opinion Method. A variant of the opinion pole and survey method is Delphi method. It consists of an attempt to arrive at a concensus in an uncertain area by questioning a group of experts repeatedly until the response appear to coverage along a single line or the issue causing disagreement are clearly defined. Each expert is given the opportunity to reach to the information or considerations advanced by others. Delphi method was originally developed at Rand Corporation of USA in the late 1940 by Olaf Helmer, Dalcey and Gordan and has been successfully used in the area of technological forecasting. It is possible to use this method where interchanging discussions are frequently occuring.

(2) Statistical Methods. Under statistical method, following are the main methods being used in demand forecasting:

(A) Mechanical Extrapolation or Trend Projection Method. These methods are, generally, based on analysis of the past sales pattern. These methods do not use costly market as such and is based on the analysis of time series. In time series, we may use:

(i) Free hand curve method

(ii) Semi-average method

(iii) Moving average method

(iv) Method of least square.

(v) Exponential or semi log trend method.

(B) Barometeric Technique (Economic Barometers). The difference between mechanical extrapolation and barometeric technique is significant. Mechanical extrapolation implies that the future is some sort or the expansion of the past and economic barometer is based on the idea that future can be predicted from certain events occurring in the present situations. Economic barometers are more important than mechanical extrapolation. These trends are reflected in the market by leading indicators. There are certain coincident indicators and lagging indicators.Coincident indicators are GNP, industrial production index etc. Lagging indicators are manufactures stock levels and consumer's credit outstanding.

Diffusion indices show the percentage of leading indicators which experienced simultaneous rise over a proceeding period.

(C) Regression Method. Regression analysis is a technique by which the relationship between quantity demand and other variables take income, price, advertisements etc. is estimated. It is a technique by which if one variable is known, the other corresponding variable can be estimated or forecasted. Regression analysis may be:

(a) Linear regression analysis

(b) Non-linear

(c) Multiple or partial regression analysis.

(D) Simultaneous Equation Method. This method is also known as the complete system approach. Under this method, simultaneous considerations of all variables are taken into consideration. It may be a system of predetermined or not determined variables. This method is beneficial in those cases where we need to estimate the future value of only predetermined variables.

FORECASTING DEMAND FOR NEW PRODUCTS

1. Project the demand for the new product as an outgrowth of an existing old product.
2. Analyse the new product as substitute for some existing product or service.
3. Estimate the demand by making direct enquiries from the ultimate purchasers, either by the use of samples or on a full scale.
4. Offer the new product for sale in sample market, *e.g.*, by direct mail or through one multiple shop organisation.
5. Estimate the rate of growth and the ultimate level of demand for the new product on the basis of the pattern of growth established products.
6. Survey consumer's reaction to a new product indirectly through the eyes of specialised dealers who are supposed to be informed about consumer's need the alternative opportunities.

These methods are not mutually exclusive and it would be desirable to try to combine several of them so that cross checking is possible. To some extent, the methods of forecasting demand for an established product may also be applied or adapted for new products.

FACTORS INVOLVED IN DEMAND FORECASTING

According to Savage and Small there are at least six factors involved in demand forecasting:

1. Period of Forecasting. How far ahead? The problem arises how long is the future period for which forecasting is being made. This problem is solved by having both short-run forecasting, usually defined as covering any period up to one year, and long run forecasting covering a period of 5, 10 or even 20 years.

How far ahead can be the long-term forecast, depending upon the nature of the industry, but beyond ten year, the future becomes so uncertain that the projection becomes rather dubious. However, because of the close link with capital expenditure forecasting, it may be necessary to look 20 years ahead in case of certain industries. For example, petroleum companies, and paper mills, etc.

A short-term forecasting may cover a period of three months, choice depends upon the nature of the business; when demand fluctuates from one month to another, a very short period should be taken.

Instead of defining short-term and long-term forecasting in terms of different periods of time, an alternative method is to associate them with certain types of decisions or objectives to be met.

Accordingly, short-term forecast is one which provides information for technical decisions, it is, therefore, concerned with day-to-day operations within the limits of resources currently available. A long-term forecast is one which provides information for major strategic decisions; it is concerned with extending or reducing the limits of resources.

2. Various Levels Demand forecasting may be undertaken at three different levels:

(a) ***Macro-Level.*** Macro-level concerned with business conditions over the whole economy is measured by an appropriate index of industrial production, national income or expenditure. Such external data constitute the basic assumptions on which the business must base its forecast.

(b) ***Industry-Level.*** Industry-level prepared by different trade associations. The association then supplies the results to their members.

(c) ***Firm-Level.*** Firm-level which is the most important forecast from the managerial view point.

3. General or Specific Forecasting. Should the forecast be general or specific? The firm may find a general forecast useful, but it usually needs to be broken down into commodity product-wise forecasts and forecasts by area of sale *e.g.* separate forecasts may be necessary for home-markets and export-markets.

4. Different Forecasting. Problems and methods of forecasting are usually different for new products from those for products already well established in the market as sales trends are known better and the competitive characteristics of the product is well understood. Thus, the methods and problems should be studied accordingly.

5. Classification of Products. It is important to classify products as producer goods, consumer durables, or consumer goods and services. Economic analysis indicates distinctive patterns of demand for each of these different categories.

6. Special Factors of the Product. In every forecast special factors peculiar to the product and the market must be taken into consideration. If the situation is complicated by uncertainty or non measurable risk and the possibility of error in the forecast must be seriously considered. Sociological factors are of great importance in some markets *e.g.* in the case of women's dresses. Likewise, the role of psychology in demand can hardly be understood what people think about the future, their own personal prospects and about products and brands are vital factors for firms and industries.

Approach to Forecasting

(1) Identify and clearly state the objectives of forecasting short-term or long-term; market share or industry as a whole.

(2) Select appropriate method of forecasting.

(3) Identify the variables affecting the demand for the product and express them in appropriate forms.

(4) Prepare the forecast and interpret the results. Interpretation is more important to the management.

(5) For forecasting the company's share in the demand two different assumption may be made :

(a) The ratio of the company's sales to the total industry's sales will continue as in the past.

(b) On the basis of an analysis of likely competition and industry trends, the company may assume a market share different from that of the past.

(6) Gather relevant data or approximations to relevant data to represent the variables.

(7) Through the use of statistical techniques, determine the most probable relationship between the dependent and the independent variables. It would, however, be useful to prepare alternative forecasts. It is more meaningful than a single forecast. As forecasts are based on certain assumption forecasts must be revised when improved information is available. In long-term forecasts the projections may be revised every year. These are sometimes known as rolling forecasts.

(8) Forecast may be made either in terms of physical units or in terms of rupees of sales volume. The latter may be converted into physical units by dividing it by the expected selling price.

(9) Forecasts may be made either in terms of product groups and then broken for individual product on the basis of past percentages. Product group may be divided into individual products in terms of sizes, brands, labels, colours etc.

(10) Forecasts may be made on annual basis and then divided month-wise or week-wise on the basis of past records.

(11) For determining the month-wise break up of the forecast sales of a new product, either *(i)* use may be made of other firms data if available, or *(ii)* some may be necessary. Similiar will be the situation when the forecast sale of a product-line have to be divided product wise.

VARIOUS METHODS OF DEMAND OR SALES FORECASTING

Business economists have developed many forecasting techniques to help managers in management decision making. No method of forecasting is complete in itself which may be applied to all enterprises, all products and in all circumstances. Broadly speaking, the use of a particular forecasting method depends upon the nature of the enterprise, the products manufactured, information system in use etc.

Moreover, two dangers must be guarded against. First, too much emphasis should not be placed on mathematical or statistical techniques of forecasting. Though statistical techniques are essential in clarifying relationships and providing techniques of analysis, they are not substitutes for judgement. The other danger is that we may go to the opposite extreme and regard foreasting as something to be best to the judgement of the so-called experts, what is needed is some commonsense meant between pure guessing and too much mathematics. The more commonly used methods of demand forecasting are discussed below :

I. Survey of Buyers' Intentions. The most direct method of estimating demand in the short-run is to ask customers what they are planning to buy for the forthcoming time period usually a year. This method, also known as "Opinion survey" is most useful when bulk of the sales is made to industries' producers. Here burden of forecasting is shifted to the customer. Yet it would not be wise to depend wholly on the buyer's estimates and they should be used cautiously in the light of the seller's own judgement. A number of biases may creep into requirements.

This method is not very useful in the case of household customers for s^veral reasons, viz., *(i)* irregularity in customers buying intentions, *(ii)* their inability to foresee their choice when faced with multiple alternatives, *(iii)* the possibility that the buyers plans may not be real but only wishful thinking, *(iv)* household customers are numerous making this method rather impracticable and costly, *(v)* a basic limitation of this method is that it is passive and does not expose and measure the variables under management's control.

II. Delphi Method. Delphi Method was originally developed at Rand Corporation of the U.S.A. in the late 1940s by Olaf Helmer, Dalkey and Golden and has been successfully used in the area of technological forecasting *i.e.*, predicting technical changes. It has proved more popular in forecasting non-economic variables.

III. Collective Opinion. Under this method, also called sales-force polling, salesman being the closest to the customers, are likely to have the most intimate feeling of the market, *i.e.*, customer reaction to the products of the firm and their sales trends. The estimate of individual salesmen are consolidated to find out the total estimated sales. They are then reviewed to eleminate the bias of optimism on the part of the some salesmen and pessimism on the part of others. These revised estimates are further examined in the light of factors like proposed changes in selling prices, product designs and advertisement programmes, expected changes in competition, changes in secular forces like purchasing power, income distribution, employment, population, etc. The final sales forecast would emerge after these factors have been taken into account. This method is known as the "collective opinion method" as it takes advantage of the collective wisdom of salesmen departmental heads like production manager, sales manager, marketing manager, managerial economist, etc., and the top executive.

Advantages

1. The method is simple and does not involve the use of statistical technique.

2. The forecasts are based on first-hand knowledge of salesman and others directly connected with sales.

3. The method may prove quite useful in forecasting sales of new products of course, here sales will have to depend more on their judgement than in the case of existing products.

Disadvantages

1. It is almost completely subjective as personal opinions can possibly influence the forecast. Salesmen may even understate the forecast if their sales quotas are to be based on it.

2. The usefulness of this method is restricted to short-term forecasting, *i.e.*, for a period of about one year. These forecasts may not be useful for long-term production planning.

3. Salesman may be unaware of the broader economic changes likely to have an impact on the future demand.

IV. Analysis of Time Series and Trend Projections. A firm which has been in existence for some time, will have accumulated considerable data on sales pertaining to different time periods. Such date when arranged chronologically yield "time series". The time series relating to sales represents the past pattern of effective demand for a particular product. Such data can be presented either in a tabular form or graphically for further analysis. The most popular method of analysis of time series is to project the trend of the time series. A trend line can be fitted through a series either visually or by means of statistical techniques such as the method of least squares. The analyst chooses a plausible algebraic relation (linear, quadratic, logarithmic, etc.) between sales and the independent variable time. The trend line is then projected into the future by extrapolation.

Advantages

1. This method is popular because it is simple and inexpensive.

2. Time series data often exhibit a presistent growth trend. The basic assumption of the trend variable under study will continue in the future.

3. This technique yields acceptable results so long as the time series shows a persisent tendency to move in the same direction.

Disadvantages

Whenever a turning point occurs, however, the trend projection breaks down. Nevertheless, a forecaster could normally expect to be right in most forecasts especially if the turning points are few and spaced at long intervals from each other.

There are primarily four sets of factors which are responsible for the characterisation of time series by fluctuations and turning points in the time series:

(i) Trend, *(ii)* Seasonal variations, *(iii)* Cyclical fluctuations and *(iv)* Irregular or random forces. The problem in forecasting is to separate and measure each of these four factors.

V. Use of Economic Indicators. The use of this approach is based on certain economic indicators, *e.g.*

(i) Construction contracts sanctioned for the demand of building materials, say, cement.

(ii) Personal income for the demand of consumer goods.

(iii) Agriculutral income for the demand of agricultural inputs, implements, fertilizers, etc.

(iv) Automobile registration for the demand of car accessories, petrol etc.

These economic indicators are published by specialized organizations like the C.S.O. which publishes national income estimates.

For the use of economic indicators, the following steps have to be taken:

1. See whether a relationship exists between the demand for a product and certain economic indicators.

2. Establish the relationship through the method of least squares and derive the regression equation. Assuming the relationship to be linear, the equation will be of the form $Y = A + bx$. There can be carvilinear relationships as well.

3. Once regression equation is derived, the value of Y, *i.e.*, demand, can be estimated for any given value of x.

4. Past relationship may not recur. Hence the need for value judgements as well. New factors may also have to be taken into consideration.

Limitations

1. Finding an appropriate economic indicator may be difficult.

2. For new products, it is inappropriate as no past data exists.

3. This method of forecasting works best where the relationship of demand with a particular indicator is characterized by a time lag.

VI. Controlled Experiments. Under this method, and effort is made to very separately certain determinants of demand which can be manipulated *e.g.*, price, advertising, etc., and conduct the experiments assuming that the other factors remain constant. Thus, the effect of demand, determinants like price, advertisement, packaging, etc., on sales can be assessed by either varying them over different markets or by varying them over different time periods in the same markets. For example, different prices would be associated with different sales and on that basis the price-quantity relationship is estimated in the form of regression, equation and used for forecasting purposes. It must be noted that the market divisions here must be homogenous with regard to income, tastes, etc.

The method of controlled experiments is still relatively new and less tried. This is due to several reasons: *1.* Such experiments are expensive as well as time-consuming. *2.* They are risky too because they may lead to unfavourable reactions on dealers, consumers and competitors. *3.* There is a great difficulty in planning the study in as much as it is not always easy to determine what conditions should be taken as constant and what factors should be regarded as variable so as to segregate and measure their influence on demand. *4.* It is difficult to satisfy the condition of homogeneity of markets. Despite these limitations, controlled experiments have sufficient potentialities to become a method for business research and analysis in future.

VII. Judgemental Approach. Management may have to use its own judgement when *(i)* analysis of time series and trend projections is not feasible because of wide fluctuaions in sales or because of anticipated changes in trend and *(ii)* Use of regression method is not possible because of management's inability to predict or even identify causal factors. Even when statistical methods are used it might be desirable to supplement them by use of judgement for the following reasons:

(a) Even the most sophisticated statistical method cannot incorporate all the potential factors affecting demand.

(b) For industrial products, demand may be concentrated in a small number of buyers, it could be taken into account only through the judgemental approach.

(c) Statistical forecasts are more reliable for larger levels of aggregations.

Thus, while it may be possible to forcast that total national demand more or less accurately it may be more difficult to accurately forecast demand by sales territory, sizes and models. In such cases, there is no alternative but to depend upon judgement for developing more detailed forecasts.

VARIOUS METHODS FOR FORECASTING DEMAND OF NEW PRODUCTS

Forecasting the demand for a new product is entirely different from forecasting demand for an established product. In the case of new products no historical data is available and therefore, the statistics cannot be applied. Only an intensive study of the economic and competitive characteristics of the product in question will provide some guidelines for demand projections in the case of new product.

Joel Den has suggested some approaches for estimating the demand for a new product. They are described below:

1. Evolutionary Approach. In this method the new product is regarded as an outgrowth and evolution of an existing old product. For example it may be assumed that colour television is the evolution of black and white television. Black and white TV is an established product and form its demand. Thus we can set some idea about the demand for colour TV sets.

2. Substitute Approach. In this method the new product is analysed as a substitute for some existing product. For example synthetic fabrics may be regarded as a substitute for cotton fabrics. The demand for the product can be looked out on the basis of a market share, by estimating the total market for all substitutes.

3. Growth Curve Approach. In this method the rate of growth and the ultimate level of demand for the new product is estimated on the basis of the pattern of growth of established product. For example by analysing growth curves of all established houseful appliances, grwoth cruve can be developed for new appliance.

4. Opinion Polling Approach. In this method, a demand for a new product is estimated by direct inquiry of the ultimate purchasers, either by the use of samples or on a full scale.

5. Sales Experience Approach. In this method the new product is offered for sale in a sample market, say a super-market in a large city. The estimates so obtained then can be 'blown up' to arrive at the total demand for the product for all channels.

6. Vicarious Approach. In this method consumers reactions to a new product is surveyed indirectly thorugh the eyes of specialised dealers who are supposedly informed about consumers needs and alternative opportunities.

Criteria of a Good Forecasting Method

1. Accuracy. It is necessary to check the accuracy of past forecasts against present performance and of present forecasts against future performance. Some comparisons of the model with what actually happens and of the assumptions with what is borne out in practice are more desirable. The accuracy of the forecast is measured by *(a)* the degree of deviations forecasts and actuals and *(b)* the extent of success in forecasting directional changes.

2. Simplicity and Comprehension. Management must be able to understand and have confidence in the techniques used. Understanding is also needed for a proper interpretation of the results. Elaborate mathematical and econometric procedures may be judged less desirable if management does not really understand what the forecaster is doing and fails to understand the procedure.

3. Economy. Costs must be weighed against the importance of the forecast to the operations of the business. A question may arise: how much money and managerial effort should be allocated to obtain a high level of forecasting accuracy? The criterion here is the economic consideration of balancing the benfits from increased accuracy against the extra cost of providing the improved forecasting.

4. Availability. The techniques employed should be able to produce meaningful results quickly; techniques which take a long time to work out may produce useful information too late for effective management decisions.

5. Maintenance of Timeliness. The forecast should be capable of being maintained on an up-to-date basis. This has three aspects:

(a) The relationships underlying the procedure should be stable so that they will carry into the future for a signficant amount of time.

(b) Current data required to use these underlying relationship should be available on timely basis.

(c) The forecasting procedure should permit changes to be made in the relationsihps as they occur.

6. Presentation To Management. In presenting of forecast to the management, a managerial economist should:

(i) Make the forecast as easy for the management to understand as possible.

(ii) Avoid using vague generalities.

(iii) Always pin-point his major assumptons and sources.

(iv) Give the possible margin of error.

(v) Avoid making undue qualifications.

(vi) Omit details about methodology and calcualtions.

(vii) Make use of charts and graphs as much as possible for easy comprehension.

❐

5

Classification of Demand or Demand Distinctions

Demand for any commodity is determined by its nature. Demand for such commodities which are indispensable for the consumer is not affected significantly by changes in their market conditions. Opposite will be the case with those commodities which are dispensable or have close substitutes in the market. Similarly, commodities which are durable have different demand than those which are non-durable. Use-characteristics of different goods also influence demand for them. A good with multiple uses generally has a higher demand than the one with single-use. We can broadly classify the goods in the following categories on the basis of difference in their nature:

(i) Demand for producers' goods and consumers' goods.

(ii) Derived demand and autonomous demand.

(iii) Demand for durable (or non-perishable) and non-durable (perishable) goods.

(iv) Industry demand and firm (or company) demand.

(v) Total demand and market segment demand.

(vi) Short-run demand and long-run demand.

(vii) Long-term trend in demand and short-run demand fluctuations.

(1) PRODUCERS' GOODS AND CONSUMERS' GOODS

Producers' goods are those which are used for the product of other goods—either consumer goods or producer goods themselves.

Examples of such goods are machines, looms, tools and implements, locomotives, ships, etc.

Consumers' goods can be defined as those which are used for final consumption. They satisfy the consumers' wants directly. Examples of consumers' goods can be ready-made clothes, prepared food residential houses, etc. Consumer goods may be further sub-divided into durable and non-durable goods.

Some of the distinctive characteristics of durable consumer; goods are given below:

(a) Certain durable consumer goods require the existence of special facilities for their use, *e.g.*, the use of cars and trucks requires the existence of petrol public stations and the use of television sets requires the prior establishment of telecasting stations. This characteristics, therefore, makes the demand for these goods dependent upon the existence of thee facilities. For example, television sets can be sold in India in the vicinity of telecasting centres only, and not in places far removed from these centres.

(b) Consumer durables are often consumed by more than one person. For example, several members of a family can use a car, radio or refrigerator. The significance of this distinctive feature lies in that the demand for these products also depends upon family needs and characteristics like size. age distribution, etc.

(c) While purchases of most non-durable consumer goods are made at fairly regular intervals, purchases of durable consumer goods are made at irregular intervals.

Producers' goods can also be classified into two categories: consumable and durable. The examples of the former are: coal, oil, etc. whereas examples of the latter are machines and equipment.

For consumers' goods, buyers' income is the factor most nearly universal, since it determines the amount of cash in the buyers' hands and strongly affects their expectations of future income. The relation of demand to price, advertising, competition and speculation hinges more on the nature of the product. Again factors that are dominant for some products may be quite irrelevant or unimportant for others.

Generally speaking, the reasons for expecting distinctive demand behaviour for producers' goods are three:

1. Buyers are profession also and hence more discriminating price wise, quality-wise and sensitive to substitutes.
2. Their motives are more purely economic; products are bought not for their own sake but for their profit prospects. As such, their purchases are less susceptible to "pressure advertising" but more sensitive to small price differences.
3. Demand, being derived from consumption or from production, fluctuates differently and generally more violently.

Though this distinction between producers' and consumers' goods serves a useful purpose, it is purely arbitrary. Whether a particular commodity is a producer good or consumer good depends upon who buys and why and hence the distinction is bound to be indistinct.

(2) AUTONOMOUS AND DERIVED DEMAND

Autonomous demand for a commodity is one that arises independent of the demand for any other commodity whereas derived demand is one that is tied to the demand for some 'parent product'. To look more closely at the distinction between the two kinds of demand, the demand for a commodity which arises directly from the biological or physical needs of the human beings may be considered as autonomous demand, *e.g.*, demand for food, clothes, shelter etc. An autonomous demand may arise also as a result of 'demonstration effect' rise in income, advertisement of new products. On the other hand, demand for a commodity that arises because of the demand for some other commodity may be considered as derived demand. For instance, demand for and, fertilisers, and agricultural tools and implements is derived demand because it is dependent nor tied with the demand for food. Similarly, demand for cotton, bricks, cement etc., is derived demand, thus, the demand for producers' goods or industrial inputs is a derived one; Besides, demand for complementary commodities which complement the use of other commodities, or for supplementary commodities, which supplement or provides additional utility from the use of other goods is a derived demand. For instance, power-regulator is a complementary goods of refrigerators and TV sets, add a chair is a complement and table glass is supplement to the use of table. Therefore, demand for power-reguiator, chair, and table-glass would be considered as derived demand. The conceptual distinction between autonomous demand (*i.e.*, demand for a 'parent product') and derived demand would be useful for businessman's point of view to the extent the formar can serve as an indicator of the latter.

(3) DURABLE GOODS AND NON-DURABLE GOODS

Durable goods give more complicated problems of demand analysis than products of a non-durable nature. Non-durable goods are sold for the current demand which are dependent on current conditions. While durable goods are sold to add to the stock of existing goods that give services over years. Hence it is a practice to separate current demand for durable goods in terms of replacement of old products and expansion of total stock.

Demand for durable goods has the characteristics of a volatile relation to business conditions. Current output of a durable product gives only a small position of the total current service demanded for that kind of product. Sales are hypersensitive to small changes in the demand for the service.

For example, if we suppose that formal automobile production is used *(a)* to replace 20 per cent of the existing stock of cars and *(b)* to expand car production by 5 percent that a 3 percent increase in the demand for motor transportation will raise the new car demand by about 25 percent. This can be explained in this way. Suppose that the existing number of cars in use is 20,000. The replacement demand at the rate of 10 per cent would be 2000. Further, the expansion demand for cars at the rate of 5 percent would amount to

1000 cars. Thus the existing total production of cars would be 3000. Now, if there is an extra increase of 3% in the demand of cars, the additional demand for cars would come to 600 cars *i.e.*, 20 per cent of the existing production of 3000 cars.

For durable goods demand analysis is not a simple process. Expansion and replacement have manifold set of demand detrainments. When expansion demand increases, value of used equipment goes up and replacement demand falls. If the expansion demand goes down, scrapped rate becomes greater than the level of new production. The most important determinant for replacement is obsolescence due to technological developments. Physical determination is of less importance in case when it is a modernity change.

For consumer products and to some extent for producer goods also, style, convenience and income play a prominent part in demand. For major innovations, demand is dependent on financial necessities and rivalry of alternative investments.

As for the purchase of durable goods, besides current prices and incomes, the consumer thinks of maintenance and operating costs in relation to his future income and his other demands with expected improved designs of the products. Hence price concessions are given to clear out existing stock that may be come out of fashion and hence may not prove to the par mark of sale specially when it has to face cut-throat competition with new models that have newly arrived in the market. So the discount rates are increased on the old stocked goods so that the new arrivals may not obstruct sales. As we see in the United States of America old car models are disposed at heavy discounts.

(4) SHORT-TERM AND LONG-TERM DEMAND

Short-term demand refers to the demand for such goods as are demanded over a short-period. In this category fall mostly the variety consumer goods, goods of seasonal use, inferior substitutes during the scarcity period of superior goods, etc. For instance, the demand for cowboy trousers, slacks, high-heel and 'platform' shoes, broad ties, was short-term demand, through the demand for the generic goods (trousers, shoes, ties, etc.) continues to remain a long-term demand. Similarly demand for umbrella, rain-coats, sum-boots, cold-drinks etc., is of seasonal nature. The demand for such goods lasts till the season lasts. Although some goods are used only seasonally but are of durable nature, *e.g.*, electric fans, woollen garments, etc. Although the demand for such goods is of durable nature, it is subject to seasonal fluctuation. Some times, demand for certain goods suddenly increases because of scarcity of their superior substitutes. For example, when supply of cooking gas suddenly decreases demand for kerosene and coal increases. In such cases, additional temporal demand is of short-term natures.

The long-term demand, on the other hand, refers to the demand which exists over a long period. The change is long-term demand is perceptible only after a long period. Most generic goods have belong-term demand. For example, demand for consumers' and producers' goods, durable and nondurable goods, is long-term demand, though their different varieties or brands may have only short-term demand.

Short-term demand depends, by and large, on the price of commodities, price of their substitutes, current' disposable income of the consumers, their ability to adjust their consumption pattern, and their susceptibility to advertisement of a new product. The long-term demand depends on the long-term income trends, availability of better substitutes, sales promotion, etc.

The short-term and long-term concepts of demand are useful in designing new product for established producers, and choice of products for the new entrepreneurs, in pricing policy in determining and phasing the advertisement expenditure.

(5) INDUSTRY DEMAND AND FIRM DEMAND

The term company demand denotes demand for a particular product of a particular firm. For example, hosiery products produced by Victor. When we add demands for a particular product of all the companies producing that product, we get what is called an industry demand. In other words, industry demand refers to the total demand for the products of a particular industry. It may be noted that we can add up the demands of the various firms only if either all the firms produce exactly the same commodity or they should be close substitutes of each other. *e.g.*. the various toothpastes, boot-polishes, etc. If the products in the industry are similar or close substitutes, we can get industry demand schedule which represents the relation of price of the product in the industry with the total quantity of the good demanded from all the firms in the industry. But it must be noted that from the point of view of a manager knowledge of industry demand is much less important as compared to that of the company demand. He needs to know the share of his company demand in the industry demand, as well as the share of his company demand *vis-a-vis* the share of other company demands in the industry. However, the industry demand is a useful guide for studying the company demand, and the projection of industry demand is the initial step in forecasting company's demand or sales.

Since the individual company faces competition from its rivals in the industry, generally, the company demand is more price elastic than the industry demand. However, the degree of price-demand relationship of company demand depends on the structure of the market. Market structure is generally classified on the basis of two aspects:

(a) the number of sellers;

(b) the degree of product differentiation.

Considering the above two aspects of market structure, we can divide the markets into the following broad categories:

(a) Monopoly. Since monopoly implies a situation where there is a single seller of a product, the firm is itself an industry there. Thus, in case of a single firm monopoly, the company demand curve is the same as the industry demand curve.

(b) Oligopoly. It is a situation where there are only a small number of firms. These firms may be selling products which are either standardised or differentiated. The formal is called homogeneous oligopoly while the latter is known as differentiated oligopoly.

(c) **Pure (or Percent) Competition.** In case of pure competition, there are a large number of buyers and sellers, with perfect knowledge of the market and perfect mobility. In such a situation, any individual firm is very small and competition is very intense. An individual company will have to sell at the prevailing price in the market, which makes demand curve for its product perfectly elastic (graphically, a horizontal straight line), while on the other hand, the industry demand curve is the usual negatively sloped one.

(d) **Monopolistic Competition.** This situation falls between monopoly and pure competition. There are many sellers (but both large in number) while there are large number of buyers. Each firm tries to introduce some differentiation in its product. This is a situation which often prevails in real life and is therefore, of maximum interest for a managerial economist.

Due to differentiation in their products, each firm has a segment of customers attached to their product, which provides the firm with some control over the market price. When the degree of product differentiation is quite significantly the firm's control over market price becomes as powerful as a monopolist. But the demand curve of a monopolistic competitor differs from that of a monopolist because the demand in case oithe former is affected by the number of rival firms, their products, prices, etc. thus, in case of monopolistic competition, the firm's demand is more volatile than the industry's demand. In other words, company demand is more price elastic, here, than the industry demand.

(6) TOTAL MARKET AND MARKET SEGMENT

Demand for a certain product has to be studied not only in its totality but also by breaking it into different segments, *viz.*, geographical areas, sub products, uses of the product, sensitivity to price, distribution channels, size of the customers, etc. This division of demand into different segments gives rise to the concept of market segment as distinguished from the total market. Thus 'total market' refers to the total demand for a product where as 'market segment' signifies a part of it.

Some problems, such a sales forecasting, call for an analysis of the total market. Other problems, notably those of pricing, promotion and distribution, call for analysis of separate market segments that have homogeneous demand characteristics. Each of these market segments may differ significantly in respect of delivered prices, net profit margins, substitutes, competition, seasonal patterns and cyclical sensitivity. For manipulating prices, promotion, product or distribution channels in order to meet or exercise sales competition, a segment concept of demand is often more appropriate than the 'total market' concept that has greater coverage.

(7) MARKET SHARE CONCEPT OF DEMAND

The company demand may also be expressed as a percentage of the industry demand. The percentage so arrived at would denote the company's market share for the product. The company demand expresses the quantity demanded in absolute terms while market share expresses it in relative terms. Suppose that at a given price, the demand for patron in the country is 5 million litres. and Indian Oil supplies 2 million litres, *i.e.* 40 per cent of the total demand for petrol. The industry demand at that price is 5 million liters, the company demand is 2 million liters and market share of the company is 40 per cent. The concept of market share becomes important because the demand being the result of vast impersonal economic forces, is usually beyond the control of the individual company, but the market share enjoyed by it is subject to manipulation. Market share information can also be helpful in persuading people to buy a company's shares.

This concept of demand is most usable in mature, well-defined industries which relatively homogeneous products, *e.g.*, steel and cement. The objective is to improve the market share of the company or at least to maintain it. The first step is to forecast industry sales. The next stage is to plan a market strategy to improve or at least maintain the market share. This is largely done by keeping abreast of competitive developments, *e.g.*, overtaking product innovators, meeting price-cutters and countering aggressive advertising.

The factors which determine the market share are:

(i) Plice-spread or Price Differential. It means the difference between the price charged by one company and the prices charged by other companies. If a company's price is lower than the price charged by other companies, it would be able to capture a great market share of the Industry demand. Therefore, the higher the price differential, the greater the market share.

It may, however, be noted that the responsiveness of the market share to price differential will be insignificant up to a point due to the thickness of the buyers to a certain extent. But as the price differential increases, there will be a tendency for the market share to increase. And the responsiveness of the market share rises sharply when the price differential increases beyond a critical point. The critical point varies with areas and possibly also with the buyer's affluence. Responsiveness of the market share also depends upon how well publicised and easily available the lower price is.

(ii) Promotional Expenditure. It denotes the amount spent for the promotion of sales by a particular company. As we have already seen, there is a tendency for the sales to increase with an increase in promotional outlays. As a result the market share is likely to go up with an increase in promotional outlays.

Very often a particular industry may undertake collective advertisement to promote the sales of the industry as a whole. *e.g.*, advertisement on behalf of the cigarette industry. To maintain its market share, particular producer will undertake an individual advertisement in addition to the aggregate advertisement.

(c) Product Improvement. It may also be adopted to increase the market share. The improvement may be oral or illusory. Sometimes, the improvement may take the form of more attractive packaging though the real contents may be the same.

FACTORS AFFECTING NON-DURABLE CONSUMER GOODS

There are three basic factors affecting demand for non-durable consumer goods:

(i) Purchasing Power. Purchasing power of consumers affects the demand of non-durables (which are mostly not necessaries). The purchasing power of consumer can be judged from their disposable income *i.e.*, personal income—direct taxes and deductions. Some people suggest the use of discretionary income in place of disposable income. Discretionary income means disposable income minus three items *i.e.*, *(a)* inputted income and income in kind, *(b)* major fixed outlay payments such as repayment of debt, rent, insurance premium etc. and *(c)* expenditure on essential items, like food, dothing etc.

(ii) Price. Price is another factor that may be concerned in demand analysis for non-durables. Here one has to consider the prices of any price differences among the products and also its substitutes and complements.

(iii) Demography. It involves the characteristics of the population, human as well as non-human, using the product. Population of children is more important *i.e.*; estimating the demand of toys or the number of automobiles on road is more important for estimating the demand of tyres and tubes. The study may be made on the basis of total market or a segment of it. Segments may be defined in terms of income, status, sex, education level, geographical location, male-female ratio, etc.

DISTINCTIVE TYPES OF ELASTICITY

From the managerial view point, it is considered useful to distinguish certain sub-types of the elasticity of each demand determinant. The important ones are: Industry elasticity, market share elasticity and expectations elasticity.

(i) Industry elasticity refers to the change in total industry sales with a change in the general level of process for the industry as a whole. The industry demand has elasticity with respect to competition from other industries. e.g., oil, gas and coal.

(ii) Market share elasticity relates the change in company's share of the industry-wide sales to the price differential between the company's price and the industry-wise price level.

(iii) Expectations elasticity refers to the responsiveness of sales to buyers' guesses about the future values of demand determinants, such as the future price of a commodity or of its substitutes, further incomes of buyers, prospects of easy availability or otherwise in the future, or future promotional outlays. Price and income expectations are perhaps the most important of them. But in the context of scarcity economy as in India, the future availability tends to become very important in the case of certain commodities like wheat and sugar.

From the viewpoint of a particular firm, the market share elasticity is perhaps the most important. It is influenced by a number of factors like rivals' changes in price and promotional efforts-qualitative as well as quantitative. Rivals may constitute a single competitor or several of them together.

(A) SUPERIOR GOODS AND INFERIOR GOODS

Superior goods and inferior goods are two divisions of the goods in the market. Generally they refers to the producer an consumer goods also. They may also be referring to durable and non-durable goods. Some producers the superior goods and these are sold promptly in the market due to goodwill of the production unit. They may charge whatever price they want. No doubt, it is more than other goods but these goods are sold quickly in the market due to their durability over other makes. For example M.R.F. tyres are more preferred by the persons as compared to other company makes because the consumers consider them of superior quality to the other makes.

(B) TOTAL MARKET DEMAND V/S MARKET SEGMENT DEMAND

The demand for a product should not only be studied on the basis of demand by all the consumers in the market (or in its totality) but the demand in a part or segment of the market should also be studied separately so as to estimate the demand of the product in that area. This part or segment should be studied as such based on geographical regions, sub-products, uses of the product, sensitivity to price of the product, and size of customers. In this way demand could be studied in parts. This gives the stuck of market segments as differentiated from total market. The total market gives the total demand for a produer while market segment refers to a part of it.

Problems like forecasting, call for an analysis of the tota market while problems like pricing, promotion and distribution call for the breaking of separate market segments that have similar demand characteristics. Each of these market segments may differ mostly in respect of delivered prices, net profit margins, substitutes, competition, seasonal patterns and cyclical sensitivity. A 'segment concept of demand is more useful than a product concept of total coverage of manipulating prices, promotion, product or distribution channel of sales competition.

(C) COMPLEMENTARY GOODS AND SUBSTITUTES

Complementary goods are those goods which contrioute to help the sale of one commodity to the other. If one commodity enjoys a large sale, it requires its complement to push its sales. For example, a person has a motorcar but motorcar cannot be driven by water only, it requires a pattern tin. Thus use or sale of cars has provided complementary goods *i.e.*, sale of petrol at petrol pumps.

This case is applicable to both producer as well as consumer items. The producer will sell a car to the purchaser and ask him to take petrol from the neares petrol pump. Thus both are complementary.

As far as substitutes are concerned if certain commodity is in more use and sudden rise in its cost takes place, people will like to have a substitute for it. The more highly competitive situation of a company, the greater the elasticity of demand of its products. If there are more than one substitute *(a)* a decline in the price will lead one's produce to replace the substitutes *(b)* an increase in the price will lead the substitutes to replace it provided price of substitutes do not change at the same time and to the same extent.

❑

6

Production Theory

The theory of production is the analysis of the relationship between inputs (*i.e.* services of land labour, capital, organisation and entrepreneur) and the output. It states the principles according to which output is supposed to vary as inputs vary or a single input varies.

Meaning of the Production Function

It reveals various types of natural resources, land, labour and capital, which will have to be employed in order to produce a unit or a given quantity of certain commodity or service, in a given period of time. In other words, it indicates varieties of resources and their unique combinations which can be transformed into desired quantities of goods and services. It reflects the state of arts technological possibilities of the production processes and the size of the production units.

Thus, the production functions is a symbolical expression of the fact that output of a firm depends on the inputs employed in the production process.

Traditionally, the Production Function has been called the law of Diminishing Returns and has been explained by economists in different ways in the last 200 years or so.

We may study the Production Functions as follows:

(a) with land as fixed factor and labour and capital as variable factors. This is Marshall's version of the law of diminishing returns.

(b) With one factor variable and all other factors fixed, this is the modern version of the law of diminishing returns.

In traditional production theory resources used for the production are now termed as inputs which may mean the use of the services of land, labour, capital and organisation in the process of production. The term output refers to the commodity produced by the various inputs. Production theory concerns itself with the problems of combining various inputs, given the state of technology, in order to produce a stipulated output. The technological relationships between inputs and outputs are known as production functions.

The production function expresses a functional relationship between quantities of inputs and outputs. It shows how and to what extent output changes with variations in inputs during a specified period of time. Basically, the production function is a schedule or table showing the amount of output obtained from various combinations of inputs, given the state of technology. Algebraically, it may be expressed in the form of an equation as

$$P = f(A, B, C, D)$$

Where P stands for the output of goods per unit of time and A, B, C, D are the various inputs of resources land, labour, capital and organization used in making the output.

The production function as determined by technical conditions of production is of two types: it may be rigid or flexible. In the short run, the technical conditions of production are rigid so that the various input resources used to produce a given output are in fixed proportions. This is, however, a rare phenomenon in production, for it is possible to change inputs in different proportions.

Even in the short run, it is possible to increase the quantities of one input while keeping the quantities of other inputs constant in order to have more output. This aspect of the production function is known as the law of variable proportions.

In the long run, it is possible for a firm to change all inputs up or down in accordance with its scale. This is known as returns to scale. The returns to scale are constant when output increases in the same proportions as the quantities of inputs increase. The returns to scale are increasing when the increase in output is more than proportional to the increase in inputs and they are decreasing if the increase in output is less than proportional to the increased inputs. Thus "the production function is a boundary relationship which indicates the present limits of the firms' technical production possibilities. The production function states that a firm cannot achieve a higher rate of output without using more inputs and that a firm cannot use fewer inputs without decreasing its rate of output. Further the production function indicates the manner in which the firm can substitute one input for another without reducing the total amount of output, and also the manner in which the firm can substitute an input for another without altering its total average of inputs."

Let us illustrate the case of constant returns to scale with the help of our production function.

$$P = f(A, B, C, D)$$

If the quantities of all inputs A, B, C, D are increased n-fold, the output P also increases n-fold. Then the production function becomes

$$nP = f(nA, nB, nC, nD)$$

This is known as the linear and homogeneous production function, or a homogeneous function of the first degree. If the homogeneous function is of the Kth degree, the production function is

$$n^k.P = f(nA, nB, nC, nD)$$

If k is equal to 1, it is a case of constant returns to scale, if it is greater than 1 it is a case of increasing returns to scale, and if it is less than 1, it is a case decreasing returns to scale.

One of the important production functions based on empirical hypothesis is the Cobb-Douglas production function. Originally it was applied to the whole manufacturing industry in America though it can be applied to the whole economy or to any of its sectors. The Cobb-Douglas production function is

$$P = K L^{a} C^{1-a}$$

Where P stands for output, L for labour, C for capital employed, and k and a are positive constants. In this function the exponents of L and C are equal to 1.

The production function exhibits technological relationships between physical inputs and outputs and is thus said to belong to the domain of engineering. Prof. Stigler does not agree with this commonly held view. The function of an entrepreneur is to sort out the right type of combination of inputs for the quantity of output he desires. For this he has to know the prices of his inputs and the technique to be used for producing a specified output within a specified period of time. All these technical possibilities are derived from applied sciences, but can not be worked out by engineers alone.

The production function presumes substitutability, complementarity and specificity characterisitcs of inputs:

(1) Substitutability. The factors of production or inputs are substitutes of one another which make it possible to vary the total output by changing the quantity of one or a few inputs, while the quantities of all other inputs are held constant. It is the substitutability of the factors of production that gives rise to the laws of variable proportions.

(2) Complementarity. The factors of production are also complementary to one another, that is, the two or more inputs are to be used together as nothing will be produced if the quantity of other of the inputs used in the production process is zero. The principles of returns to scale is another manifestation of complementarity of inputs as it reveals that the quantity of all inputs are to be increased simultaneously in order to attain a higher scale of total output.

(3) Specificity. It reveals that the inputs are specific to the production of a particular product. Machines and equipments, specialised workers and raw materials are a few examples of the specificity of factors of production. The specificity may not be complete as factors may be used for production of other commodities too. This reveals that in the production process none of the factors can be ignored and in some cases ignorance to even slightest extent is not possible if the factors are perfectly specific.

Production involves time, hence, the way the inputs are combined is determined to a large extent by the time period under consideration. The greater the time period, the greater the freedom the producer has to vary the quantities of various inputs used in the production process. In the production function, variation in total output by varying the quantities of all inputs is possible only in the long run whereas the variation in total output by varying the quantity of single input may be possible even in short run. Thus, the former is known as return to scale while the latter is known as laws of Returns.

FACTOR-ELASTICITY OF SUBSTITUTION

If we suppose a situation in which the relative prices change and one of the factors, labour, becomes relatively cheaper than the other factor *viz.*, capital, a change in the price of one factor, the price of the others remaining unchanged, will necessitate a readjustment of factor proportions. For the change in price ratios will destory the equality of price ratios and the rate of substitution. But this readjustment of factor proportions *i.e.* how much more of the cheaper factor will substitute. How much of the costly factor will depend upon what is known as elasticity of substitution between two factors.

By the elasticity of substitution between any two factors, we mean the relative extent to which one factor will be replaced by another in response to a change in their relative price. For example, if wages fall the producer will substitute labour for capital. How fast and how will he be able to substitute labour for capital will naturally depend upon the marginal rate of technical substitution between the factors and the change in prices.

Elasticity of substitution measures the degree of substitutablitiy between two factors. Prof. J.R. Hicks, the inventor of this concept, defines it as a "measure of the case with which the varying factors can be substituted for others." If the two factors, capital and labour are required in fixed proportions (1 machine + 2 workers) to give a unit of product, then their elasticity of substitution is zero. If labour and capital are identical so that one is almost a perfect substitute for the other, then the elasticity of substitution between them is infinite.

When an increase in the quantity of one factor raises the marginal product of the other factor in the same proportion as the total product, then elasticity of substitution is unity. In other words, when with the increase in the quantity a labour, the marginal productivity of capital increases in the same proportion in which the total output increases, the elasticity of substitution is said to be unity.

Mrs. Joan Robinson, however, defines elasticity of substitution as "the proportionate change in the ratio of the amounts of the factors divided by the proportionate change in the ratio of their marginal physical productivities." If labour (L) and capital (C) are the two factors and the ratio of their marginal physical productivities is denoted by r, then the elasticity of substitution (es) is

$$es = \frac{d(C/L)}{C/L} \div \frac{dr}{r}$$

Where d refers to change.

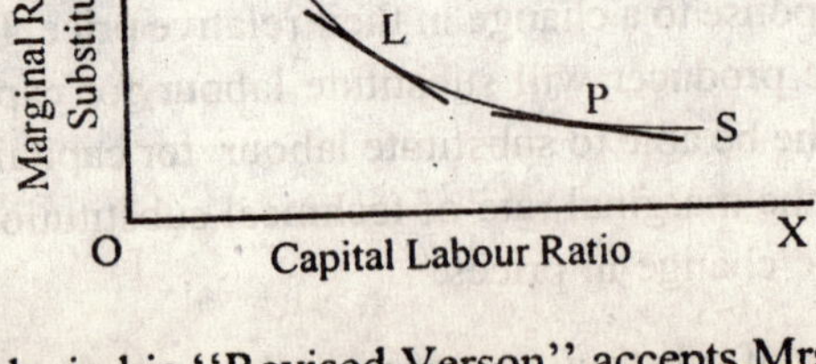

Prof. Hicks in his "Revised Verson" accepts Mrs. Robinson's definition when he says that under perfect competition and constant returns to scale "where there are only two factors, we can thus draw a curve, measuring along one axis the ratio of the quantities of factors used, along the other the ratio of the values per unit of the factors. The elasticity of this curve we call the elasticity of substitution."

Since the ratio of the marginal physical productivities of the two factors are known as the marginal rate of technical substitution (MRTS), the concept of elasticity of substitution can be defined in terms of the isoquant analysis as the proportionate change in the ratio of the factors divided by proportionate change marginal rate of technical substitution. Mathematically, the elasticity of substitution (es) between two factors capital and labour is

$$es = \frac{d(C/L)}{d(MRTS)} \times \frac{MRTS}{C/L}$$

This definition shows that the marginal rate of technical substitution varies inversely with the proportion of the factors. If we plot the marginal rate of technical substitution on the Y-axis and the capital-labour ratio on the x-axis, the resulting curve MS is the substitution curve which measures the elasticity of substitution on figure.

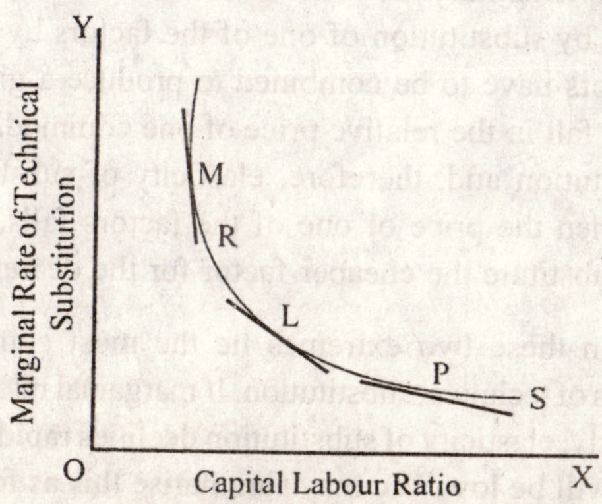

The range over which the substitution curve MS is flat, the elasticity of substitution is very high as between L and P. Capital and labour are good substitutes in this case. Where the substitution curve is steep, the elasticity of substitution is low, as between R and L on the MS curve. Capital and Labour are not good substitutes here. At point M where the substitution curve is veritcal the elasticity of substitution becomes zero because a given percentage change in MRTS brings no change in the capital-labour ratio. S is the point of infinite elasticity of substitution where a given percentage change in MRTS brings an infinitely large change in the capital-labour ratio. Around point L the elasticity of substitution is unity because a given percentage change in the MRTS brings an equal change in the capital labour ratio.

If two factors are perfect substitutes, production can be carried through either of the two factors or through only one of them; in fact increase in one factor will be accompained by a constant decrease of the other. Hence the marginal rate of substitution between two factors which are perfect substitutes will be constant or uniform and therefore, the fall in the price of one of the factors will induce the producer to substitute the costly factor completely by the cheaper factor; in such a case elasticity of substitution between two factors is infinity. On the other hand, suppose two factors of production are complementary, in the sense that both to be used in fixed proportions to produce a given output. The marginal rate of substitution between perfectly complementary factors is said to be infinite for, production is impossible by substitution of one of the factors by another, since both the factors have to be combined to produce a given output. In such a case a fall in the relative price of one commodity cannot lead to any substitution and, therefore, elasticity of substitution is zero (for, even when the price of one of the factors falls, it will not be possible to substitute the cheaper factor for the dearer one.)

Between these two extremes lie the most common types of marginal rates of technical substitution. If margainal rate of substitution declines slowly, elasticity of substitution declines rapidly, elasticity of substitution will be low. We may summarise this as follows :

(1) Every producer should be careful in combining factors of production. If he wants to secure maximum possible output with the least cost combination.

(2) The best or least cost combination of factors is indicated by the equality of price ratio between factors of production and the marginal rate of technical substitution between them.

(3) The best combination is disturbed when the price ratios change. How the different factors will be combined, when the ratios change, will depend upon the elasticity of substitution between the two factors which in trun depends upon the marginal rate of technical substitution.

(4) Between any two factors which are perfect substitutes for each other, the marginal rate of technical substitution is constant or uniform and hence elasticity of substitution is infinite.

(5) Between any two factors which are perfect complementaries, the elasticity of substitution is zero.

(6) In all other cases, in which the marginal rate of technical substitution is between infinite and zero, elasticity of substitution will be high or low, according to circumstances.

From the above discussion of the elasticity of substitution, it can be said that when the elasticity of substitution is unity, production obeys the law of constant returns, elasticity greater than unity indicates increasing returns and elasticity less than unity is associated with diminishing returns.

ESTIMATION OF PRODUCTION FUNCTION

The statistical investigations into the laws of production by C.W. Cobb and P.H. Douglas are of great importance in the field of economics. Their production function is used as a fairly universal law of production. They have estimated it in numerous samples of manufacturing industries throughout the world. This exponential type of production function ($X = A\ L^{\alpha} K^{\beta} U$) has no more claim to general validity as a description of technology than other mathematical functions. Moreover, it possesses certain interesting properties which make it a very convenient choice of a researcher. Even before the research of C.W. Cobb and P.H. Douglas, the similar type of production function had been used by many economists. But it was clearly developed and empirically verified by these two persons, Cobb and Douglas. That is why this function is almost always referred to as the "Cobb-Douglas Production Function."

The general form of Cobb-Douglas production function is

$$P = KL^{a} - C^{1-a}$$

where

P = output

L = labour input,

C = capital input,

K, a = positive constant

Also L > o, C > o, a >o, 1-a > o

The production function solved by Cobb - Douglas had 3/4 contribution of labour to the increase in manufacturing industry and 1/4 of capital. Thus, the Cobb-Douglas production in which

$$P = KL^{3/4} C^{1/4}$$

shows constant returns to scale because the total of the values of L and C is equal to one (3/4 + 1/4). To prove it, let us increase the quantities of labour and capital by g times. Then output

$$P = k(gL)^{a} (gC)^{1-a}$$

$$= k(g^{a} L^{a}) (g^{1-a} C^{1-a})$$

$$= Kg(L^{a}) (C^{1-a})$$

$$= gkL^{a} C^{1-a} = gP$$

$$[\therefore g = g^{a}g^{1-a}]$$

$$[\therefore P = L^{a} C^{1-a}]$$

Thus, the output P has become gp when the inputs are increased by g times. It shows that doubling the inputs, doubles the output. It implies that the Cobb-Douglas production function is linear and homogeneous.

One method is to take the scale line or Expansion Path connecting the equilibrium points O, P, R, OS is the scale line or expansion path joining these points. It shows that the isoquants 100, 200 and 300 are equidistant. Thus, on the scale line OS, OQ = QP = PR which shows that when the capital and labour are increased in equal proportions, the output also increases in the same proportion.

David Durand proposed that the restricted function of $P = K^a - C^{l-a}$ which assumed the existence of constant returns be abandoned for one in which the exponent for capital was independently determined. In that case, it would then be possible for the sum of the two exponents to be either greater or less than unity and hence to show the actual returns to scale which may be increasing, diminshing or constant. Hence the later formula of the Cobb-Douglas function is

$$P = KL^a - C^b$$

Thus, in the Cobb-Douglas function, the sum of the exponents show the degree of "returns to scale" in Production.

$a + b > 1$ increasing returns to scale.

$a + b = 1$ constant returns to scale.

$a + b < 1$ dercreasing returns to scale.

Properties of Cobb-Douglas Production Function

These properties are the following:

(i) Constant returns to scale prevails in the economy.

(ii) Elasticity of substitution is equal to one.

(iii) Expansion path generated by Cobb-Douglas production function is linear and passes through the origin.

(iv) a and 1-a represent the labour share and capital share respectively in output.

(v) a and 1-a are also the elasticities of output with respect to labour and capital respectively.

(vi) If one of the input is zero, output will also be zero.

Criticism. The Cobb Douglas function has been criticised on certain grounds.

(i) The total output is assumed to be the function of labour and capital only ignoring all other factors of production or inputs.

(ii) It regards all units of labour to be homogeneous.

(iii) It is based on industry-to-industry variations but plant to plant or firm to firm variation within an industry would seem to provide better results.

(iv) It is criticised because of shows constant return to scale. But constant returns to scale are not an actually because either increasing or decreasing return to scale generally applicable to production. This is why David Durand made suggestions.

Thus on the basis of the above criticism the practicability of Cobb-Douglas production function in the manufacturing industry seemed to be a doubtful proposition.

However, despite these limitations "Statistical investigations into the laws of production by C.W. Cobb and P.H. Douglas are among the most celebrated in the history of Econometries."

IMPORTANT CONCEPTS USED IN PRODUCTION FUNCTION

In Production Function a 'Firm' employs the services of the four factors of Production *viz* land, labour, capital and entreprise. For example if parts have to be produced, some one will be required to organise the Production unit, he will be called "entrepreneur. Thus entrepreneur will hire or purchase Land or Building machines and other equipment, cloth and service, of tailors, cutters, designers etc. These different persons will pool these resources together and produce pants. The Production of Pants known as "output" will be the result of the joint efforts of all these factors of production known as inputs".

In case if the output of Pants has to be increased additional cloth and labour has to be produced with out any change in other factors of Production. On this basis the various factors of Production can be classified into two parts:

(a) Fixed Factor of Production are those factors of inputs whose quantity need not be changed at different levels of output land, top management etc.

(b) Variable Factors of Production are those factor of inputs whose quantity will differ at different levels of output *e.g.* labour raw materials, capital etc.

Production has also a time dimension. Production and Planning take time. Farmers cannot change crop in midseason, Pipeline cannot be built overnight, fertiliser or cement plants take years to start and so on. The response of Production to a change in demand for some commodity is to be seen in this perspective. We may distinguish these two different time periods in Production Function as

(a) Short-run. In the short-run, some factors of inputs are fixed while the others are variable. The Production can be increased only by increasing the quantity of the variable factors, the time is so limited that the firms cannot hire additional units of the fixed factors. This sets limit to the maximum quantity of output that a firm can turn out.

(b) Long-run. In the long run all the factors of Production become Variable. A firm can instal a new plant or raise a new building in response to new demand.

The short-run and long run period is rather an "operational concept". This "operational time" interval will differ between different industries depending on the nature of the processes and the kind of equipment used.

Level of Production and Scale or Production

The level of production can be changed by changing the factor proportions in which the various inputs are used. In the short run, as we know, some factors are of the fixed nature, while others are variable. The level of production can be increased by increasing the quantity of the variable factors.

The law of proportions explains the relationship between inputs and outputs when some of the factors are fixed while the other is variable. For example inputs like plant, equipment and land are fixed while the other is variable. For example inputs like plant, equipment and land are fixed while labour is a variable input. It is common experience of every producer that when the proportion between fixed and variable inputs is changed by increasing the quantity of variable inputs the resultant addition to the total output may be at increasing constant or decreasing rate initially. But ultimately, total out put increases at a diminishing rate. Thus the theory of production seeks to explain the relationship between quantity of inputs and output.

Production is the backbone of economic activity. Production may be called the process of adding values to the natural resources or providing services to the people. It is essential that we define the three concepts of output or product very much used in the theory of production.

There are three basic concepts of product:

1. Total Product (TP). Total product is the total amount of a commodity produced during a given period of time by a given number of the factors of production. In other words, total product means the total physical output produced by a set of inputs.

Total product can be estimated in two ways:

(i) As the summation of marginal products of various units of a factor;

Or

(ii) As the average product multiplied by the number of units of a factor employed.

Hence,

$$TP = \Sigma MP$$

Or

$$TP = AP \times N$$

Here, TP = Total Product

Σ MP = Sum total of marginal products

AP = Average Product

N = Number of units of a factor

2. Average Product. (AP) Average product of a factor is the total product divided by the number of units of a factor. Thus, average product means the per unit output.

$$AP = \frac{TP}{N}$$

Here, AP = Average Product, TP = Total Product; N = Number of units of factor

3. Marginal Product. (MP) Marginal product is the change in total product resulting from the use of one more (or one less) unit of the variable factor. In short it is called as incremental product. The marginal product thus measures the rate at which total product is changing as one factor is varied.

Hence, $MP = \frac{\Delta TP}{\Delta F}$

Here, MP = Marginal Product

ΔTP = Change in the total product

ΔF = Change in factor input that caused TP to change.

Marginal Product can also be calculated with the help of the following formula:

$$MP = TP_n - TP_{n-1}$$

Here, MP = Marginal Product

TP_n = Total product of the n units of a factor

TP_{n-1} = Total product of the n – 1 units of a factor

The computation of all the three concepts has been explained in the following table below showing the output data when one of the factors is variable (labour) and the other factors are fixed.

Schedule Showing the Different Concepts of the Product

Land Fixed Factor (Acre)	*Labour Variable Factor (Units)*	*Total Product (Units)*	*Marginal Product (Units)*	*Average Product (Units)*	
2	0	0	–	–	
2	1	8	8	8	I Stage
2	2	20	12	10	I Stage
2	3	36	16	12	I Stage
2	4	48	12	12	II Stage
2	5	55	7	11	II Stage
2	6	60	5	10	II Stage
2	7	60	0	8.6	III Stage
2	8	56	–4	7	III Stage
2	9	45	–11	5	III Stage

Shapes of TP, AP and MP Curves

Following diagrams show the shapes of total product, average product and marginal product curves.

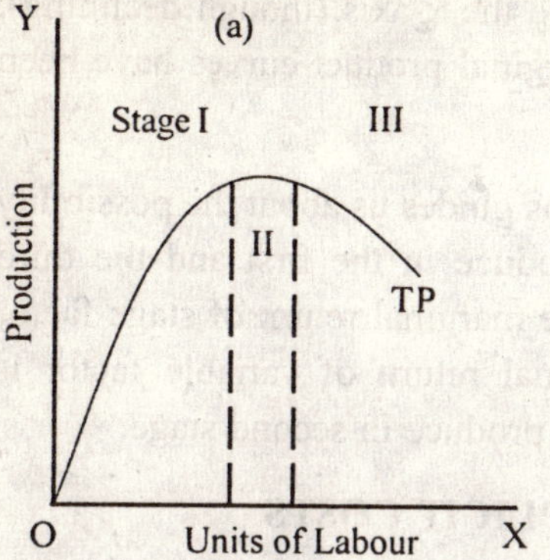

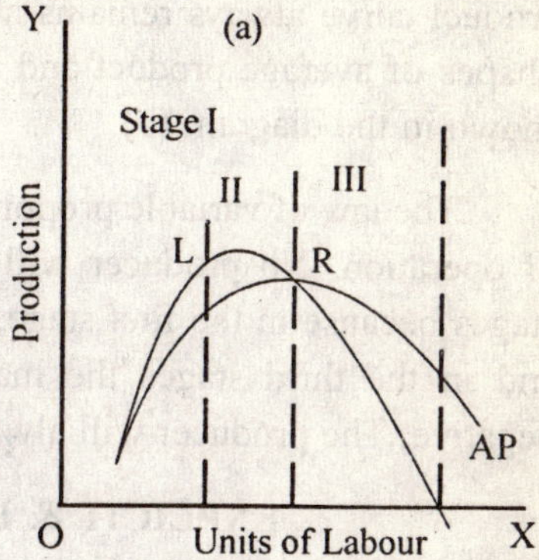

(i) At the First Stage. It is very evident from our above mentioned table that as we increase the units of labour on a fixed quantity of land, the total product first rises with an increasing rate (upto 3 units of labour at I Stage)

(ii) At Second Stage. Thereafter (upto 6 units of labour at II Stage) though it increases but at a diminishing rate. After it when we employ seventh unit of labour, it (*i.e.*, total product.)

(iii) At Third Stage. Reaches the maximum and, thereafter, from eighth units it starts declining. Thus, total product passes through three stages. Because of this type of trend of change in total product the shape of the total product curve will be like the curve shown in diagram.

Total product curve rises rapidly at first, then gradually level off, and finally turns down.

With the increase in the units of labour both average product and marginal product first rise, then after reaching their maximum start to decline. Hence the average product and marginal product curves are inversely U-shaped curves. With the increase in the units or a variable factor marginal product continues to decline and with its declining trend it reaches zero and even negative. Hence, marginal product curve after cutting the x-axis goes below to it. But on the other, average product no doubt declines as the variable factor increases but it never becomes zero or negative, hence average product curve always remains above the x-axis (though declining). Shapes of average product and marginal product curves have been shown in the diagram (b).

The law of variable proportions guides us about the possibility of operation. No producer will produce in the first and the third stages because in the first stage, the marginal return of stage factor and in the third stages the marginal return of variable factor is negative. The producer will always produce in second stage.

EXPLICIT & IMPLICIT COSTS

The term "cost" usually refers to money costs, real cost, private and special costs, and opportunity cost. In our day to day life we are mostly concerned with money costs in the matter of the production of commodity in a firm. Money costs are the money outlays of a firm on the production of a commodity. They include wages and salaries paid to labour. Payments in relation to rent, advertising and insurance; outlays on capital equipment (machinery etc.) Expenditure on transportation, the taxes and interest on borrowed money.

If the payment of wages, interest, rent etc. is made to 'outside' agent who have supplied labour, capital, land etc., the payments are called explict costs. If the entrepreneur invests his own savings in his bussiness, uses his own building and acts as a manager he does not pay interest, rent and salaries on these accounts to any "outside agent". But we must allow interest on his own capital, rent on his own building etc. as the entreprenur had allowed others to use these "factors", he would have earned remuneration on them, the payments for such factors are called "implict costs" or "imputed costs". The implict costs of producing particular commodity consist of the above mentioned factors of Production.

Thus it is evident that the total cost of production of a firm include both the Explict and Implict costs. Explicit costs are those expenses which are incured by the firm in buying goods and services directly. Implict costs are the imputed value of the entrepreneurs own resources and services which he could earn in the best alternative uses. Both explicit costs and implicit costs must be taken into account while calculating money costs, or expenses of production.

These total costs of production are devided into two parts:

(a) Variable costs and (b) Fixed costs

The variable costs are those expenses of production which change with the change in the firm's output. Marshall called these variable costs as prime costs of production *e.g.*, labour power and raw material etc.

Fixed costs, called supplementary costs by Marshall are those expenses of production which do not change with the change in output, *e.g.*, rent interest, salary depreciation etc.

Real costs-money costs are the expenses of production from the point of view of the producer. But they tell us nothing about what lies behind these costs. Marshall and others have given thought to real costs and gone behind the money costs. Marshall thought that the efforts and sacrifices undergone by the various members of the society producing a commodity are the real costs of production. The efforts and sacrifices made by the capitalist to save and invest by the workers in fore-going leisure and by the landlords in the use of land, all constitute real costs.

It is important from the social point of view to study what lies behind the money costs. Marshall says. "The exertions of all the different kinds of labour that are directly or indirectly involved in making it, together with the abstinence or rather the waitings required for saving the capital used in making it, all these efforts and sacrifices together will be called the real cost of production of the commodity." In other words real costs consider the disutilities of rendering the services. When we put in labour, there is pain or discomfort involved in it. The owner of a firm is always worried about whether his business would fetch him what he wants. If we consider capital, very act of saving involves the sacrifice of present consumption. But as saving increases more and more and the expense of present consumption, disutility of saving *i.e.* unpleasantness in saving, increases. Even in the Keynesian theory of interest, there is the idea of real cost. When we lend money, we part with liquidity-interest is the price for the dicomfort involved in parting with liquidity.

The real costs are psychological cost, and as such they do not lead themselves to exact measurement. Again money costs are real costs. But real costs seldom equal money costs of production. Marshall himself admitted and when he wrote, "If the purchasing power of money in terms of effort has remained about constant, and if the rate of remuneration for waiting has remained about constant, and if the rate money measure of costs corresponds to real costs; but such a correspondence is never to be assumed lightly." The price of goods do not reflect the disutility of different kinds used in their production. If it were so, the wages of labour will have to be according to the marginal disutility of labour. But wages are determined by the marginal productivity of labour and not by the disutility of different kinds used in their production. if it were so, the wages of labour will have to be according to the marginal disutility of labour. But wages are determined by the marginal productivity of labour and not by the disutility of labour. Thus the money costs and the real costs of production do not correspond with each other in the short run or the long run. Rather it leads us "into quagmire of unreality and dubious hypothesis."

Private, External and Social Costs

Private costs refer to all those expenses which are incurred by a firm (or a produce) in producing a commodity. The costs which fall on the society during the course of producing a commodity are called social costs. In social costs we include not only the costs to the firm or the producer but also the costs borne by the society in order to produce that commodity. In other words, along with the opportunity costs, social costs take into consideration the adverse effect on the welfare of the members of the society also in producing a commodity. That is why the doctrine of social costs is wider than the private costs.

We know that when an economic activity is undertaken it affects not only the persons involved in it but it also affects the other sections of the society. When costs are calculated from the standpoint of the persons engaged in an economic activity, they are called private costs. On the other, when costs are calculated from the standpoint of the society as a whole, they become social costs. In this way there is a difference between private costs and social costs. In some cases social costs can be higher than private costs and in other cases they may be lower than private-costs. Now we shall try to understand this difference with the help of some practical examples.

Examples where social cost are higher than private costs:

(i) For a factory-owner private costs mean the expenses on raw materials, power, wages, transport, publicity, capital-equipments, etc.

Social costs include washing bills for cloths, medical bills and pollution due to smoke that emits from the chimneys of the factory.

(ii) In the case of car driving, private costs include expenses on petrol, depreciation of tyres and other spare parts, etc.

Social costs include road maintenance, road accidents, etc.

Examples where social costs are lower than private costs:

In the case of engineering colleges, medical colleges, training institutes dams and canals, social costs are smaller (*i.e.*, social benefits are greater) than the private costs (*i.e.*, expenses incurred on them).

The doctrine of social cost is very important yet it could not form the basis for calculating the cost in practical life. It requires more research in this field. Uptill now most of the calculations in the field of economics are done on the basis of private costs.

Sometimes, there is deviation between the cost incurred by a firm and the cost that must be incurred by the society. For example, a factory may dispose of its untreated waste into a river or take such a method of waste disposal which may minimise the private cost, but it does impose a cost to the society in the form of polluted water ways. A cost that not borne by the producer, but is incurred by others in society is called an External cost.

The true cost to the society must include all costs regardless of who bears them. Thus the social cost is the sum of private and external cost. A firm may also create in the process of production, some benefits to society for which it is not directly paid *e.g.*, the apple blossoms increases the output of nearly honey production.

Thus, the apple growers create external benefits to the honey producers. These are knwon as Externalities. In brief if social cost is more than private cost there is an external cost or negative externality if social cost is less than private cost, there is an external benefit or positive externality.

Besides, there are so many examples which show that the private costs fall short of social cost; combination of water in mining and industrial areas; in pollution due to smoke let loose by factories, the noise caused by radio and gramophone music; occupational diseases, etc. But we can think of the cases when private cost is greater than the social cost. The production may mean free or unpaid for benefits to the economy as a whole. The private business and technological institution bear the cost of running them (private costs), but the society or economy at large gains. A private firm may set up an electricity plant or a dam. It will provide cheaper power and irrigational facilities to society. Private research by a firm or an institution involves cost for it. But others also gain from result of research-the economy as a whole gains.

The Concept of Opportunity Costs

It is also called alternative cost, or displacement cost, or transfer cost which was introduced by Von Wieser and was popularised by Davenport. This concept of cost is based on the idea of choice. It is based on the fact that our means of resources have alternative uses. Opportunity cost is determined by the next best alternatives-the best one and next best one. It is our effort to put resources to the best use, in doing so, we sacrifice the next best use. The next best use sacrificed is the opportunity cost of putting the resources to the best use.

Thus, opportunity cost for a commodity is the amount of other goods which have to be given up in order to produce one additional unit of that commodity. According to Prof. Benson, "The opportunity cost of anything is the next best alternative that could be produced instead by the same factors, or by an equivalent group of factors, costing the same amount of Money." In short opportunity cost is the cost of foregone alternatives.

Closely viewed, in most of the cases, opportunity cost has a psychological foundation. We have to give up not only the pleasure but also goods or an amount of money. Opportunity cost appears as a clear phsychological phenomenon when a consumer who purchases a commodity forgoes another goods which he also wants. Thus the economising individuals gives up certain satisfactions.

It is possible that the next best alternative goods is in such great demand that its exclusion involves a serious and concrete sacrifice for a given individual.

Importance of Opportunity Cost

(1) The concept of opportunity cost is of great importance for the individual as also for the economy at large. The quantities of economic resources are limited in relation to human wants. Thus when resources are employed by a firm in the production of a commodity, it means certain amounts of other goods, which the resoruces in question help in producing, must be sacrificed by society. With certain resources society can produce gun or butter. If the choice fall upon guns, and resources are employed for the manufacture of guns, society has to go without butter. Thus for the economy as a whole, the opportunity cost of guns is better.

(2) The idea of opportunity cost emerges in various felds. There is opportunity cost when a consumer purchases one article rather than another, it is there in the labourer's choice of a job it exists when the investor has to make a choice regarding where he should invest his savings; and so on.

(3) The opportunity cost will always mean displacement of an article which ranks next in the consumer's scale of preferences. The opportunity cost of enjoying a movie may be the sacrifice of a book (both costing the same amount of money). The opportunity cost of working in a distillery for a labourer is the wages he could get in a sugar mill. A factor of production expects as much compensation in one employment as it can get in the alternative employment.

(4) The concept of opportunity cost is of great significance in the theory of value. The cost of resources of a firm are really the values of these resources in their best alternative-*i.e.*, next best uses. To secure the services of resources the firm will have to pay them as much as they can earn in next best uses. The cost of labour in the manufacture of sewing machines must be as much as the value of washing machines which the same labour could have produced. If labour is not paid that much, it will continue to be employed in the manufacture of washing machines, and will not be available for manufacturing sewing machines.

(5) The values or prices of goods and services are according to their opportunity costs. Suppose that with given resources, a firm can produce 100 tables or 200 chairs. If it is so, the value of 100 tables must in the final analysis be equal to 200 chairs or *vice-versa*. Put in terms of money, the price of one table will tend to be the same as that of two chairs.

(6) In the case of services of factors, opportunity costs have a bearing on the prices of goods which they help to produce. The opportunity cost of labour (the wages it can earn in the next best employment) will affect market wage-rate and thus the cost of production and the price of the goods which labour produces.

(7) It is however, unspecialized productive agent or services which help determine the prices of the product they produce. Thus an unspecialized service is a price determining service. An unspecialized productive agent is one that has different uses, that is, it can serve in various lines of production. Suppose an unspecialized agent can work in various capacities. But his earning or wages in one field will be governed by his earning in other fields, such a productive agent will not accept much less in one occupation than in others. The earning in one occupation will be controlled by its earning in other occupations.

(8) The specialised agent can render the best service in one particular occupation. There is sizable difference between its earning in the best occupation and in any alternative occupation. In fact the best occupation of such an agent is without an occupation which can be considered a close one, or next best one. Thus the specialised serivce is price determined service. Its earning or its cost to the firm would depend upon the demand for what it produces. The earnings of unspecialised service influence the price of the product of the service, the earnings of the specialized service are influenced by the price of its product.

Opportunity cost rises above the bounds of an economy system. In every economy the alternative sacrificed is an opportunity cost. Even in Robinson Crusoe economy-isolated economy-there is such a cost. The opportunity cost of repairing the hut is the loss of fish which Robinson Crusoe might have cuaght. A communist society has also to choose between more of tanks and more of tractors. Thus, there may not be opportunity cost of factors of production from the point of view of an individual, but from the standpoint of the economy opportunity cost of factors of production is of paramount importance even in communist societies.

Uses of Marginal Cost in Pricing Decisions

The total costs of a product consists of two elements-namely, variable costs and fixed costs. The variable costs varies directly in proportion to change in the volume of output, which means that variable cost per unit remains constant regardless of the level of output. On the other hand, fixed costs remain fixed at the same level regardless of changes in the volume of output. In this way, fixed costs are period costs and they go down per unit with the upward change in the level of output. These variable costs are known as marginal costs also. The main components of variable costs are direct marginal costs, direct labour, and variable overheads, Thus, marginal costs are the direct labour, and variable overheads. Thus, marginal costs are the direct costs of production and they are main components of total costs.

The technique of marginal costing is valuable aid to management in taking many policy decisions. The information provided by the total cost method may not be sufficient in solving the marginal problems. The following are some of the managerial problems where marginal cost analysis becomes useful:

1. Pricing Decisions
2. Make or buy decisions.
3. Key of limiting factor,
4. Effect or change in sales price.
5. Maintaining a desired level of profit.
6. Selection of suitable and profitable product mix.
7. Alternative methods of production.

Here, we shall describe contribution of marginal costing to pricing decisions only. Although price are controlled more by market conditions and other economic factors than by decisions of management, yet fixation of selling prices is one of the most important functions of management. Marginal costing is useful in pricing decisions in the following circumstances:

1. Determination of Selling Price at Different Volume of Output. If the total revenue can be projected on the basis of anticipated prices and volumes of production the increase in revenue at different levels of production and at different prices can be compared with the marginal costs at those levels of activity. Thus the selling price which will maximise profits can be determined easily by comparing the marginal costs and incremental revenue.

(2) Pricing in Depression. Prices fall during depression and the product may be sold below the total cost. In case, there is considerable but temporary fall in the demand on account depressions leading to the use for a drastic reduction in prices temporairly, the minimum selling price can be fixed at he marginal cost. If the selling prices at which the goods can be sold be continued.

(3) Submitting Tenders and Quotations. When a tender is submitted, the additional production involved will mean an increase in total cost. To make a competitive bid, the minimum prices has to be quoted. The Marginal Cost indicates the floor below which the quotation will be unprofitable. Thus, with the help of marginal cost analysis, any price above the marginal cost may be quoted so as to increase the total profit, provided the quoted price does not lower the normal price for the rest of the market.

(4) Acceptance of Special Order. If some special order is proposed and the price offered is less than the average total cost, a comparison of the additional revenue and marginal costs is necessary to decide whether the order is worthwhile to accept. The order from a local merchant should not be accepted at a price below normal price because it will affect relationship of the concept with other consumers. But in case of foreign markets, goods may be sold at a price below normal costs price keeping in view the direct and indirect benefits of exporting such as import quotas, subsides from government, prestige of exporting, etc.

(5) Pricing Decisions in Other Circumstances. Management is offenly confornted with the problems of cut in prices of products from time to time on account of competition, expansion programme or government regulations, etc. Marginal cost analysis helps in pricing decisions in these circmstances by adding a margin in marginal costs which may be sufficient to conribute towards fixed expenses and profits.

CONCEPTS OF SHORT RUN AND LONG RUN COST CURVES

A short period may be defined as a period in which the productive capacity of a firm remains unchanged. Let us take a case in which a firm is fully utilising its productive capacity in the shape of plant and other equipment. It is possible for the demand for the output of the firm to undergo changes even in this case. Suppose the demand increases. The producer cannot increase his output immediately for such an increase is possible only when the productive capacity can be increased but it cannot be adjusted to the increased demand all at once. Increase of productive capacity requires more or bigger which are not immediately possible. The first thing which the producer must find out is whether the increase in demand is only temporary or whether it will stay. If the increase in demand is expected to stay, the producer will take steps to order more and new plants and equipments and, having procured them, to instal them. This will naturally take time. The same thing happens when the demand for the product falls down. It will not be possible to reduce the productive capacity immediately.

In short period, production can be changed but not according to the change in the conditions of demand. There are two types of factors in short run—*(1)* fixed factors *e.g.* machinery and equipment, organisation, techniques of production etc. *(2)* Variable factors *e.g.* fuel, temporary and unskilled labour, number of shifts, raw materials. Naturally there are two types of costs in the short period. Needless to emphasise here that these periods are not defined by same specified length of time, but rather, are determined by the variability of factors of production. In the short run, a firm incurs some costs that are associated with variable factors and others that result from fixed factors. The former are called variable costs and the latter represent fixed costs. Variable costs (VC) change as the level of output changes and therefore, can be expressed as a function of output Q that is VC = f (Q). Variable costs typically include such things as raw material, labour and utilities. But the increases in variable costs associated with each unit increase in output are not constant due to the operation of laws of variable proportions. Fixed costs on the other hand, are not a function of the level of output and are constant in the short run that if FC = K (property taxes, the cost of leases on land, buildings and some types of equipment, interest changes on the long term borrowed funds, insurance charges etc.) The distinction between fixed and variable costs is of great significance to the business manager. Variable cost are those costs which business can control or alter in the short run by changing levels of production. Fixed costs are clearly beyond business executives control, such costs are incurred in the short run and must be paid regardless of the level of output.

$$TC = FC + VC \qquad ...(1)$$

$$TC = K\ (Const) + f\ (R) \qquad ...(2)$$

$$VC = f\ (Q)$$

Average fixed cost (AFC) is derived by dividing total fixed cost by the corresponding output (Q). That is

$$AFC = \frac{TFC}{Q}$$

Total fixed cost remains constant whatever be the value of output. AFC will tend to approach infinity as the output approach to zero. AFC curve is a rectangular hyperbola. AFC is also known as an asymptotic hyperbola.

Average variable cost is found by dividing total variable cost by the corresponding output (Q);

$$AVC = \frac{TFC}{Q}$$

AVC declines initially, reaches a minimum and then increases again. Due to the operation of laws of variable proportions in the beginning VC increases in a lesser proportion and after a point it increases in a higher proportion. Graphically AVC is a U shaped or saucer shaped curve. Because total variable cost reflects the law of diminishing returns, so must the AVC figures. Because of increasing returns initially, it takes fewer and fewer additional variable resources to produce each of additional output (variable cost per unit decline). After AVC hitting a minimum, AVC rises as diminishing returns necessitate the use of more and more variable resources to produce each additional unit of output.

Average total cost (ATC) can be found by dividing total cost by total output.

$$ATC = \frac{TC}{Q} = AFC + AVC$$

ATC is found by adding vertically AFC and AVC. Thus the vertical distance between the ATC and AVC curves reflect AFC at any level of output. As the output increases, AFC decreases that is why the distance between ATC and AVC decreases.

Marginal Cost (MC) is defined as the extra or additional cost of producing one more unit of output. MC can be determined for each additional unit of output simiply by noting the change in total cost which that unit's production entails—

$$MC = \frac{\text{Change in TC}}{\text{Change in Q}} = \frac{\Delta TC}{\Delta Q}$$

$$MC = \frac{\delta}{\delta Q}(TC) = \text{Slope of TC Curve}$$

The concept of marginal cost is very important because it designates those cost over which the firm has the most direct control. More specifically, MC indicates those costs which are incurred in the product of the last unit (Average cost figure do not provide this information). Marginal cost declines sharply, reaches a minimum and then rises rather sharply. This mirrors the fact that variable cost (TC also) increases first by decreasing amounts and then by increasing amounts. The law of diminishing returns implies eventually increasing marginal cost and increasing average variable cost. Short run AVC curve are often U shaped. A short run cost curve show how costs vary with output for a given quantity of fixed factor—say a given size of plant. There is a different short run cost curve for each quantity of the fixed factor.

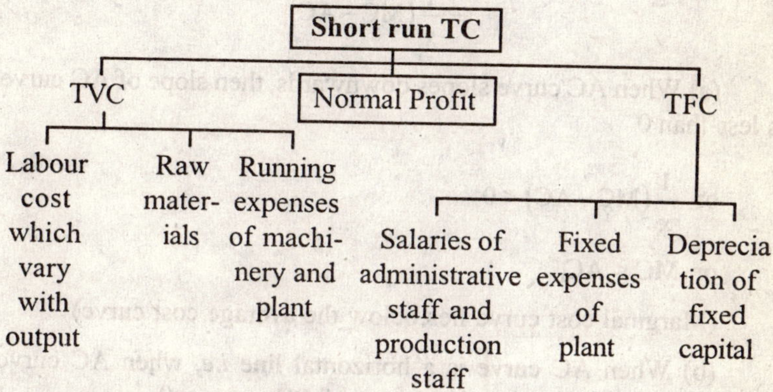

Mathematical Application—

$$AC = \frac{\text{Total Cost}}{\text{Output}} = \frac{\pi}{x}$$

Total Cost p = AC . x

Marginal cost is defined as the rate of change in total cost with respect to output $MC = \frac{d\pi}{dx}$

Slope of TC and AC curve

$$p. = f(x)$$

$$\text{Slope of AC curve} = \frac{d}{dx}(\pi / x)$$

$$= \frac{x - \frac{d\pi}{dx} - \pi}{x^2}$$

$$= \frac{1}{x}\frac{d\pi}{dx} - \frac{\pi}{x^2}$$

$$= \frac{1}{x}\left(\frac{d\pi}{dx} - \frac{\pi}{x}\right)$$

$$= \frac{1}{x}(MC - AC)$$

(a) When AC curve slopes downwards, then slope of AC curve is less than 0

or $\frac{1}{x}(MC - AC) < 0$

or $MC < AC$

(Marginal cost curve lies below the average cost curve)

(b) When AC curve is a horizontal line *i.e.* when AC curve reaches a minimum point, then slope of AC curve = 0

$$\frac{d}{dx}(\pi / x) = 0 \text{ or } MC - AC = 0 \text{ or } MC = AC$$

When AC curve is a horizontal line then MC curve is equal to AC (c) When AC curve slopes upwards, then slope of AC curve

$$> 0 \frac{d}{dx}(\pi / x) > 0 \ MC - AC > 0 \text{ or } MC > AC$$

Marginal cost curve lies above average cost curve.

Cost Elasticity. Let us suppose the cost function of a firm producing x units by given by p = f (x)

elasticity of demand is given by $= \frac{p}{x} - \frac{dx}{d\pi} = \frac{d(\log x)}{d(\log p)}$

[demand function is x = f (p)]

elasticity of total cost is given by $= \frac{x}{\pi} - \frac{d\pi}{dx} = \frac{d\log(\pi)}{d(\log x)}$

Thus cost elasticity is the ratio of relative change in total cost to the relative change in output. In other words cost elasticity is the ratio of MC to AC.

$$= \frac{MC}{AC}$$

Also AC = p/x, then elasticity of AC

$$\text{Elasticity of average cost} = \frac{x}{AC}\frac{d}{dx}(AC)$$

$$= \frac{x}{\pi / x}\frac{d}{dx}(\pi / x)$$

$$= \frac{\frac{x^2}{\pi}\left(x\frac{d\pi}{dx} - \pi\frac{d}{dx}(x)\right)}{x^2}$$

$$= \frac{1}{\pi}\left(x\frac{d\pi}{dx} - \pi\right)$$

$$= \frac{x}{\pi}\frac{d\pi}{dx} - \frac{\pi}{\pi}$$

= elasticity of total cost-1

$$\text{Elasticity of AC} = \frac{x}{AC}\frac{d}{dx}(AC) = \frac{x}{AC}\frac{d}{dx}(\pi / x)$$

$$= \frac{x}{AC}.\frac{1}{x^2}\left(x\frac{d\pi}{dx} - \pi\right)$$

$$= \frac{1}{AC}\left(\frac{d\pi}{dx} - \pi / x\right)$$

$$= \frac{1}{AC}[MC - AC]$$

LAWS OF PRODUCTION OR LAWS OF RETURNS

Traditionally, the production function has been called the law of diminishing returns and has been explained by economists in different ways in the last 200 years or so. We may study the production function as follows:

Laws of Production or Laws of Return

(a) With land as the fixed factor and labour and capital as variable factors, this is Marshall's version of law of diminishing returns.

(b) With one factor variable and all other factors fixed. This is modern version of law of diminishing returns known as law of variable proportions.

(c) With all factors variable, this is the law of Return to scale. On the basis of different stages of the law of variable proportions generally three laws of returns are described : Law of increasing returns, Law of constant returns; and Law of the diminishing returns. In fact, laws of returns are the simplified forms of the law of variable proportions. However, there are some minor differences between the three stages of the law of variable proportions and the three laws of returns. The boundaries of these laws of returns are some what different from the three stages of the law of variable proportions. Beside, laws of returns do not include the negative stage. Early economists have discussed the theory of production on the basis of these laws of returns and among them also they emphasised more on the law of diminishing returns. Hence, it will be useful to study these laws of returns.

As we have already said that the change in factor-proportions affects the amount of output. This effect may take three forms and that is why the laws of production have three variants.

1. Law of Diminishing Returns

This law has two versions: classical version and modern version.

(i) Classcial Version. This version was propounded and exposed by Prof. Ricardo, Malthus, Marshall and others. According to classical version this law is concerned mainly with land agriculture. As Marshall puts it, "An increase in the capital and labour applied in the cultivation of land causes in general, a less than proportionate increase in the amount of product raised, unless it happens to coincide with an improvement in the art of agriculture."

(ii) Modern Version. According to modern economists, it is applicable not only in agriculture but in all the fields of production. This version is explained by Mrs. John Robinsons, Behanm, Samuelsons, Boulding and other modern economists. Prof. Boulding has defined this law in these words, "As we increase the quantity of any one input which is combined with a fixed quantity of the other inputs the marginal physical productivity of the variable input must eventually decline."

In short, when the increasing quantities of a variable factor are applied to given quantities of fixed factors, the marginal product falls, it is termed as laws of diminishing returns. This is illustrated in the following table and diagram:

EXAMPLE

Fixed Factor Land (Acres) (1)	*Variable Factor Labours (Units) (2)*	*Total Product (kg.) (3)*	*Average Product*	*Marginal Product (Rs.) (4)*
1	1	50	50	50
1	2	90	45	40
1	3	120	40	30
1	4	145	36	25
1	5	165	33	20

The law of diminishing returns, as it is usually formulated states that with a fixed amount of any factor of production successive increase in the amounts of other factor will, after a point, yield diminishing increment of output. "Thus from the above schedule and figure it is clear that if one factor is held constant and is perfectly inelastic, and if another factor is varied, the total output will increase at an increasing rate in the first instance and then at dimnishing rate, the average and marginal output will rise up to a certain stage, and they will eventually decline.

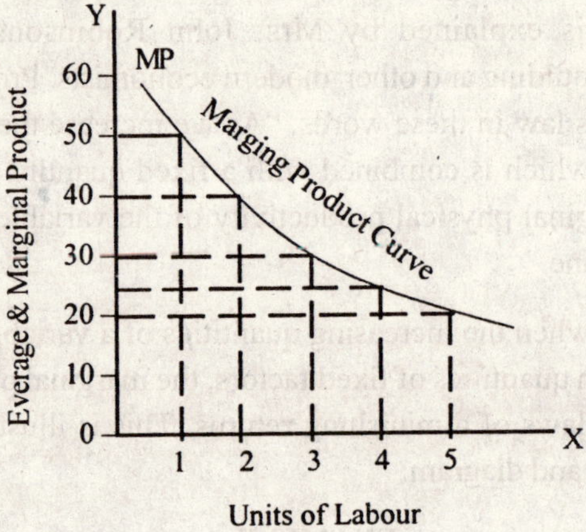

Our above example makes it clear that with the increase in the units of labour to a fixed plot of land, marginal product goes on diminishing. In other words, increase in total output is less than proportionate to the increase in the units of labour. In the diagram marginal product (MP) curve slopes downwards from left to the right which indicates the diminishing returns.

Causes for the Operation of the Law

Why does the law of diminishing returns operate? Following are given as its main reasons:

(i) Fixed Factor. The quantity of the fixed factor-input per unit of the variable input falls as more and more of the latter is put to use successive unit of the variable input, therefore, must add decreasing amounts to the total output as they have less of the fixed input to work *e.g.* land is a fixed factor.

(ii) Scarcity of Factors. Factors of production are scarce and limited in supply. If factors had not been limited, this law would also not have come into existence.

(iii) Imperfect Substitutes. Factors of production cannot be substituted fully. For example, labour or capital cannot be substituted in place of land.

(iv) Optimum Combination. There is optimum combination of different factors that gives the maximum output. When we increase a particular factor of production beyond this optimum combination, marginal product of that variable factor declines naturally.

Samuelson has regarded the law of dimnishing returns as a natural law. Since this law is applicable in all the fields of production, it is called as the universal law of production. Many principles of economics such as the Malhusian theory of distribution are based on the assumption of the law of diminishing returns. Though this law is applicable in all fields yet it is more applicable in the fields of agriculture. The main reason behind this is that in agriculture nature plays a greater role than the man. In the words of Wick Steed the law of diminishing returns "is as universal as the law of life itself." The universal applicability of this law has transcended economics to the realm of science. Above all, it is of fundamental importance for understanding the problems of under developed countries.

2. Law of the Constant Returns

The law of constant returns established relationship between the law of increasing returns and diminishing returns. The law may be defined in the words of Prof. Stegler as follows. "When all the productive services are increased in a given proportion, the product is increased in the same proportion." The law of constant return is also known as the law of constant costs as the costs remain constant. When production increases in the same proportion as the increases in variable factor, it is the case of law of constant returns.

In other words, with increase in variable factor marginal product of the variable factor remains constant. This law is illustrated in the following example and diagram

EXAMPLE

Fixed Factor	*Variable Factor labour (Units)*	*Total production of vests (Units)*	*Average production (Units)*	*MP of vests (Units)*
Machine	1	25	25	25
and other	2	50	25	25
factors	3	75	25	25
remain	4	100	25	25
constant	5	125	25	25

In diagram above there is only one line for average output and marginal output parallel to OX. It is evident from the example that as we increase the units of labour in a hosiery unit producing vests, the marginal product always remains 25 vests.

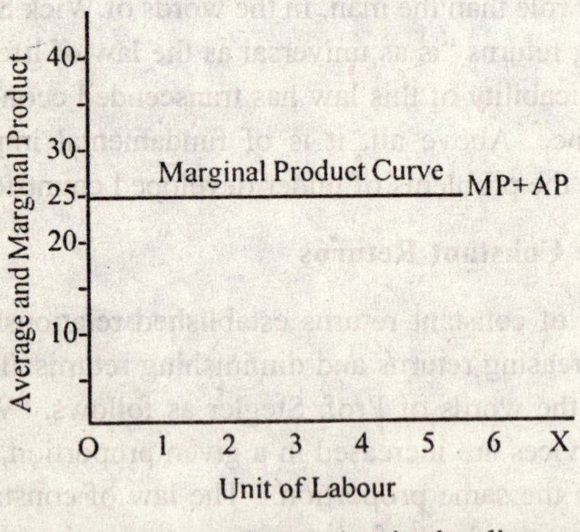

Hence the marginal product curve in the diagram is horizontal and parallel to the X-axis which shows the constant returns. As a result of its marginal cost also remains constant.

In actual word this law is a rare phenomenon. But sometimes we see the operation of law in hosiery industries, though it does not last long. However, the law of constant returns is important because its operation in an enterprise reflects an ideal or optimum combination of the various factors of production. In such situation the total output increases at a fixed rate and the average output and marginal output are same.

3. Law of Increasing Returns

The law states that with an increase in the quantity of the variable factors of production, the total output increases with an increase in the marginal output and the average output. Prof. Marshall has put the law as under : "An increase of labour and capital leads generally to improve organisation, which increase the efficiency of work of labour and capital."

When production increases more than proportionate to the increase in variable factor, it is known as the law of increasing returns. In other word, marginal product increases with the increases in quantities of variable factor. This law has been explained through the following example and diagram.

EXAMPLE

Fixed Factor	*Variable Factor Labour (Units)*	*Total Production of cloth (Metres)*	*Average Product of cloth (Metres)*	*MP of Vests (Metres)*
Machine	1	20	20	20
and other	2	45	22.5	25
factors	3	75	25	30
remain	4	115	29	40
constant	5	165	33	50

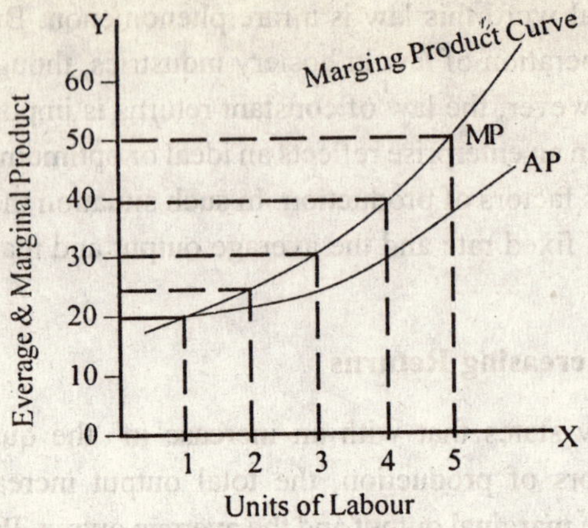

According to example and diagram marginal production of cloth increases with the increases in the units of labour. This is shown by an upward sloping marginal product curve in thc diagram.

Causes for the Opertion of the Law

(i) Indivisibility of Factors. There are some factors which cannot be purchased in parts. For example, if no generator is available in the market less than the size of 15 horse power then we have to purchase and use this generator. If at present we are not using this generator to its full capacity then with the increase in production marginal cost will decline.

(ii) Increase in Effeciency. If the efficiency of fixed factor increases with the increase in the quantities of variable factor, the law of increasing retuns will apply.

(iii) Fixed Factors. The cost of fixed factors is also fixed. Hence, with the increase in output per unit fixed cost will decline which in turn will lower the over all average cost also up to a certain limit.

(iv) Division of Labour. If the increase in the units of labour brings greater division of labour and specialisation in the production, it will also create the conditions of increasing returns.

(v) Optimum Combination. If to achieve optimum combination of various factors of production, the increase in the quantities of a particular factor is required it will also bring increasing returns.

RETURN TO SCALE

In the long run all factors are variable, hence the expansion of output may be achieved by varying all factor-inputs, when we change all factor-inputs in the same proportion, the scale of production is also changed. The study of the effects of change in the scale of production on the amount of output comes under the head of returns to scale.

Thus, the term **returns to scale** refers to the changes in output as all factor-inputs change by the same proportion in the long run.

In other words, the law expressing the relationship between varying scales of production and quantities of output is called returns to scale. In short, returns to scale refer to the effects of scale relationship.

Now the question is at what rate the output will increase when all factor-inputs are varied in the same proportion. There can be three possibilities in this regard. The increase in output may be more than, equal to, or less than proportional to the increase in factor-inputs. Accordingly, returns to scale are also of three types-increasing return to scale, constant returns to scale and diminishing returns to scale.

(1) Increasing Return to Scale

Increasing returns to scale refers to a situation where the total output increases in a greater proportion than the increase in units of factor inputs.

When the increase in output is more than proportionate to the given increase in the quantities of all factor-inputs, it is termed as increasing returns to scale.

For instance, if the increase in factor-inputs is 100 per cent and the resultant increase in output is 150 per cent, it is increasing returns to scale. We give an illustration of increasing returns to scale by a diagram. From O three lines OS, OQ and OR are drawn cutting the isoproduct curve 1, curve 2, curve 3 at various points. Increasing returns to scale is shown as:

OR > RT > TG

or OR' > R'T' > T'G'

or O'R' > R'T' > T 'G'

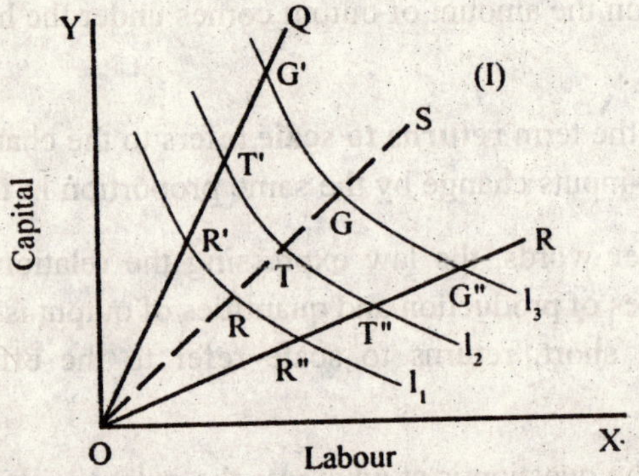

It means in this case, a doubling of inputs results in more than doubling of output. It is explained in the following example–

Scale of Production (machine + Labour)	*Total Output (Units)*
1 Machine + 2 Labour	100
2 Machine + 4 Labour	250

Causes for the Operation of Increasing Returns to Scale

Why does increasing returns to scale operate? The reasons for the operation of increasing returns to scale are found in the form of economies of large-scale production. They are:

(i) Labour Economies. They are also known as the economies of specialisation and division of labour. Division of labour and specialisation are possible more in large-scale operation. Different types of workers can specialise and do the job for which they are more suited. A worker acquires greater skill by devoting his attention to a particular job. Quality and speed of work both improve. This results in a sharp increase in output per man. Thus in short, with growing scale come, increasing specialiation and increasing returns to scale.

(ii) Technical Economies. The main technical economies result from the indivisibilities which are a characteristic of the modern industrial techniques of production. Several capital goods, because of the strength and weight required, will work only if they are of a certain minimum size. It may be technically possible to build smaller models of them; but it will not always be possible to use such models. Besides this, there is a general principle that as the size of a capital good is increased, its total output capacity increases far more rapidly than the cost of making it. To double the size and output capacity of a blast furnace for instance, we do not have to double the materials required. This is known as the principle of indivisibility.

(iii) Marketing Economies. Advertising space (in newspapers and magazines) and time (on television and radio), and the number of salesmen do not have to rise proportionately with the sales. Thus the selling cost per unit of output fall with scale.

(iv) Managerial Economies. Managerial economies arise from specialisation of management and machanisation of managerial function. Large firms make possible the division of managerial tasks. This division of decision-making in large firms has been found very effective in the increase of the efficiency of management. Besides, large firms apply techniques of management involving a high degree of mechanisation, such as telephones, telex machines, television screens and computers. These techniques save time and speed up the proceeding of informations.

As the business firms continues to expand it gradually exhausts the economies which cause the operation of increasing returns to scale. Beyond this point, further increase in the scale of operation are accompained by constant returns to scale.

(v) Economies Related to Transport and Storage Costs. Because a large firm uses its own transport means and larger vehicles, the per units transport costs would fall. Similarly, storage costs will also fall with the size.

As a result of all these economies firm's long run average and marginal cost decline with the increase in output and scale of production.

(2) Constant Returns to Scale

Thus the constant returns to scale means that if all factor-inputs are varied at a certain percentage rate, output will change by the same rate.

Or, when the increase in output is proportional to the increase in the quantities of all factor-inputs, it is termed as constant returns to scale.

The constant returns to scale sometimes referred to by economists in managerial language, a production curve showing constant returns to scale is often called "Linear and homogeneous" or "homogeneous of the first degree". The Cobb-Douglas production function evolved by American economists, Paul Douglas and C.W. Cobb is a linear and homogeneous function. Fig. illustrates constant returns to scale.

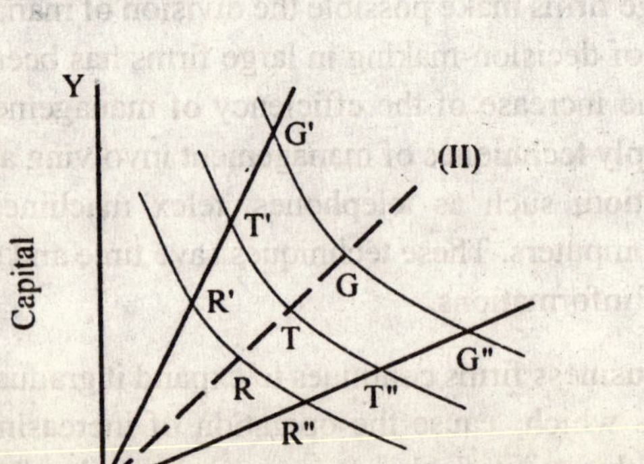

or O'R' = R'T' = T'G'.

OR = RT = TG

or O"R" = R"T" = T"G".

(3) Diminshing Returns to Scale

When the increase in output is less than proportionate to the given increase in the quantities of all factor-inputs, it is termed as diminishing returns to scale. For instance, if the increase in factor-inputs is 20 per cent and the resultant increase in output is less than 20 per cent (say 15 per cent) or a doubling of inputs causes a less than a doubling of output, it is diminishing returns to scale. This is explained in the following example–

Scale of Production (Machine + Labour)	*Total Output (Units)*
1 Machine + 2 Labour	100
2 Machine + 4 Labour	150

The result is diminishing return to scale. Diminishing returns to scale implies that for a given increase in output longer increase in the amount of input factors is required. In other words, proportionate increase in input factors will be more than proportionate increase in output. Fig illustrates the application of diminishing returns to scale.

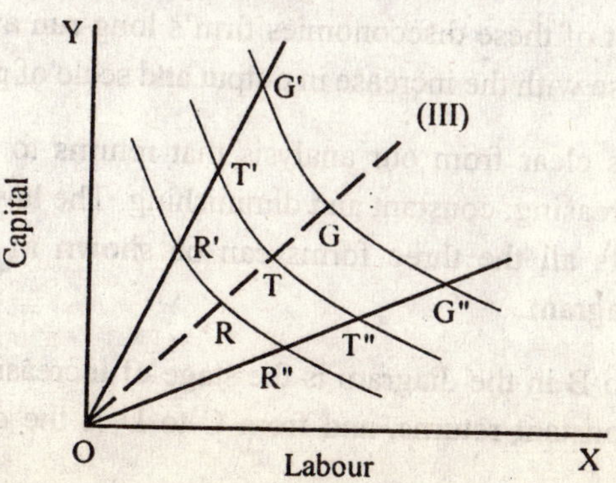

Here OR < RT < TG

O'R' < R 'T' < T 'G'

O "R" < R "T" < T "G"

CAUSES FOR THE OPERATION OF DIMINISHING RETURNS TO SCALE

As a firm expands its output, after a certain point, it encounters growing diseconomies. These diseconomies, ultimately, more than cancel out the economies of large scale production and lower down the long run average production. The economies of production are swamped by diseconomies of production. The main diseconomies are:

(i) Managerial Diseconomies. These diseconomies occur primarily because of increasing managerial difficulties. As the output grows, top management becomes eventually overburdened and hence less efficient in its role as co-ordinator and ultimate decision-maker.

(ii) Diseconomies due to exhaustible natural resources. Another cause for diminishing returns to scale may be found in the exhaustible natural resources, doubling the fishing fleet may not lead to a doubling of the catch of fish; or doubling the plant in mining or on an oil-extraction field may not lead to a doubling of output.

As a result of these diseconomies firm's long-run average and marginal cost rise with the increase in output and scale of production.

Thus, it is clear from our analysis that returns to scale have three forms-increasing, constant and diminishing. The law of returns to scale with its all the three forms can be shown in one single example and diagram.

From A to B in the diagram is the stage of increasing returns; from B to C constant returns, and from C to D is the diminishing returns to scale.

EXAMPLE

Units	*Scale of Production*	*Total Production*	*Marginal Production*	*Return to Scale*
1.	1 Labour + 2 Acres Land	8	8	Increasing Returns
2.	2 Labour + 4 Acres Land	17	9	
3.	3 Labour + 6 Acres Land	27	10	
4.	4 Labour + 8 Acres Land	38	11	Constant Returns
5.	5 Labour + 10 Acres Land	49	11	
6.	6 Labour + 12 Acres Land	59	10	Diminishing Returns
7.	7 Labour + 14 Acres Land	68	9	
8.	8 Labour + 16 Acres Land	76	8	

The main reason for the operation of the different forms of returns to scale is found in economies and diseconomies. When economies exceed the diseconomies, the stage of increasing returns operates; when economies and dis-economies equals each other, it becomes the stage of constant returns to scale; and when diseconomies exceeds the economies, then comes the stage of diminishing returns to scale.

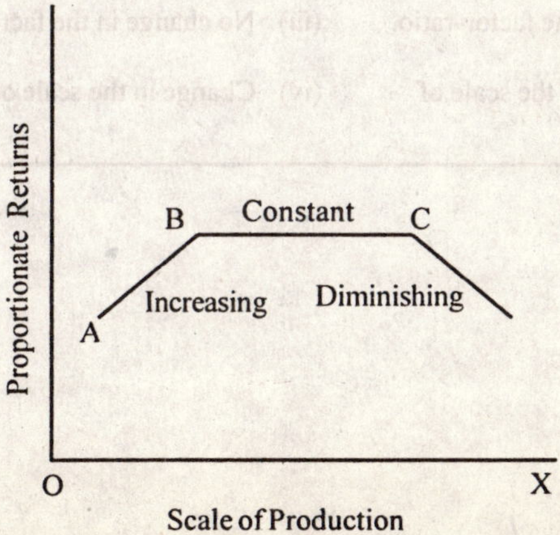

Distinction Between Returns to a Variable Factor and Returns to Scale

I. Returns to a variable Factor. The law of returns to a variable factor states that with the increase in the units of a variable factor, keeping other factors constant, the increase in total production becomes, after some point, smaller and smaller.

In this case marginal product first increases, then becomes constant and finally it declines and becomes negative. Thus, the law has three stages: increasing marginal returns; diminishing marginal returns and negative returns.

II. Returns to Scale. The term returns to scale refers to the changes in output as all factor-inputs change by the same proportion in the long run.

The increase in output may be more than, equal to, or less that proportional to the given increase in factor-inputs, hence returns to scale are of three forms-increasing, constant and diminishing.

Returns to a Variable Factor	*Returns to Scale*
(i) Operates in the short run	(i) Operates in the long run.
(ii) Only the quantities of one factor are varied	(ii) All factor-inputs are varied in the same proportion.
(iii) Changes in the factor-ratio.	(iii) No change in the factor-ratio.
(iv) No change in the scale of pıoduction.	(iv) Change in the scale of production.

❐

7

Cost Curves

ASPECTS OF COST OUTPUT RELATIONSHIP

Cost-output relations play an important role in business decisions pertaining to cost-minimisation or profit-maximisation and optimisation of output. Cost-output relations are expressed through a cost function.

$$TC = f(Q)$$

where TC = total cost, and Q = quantity produced.

Cost functions depend on *(i)* production function; and *(ii)* market-supply function specifies the technical input-combination and its relation to the output. Production function of a firm combined with the supply function of inputs or prices of inputs determines the cost function of the firm. Thus cost function is a function derived from the production function and the market supply function.

Cost-output relations depend on the nature of cost function. Change in cost function. Change in cost function brings a change in the cost-output relations. Since cost function is dependent on the production function, it may change due to change in the latter. Since a production function can take different forms depending on how many variable are held constant, cost functions can also take different forms. Whether certain variables in the function can be held constant or not depends on whether short or long-run is considered for the production function. Accordingly, there can be two kinds of cost functions: *(i)* Short-run cost-function and *(ii)* Long-run cost function. Cost output relations, or cost behaviour in relation to the different levels of output will be discussed here under both kinds of cost-functions.

Costs in the Short-Run

The short-run cost-output relationship refers to a particular scale of operation or to a fixed plant. That is it indicates variations in cost over output for the plant of a given capacity and their relationship will vary with plants of varying capacity.

For decision-making, one needs to know not only the relationship between total cost and output but also separately between various types of costs and output. Thus, the short-run cost-output relationship needs to be discussed in terms of

(i) Total cost and output,

(ii) Average costs and output; and

(iii) Marginal cost and output.

(i) Short-run Total Cost and Output

Once the firm has invested resources into the factors such as capital equipment, building, top management personnel and other fixed assets, their amounts cannot be so easily changed. Thus, in the short-run there are certain resources whose amount cannot be changed when the desired rate of output changes (called fixed factors), while there are other resources whose quantity used can be changed almost instantaneously with output change (called variable factors). Since certain factors do not change with the change in output, the cost to the firm of these resources is also fixed. Hence fixed cost does not vary with output. Thus, the larger the quantity

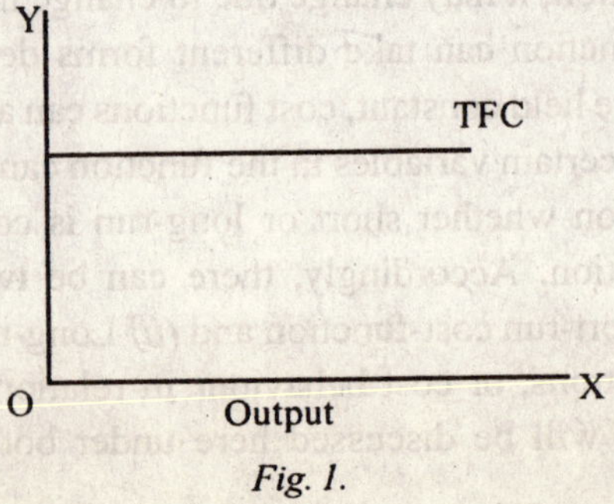

Fig. 1.

produced, the lower will be the fixed cost per unit and marginal fixed cost will always be zero. On the other hand, those factors whose quantity can be changed in the short-run their cost is known as variable cost. Thus, the total cost of a business is the sum of its total variable costs (TVC) and total fixed cost (TFC). This is,

$$TC = TFC + TVC$$

The total fixed costs include:

(a) Salaries of administrative staff.

(b) Depreciation (wear and tear) of machinery.

(c) Expenses for building depreciation and repairs.

(d) Expenses for land maintenance and depreciation (if any).

Another element that may be treated as fixed costs is the normal profit, which is a lumpsum including a percentage return on fixed capital and allowance for risk.

The total variable costs include:

(a) The raw materials.

(b) The cost of direct labour.

(c) The running expenses of fixed capital.

such as full, ordinary repairs and routine maintenance.

The total fixed cost is graphically denoted by a straight line parallel to the output axis. It will be seen in the following Fig. 1 that total fixed cost curve (TFC) starts from a point of the Y-axis meaning thereby that the total fixed cost will be incurred even if the output is zero.

The total variable cost is the traditional theory of the firm has broadly an inverse S shape which reflects the law of variable proportions. According to this law, at the initial stages of production with a given plant a more of the variable factor(s) is employed its productivity increases and the average variable cost falls. (Fig. 2)

As per economic theory, the nature of total variable cost is such that in the beginning as output increases, total variable cost increases at addressing rate, then at a constant rate and eventually at an increasing rate. Thus the increase in total variable cost goes on diminishing up to a certain level of output, then remains constant for some range of output, and then if starts rising. This is so because the need for the variable factor inputs for increased output behaves in a similar fashion and there is the operation of the law of diminishing return. It may be recalled that according to this law as more and more units of a variable factor of production are used along with a fixed factor or production the marginal product of that variable factor first increases, then remains constant and finally starts diminishing. Thus, given the factor prices, the increment in total variable cost first falls as output increases, then remains constant and eventually increases as output increases. It should be noted that though the general behaviour of thc variable cost function is of the nature described above, its exact behaviour may vary from product to product and will have to be verified empirically.

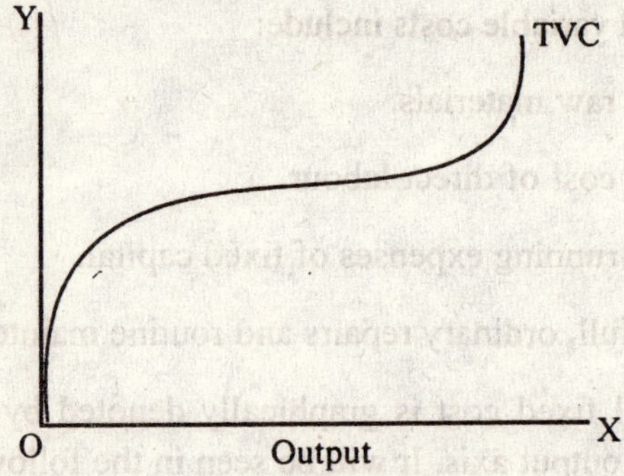

Fig. 2.

In the following Fig. the shape of the total variable cost curve (TVC) is principle determined by the productivity of the variable input. Up to Q_1 level of output, TVC increases at a decreasing rate. After Q_1, TVC increases at an increasing rate. This increase in rate is due to fixity of supply of the other inputs. Below Q_1 output level, the variable inputs cannot fully utilise the capacity inherent in fixed input. So, output can, be increased proportionately more then the increases in variable inputs. Beyond Q_1 output level, the diminishing returns to the fixed input set in. As a result the increase in variable inputs can add proportionately less to output.

As stated above the total fixed costs remain unchanged with output, the TFC curve remains horizontal line at all levels.

TC curve has been obtained by adding up vertically total fixed costs curve and total variable cost curve because the total cost is the lateral summation of the TFC and TVC curves as seen in the diagram. It will be seen that the vertical distance between the TVC curve and TC curve is constant throughout. This is because the vertical distance between the TVC and TC curve represents the amount of total fixed cost which remains unchanged as output is increased in the short-run.

(ii) Short-run Average Costs and Output

We have explained above the short-run total cost curves. However, the cost concept is more frequently used both by businessmen and econumists in the form of cost per unit or average cost rather than as totals. We, therefore, pass on to the study of short-run average cost curves.

(a) Average Fixed Cost (AFC). Average fixed cost is the total fjxed cost divided by the number of units of output produced. Therefore, where Q represents the number of units of output produced.

$$AFC = \frac{TFC}{Q}$$

Thus, average fixed cost is the fixed cost per unit of output. Since total fixed cost is a constant quantity, average fixed cost will steadily fall as output increases. Therefore, average fixed cost curve slopes downward throughout its length. As output increases, the total fixed cost spreads over more and more units and therefore average fixed cost becomes less and less. When output hecomes very large, average fixed cost approaches zero. Average fixed cost curve, which is a rectangular hyperbola, showing at all its points, the same magnitude, is shown in the upper Fig.3(b).

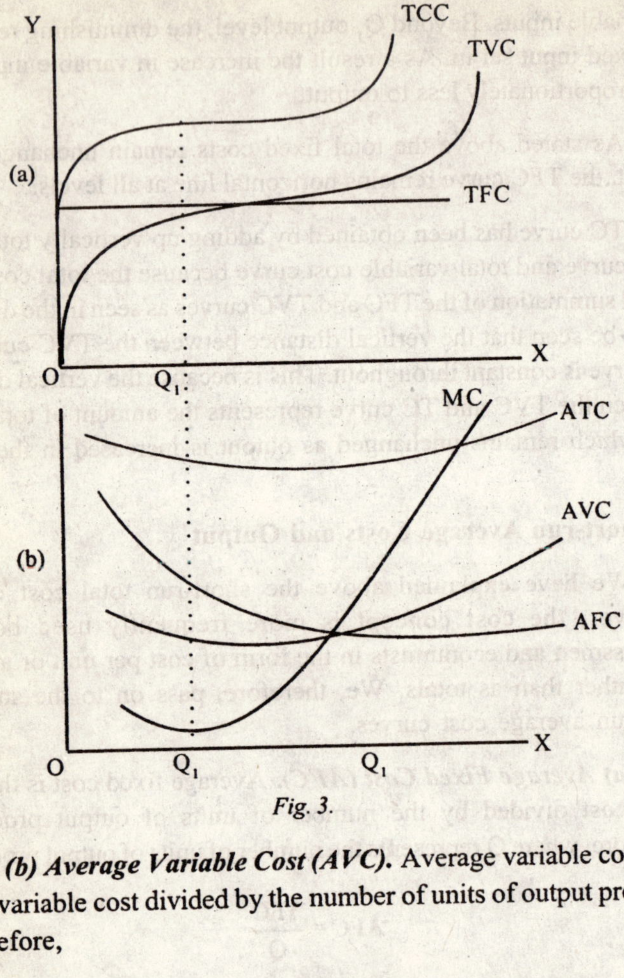

Fig. 3.

(b) Average Variable Cost (AVC). Average variable cost is the total variable cost divided by the number of units of output produced. Therefore,

$$AVC = \frac{TVC}{Q}$$

Thus average variable cost is variable cost per unit of output. We know that the total variable cost (TVC) at any output level consists of the payments to the variable factors used to produce that output. Therefore TVC = $P_1V_1 + P_2V_2 + ... P_nV_n$ wheel P is the unit price and V is the amount of the variable input. Average variable cost for a level of output (Q), given P is

$$AVC = \frac{TVC}{Q} = \frac{PV}{Q} = \left[P\frac{V}{Q}\right]$$

The term V is the number of units of input divided by the number of units of output. Since the Average Product (AP) of an input is total output divided by the number of units of input (V). So we can write,

$$\frac{V}{Q} = \frac{1}{Q/V} = \frac{1}{AP}$$

$$AVC = P\left[\frac{V}{Q}\right] = P\left[\frac{1}{AP}\right]$$

That is, average variable cost is the price of the input multiplied by the reciprocal of the average product of the input. We know that due to first increasing and then decreasing managerial return to the variable input, average product initially rises, reaches a maximum and then declines. Since average variable cost is 1/AP, the average variable cost normally falls, reaches a minimum and then rises. It first declines and then rises for reasons similar to those operating in case of TVC. This is shown in upper Fig.

(c) Average Total Cost (ATC). The average total cost or what is called simply average cost is the total cost divided by the number of units output produced. Therefore,

$$ATC = \frac{TC}{Q}$$

Since the. total cost is the sum of total variable cost and total fixed cost, the average total cost is also the sum of average variable cost anq average fixed cost.

This can be proved as follows:

$$ATC = \frac{TC}{Q}$$

Since TC = TVC + TFC

Therefore,

$$ATC = \frac{TVC + TFC}{Q}$$

$$= \frac{TVC}{Q} + \frac{TFC}{Q}$$

$$= AVC + AFC$$

Average total cost is also known as unit cost, since it is cost per unit of output produced.

The behaviour of the average total cost curve will depend on the behaviour of the average variable cost curve and average fixed cost curve. In the beginning both AVC and AFC curves fall. The ATC curve therefore falls sharply in the beginning. When AVC curve begins rising, but AFC curve is falling steadily, the ATC curve continues to fall. But as output increases, there is a sharp rise in AVC which more than offsets the fall in AFC. Therefore, the ATC curve rises after a point. This is shown in Fig.

(d) Marginal Cost (M). Marginal cost is the addition to the total cost caused by producing one more unit of output. In other words, marginal cost is the addition to the total cost of producing in units instead of n -1 units. In symbols, since, marginal cost is

$$MC_n = TC_n - TC_{n-1}$$

rate of change in total cost with respect to a unit change in output *i.e.*,

$$MC = \frac{d(TC)}{dQ}$$

where d in the numerator and denominator indicates the change in TC and Q respectively.

It is worth pointing out that marginal cost is independent of the fixed cost. Since fixed costs do not change with output, there are no marginal fixed costs when output increases in the short-run. It is only the variable costs that vary with output in the short-run. Therefore, marginal costs are in fact due to the changes in variable costs.

$$MC = \frac{d(TVC)}{dQ}$$

The independence of the margin cost from the fixed cost can be proved algebracillay as follows:

$$MC_n = TC_n - TC_{n-1}$$
$$= (TVC_n + TFC) - (TVC_{n-1} + TFC)$$
$$= TVC_n - TFC - TVC_{n-1} - TFC$$
$$= TVC_n - TVC_{n-1}$$

Hence, marginal cost is the addition to the total variable costs when output is increased from n – 1 units to n units of output. It follow therefore that the marginal cost is independent of the amount of the fixed costs.

In the above Fig., MC is the slope of the TC curve. As TC curve first rises at a decreasing rate and later on at an increasing rate, MC curve will also, therefore, first decline and then rise.

The properties of the average cost (AVC, AFC, ATC) and marginal cost can briefly be described as follows:

(i) AFC declines continuously, approaching both axes asymptotically.

(ii) AVC first declines, reaches a Q minimum and rises thereafter when AVC attains its minimum, MC equals AVC.

(iii) As AFC approaches asymptotically the horizontal axis, AVC approaches ATC asymptotically.

(iv) ATC first declines, reaches a minimum and rises thereafter, When ATC attains its minimum, MC equals ATC.

(v) MC first declines, reaches a minimum and rise thereafter, MC equals AVC and ATC when these curves attain their minimum values. Furthermore, MC lies below both AVC and ATC over the ranges in which AVC and ATC decline; it lies above them when they are rising.

COST-OUTPUT RELATIONSHIP IN THE LONG-RUN

Long-run Costs

In order to study the cost-output relationship in the long-run, it would be necessary to explain the concept of Long-run Costs.

The long-run, as we have already seen earlier, is a period long enough to make all costs variable including such as its as are fixed in the short run. In the short-run, variations in output are possible only within the range permitted by the existing fixed plant and equipment. But in the long-run entrepreneur has before him a number of alternatives which include the construction of various kinds and sizes of plants. Thus there are not fixed costs since the firm has sufficient time to fully adapt its plant. And all costs become variable. In view of this, the long—run costs would refer to the costs of producing different levels of output by changes in the size of plant of scale of production. The long-run cost-output relationship is shown graphically by the long-run cost curve—a curve showing how costs would change when the scale of production is changed.

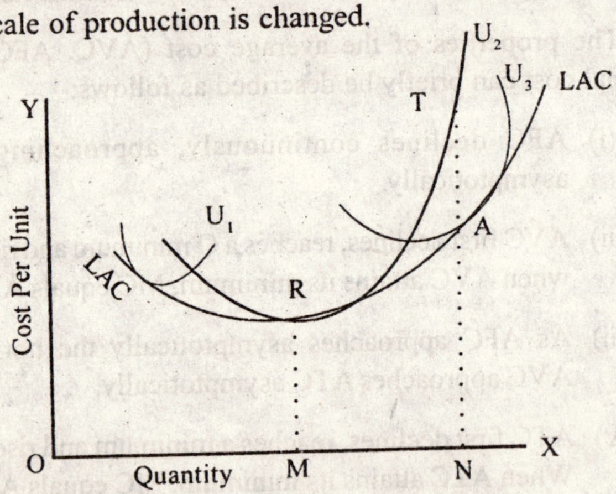

Fig. 4.

The concept of long-run costs can be further explained with the help of an illustration. Suppose that at a particular time, a firm operates under average total costs curve U_2 and produce OM. Now it is desired to produce ON. If the firm continues under the old scale, its average cost will be NT. If the scale of the firm is altered, the new cost curve would be U_3. The average cost of producing ON would then be NA. NA is less than NT. So the new scale is preferable to the old one and should be adopted. In the long run, the average cost of producing ON output in NA. This may be called as the long-run cost of producing ON output. It may be noted here that we shall can NA as the long-run cost only so long as the U_3 scale is in the planning stage and has not actually been adopted. The moment the scale is installed, the NA cost would be the short-run cost of producing ON output.

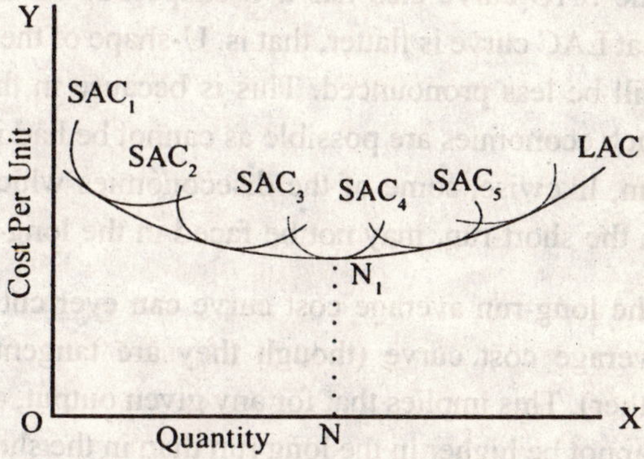

Fig. 5.

To draw a long-run cost curve, we have to start with a number of short-run average cost curves (SAC curves), each such curve representing a particular scale or size of the plant, including the optimum scale. One can draw the long-run cost curve which would be tangential to the entire family of SAC curves, that is, it would touch each SAC curve at one point. In this connection the following points are to be noted:

(i) The LAC curve is tangential to the various SAC curves. It is said to envelop them and is often called as the "Envelope Curve" since no point on an SAC curve can ever be below the LAC curve.

(ii) The LAC curve is U-shaped or like a 'dish'. The U-shape of the LAC curve implies lower and lower average cost in the beginning until the optimum scale of the enterprise is reached, and successively high average costs thereafter, *i.e.*, with plants larger than that of optimum scale.

The tendency for the long-run average costs to fall as the firm expands its scale of operations is a reflection of cost economies available with the increase in size, while the ultimate rise in the long-run cost curve is due largely to the eventual setting in of diseconomies of scale.

The SAC curve also has a U-shape but the difference is that LAC curve is flatter, that is, U-shape of the LAC curve will be less pronounced. This is because in the long-run, such economies are possible as cannot be had in the short-run, likewise, some of the diseconomies which are faced in the short-run, may not be faced in the long-run.

(iii) The long-run average cost curve can ever cut a short-run average cost curve (though they are tangential to each other). This implies that for any given output, average cost cannot be higher in the long run than in the short-run. This is because any adjustment which will reduce costs and which it is possible to make in the short-run can also be made in the long-run. On the other hand, it is not aiways possible in the short-run to produce a given output in the cheapest possible way.

(iv) LAC curve will touch the 'optimum scale' curve at the latter's least cost point, *i.e.*, N_1.

(v) LAC curve will touch SAC curves lying to the left of the optimum scale curve at the left of their least-cost points.

(vi) LAC curve will touch SAC curves lying to the right of the optimum scale curve at the right of their least-cost points.

Thus it will be seen that LAC curve is tangential to the minimum cost point in the case of the optimum scale AC and not in the case of other SAC curves.

CHARACTERISTICS OF LAC CURVE

The following characteristics of LAC curve should be noted:

(i) The LAC curve is tangential to the various SAC curves. It is drawn to cover them and is often known as Envelope curve as no point on SAC curve can ever be below the LAC curve.

(ii) The LAC' curve is U-shaped or like a dish. This U-shape of the LAC curve implies lower and lower averages costs in the beginning until the optimum scale of the enterprise is reached and successively higher average costs thereafter *i.e.*, with plants larger than that of the optimum scale.

The tendency for the long-run average costs to fall as the firm expands its operation scale is a reflection of cost economies available with the increase in size, while the ultimate size in the long-run curve is due largely to the eventual setting in of diseconomies of scale.

The SAC curve is also U-shaped but the difference is that LAC curve is fatter, that is U-shape of the LAC curve will be less pronounced. This is because in the long-run such economies are possible as cannot be had in the short run.

(iii) The long run average cost curve can never cut a short run curve though they are tengential to each other. This implies that for any given output, average cost cannot be higher in the long-run than in the short-run. This is because any adjustment that will reduce costs and which it is possible to make in the short run can also be made in the long run. On the other side, it is to always possible in the shortrun to produce a given output in the cheapest possible way.

(iv) LAC curve will touch the optimum scale curve at the latter's least cost point *i.e.*, N.

(v) LAC curve will touch SCA curves lying to the left of the optimum scale curve at the left of their least cost points.

(vi) LAC curve will touch SAC curves lying at the right of the optimum scale curve at the right their least cost points.

Thus one will find the LAC curve is tangential to the minimum cost point in case of optimum scale SAC and not in case of other SAC curves.

DO FIRMS OPERATE AT OPTIMAL SCALE?

It is only in the long-run that a firm can decide about the optimum scale of plant, because in the short-run the plant size is give and what the finn can best do is to decide its optimum utilisation. But often firms do not operate at optimum scale because of the following reasons:

(i) Optimal scale is, many a time, violated when either the market for the produced good is too small or too big so that the firm is constrained in the first case and over-enthusiastic in the second case. So in these cases there may be a partial or more-than-full capacity outputs.

(ii) Sometimes the firms purposefully hold back output to create scarcity and thus force up the prices of their commodity. Such a situation arises when there is a lack of competition in the market for that commodity.

(iii) The firms sometimes 'over-expand' to either push out the rivals from the market or to keep the potential rivals out of the market. Such a strategy may be called 'market dominance' strategy.

(iv) There may be government's control (direct or Indirect) or the fear of government intervention that may force the firms to produce less than the optimum capacity. For example, the car production in India is at much less than optimum capacity because the government's regulations specify their levels of output.

(v) Market conditions, technology and prices of factor inputs do not remain fixed. The firms need to make adjustments to these changed conditions to remain at the optimal levels of output. But generally there is a time-lag between the change in conditions and necessary adjustments of the firm. By the time the firm is able to make adjustments to a particular change, another change takes place in the mean time. Thus, the particular firms keep on trying to move towards the optimal scale but often do to reach it.

DETERMINANTS OF A COST FUNCTION

The main determinants of a cost function are the following:

(i) Size of Plant. Plant size is an important variable influencing cost. The relation between scale of operations or size of plant to the unit cost is negative in the sense that as the former increases, unit cost decreases and *vice-versa*. Such a function shall be a downward falling cost function, which may fall in steps depending upon the different sizes of plants taken into account. Such a cost function is more concerned with engineering estimates of cost.

(ii) Output Level. Level of output and total cost are obviously related. Total cost increase with increase in output. But average and marginal costs may not do so. These first decline and then increase with increase in output. The average total cost or marginal cost functions are derived by relating the relevant costs wiih the level of capacity utilisation of a given sized plant. Since such a function forms a 'U' shaped curve, quadratic or cubic function is the more appropriate one.

(iii) Price of Inputs. Obdously, prices of inputs and changes in them affect cost, depending on the relative usage of the inputs and relative changes in their prices. A factor which forms a major element of production process when becomes relatively costly, it raises the cost significantly.

(iv) Technology. More efficient technology would certainly be cost-saving one. Technology is often quantified as capital-output ratio. Generally a modern technology is take as the one with higher capital-output ratio.

(v) Managerial Efficiency. Although the cost is influenced a great deal by managerial efficiency, it is difficult to quantify it. However, a change in cost at two points of time may explain how organisational or managerial changes within the firm have brought about cost efficiency provided it is possible to exclude the effect of other factors.

METHODS OF ESTIMATING COST FUNCTIONS

Several methods exist for the measurement of the actual cost-output relation for a particular firm or a group of firms, but the three broad approaches—accounting, engineering and statistical—are the most important and commonly used.

(i) Accounting Method. This method is used by the cost accountants. Essentially, in this method the data is classified into various cost categories (*i.e.*, fixed, variable and semi-variable) and then observations of cost are taken at the extreme and various intermediate output levels. They by plotting them on a graph and joining them by a line the linear or curvilinear cost functions are estimated. It must be noted that in building up cost functions from basic data in this way, no attention is generally paid to build up a hypothesis or to find out the changes in conditions which influence costs.

(ii) Engineering Method. In the engineering approach, the cost functions are estimated with the help of physical relationships such as weight of supplies and materials used in a process, rated capacity of an equipment, etc. Emphasis is placed primarily on these physical relationships and they are then converted into money terms (*i.e.*, rupees) to arrive at an estimate of costs. The method may he useful if good historical data is difficult to obtain. But this method requires a should understanding of engineering and needs detailed sampling of the different process under controlled conditions, which may not always be possible.

(iii) Statistical or Econometric Method. This method uses statistical techniques on economic data to find the nature of cost-output relationship. The economic data may relate to past records of a firm (called, the historical data) or to the different firms in the same business at a point of time (called, the cross-section data). If we use the historicai data we generally get a short-run cost function, while if we take recourse to the cross-section data we derive a long-run cost function. It must be understood that the three approaches discussed above are not competitive, but are rather complementary to each other. They supplement each other. The choice of any method depends upon the purpose of stuck, time and expense considerations.

ECONOMIES OF SCALE

Marshall classified the economies of large-scale production into two types:

(i) External Economies, and

(ii) Internal Economies.

(i) External Economies are those which are available to all the firms in an industry, *e.g.*, the construction of a railway-line in a certain region which would reduce transport cost for all the firms, the discovery of a new machine which can be purchased by all the firms, the emergence of repair industries, rise of industrials utilising by-products, and the establishment of special technical schools for training skilled labour are research institutes, etc. These economies arise from the expansion in the size of an industry-involving an increase in the number and size of the firms engaged in it.

(ii) Internal Economies are the economies which are available to a particular firm and give it an advantage over other firms engaged in the industry. Internal economies arise from the expansion of the size of a particular firm. From the managerial point of view, internal economies are more important as they can be effected by managerial decisions of an individual firm to change it s size or scale or otherwise.

TYPES OF INTERNAL ECONOMIES

(a) Labour Economies

If a firm decides to expand its scale of output, it will be possible for it to reduce the labour costs per unit by practising division of labour.

Economies of division of lahour arise because of *(i)* an increase in the skill of workers, and *(ii)* the saving of time involved in changing from one operating to the other. Again, in many cases, a large firm may find it economical to have a number of operations performed mechanically rather than manually. These economies will be the greatest in firms where the product is complex and the manufacturing processes are capable of being sub-divided.

(b) Technical Economies

There are economies derived from the use of subsize machines and such scientific processes as can be carried out in large production units. A small establishment cannot afford to use such machines and processes, for their ruse would bring a saving only when they are used intensively. On the other hand, their use will be quite uneconomical if they were to lie idlc over a considerable part of the time. For example, a large electroplating plant costs a great deal to keep it in operation. Therefore, the cost per unit will be low only if the output is large. Similarly, a machine pressing out the side of a motor car will take a week or more to be put ready for operation to produce a particular design. The greater the output of cars of this particular design, the lower the cost per unit of 'getting the machine ready for operation'. Likewise, if a die is made to produce a particular model of cars, the cost of die per unit of cars will depend upon the output of the cars. Very often large firms may find it economical to produce or manufacture parts an components for their product rather than buy them for outside sources. For example, Hind Cydes, unlike small manufacturers, produced parts and components themselves. Again, large firms may find it profitable to utilise their by-products and waste products. For example, Tatas use the smoke from their furnaces to manufacture coal-tar, naphthalene, etc. A small firm's output of smoke would not be large enough to justify setting up the equipment necessary to do so.

(c) Managerial Economies

When the size of the firm increases, the efficiency of management usually increases because there can be greater specialisation in managerial staff. In a large firm, experts can be appointed to look after the various sections or divisions of the business, such as purchasing, sales, production, financing, personnel, etc. But a small firm cannot provide full-time employment to these experts. Naturally, the various aspects of the business have to be looked after by a few persons only who may not necessarily be experts. Moreover, a large firm can afford to set up data processing and mechanised accounting, etc., whereas small firms cannot afford to do so.

(d) Marketing Economies

A large firm can secure economies in its purchasing and sales. It can purchase its requirements in hulk and thereby get better terms. It usually receives prompt deliveries, careful attention and special facilities from its suppliers. This is sometimes due to the fact that a large buyer can exert more pressure, at times coercive in nature, for specially favoured treatment. it can also get concessions from transport agencies. Moreover, it can appoint expert buyers and expert salesmen. Finally, a large firm can spread its advertising cost over bigger output because advertising costs do not rise in proportion to a rise in sales.

(e) Economies of Vertical Integration

A large firm may decide to have vertical integration by combining a number of stages of production. This integration has the advantage that the flow of goods through various stages in production processes is more readily controlled. Steady supplies of raw materials, on the one hand, and steady outlets for these raw materials, on the other, make production planning more certain and less subject to erratic and unpredictable changes. Vertical integration may also facilitate cost control as most of the costs become controllable costs for the enterprise. Transport costs may also be reduced by so planning transportation that cross-hauling is reduced to the minimum.

(f) Financial Economies

A large firm can offer better security and is, therefore, in a position to secure better and easier credit facilities both from its suppliers and its bankers due to a better image, it enjoys easier access to the capital market.

(g) Economies of Risk-spreading

The larger the size of the business , the greater is the scope for spreading of risks through diversification. Diversification is possible on two lines:

(i) ***Diversification of Output.*** If there are many products, the loss in the sale of one product may be covered by the profits from others. By diversification, the firm avoids what may be called putting 'all eggs in the same basket'. Vickers Ltd., for example, make aircraft, ships, armaments, food-processing plant, rubber, plastics, paints, instruments and a wide range of other products. Many of the larger firms have taken to diversification. India Tobacco have diversified to include marine products and hotel business In their operations.

(ii) ***Diversification of Markets.*** The larger producer is generally in a position to sell his goods in many different and even far-off place. By depending upon one market, he runs the risk of heavy loss if sales in that market decline for one reason or the other.

❐

8

Cost Analysis

In its most elementary form, cost refers to the sacrifice incurred whenever an exchange or transformation of resources takes place. Many of the difficulties and controversies associated with the concept of cost arise when one attempts to measure this sacrifice. The appropriate manner to measure costs is a function of the purpose for which the information is to be used.

Accounting v/s Economic Costs

Accountants have been primarily concerned with measuring costs for financial reporting purposes. As a result, they define and measure cost by the historical outlay of funds that takes place in the exchange or transformation of a resource. Thus, whenever A sells a producer to commodity to B, the price paid by B, expressed in rupees, measures the cost of the product to B. When A exchanges labour services, for money or other items of value, the wages that A receives represent the cost of A's services to the employer. Similarly, the interest paid to the bondholder or lending institution is used to measure the cost of funds to the borrower.

Economists have been mainly concerned with measuring costs for decision-making purposes. The objective is to determine the present and future costs of resources associated with various alternative courses of action. Such as objective requires a consideration of the opportunities forgone (or sacrificed) whenever a resource is used in a given course of action. Cost is a function of the value of a resource in its best alternative use. Consequently, the outlay of funds incurred in obtaining a resource may not always be the appropriate measure of cost in a decision problem.

The opportunity cost of using a given quantity of resource (inputs) to produce a unit of Good A is the number of units of the next best alternative that must be sacrificed or forgone as a result of the decision to produce A. If the resources (labour, materials, equipment) needed to build ten houses (of a specified size and quality) can also be used to build one office building (likewise of a specified size and quality), then the opportunity cost of the decision to build toe office building is equal to the ten houses that have to be forgone. With a fixed quantity of resources available to the organisation, resources used in the production of one good cannot be used in the production of other goods.

In calculating the cost to the firm of producting a given quantity of output, economists include some additional costs that are typically not reflected in the cost figures appearing in the financial reports of the firm. Both the accounting cost and the economic cost of a product will include such explicit costs as labour, raw materials, supplies, rent, interest, and utilities. Economists also include several implicit costs. The implicit costs consist of the opportunity costs of time and capital that the owner-manager has invested in producing the given quantity of output. The opportunity cost of the owner's time is measured by the most attractive salary or other form of compensation that the owner could have received by operating or managing a similar kind of fitm for another investor. The opportunity cost of the capital employed in producing the given quantity of output is measured by the profit or return that could have been received if the owner had chosen to employ capital in the best alternative investment of comparable risk.

FACTORS AFFECTING THE COST

An entrepreneur has to take some very important decisions before setting up a new venture. These decisions have a close bearing on the cost of production pf the product in the long run. He has to decide the site of the works, the nature of production, scope and size of the market that will be served and the size of the plant. All these decisions are of such nature that once take cannot be altered time and again. All these decisions affect the cost of production in the long run.

The entrepreneur, therefore, should study the various forces (factors) which may affect the cost behaviour in the long run. Generally there are three types of factors which influence the cost of production *e.g.*, *(i)* Location, *(ii)* Scope, and *(iii)* Size. A complete analysis of these factors, will certainly help the entrepreneur to earn maximum profits by reducing the costs.

(i) Location

Dr. M. Visvesvariya has pointed out to nine M's which must be taken into consideration before taking any decision in regard to location of the new unit. These are money, material men, market, machinery, motive power, management, means of transport and momentum of early start. The success of the new enterprise very much rests on the selection of suitable site. In the selection of the site the following factors should be kept in view.

(a) **Availability of Raw Materials.** The place selected should be such where the raw materials are available easily. There should be an easy approach to the place of raw materials. Iron and steel industry in Bihar textile factories in Gujrat and Maharashtra. Jute works in Bengal owe their success on account of easy availability of raw materials. It reduces the cost of transportation.

(b) **Nearness to the Market.** Manufacturing a thing successfully is to sufficient. It is also necessary that the output should find ready market and that the product is sold at a price to yield reasonable profit. This is possible only when the market is not far away. Nearness of the market ensures transportation cost less and minimum wastage.

(c) **Nearness to Sources of Operating Power.** Every industry requires fuel for working the machinery and unless the region has rich fuel resources it can not develop an industrial area. Various sources of power now available are coal, hydroelectricity and oil etc. Coal is the cheapest source of power, but it is very bulky and involves high transportation costs.

(d) **Labour Supplies.** For the successful and uninterrupted working of a factory, availability of adequate supply of labour of the right type at reasonable wages is also very essential. There are some industries in which the inherited skill of the workers is an important factor in the process of manufacturing. The development of the dying and printing industry in Fraukhabad and the glass industry in Ferozabad have been mainly located there due to the availability of skilled labour in these towns.

(e) **Transportation.** Every manufacturing industry requires cheap and efficient means of transportation for the movement of both raw materials from the source of supply to the factory and finished products from the factory to the markets or the centres of consumption.

The location of the plant, should therefore, be at a place where adequate transport facilities are available at cheaper rate.

(f) **Finance.** No productive activity is possible without the availability of adequate capital. Banks, Stock Exchanges and other similar institutions help in capital formation and expansion of industry by providing financial help to it from time to time.

(g) **Climate.** Certain industries for their successful working require a special type of climate. For example, cotton textile industry require humid climate while the photographic goods industry flourishes best in regions of dry climate. Climate also affects the efficiency of labour.

(h) **Industrial Inertia or Momentum of Early Start.** There is tendency for an established industry to remain localised in a particular areas in which in also even after some of the original advantages possessed by that area for such work have cost their previous importance.

If however, the entrepreneur acts rationally and has necessary knowledge, he will choose the location which offers the lowest cost per unit of output.

(i) **Personal Preferences.** Location of any industry may some times be decided according to the personal preferences and prejudices of the industrial enterprises.

(j) **Government Policy.** These days the government plays an important role in determining the location of new industries.

In addition to the factors discussed above, cost of land and building for setting up the factory, topography of the area, the possibilities of future expansion etc. are some other factars which influence the decision-making regarding location of industry.

(ii) Scope

It is advisable to plan before hand the scope of activities of the firm before hand. On the basis of further experience the plan may be revised from time to time in deciding about the scope. The following points should be take it consideration in this regard:

(a) What techniques have to be followed in production ? What parts have to he manufactured in the factor itself and for What parts should depend on other firm?

(b) Should all the process involved in the production be carried in the factory or some have to depend upon contracts?

(c) Has the firm to produce the raw material itself or should it depend upon other firms?

(d) How far the firm should specialise in production or should it depend upon other firms?

(e) Should all the connected goods with the main product be manufactured by the firm itself and the business scope be expanded?

(f) Should the marketing of the product be organised by the firm itself of should it depend Upon other agencies for marketing?

(g) Should the after-sale service to the consumers be undertaken by the firm itself or should firm enter into some agreement with other firm for this important responsibility?

The firm has to take decision on the above question and other allied problems finally setting up the unit keeping in view that the unit cost producing and distributing of the product or service should be the lowest and the changes of making maximum profits are the brightest.

(iii) Size

The success and efficiency of the firm also depends on its suitable size. The size of the firm should be optimum as to ensure maximum profitability. The optimum size of the firm is that joining which results in the lowest production cost and maximum efficiency. At this optimum point of output all the technical, managerial marketing factors are well balanced. If should be noted that optimum size of the firm is not fixed but goes on alterting with the improved techniques of production and managerial experience.

NEED AND SIGNIFICANCE OF COST IN MANAGERIAL DECISION-MAKING

In Managerial Economics, demand estimation and forecasting demand in the future form a very essential part of decision-making. But there is another area which is of great importance to managerial economics *viz.* The cost of production. The cost which a firm incurs in the process of production of its goods and services is an important variable for decision-making. Total cost together with total revenue determine the profit level of a business concern. To this end, managers try to produce optimum levels of output, use the least-cost combination factors of production, increase factor productivities and improve organisational efficiency.

The solution of various economic problems needs cost figures different from what are available in the balance sheets, income-statements, etc. of the firm. The accounting cost figures serve the legal, financial and tax needs of the firm but are not directly very helpful for managerial decisions. For, the management needs costs in terms of their source, period, rate of change with respect to output, the degree of their controllability etc.

It must be pointed out that all types of costs do not matter much rather future costs matter most in managerial decision-making.

The other costs are relevant only if the management is to continue with its past or present policies in future too, and if the environment in which the firm operates remains unchanged. Further, only those costs which are affected by the decision of the management need by analysed; while expenses that remain unchanged should ignored in the decision-making process.

Cost of production provides the floor to pricing. It provides a basis for managerial decision with respect to the price the firm must quote to its prospective customers; in deciding whether to accept a particular order or not; whether to abandon an old or establish a new product line; whether or not to increase the volume of specific outputs; to use idle capacity or rent facilities to outsiders; and whether to make a particular product or buy it. There are no straight and simple rules for such decisions and it is necessary to study production and cost analysis thoroughly to arrive at these decisions. The costs which firms incur are payments to various factors of production and hence they indicate incomes of these factors also. An understanding of cost thus helps to undershot and the distribution of factor incomes as well.

We know that a particular cost behaviour is the result of manufacturers, some controllable while others non-controllable, by the firm. Just like production-function, we can also write a cost function. Cost function as be taken for the enterprise as a whole or for each of its departments, depending upon the requirement of the management using the cost function. Since detenninants of cost vary from situation to situation and enterprise to enterprise, it is not possible to state any general set of determinants of costs. Each management must, therefore, have to identify for itself the various determinants relevant to that particular situation. However a few determinants, which seem important in modem business, are plant size, utilisation of the plant, technology, prices of the various inputs, size of lot, stability of production level, management and labour efficiency.

Making of effective and right decisions depends much on the proper calculation of costs. If different types of costs are not properly understood, the managerial decisions are found to be wrong and misleading.

COST CONCEPTS

The kind of cost concept to be used in a particular situation depends upon the business decision to be made. Cost considerations enter into almost every business decision, and it is important, though sometimes difficult, to use the right kind of cost. Hence an understanding of the meaning of various concepts is essential for clear business thinking. Defining and distinguishing cost concepts are necessary to emphasise *(i)* that cost estimates produced by conventional financial accounting are not appropriate for all managerial uses, and *(ii)* that different business problems call for different kinds of costs. Different combinations of cost ingredients are appropriate for various kinds of management problems.

(i) Actual Cost and Opportunity Cost. Actual costs mean the actual expenditure incurred for acquiring or producing a good or service. Thee costs are the costs that are generally recorded in the books of account, wages paid, cost of materials purchased, interest paid, etc. These costs are also commonly known as Absolute Costs or Outlay Costs.

In contradistinction, opportunity cost of a good or service is measured in terms of revenue which could have been earned by employing that good or service in some other alternative uses. Opportunity cost can be defined as the revenue foregone by not making the best alternative use. Thus, the opportunity cost of yarn produced by a composite spinning and weaving mill and used in the weaving section would be the price that could have been obtained by selling the yarn in the market. This opportunity cost is different from the actual cost of producing the yarn in the spinning section. So also, if a company retains part of its profits to finance growth rather than pay higher dividends to its shareholders, the opportunity cost of this additional finance is alternative return the shareholders would have earned if the retained profits had been invested elsewhere.

Very often, there are cases where a particular resource of factor of production has no alternative use. Its opportunity cost will be nil irrespective of its utility in the existing use. For example, if a firm receives an export order when its capacity is not fully utilised, the opportunity cost of using the plant for export production would be nil or zero. This is so because the unutilised capacity of the plant has no alternative use. Similarly, the opportunity cost of a product having specialised use is zero.

In managerial decision-making, quite often it becomes necessary to consider not the actual cost of a commodity but its opportunity cost. For example, to determine the profitability of the weaving section of a composite textile mill, we have to consider the opportunity cost of the yarn and to the actual cost thereof.

The concept of opportunity cost is more important and useful to management in making a decision among alternatives. For example, suppose A has two alternatives before him: *(i)* having a shop in the central locality of the town after paying a pugree of Rs. 10,000, and *(ii)* having a shop in any other locality without any pugree. While comparing the two alternatives, A will have to take into consideration the additional earnings that he can make by having a shop in the central locality and the profits he can achieve by employing the amount of pugree elsewhere. Thus the opportunity cost of having a shop in the central locality is Rs. 10,000 plus interest forgone there on. A stage corporation was offered a choice of either 50 acres of land free of cost in a remote area or 2 acres at Rs. 50,000 near the town. The opportunity cost of the free land consisted of *(a)* cost of building roads, and *(b)* being permanently away from the railway station. In effect, opportunity cost is an imputed cost.

As Dean has put it, "In business problems, the message of opportunity costs is that it is dangerous to confine cost knowledge to what the firm is doing. What the firm is not doing is frequently the critical cost consideration which it is perilous but easy to ignore.

(ii) Business Costs and Fun Costs. Business costs include all the expenses which are incurred in crying out the business. The concept of business costs is similar to the actual or real costs. Business costs 'include all the payments and contractual obligations made by the firm together with the book cost of depreciation on plant and equipment'. Both these concepts are used in calculating the profits and loses in the business in filing returns for income-tax, and for other legal proposes.

The concept of full costs, includes two other costs: alternative cost and normal profit. Alternative cost will include the expected earning from the next best use of the resources, or the market rate of interest on the total money capital, and also the value of entrepreneur's own services which are not charged in the current business. Normal profit is a necessary minimum earning, in addition to alternative cost, which a firm must get to remain in its present occupation.

(iii) Explicit and Implicit Costs. Explicit costs are those expenses which are actually paid by the firm. In other words, thee are paid-out costs. These costs appear in the accounting records of the firm.

On the other hand, implicit costs or imputed costs are theoretical costs in the sense that they go unrecognised by the accounting system. These cots may be defined as the earnings of those employed resources which belong to the owner himself. For example, the interest payment on borrowed funds is an explicit cost and enters the accounting record, but the amount of interest which the employer could have earned (and which he foregoes when the uses his capital in his firm) is his implicit cost. Similarly, the amount of rent, wages, utility expenses, etc., which are paid-out are the explicitly costs of the firm, while the wages, rent, etc., which are due to the entrepreneur for employing his own resources in the firm, are all implicit costs.

The explicit costs are important for the calculating of profit and loss account, but for economic decision-making the firm takes into account both the explicit as well as implicit costs.

(iv) Future and Past Costs. Futurity is an important aspect of all business. Future costs, on the other hand, are the estimates of time adjusted past or present costs. Future costs are reasonable expected to be incurred in some future period or periods. Their actual incurrence is a forecast and their management is an estimate. They are the only costs that matter for managerial clecisions because they are only subject to management control. The major managerial uses where future costs are relevant are: cost control, projection of future profit and loss statements appraisal of capital expenditure, introduction of new products, expansion programmes and pricing.

Past costs are actual costs incurred in the past and they are always contained in the income statements. Their measurement is essentially a record keeping activity. These costs can only be observed and evaluated in retrospect. Past costs are, therefore, those unadjusted historical cost data which has been recorded in the books.

(v) Incremental Costs (Differential Costs) and Sunk Costs. Incremental cost is the additional cost due to a change in the level or nature of business activity. The change may take several forms, *e.g.*, addition of a new product-line, changing the channel of distribution, adding a new machine, replacing a machine by a better machine, expansion into additional markets, etc. Thus, the question of incremental or differential cost would not arise when a business to be set up afresh. It arises only when a change is contemplated in the existing business.

Sunk cost is one which is not affected or altered by a change in the level or nature of husiness activity. It will remain the same whatever the level of activity. The most important example of sunk cost is the amortisation of past expenses, *e.g.*, depreciation.

The distinction between sunk cost and incremental cost assumes importance in evaluating alternatives. Incremental costs will be different in the case of different alternatives. Hence incremental costs are relevant to the management in the analysis for decision-making. Sunk cost, on the other hand, will remain the same irrespective of the alternative selected. Thus it need not be considered by the management in evaluating the alternatives as it is common to all of them.

Whether a cost is a sunk cost or differential cost is a question of fact and can be determined only in the light of the circumstances of each individual case. Thus a particular cost item can be a sunk cost in one case and a differential cost in another. Sometimes differential costs are considered as synonymous with variable costs and sunk costs as synonymous with fixed costs. But this need not always be the case.

(vi) Book Costs and Out-of-Pocket Costs. Out-of-pocket costs are those expenses which are current cash payments to outsiders, whereas the book costs do not require these current cash payments. All the explicit costs like payment of rent, wages, salaries, interest, transport charges, etc., fall in the category of out-of-pocket costs. On the other hand, there are those business costs which do not involve any cash payments but for them a provision is made in the books of account to include them in profit and loss accounts and take tax advantages. These are known as the book costs. The examples of book costs are the provisions for depreciation and for unpaid amount of the interest on the owner's capital employed in the firm. In a way these are imputed costs or the payments by a firm to itself.

(vii) Replacement and Historical Costs. Historical cost of asset states the cost of plant, equipment and materials at the price paid originally for them, while the replacement cost states the cost that the firm would have to incur if it wants to replace or acquire the same asset now. For example, if the price of bronze at the time of purchase, say, in 1974 was Rs. 25 a Kg. and if the present price is Rs. 28 a kg. the original cost of Rs. 25 is the historical cost while Rs. 28 is the replacement cost. Replacement cost means the price that would have to be paid currently for acquiring the same plant.

(viii) Total, Average and Marginal Cost. Total cost represents the value of the total resource requirements for the production of goods and services. It refers to the total outlays of money expenditure, both explicitly and implicitly, on the resources used to produce a given level of output. The total cost for a given output is given by the cost function.

Average cost is statistical nature, rather than being an actual cost. It is obtained simply by dividing the total cost (TC), by the total output (Q), *i.e.* $\frac{TC}{Q}$ = average cost.

Marginal cost is the addition to the total cost on account of producing an additional unit of the product or, marginal cost is the cost of marginal unit produced.

Total, average and marginal cost concepts are used in the economic analysis of the firm's productive activities.

(ix) Accounting (or, Private), Economic and Social Costs. Accounting costs are the actual or outlay cots. These costs point out how much expenditure has already been incurred on a particular process or on production as such. Since these costs related to the past, these are generally sunk costs. The accounting costs are useful for managing taxation needs as well as to calculate profit or loss of the firm. On the other hand, economic cost are the ones which help in the decision-making process. They are in the nature of the incremental costs—both the imputed and the explicit costs and the opportunity costs. Since economic costs are used for business-decisions they relate to future, as the only costs that matter for business decisions are the future costs.

Economic costs can be calculated at two levels: micro-level and macro-level. The micro-level economic costs related to functioning of a firm as a production unit, while the macro-level economic costs are the ones that are generated by the decisions of the firm but are paid by the society and not the firm. For example, if the decision of a firm to expand its output leads to increase in its costs, this cost will be of the former type, known as private costs. Whereas, if it also leads to certain costs to the society, may be in the nature of greater pollution, greater congestion, etc., these costs which are external to the firm are social costs from society's point of view. Thus, private costs are those which are actually incurred or provided for by an individual or a firm for its business activity. Social cost, on the other hand. is the total cost to the society on account of production of a good. Thus, the economic costs include both the private and social costs. However, the net social cost is the total social cost minus the private cost.

It is the responsibility of a business firm not only to try to minimise his private cost but to minimise the net social cost.

(x) Fixed and Variable Costs. Total costs could be divided into two components: fixed costs and variable costs. Fixed costs remain constant in total regardless of changes in volume up to a certain level of output. They are not affected by changes in the volume of production. They will have to be incurred even when output is nil. There is an inverse relationship between volume and fixed costs per unit. Thus total fixed costs do not change with a change in volume but vary per unit of volume inversely with volume. If the total production increases, fixed costs per unit will go down and *vice versa*. Total variable costs vary in direct proportion to changes in volume. An increase in volume means a proportionate increase in the total variable costs and decrease in volume results in a proportionate decline in the total variable costs. There is a linear relationship between volume and total variable costs, but variable costs are constant per unit.

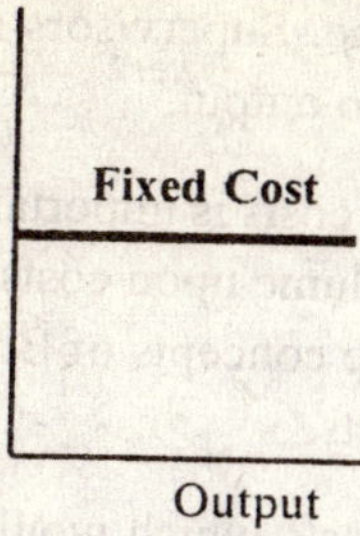

Fig. 1 (a) A completely fixed cost remaining unchanged irrespective of output.

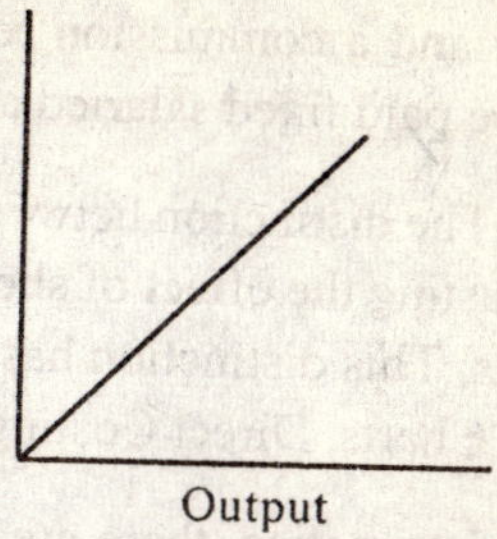

Fig. 1 (b) A completely variable cost increasing in direct proportion to output

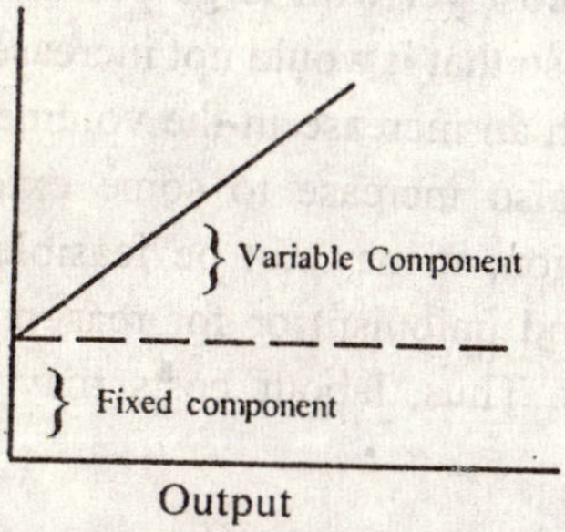

Fig. 1 (c) Shows a semi-variable cost combining fixed and variable components.

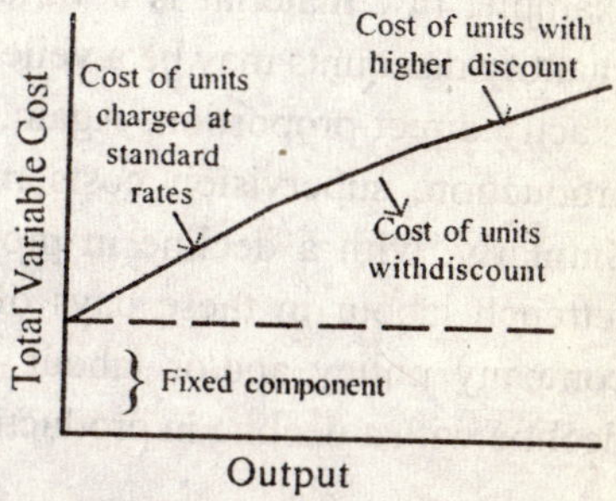

Fig. 1 (d) Give a more complicated type of semi-variable cost, where there is a fixed charge and a variable cost with quantity discount for greater volume.

The distinction between fixed and variable costs, however, is to a watertight one. Which cost is fixed and which is variable may be different in each different decision. Again, it may be noted that the variability of costs is in relation to output and not to the time factor though in the long run, all costs tend to be variable. What is fixed at one level of output may become variable at another level of output.

Many costs fall between the two extremes of being fixed or variable. They are called as semi-variable costs. They are neither perfectly variable nor absolutely fixed in relation to changes in volume. They change in the same direction as volume but in direct proportion thereto. To take an example, electricity bills often include both a fixed charge and a charge based on consumption—this is known as two-part tariff. Again, a salesman may get both a monthly salary and a commission related to sales volume. Supervisors may also be paid fixed salaried and business related to output.

The distinction between fixed and variable costs is important in forecasting the effect of short-run changes in volume upon costs and profits. This distinction has also given rise to the concepts of Break-Even Charts, Direct Costing and Flexible Budgets.

In practice, there are cooperativeiy few costs which would be perfectly variable or absolutely fixed over all ranges of outputs. But for analytical purposes, they are most often assumed to be so. For example, raw material is a variable cost yet with large purchases, quantity discounts may be a veiled of so that it would not increase in exactly direct proportion. Again, with an increase in the volume of production, supervision costs may also increase to some extent. Similarly, with a decline in production, it may not be feasible to retrench labour in these days of trend unionism or for reasons of company policy and/or labour laws. Thus, labour costs may not decline with a decline in production.

(xi) Direct and Indirect Cost. There are some costs which can be directly attributed to the production of a unit of a given product. Such costs are direct costs and can easily be separated, ascertained and imputed to a unit of output. This is because these costs vary with the output units. However, there are other costs which cannot be separated and clearly attributed to individual units of production. These costs are therefore, classified as indirect costs in the accounting process. For example, electricity charge may not be separable department-wise in a single product firm or even product-wise in a multiple product firm. The cost or raw material may be traceable product-wise even in a multiple product firm. In a university. the salary of a Vice-chancellor is not traceable department-wise while that of a professor may be traceable department-wise.

Since all the direct costs are linked to a particular product/ process/department, they vary with changes in them. In other words, all direct costs are variable. On the other hand indirect costs may or may not be variable. Common costs may or may not change as a result of the proposed changes in production level, production process or marketing process. So, indirect costs are both variable and fixed types.

(xii) Shut-down and Abandonment Cost. Shut-down costs are required to be incurred when the production operations are suspended and will not be necessary, if the production operations continue. For example, if the production is suspended, the plant, machinery or equipment will have to be protected by putting up sheds, using tarpaulin, plastic sheets etc. Such costs are called shut-down costs.

When any plant is to be permanently closed down, some costs are to be incurred for disposing of the fixed assets. These costs are called abandonment costs.

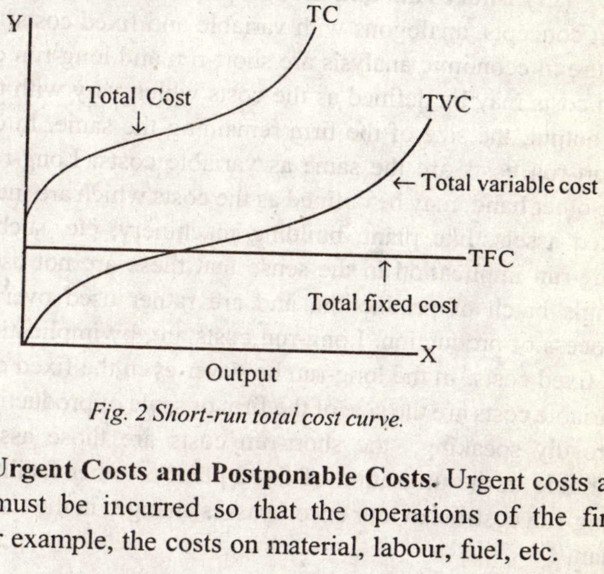

Fig. 2 Short-run total cost curve.

(xiii) Urgent Costs and Postponable Costs. Urgent costs are those that must be incurred so that the operations of the firm continue, for example, the costs on material, labour, fuel, etc.

Those costs whose postponement does not affect, at least for some time, the operational efficiency of the firm are known as postponable costs, *e.g.*, the maintenance of building, machinery, etc.

This distinction of cost becomes quite obvious during the period of war or inflation when firm want to produce the maximum and postpone the maintenance to their plants, buildings, etc.

(xiv) Controllable Costs and Non-controllable Costs. Controllable costs are those that are subject to control or check by executive vigilance, while non-controllable costs are those that cannot be subjected to administrative control or supervision. But a cost which is non-controllable at one level of the executive may be regarded as controllable at some other level. May be that controllability in case of some costs depends on more than one executive. For example, the purchase department of a firm pays for the material while the production department uses it. Thus, controllability of costs is related to the levels of executive responsibility under consideration. Generally, the direct material, labour, fuel costs, etc., are controllable; though some or the overhead costs are also controllable.

(xv) Short-run and Long-run Costs. Two other important cost concepts, analogous with variable and fixed costs; which often figure in economic analysis are short-run and long-run costs. Short-run costs may be defined as the costs which vary with the variation of output, the size of the firm remaining the same. In other words, short-run costs are the same as variable costs. Long-run costs, on the other hand, may be defined as the costs which are incurred on the fixed assets, like plant, building machinery, etc. such costs have long-run implication in the sense that these are not used up in the single batch of production, and are rather used over time in the process of production. Long-run costs are, by implication, the same as fixed costs. In the long-run however even the fixed costs become variable costs are the size of the firm or scale of production increases. Broadly speaking, 'the short-run costs are those associated with variable in the utilisation of fixed plant or other facilities, whereas long-run cost-behaviour encompasses changes in the size and kind of plant'.

RELATIONSHIP BETWEEN MARGINAL COSTS, AVERAGE COSTS AND TOTAL COSTS

Total cost of a firm is the sum total of all the explicit plus implicit expenditures incurred for producing a given level of output. It represents the money value of the total resources required for production of goods and services by the firm.

Average cost is the cost per unit of output, assuming that production of each unit of output incurs the same cost. That is, average cost equals the total cost divided by the number of units produced.

Marginal costs are the incremental costs. That is, these are the extra costs incurred when there is a small addition to the existing output of goods and services. For example, if the total cost of a firm is Rs. 2,000 when it produces 10 units of a good, but when 11 units of the goods are produced it increases to Rs. 2,100 then the marginal cost of 11th unit is.

$$\text{Rs. } 2{,}100 - \text{Rs. } 2{,}000 = \text{Rs. } 100.$$

In other words, marginal cost of nth unit (MC_n) is

$$MC_n = TC_n - TC_{n-1}$$

Where TC_n refers to total cost of nth unit; and

TC_{n-1} refers to total cost of (n - 1)th unit.

The relationship between MC, AC and TC can be further seen with the help of Table.

Table

Units of good produced		*Total Cost (TC)*	*Average Cost*
(AC) =	*Marginal Cost*	$\frac{\textit{Total Cost}}{\textit{No. of Units Produced}}$	*($TC_n - TC_{n-1}$)*
(1)	(2)	col. 2 col.	1 = col. 3(4)
10	2,000	200.0	—
11	2,100	190.9	100
12	2,180	181.7	80
13	2,250	173.1	70
14	2,350	167.9	100
15	2,500	166.6	150

SOME ILLUSTRATIONS

Illustration: 1

From the following data, find out fixed and variable components of semi-veriable costs by High Low Method:

Production Quantity	*Semi-variable Costs*
100	1,400
200	1,800
300	2,200
400	2,600

Solution:

$$\text{Variable Cost per unit (or V)} = \frac{\text{Difference of Cost}}{\text{Difference of Volume}}$$

$$= \frac{\text{Rs. } 2,600 - \text{Rs. } 1,400}{400 - 100}$$

$$= \frac{\text{Rs. } 1,200}{300} = \text{Rs. } 4$$

Fixed Costs (or F) = Total Semi-variable Cost – Total Variable Cost

Say, On 100 Production Quantity:

$$F = 1,400 - \text{Rs. } 4\ (100)$$

$$= 1,400 - 400 = \text{Rs. } 1,000$$

Illustration: 2

A plant produces a product which costs Rs. 3.00 per unit when produced in quantities of 10,000 and Rs. 2.25 per unit when produced in quantities of 20,000. What are the total fixed costs?

What shall be the cost per unit if the firm produces 16,000 units?

Solution:

Average Total Cost at = 3.00

10,000 units

Hence, Total Cost of = 10,000 X Rs. 3 = Rs. 30,000

10,000 units

Average Total Cost at = 20,000 x Rs. 2.25 = Rs. 45,000

20,000 units

$$\text{Average Variable Cost} = \frac{\text{Difference of Total Costs}}{\text{Difference of Volume}}$$

$$= \frac{\text{Rs. } 45,000 - \text{Rs. } 30,000}{20,000 - 10,000} = \text{Rs. } 1.50$$

Calculation of Total Fixed Cost:

Total Fixed Cost = Total Cost – Total Variable Cost

We can calculate TFC at either of the two volumes.

At 10,000 units:

Total Fixed Cost = Rs. 30,000 – 10,000 × Rs. 1.50

= Rs. 30,000 – Rs. 15,000 = Rs. 15,000

Calculation of ATC at 16,000 units:

Total Cost at 16,000 units = Fixed Cost + V. C.

= Rs. 15,000 + 1.50 × 16,000

= Rs. 15,000 + 24,000

= Rs. 39,000

$$\text{Average Total Cost at 16,000 units} = \frac{\text{Total Cost}}{\text{Total Output}}$$

$$= \frac{39,000}{16,000} = 2.437$$

Illustration: 3

The expenses of Taj Hotel are partly fixed and partly vary with the number of customers. Each customer pays Rs. 520 a month. The profits are Rs. 72 per head per month when there are 80 customers and Rs. 80 when there are 100 customers. What will be the profit per head per month if there are 150 customer?

Solution:

	80 Customers	*100 Customers*
	Rs.	*Rs.*
Total Revenue per month	520 × 80 = 41,600	520 × 100 = 52,000
Total Profit per month	72 × 80 = 5,760	80 × 100 = 8,000
Total Expenses per month	35,840	44,000

Variable Expenses per customer per month

$$= \frac{\text{Difference of Total Expenses}}{\text{Difference of Customer Number}}$$

$$= \frac{44{,}000 - 35{,}840}{100 - 80} = \frac{8{,}160}{20}$$

$$= \text{Rs. } 408$$

Fixed Expenses per month = Total Expenses – Total Variable Expenses

For 80 customers Fixed Expenses = 35,840 – 80 × 408

= 35,840 – 32,640

= Rs. 3,200

Calculation of profit per head per month on 150 customers

Profit p.m. = Total Revenue – (Total Variable Expenses + Fixed Expenses)

$$= (150 \times 520) - [(150 \times 408) + 3{,}200]$$

$$= 78{,}000 - (61{,}200 + 3{,}200) = \text{Rs. } 13{,}600$$

$$\text{Profit per head per month} = \frac{\text{Rs. } 13{,}600}{150} = \text{Rs. } 90.67$$

Illustration : 4

A manufacturer produces 2,00,000 units of a product at a cost of Rs. 3.25 per unit. Later on he produces 2,75,000 units of a product at a cost of Rs. 3.20 per unit when its fixed overheads have increased by 10%. Find out marginal cost per unit and original fixed overheads. Also extimate the cost of 3,50,000 units, assuming no further change in costs.

Solution:

Total Cost of 2,00,000 units = 2,00,000 Rs. 3.25 = Rs. 6,50,000

Total Cost of 2,75,000 units = 2,75,000 Rs. 3.20 = Rs. 8,80,000

Let x be the marginal (variable) cost and y be the original fixed overheads.

Then, $2{,}00{,}000 \times x + y = 6{,}50{,}000$

and $2{,}75{,}000 \times x + y + 10\% \text{ of } y = 8{,}80{,}000$

or $2{,}00{,}000\, x + y = 6{,}50{,}000$ ...(1)

$2{,}75{,}000\, x + 1.1\, y = 8{,}80{,}000$ ...(2)

Multiplying equation (1) by 1.1 and (2) by 1, we get,

$$2{,}20{,}000\, x + 1.1\, y = 7{,}15{,}000$$

$$\_\,2{,}75{,}000\, x + \_\,1.1\, y = \_\,8{,}80{,}000$$

Deducting

$$-\,55{,}000\, x = -\,1.65{,}000$$

$$\therefore x = -\,1{,}65{,}000 - 55{,}000 = \text{Rs. } 3$$

Putting the value of x in equation 1, we get,

$$2{,}00{,}000 \bullet 3 + y = 6{,}50{,}000$$

$\therefore\ y = 6{,}50{,}000 - 6{,}00{,}000 =$ Rs. 50,000

Calculation of total cost of 3,50,000 units of output:

Variable Costs = 3,50,000 • Rs. 3 = Rs. 10,50,000

Fixed Costs = 50,000 + 10% of 50,000 = 55,000

Total Cost = 11,05,000

Illustration: 5

Mr. Ramesh Kumar is considering whether to trade in his car for a new. He bought the car two years ago for Rs. 1,80,000. He still owes Rs. 80,000 to the bank from which he borrowed money to purchase the car at an interest rate of 8 per cent. The new car he wants will cost Rs. 2,10,000. He will be allowed Rs. 90,000 on the trade-in of his old car. For financing the purchase, he will have to borrow again from the Bank, this time at the rate of 9 per cent. Which costs are differential for Mr. Ramesh Kumar and which are sunk? What would be the incremental cost (or cost saving) of the decision to buy the new car rather than to keep the old one?

Solution:

Sunk Cost:

Interest on old bank borriwings (8% on Rs. 80,000) = Rs. 6,400 p.a.

Incremental Cost:

Cash Price of new car	Rs. 2,10,000
Less Trade-in of old car	Rs. 90,000
Incremental Outlay	Rs. 1,20,000

Differential Cost:

Interest on new bank borrowings (9% on Rs. 1,20,000) = Rs. 10,800 p.a.

Illustration: 6

Bajaj Auto Company manufactures a scooter component. It normally produces and sells about 1,000 components a day at an average cost of Rs. 14 and a wholesale price of Rs. 21. The company has an unexpected opportunity to sell additional components under private levels to three different retailers. Thus, Ravi Stores offers to buy 100 components at Rs. 19 each, Dhirendra Stores offers to buy 100 commponents would by Rs. 15 for the first 100 components, Rs. 16 for the second 100 components and Rs. 17 for the third 100 components.

(i) Which of these orders should the company accept?

(ii) What fundamental principle is involved here?

Solution:

(i)

		MR	MC
For First	100 units	19	15
For Second	100 units	17	16
For Third	100 units	16	17

From the above it is clear that the company should accept the first two orders from Ravi Stores and Dhirendra Stores, as their marginal revenues are more than the marginl costs.

(ii) Here the fundamental principle involved is that the additional production should be continued so long as MR MC.

❐

9

Market Structure

In common usage the word market designates a place where certain things are bought and sold. But when we talk about the word market in economics, we extend our concept of market well beyond the idea of single place to which the householder goes to buy something. For our present purpose, we define a market as an area over which buyers and sellers negotiate the exchange of a well-defined commodity. For a single market to exist, it must be possible for buyers and sellers to communicate with each other and to make meaningful deals over the whole market.

Several economists have attempted to define the term market as used in economics. Some of them are as under:

According to **Curnot**, "Economists understand by the term market not any particular market-place in which things are bought and sold, but the whole of any region in which buyers and sellers are in such free intercourse with one another that the price of the same goods tends to equality easily and quickly."

In the eyes of **Prof. Chapman,** "The term market refers not necessarily to a place but always to a commodity and the buyers and sellers who are in direct competition with one another."

In simple words, the term market refers to a structure in which the buyers and sellers of the commodity remain in close contact.

FEATURES OF MARKET

On the basis above-mentioned definitions we can mention following main features of the market:

(1) Commodity. For the existence of market, a commodity is essential which is to be bought and sold. There cannot be a market without commodity.

(2) Buyers and Sellers. Buyers and sellers are also essential for market. Without buyers and sellers the sale-purchase activity cannot be conducted which is essential part of a market.

(3) Area. There should be an area in which buyers and sellers of the commodity live in. It is not essential that the buyers and sellers should come to a particular place to transact the business.

(4) Close Contact. There should be close contact and communication between buyers and sellers. This communication may be established by any method. For example, in olden days this contact and communication was possible only when the buyers and sellers of a particular commodity could come at a particular place. But now with the developed means of communication physical presence of buyers and sellers at one particular place is not essential. They can contact with each other through letters, telegrams, telephones, etc. In the boundary of a market we include only those buyers and sellers who can maintain regular close contacts. For instance, India's farmers (or sellers of grains) have no close contacts with the consumers (or buyers) of England, hence though they are the buyers and sellers of grains yet do not come under the purview of a market.

(5) Competition. There should be some competition among buyers and sellers of the commodity in a market.

From the viewpoint of price analysis, it is very important for business management to gain a proper understanding of the nature and process of competition in the modern industrial society. Firstly, the management should understand the rationale of the free enterprise system within which its own business decisions have to be made and the purpose, aims and limitations of that system. Secondly, it must have full knowledge of the market and market situations in which its own business operates and of the policies appropriate to those market situations: Thirdly, it is necessary to have an understanding of the competitive process and how the variables in the process—price, product innovation and promotional activity-may be manipulated in enlarging the firm's market share. Fourthly, the firms having monopoly power should be familiar with the nature and the purpose of the law relating to monopoly and restrictive practices. What is more important, the management must also be alert and recognize when market conditions change. Although there is no substitute for the intimate knowledge of the ways of the competitors acquired by experienced executives, an understanding of the nature of competition can provide an insight into the probable behaviour patterns of the competitors. It will be useful to distinguish the following types of market situations to study how prices are determined:

1. Perfect Competition

Economists have defined perfect competition in various ways. Some importance definitions are as follows:

According to Prof. Benham, "A market is said to be perfect when all the potential sellers and buyers are promptly aware of the price at which transactions take place and all the offers made by other sellers and buyers, and when any buyer can purchase from any seller, and vice versa." Under such conditions the price of a commodity will tend to be the same (after allowing for costs of transport and taxes) all over the market.

According to Mrs. John Robinson, "Perfect competition prevails when the demand for the output of each producer is perfectly elastic. This entails first, that the number of sellers is large, so that the output of any one seller is a negligible small proportion of the commodity and second, that buyers are all alike in respect of their choice between rival sellers so that the market is perfect."

These definitions explain that perfect competitions in a market situation where a large number of buyers and sellers gather to exchange identical products, they have full knowledge of the market conditions and the price tends to be equal all over the market.

Features or Characteristics of Perfect Competition

The following are the main characteristics of perfect competition:

(a) Existence of Large Number of Buyers and Sellers. The number of buyers and sellers is so large that no individual buyer or seller can influence the market price and output by his independent action. Every buyer and seller purchases or sells a very insignificant amount of the total output. The individual firm must take the price as given. It is a 'price taker' not the 'price fixer .'

(b) Homogeneous Products. A firm produces a product which is accepted by customers as homogeneous or identical. The firm cannot differentiate among buyers. It will not earn profit or suffer loss by selling its product to a particular buyer. An individual firm cannot change any other price more than that already prevailing in the market.

(c) Free Entry and Exit of the Firms. Every firm is free to join or leave the industry. If the industry is making profits new firms can enter the market to share these profits. Similarly, if the industry suffers losses, the individual firm may decide to quit the market.

(d) Perfect Knowledge. There is perfect and complete knowledge on the part of all buyers and sellers about the conditions in the market. For a market to be perfect it is essential that all buyers and sellers should be aware of what is happening in any part of the market.

(e) Perfect Mobility. There is perfect mobility of factors of production geographically (*i.e.*,) from one place to the other as well as occupationally (*i.e.*, from one job to the other).

(f) No Transport Cost. It is necessary that the commodity of the perfect competition market should be capable of being easily transported from one part of the market to another. It is presumed that the transportation cost from one part of the market to another part is zero.

(g) Horizontal AR = MR Curve. In a pure and perfect competition market the average revenue = Marginal revenue curve of the firm becomes a horizontal curve parallel to the X-axis which shows infinite elastic demand. It is shown in the diagram. The shape of the AR curve (or demand curve) suggests that a firm under perfect competition is price-taker and not a price-maker. In other words, the market price will not be affected by the independent actions of a single firm. Different firms working under perfect competition market cannot have different prices, all firms have to keep the same price for the product.

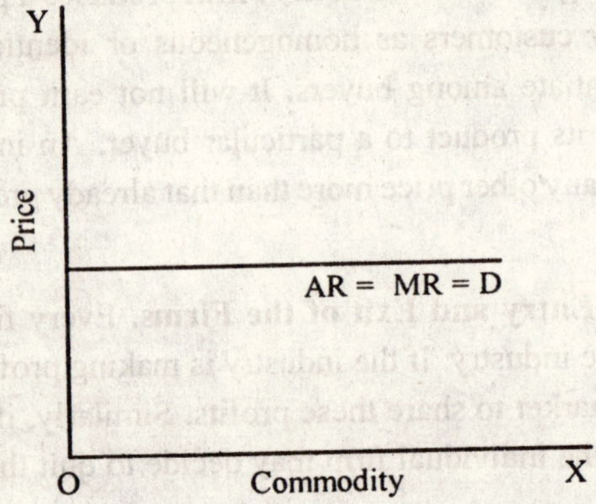

Is Perfect Competition a Myth

Does perfect competition exist in the real world or is it a myth? Is it an important 'question to be probed ? Some economists have cited, agricultural commodity market, gold market and share market as the examples of perfect competition market. But when we adjudge these markets on the basis of the salient features of perfect competition market they also do not come to that level. In the real world we do not find any market to which we can term as perfect competition market. It is because of the following reasons:

(i) Real world markets do not have the number of buyers and sellers so large that no buyer or seller can influence the market. Some buyers and sellers of the commodity are so big that they definitely influence the market.

(ii) There is no such thing as 'homogeneous product' in the real world situation which can be produced by all the firms in the market. For instance, if farmers produce wheat that does not imply that the wheat produced by all the farmers would be of the same quality.

(iii) In the real world firms do not enjoy the complete freedom even in entry or exit the industry. There are number of difficulties that the firms have to face.

(iv) Buyers and sellers cannot have the perfect knowledge regarding market conditions because of many reasons.

(v) Perfect mobility of factors of production is also not possible. Especially there are number of difficulties in the way of labourers to change place or occupation.

(vi) Transport cost will also be there when we will transport goods from one place to the other.

Thus out of the essential conditions of perfect competition, no condition is found in the real world situation. And that is why the concept of perfect competition is called an imaginary concept or a myth. If it is myth, why is it studied in economics ? The fact that perfect competition is not a real world situation does not reduce the usefulness of this model. Though perfect competition is rare, we still study it for the following important reasons:

(i) Simple Analysis. It furnishes us a simple and logical analysis to understand the process of price determination.

(ii) Ideal Situation. The theory of perfect competition provides a norm against which the actual performance of the economy can be checked or evaluated perfect competition being considered the most efficient one. For instance, price and output determined under perfect competition shall be ideal situations. Now by comparing the actual price and output of the country with this ideal we can find out the deviations from it and accordingly can plan policy formulations.

(iii) **Price Control.** The concept of perfect competition is also helpful to the government in its task of price-fixation and price-control. It will be difficult to fix price below the level of perfect competition price, hence it should be kept in mind while fixing the price by the government.

Thus, it is clear that in spite of the fact that perfect competition is not cent per cent real world situation, it is an important and useful concept in economics. We can find a number of markets in the real world which are very close to the norms of perfect competition market. On the basis of empirical observations, Prof. Leftwitch, Stigler and many other economists are of the opinion that markets are gradually moving towards, perfect competition.

2. Monopoly

The market form of monopoly is the opposite extreme from that of perfect competition. It exists whenever an industry is in the hands of single producer. In the case of perfect competition there are so many individual producers that no one of them has any power over the market and any one firm can increase or diminish its production without affecting the market price. A monopoly, on the other hand, has power to influence the market price. By reducing its output, it can force the price up, and by increasing its output it can force the price down.

The word MONOPOLY is made of two words; MONO +POLY. Here 'Mono' means one and 'Poly' implies the seller, thereby the literal meaning of the word Monopoly is one seller or one producer. Thus, pure monopoly refers to that form of market organisation wherein there is single firm (or producer) producing a commodity for which there are no good or close substitutes. According to Watson, "A monopolist is the only producer of a product that has no close substitutes." Changes in prices and outputs of other goods sold in the economy must leave the monopolist unaffected. Conversely, changes in the monopolist's price and output must leave the other producers of the economy unaffected.

Features of Monopoly

(i) Single Producer. There is a single firm producing the commodity in the market.

(ii) No Close Substitutes. For the monopoly to exist single producer is the necessary condition but not a sufficient one. It is also essential that there should be no close substitute of the commodity in the market. This second condition would be even more difficult to fulfil than the first, since there are few things for which there is no substitute. For instance, Usha are produced by a single firm alone but there are close substitutes of Usha fans that are available in the market in the form of Relifans, Khaitan Ashoka, Crompton, etc. Hence, though the firm producing Usha fans is single yet it cannot be termed a monopoly firm. It is, therefore, essential for a monopoly to exist that there should be no close substitutes available in the market. This condition can be stated in other words as that the cross elasticity of demand for the output of the firm with respect to the price of every firm's product is zero.

(iii) Barriers to the Entry. The entry into the industry is completely barred or made impossible. If new firms are admitted into the industry, monopoly itself breaks down. This ban on entry may be legal, natural or institutional but it must essentially be there.

(iv) Firm and Industry. Since in monopoly there is single firm producing the commodity, hence the difference between firm and industry vanishes automatically.

(v) Downward Sloping AR and MR Curves. The monopoly firm is like an industry, and faces a downward sloping demand curve for its product; thus, it has to lower its price in order to sell more. For, it is this nature of demand curve that determines the nature of average and marginal revenue curves. Under perfect competition, we know, average revenue and marginal revenue curves coincide in a horizontal line. But that is not so under monopoly. With a monopoly, however, the average revenue curve, which is the same as the market demand curve, is downward sloping. Furthermore, the marginal

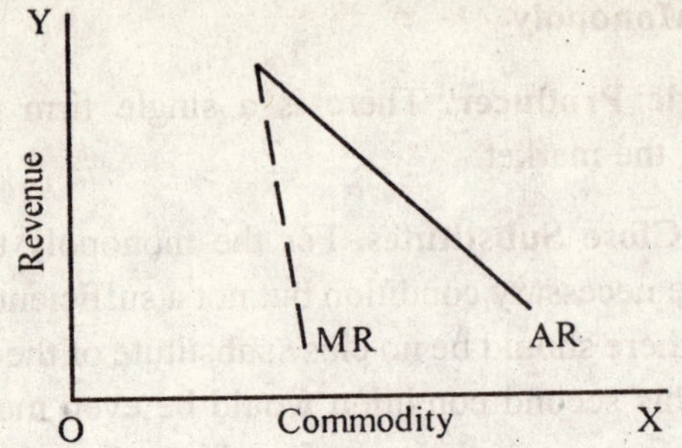

revenue curve does not coincide with the average revenue curve rather, it remains below it. Thus, for a monopolist firm both AR and MR curves are downward sloping and MR remains below AR as shown in the diagram.

The downward sloping shape of the AR curve clearly indicates that a monopoly firm is a price-maker.

(vi) Price-discrimination is Possible. Under the conditions of monopoly price-discrimination is possible. It implies that a monopolist can sell its product at different prices to different customers.

In short, monopoly depends basically on two factors:

(i) Absence of close substitutes; and

(ii) Restriction on competition.

Pure and Simple Monopoly

Economists, ordinarily, differentiate between two forms of monopoly. Pure monopoly and Simple monopoly. Pure monopoly is that market situation wherein there is only one producer of the commodity and the cross elasticity of demand is zero. In this situation total revenue at all levels of price and output remains the same. Hence the average revenue of the firm takes the shape of rectangular hyperbola. Here the monopolist is so powerful that he can extract the whole income from the consumers. In this situation producer would like to produce the minimum and he will fix the maximum price in order to exact its total revenue. But like perfect competition it is also an extreme and imaginary situation. It is not found in the real world situation.

On the other hand, simple monopoly is a market situation in which there is only one producer of the commodity and the cross elasticity of demand is not zero but small. In this situation firm can vary its price but its total revenue in all circumstances does not remain constant. AR and MR curves of this type of firm are downward sloping curves as shown in the preceding diagram. We ordinarily study only this type of monopoly.

Conditions for the Existence, Origin and Growth of Monopoly

For the monopoly to exist three following conditions must be fulfilled:

(i) Only one producer;

(ii) No close substitute and

(iii) Strong barriers to the entry into the industry.

The factors responsible for the origin and growth of monopoly are many and varied-natural, legal and institutional, technological, etc. Natural factors relate to the concentration of deposits of a particular mineral in a small area, as in the case of gold, copper ,salt, potash, diamonds, petroleum, etc.

In these days technological factors have become more important. In some industries requiring huge investment with long gestation period, the economies of large-scale production are so pronounced that the operation of market forces tend to lead to creation of monopoly, particularly when the size of the market is not very large.

Then there are legal monopolies, created by the state through "patent" laws and otherwise.

Distinction between Perfect Competition and Monopoly

A market wherein perfect competition between large number of buyers and large number of sellers of a homogeneous production is found, it is termed as perfect competition market.

A Market which has single producer of the commodity and no close substitutes is called monopoly market.

Perfect Competition	Monopoly
1. Large number of firms	1. Single firm.
2. A firm cannot adopt independent price policy. It is price-taker and not the price-maker.	2. Firm can have independent price policy. It is price-maker.
3. AR and MR curves are one and the same and parallel to the X-axis. AR = MR	3. AR and MR curves are downward sloping curves and MR curve always remains below the AR curve MR < AR
4. Price-discrimination is not possible *i.e.*, a firm here charges the same price from all customers	4. Price-discrimination is possible
5. Full freedom to entry or exit.	5. Restriction on the entry.
6. Firm can get only normal profits in the long run.	6. Firm can earn supernormal profits in the long run.

3. Monopolistic Competition

Economists found that perfect competition and pure monopoly were unrealistic market situations. The actual market situations are somewhere between perfect competition and pure monopoly. The theory of Monopolistic Competition was first propounded and popularised by an American economist E. H. Chamberlin. Sometimes monopolist competition is termed as Imperfect Competition also.

As Stonier and Hague put. "It means the large group or firms making very similar products. Here there is keen but not perfect competition between many firms making very similar products (products are not homogeneous as in perfect competition or remote substitutes as in monopoly, but they are differentiated)".

In the words of Prof. Leftwitch, "Monopolistic competition is a market situation in which there are many sellers of a particular product but the product of each seller is in some way differentiated in the minds of consumers from the products of every other seller."

In the words of Dominick Salvatore, "Monopolistic competition refers to the market organisation in which there are many firms selling closely related but identical commodities."

Thus monopolistic competition refers to the market situation in which many firms producing differentiated products (closely related but no identical products) compete with each other for the sale of their products. So defined, monopolistic competition is a market situation with some elements of pure competition and some elements of pure monopoly. This explains the essential nature of monopolistic competition. It is competition between a large number of firms, each of them enjoying a measure of monopoly power. That is why, monopolistic competition is sometimes described as "Polypoly."

Features of Monopolistic Competition

(i) Many Sellers. There are large number of firms producing commodity in the market. Large number here implies that there are so many firms that the activities of one firm has no perceptible cffect on the other firms in the industry. Each firm controls a very small or negligible share of the total output of the industry. The competitive element results from the fact that there are many firms in the market.

(ii) Freedom of Entry or Exit. Every firm is free to enter into the industry and come out from the industry as and when it wishes.

(iii) Product Differentiation. Product differentation is the most important feature of a monopolistic competition market. Under monopolistic competition products of different firm are neither completely homogeneous as in perfect competition nor entirely distinct as in monopoly. Here each firm produces a product that is somewhat different from the products of its competitors, but it is not entirely distinct, it is very close to the products of other firms. Products of two or more firms, are not exact substitutes but also are not entirely different. They are each other's close substitutes. But each firm is known for its own product, which has some distinction. For its product, the firm is a monopolist. But because of close substitutes, it faces competition with other firms. In fact, absence of differentiation would mean pure competition and perfect differentiation would mean pure monopoly. Partial differentiation, therefore, defines the nature of monopolistic competition.

There might, for example, be a large number of competing firms producing different brands of soap, all similar but by no means identical products. Each soap would differ in physical composition from competing soaps; it would also have different packing, and as the advertisers-say, a different 'brand image' from its competitors.

Thus, products may be differentiated in many ways, *e.g.* by changing in brand name, trademark, design, packing, colour, size, weight, measurement, etc. We are giving some examples of product differentiation below so that the term could be understood more clearly:

Cycle-Atlas, Estern Star, Hind, Hero, A-One etc.

-Sewing Machines-Usha, Luxmi, Singer, etc.

-Cigarettes-Wills, Gold Flake, Bristol, Taj, etc.

-Soap-Lux, Rexona, Hamam, Jai, Lifeboy, Pears, etc.

-Tea-Brooke Bond, Lipton, Modies, Tata, etc.

We can find a number of examples of such differentiated products. Cross elasticity of demand between such commodities is very high.

(iv) Each firm is a monopolist for its product. Every firm has a monopoly over the production of its product *i.e.*, no other firm can manufacture the product of this brand name. For instance no firm other that the Atlas Cycle Company can manufacture Atlas Cycle or no firm other than Hindustan Lever can manufacture Lux toilet soap.

(v) Consumer exhibits market preference. In this market situation a consumer exhibits market preference for a particular product in the market. For instance, some consumers prefer Brooke Bond tea while others prefer Lipton.

Those who prefer a particular product would like to purchase it at even somewhat higher price.

(vi) Selling Costs. Selling costs have an important place in this market. Every firm seeks to modify consumers' preferences through advertisements and salesmanship. This gives rise to what is called selling costs. Thus there is non-price competition among firms under monopolistic competition.

(vii) Independent Price Policy and Downward Sloping of AR-MR Curves. A firm under monopolistic competition can have an independent price policy. It is price maker for its product. Hence the

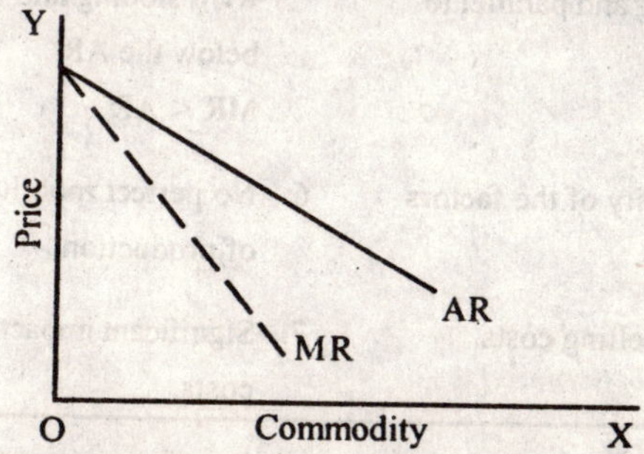

AR and MR curves facing a firm under monopolistic competition will be downward sloping similar to the monopoly. But there is an important difference between the AR curves under monopoly and monopolistic competition. The AR curve under

monopolistic competition is somewhat flatter than in the monopoly. AR and MR curves of a firm under monopolistic competition are illustrated in the diagram:

Distinction between Perfect Competition and Monopolistic Competition (or Imperfect Competition)

Perfect Competition	Monopolistic Competition or Imperfect Competition
(1)	*(2)*
1. Large number of firms.	1. Many firms.
2. Homogeneous product.	2. Product-differentiation.

(1)	*(2)*
3. Perfect competition among the sellers in the market.	3. Both the situation exist side by side-competition between sellers as well as monopoly of the firm.
4. A firm cannot have independent price policy, it is price taker, not the price-maker.	4. A firm can have independent price policy. It is price maker.
5. AR and MR curves are one and the same thing and parallel to the X-axis. AR = MR	5. AR and MR curves are downward sloping and MR remains below the AR. MR < AR
6. Perfect mobility of the factors of production.	6. No perfect mobility of the factors of production.
7. No effect of selling costs.	7. Significant impact of selling costs.

Distinction between Monopoly and Monopolistic Competition

Monopoly	**Monopolistic Competition**
1. Single Firm.	1. Many firms.
2. Homogeneous product.	2. Product-differentiation.
3. No close substitute of the commodity.	3. Many close substitutes.
4. Price-discrimination is possible.	4. Price-discrimination by an individual firm is not possible.
5. No significant effect of selling cost.	5. Significant effect of selling costs.
6. Complete restriction on the entry of the firm.	6. Freedom of entry.

4. Oligopoly

Oligopoly is a market situation wherein the number of producers (or sellers) of the commodity is so small that every seller has a perceptible effect on others and influences the market.

Large-scale manufacturing sector of modern economies is mainly oligopolistic in structure. The most important characteristic features of oligopoly is interdependence among its firms. This is due to small number of firms. Each of these firms contributes a significant portion of the total sale, with the result that when one of them lowers its price, undertakes a successful advertising campaign; or introduces a better model, the demand curve faced by other firms will shift down. Hence the rivals may immediately react. An intelligent producer, therefore, will take into consideration, or make an estimate of the reaction of his rivals before making any significant change in his output-price policy. But as there may be many different reaction patterns of the rivals to the actions of this (first) firm, we cannot neatly define the demand curve faced by our oligopolist, unless and untill we assume a specific reaction pattern, and therefore our solution is indeterminate.

Features of oligopoly are as follows:

(i) A few sellers.

(ii) Every seller has perceptible effect on other sellers.

(iii) Homogeneous product or product differentiation (both are possible).

(iv) No easy entry into the industry.

(v) Interdependence among various firms.

(vi) Non-price competition occupies a central place in such market situations.

(vii) Price-war and price-rigidity.

(viii) Price-output decisions are very difficult and indeterminate.

Types of Oligopoly

There are two important sub-types of oligopoly:

(a) Oligopoly without product-differentiation or with homogeneous product-it is called pure oligopoly.

(b) Oligopoly with product-differentiation is known as differentiated oligopoly (a special case under monopolistic competition).

5. Duopoly

If there are only two producers (or sellers) of a commodity, it is called duopoly. There is open competition between these two producers and each influences the market. Price-output determination in this form of market is similar to that of oligopoly.

Classifications of Market on the Basis of Time

(1) Very Short-period or Daily Market. Very short period market is that wherein the amount of output cannot be varied in response to the change in demand. In this market supply is limited to the stocks. Markets of perishable commodities and seasonal crops come under this category, for example, the supply of milk, fruits, vegetables, wheat, etc. cannot be varied immediately in response to change in their demands. Hence the price of such commodities is affected more by demand than supply. This price is known as market price.

(2) Short-period Market. It is market situation in which the production of a commodity can be varied only by changing variable factors in response to changes in its demand. Hence the size of the plant and fixed competition factors cannot be changed.

(3) Long-period Market. It is a market situation where output can be fully varied in accordance with the demand. Here all factors of production are variable including the scale of plant. With the increase in demand new firms can enter into the industry and increase the output and with the fall in demand some firms may close down their production. In this market situation price of the commodity is affected more by supply than the demand. This price is termed as Normal Price.

Perfect Competition and the Demand Curve

In perfect competition since there are many firms selling identical products with no one firm large enough relative to the entire market to influence the total supply of the product, no single firm has any control over the market price. If one firm decides to expand its output, it will not make any perceptible difference in the supply of the product and there may not be any change in the market price. Similarly, if one firm drops out of the market, the supply is decreased so insignificantly that it is of no consequence from the point of view of change in the price. Thus the demand curve facing a firm in a perfectly comeptitive market is horizontal at the prevailing market price.

At any price higher than the prevailing market price the firm will find no buyers and thus can sell nothing. Since all the firms in the industry sell identical products, the buyers will turn to only those firms which charge the market price and will simply ignore that firm which has raised its selling price above that level. Under the circumstances no firm will be irrational enough to raise the price above the prevailing market price. Further, a firm's share in the total market supply is so small that it can sell its entire output at the prevailing market price. Therefore, it has no reason to lower down its price. In case a firm in a perfectly competitive market decides to lower down the price of its product below that of the other firms, it will find itself faced with the entire group of buyers whose demand it cannot meet.

Generally perfectly competitive markets are non-existent. Economists, however, assert that markets for some agricultural products are reasonably close to what are theoretically considered as perfectly competitive markets. A farmer producing wheat normally faces a perfectly elastic demand curve. When he carries his wheat to the market, he is offered the prevailing market price. At this price he can sell all that he desires to sell, and he need not reduce the price for clearing his stock of wheat. On the other hand, if he asks for more than the market price and sticks to his request, he will not find any buyer for his product and he will have to return home with all the wheat which he had carried to the market.

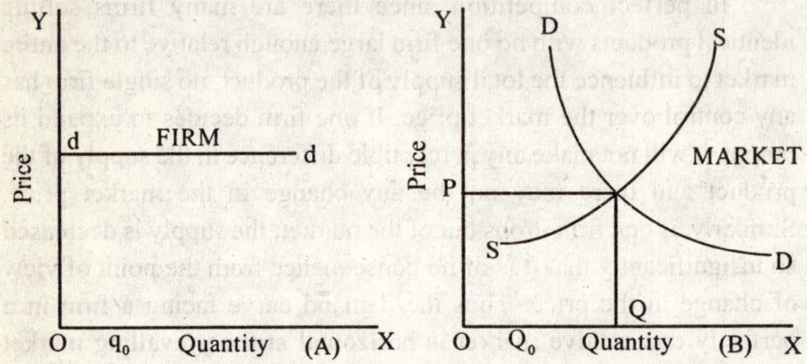

Fig. 1 : The Demand Curve Facing the firm under a Perfectly Competitive Market

In Figure 1A, the firm in a perfectly competitive market faces the demand curve dd. Since this demand curve is horizontal, that is, parallel to X-axis, the demand is perfectly elastic at the market price OP. The firm's demand curve is also its average revenue curve. In perfect competition since the firm's average revenue curve is horizontal, its marginal revenue curve coincides with its average revenue curve. The market demand curve DD and the market supply curve SS are shown in Figure 1B. They intersect each other at point E and thus the price that prevails in the market is OP. The price axes of the two figures, that is, 1(A) and 1(B) are identical; but quantity measurements of the market diagram are very much compressed as compared to those of the firm diagram. For example, if OQ in Figure 1(A) mesures 10 units of the product for the firm, OQ_o in Figure 1(B) measures 10 million units of the product for the market as a whole.

In perfect competition, a firm can do nothing whereby the demand curve which it faces and the prevailing market price change. It will have to accept both as given. However, any forces that change the market demand or the market supply will change the market price of the product and, as a result, the demand curve faced by the firm will also change.

MONOPOLY AND THE DEMAND CURVE

If in some market there is a single firm which sells a product for which there are no substitutes, it is called monopoly. This implies that the whole market for the product is available to the firm. From the production point of view there is no distinction between the firm and the industry. In a monopolistic market the demand curve faced by the monopolist has a negative slope and is the same as the market demand curve for the product.

Figure 2. shows the demand curve facing the firm in monopoly. It is also the market demand curve for the product.

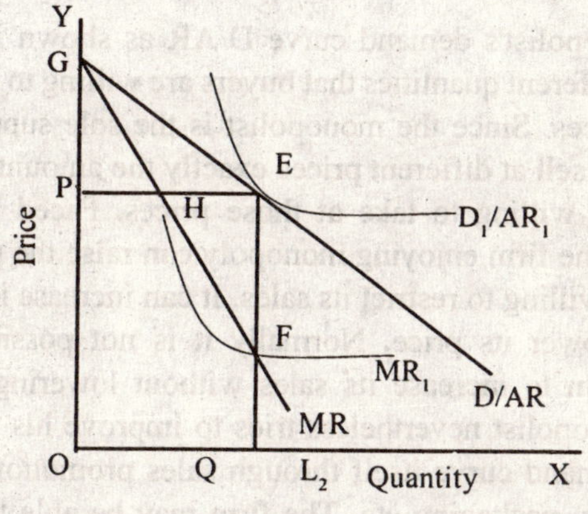

Fig. 2.

The quantity a monopolist can sell, given the nature of his product, consumers' income etc., depends on the price he charges. At a higher price he can sell a smaller quantity than at a lower price. This is reflected in the downward sloping demand curve facing him. The monopolist's demand curve is also called his average revenue curve. If the monopolist's demand curve is linear and given by the curve labelled AR in Figure 2, at price OP his sales will amount to OQ, and the total revenue will be equal to area of the rectangle OPEQ. Total revenue when sales of the monopolist equal OQ can alternatively be represented by the area under the marginal revenue curve OGFQ. Hence the area of the rectanlge OPEQ is equal to area under the marginal revenue curve OGFQ. Since area OPHFQ is common to both, triangles GPH and FEH are equal in area. They are also similar and thus congruent. Therefore, PH is equal to HE and PG is equal to EF. When output is OQ, marginal revenue is equal to average revenue at that output minus EF. Since the marginal revenue curve is linear when the average revenue curve is linear, we can derive the full marginal revenue curve by finding one more point on the marginal revenue curve. Such a point could be H, the point that bisects the line joining the average revenue curve to the ordinate at the price corresponding to sales amounting to OQ. If the monopolist's average revenue curve is non-linear, then marginal revenue curve cannot be derived by obtaining just two points and joining them by a straight line.

The monopolist's demand curve D/AR as shown in Figure 2 indicates the different quantities that buyers are willing to purchase at all possible prices. Since the monopolist is the sole supplier of the product, he can sell at different prices exactly the amount of product that buyers are willing to take at those prices. Faced by a given demand curve the firm enjoying monopoly can raise the price of the product if it is willing to restrict its sales. It can increase its sales if it is willing to lower its price. Normally it is not possible for the monopolist, firm to increase its sales without lowering down the price. The monopolist nevertheless tries to improve his position by altering his demand curve itself through sales promotion activities, *e.g.*, advertising, packaging etc. The firm may be able to pursuade more people to buy its product, and make its demand less elastic if it can convince the buyers that they cannot manage without the product. The monopolist can also think of altering the nature of the product, possibly offering different varieties to cater to the wants of different user groups.

Monopolistic Competition and the Demand Curve

In monopolistic competition there are a large number of sellers of a product but from the point of view of the buyers the product of each seller is in some way differentiated from the product of other sellers. The shape of the demand curve faced by the firm under monopolistic competition can be easily deduced from product differentiation. In the absence of product differentiation the firms shall be selling a standardised product. In these circumstances, firm will be facing a horizontal demand curve as shown in Figure 1(a). But when each one of the large number of sellers sells a differentiated product, buyers become more or less attached to particular branch names. For example, at any given price for Cibaca Top some consumers will be on the margin of switching over to other brands, while others remain attached to Cibaca Top with different degrees of firmness.

An individual firm's demand curve under monopolistic competition will be relatively flat when viewed from the abscissa.

The demand curve which a firm normally faces in monopolistically competitive industry is highly elastic. Such a demand curve has been shown in Figure 3. Suppose the firm sells OQ quantity of its product at price OP. If the firm raises the price some consumers will switch to other brands which are relatively low priced and at the same time very good substitutes for the firm's product. It may be noted that a price rise which is not too large (PP_1) will induce all the buyers of the firm's product to abandon it completely. Similarly if the firm lowers the price below OP, it will attract marginal customers of the other sellers. It will not have to reduce price much to ensure a substantial increase in the demand for its product.

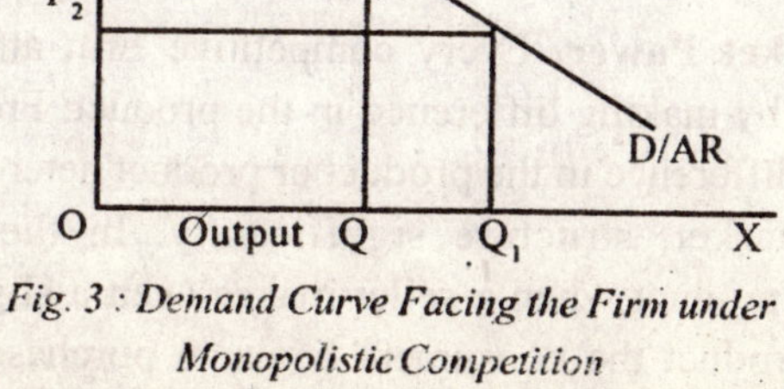

Fig. 3 : Demand Curve Facing the Firm under Monopolistic Competition

The price reductions by a firm that attract customers away from the other firms do not evoke any retaliatory action on the part of the other firms in a monopolistically competitive industry. The reason for the absence of any reaction to the price reductions by a firm is that in monopolistically competitive industry there are many firms and if some firm through its price reduction policy attracts some customers of the other firms, the loss to each of these firms is so small that it goes unnoticed. However, the gain to the firm that reduces the price may be substantial.

ELEMENTS OF MARKET CONDUCT

The term market structure refers to the type constituents and nature of an industry. It includes the relative and absolute size of firms, active in industry, easiness in the entry into business, the demand curve of the firm products etc. There are two extremities of the market structure on this basis, on one end there is a market of perfect competition and on the other perfect monopoly market. In between these two extremities there are monopolistic competition, oligopoly, duopoly etc.

(a) Seller and Buyer Concentration. Here seller concentration means in certain industry the number of active firms is very limited and these few firms produce a large part of the total supply. In other words, these firms possess the market power in a sense that any one of these firms can affect the market price by making change in the quantity of its product. In full competition, each firm produces a very small part of the total production. Hence, it cannot affect the market price. In this type of market, the seller concentration is zero. So, as we move from the perfect competitive market towards pure monopolist market, the quantity of seller concentration increases.

(b) Market Power. Every competitive firm attempts to get market power by making difference in the product. From economic point of view difference in the product or product heterogeneousness affects the market, structure significantly. In the position of homogeneous product when a seller makes even a slight change in the price of product the consumers begin to purchase the product sold by other producers. In other words the firm producing homogeneous product has to face the perfectly elastic demand curve. On the contrary in the position of heterogeneous products any single firm can increase some price without being affected due to the preferences of the consumer.

(c) Product Differentiation. In the perfect competition market all firms sell the same or homogeneous product. But in the market, in reality a single product is sold by the different producers, claiming that all products (such as toothpaste) are not same. The producers bring variety by means of brand name, packaging, size, colour, taste, weight etc. In spite of no locational differences, variety is seen by means of retailer service, home delivery, credit facility etc.

(d) Barriers in Entry. Sellers concentration indicates that how some firms acquire dominance in an industry, consequently the real competition between the firms is lessened or limited. If there are some barriers in the entry of new firms, then the prospective competition is also limited. The types of such barriers are as follows:

(i) Cost profit to the present firm which is not available to the new firms.

(ii) Legal barriers in entry.

(iii) Product difference and advertisement etc. cause the presence of strong preference among consumers for the products sold by the established firms.

(e) Other Elements. Apart from these main elements, there are some other elements to be considered. One of them is the growth rate of market demand. In this situation the firms are somewhat idle. On the contrary in a rapidly growing industry the firms also become more competitive. In the growing market every firm is struggling and striving for more demand.

If there is more elasticity of the price demand of a product, the firm will be motivated to lessen the price in order to increase ones portion in the total sale. In the condition of oligopoly when a firm decreases price other firms also do the same. Then all firms derive benefit in the condition of more elastic demand. If the product demand is inelastic no firm will tend to change price.

Market Performance

Market performance means the evaluation of the derivation of the behaviour of any industry when it behaves differently than the established superior laws of the market. It is assumed that in the position of the perfect competition only an industry can perform well. But when the market is derivated from the condition of perfect competition, then the market behaviour also changes.

Now the question arises, as to how a market performance can be evaluated in any industry? Certain acceptable indicators are as follows:

1. Profitability. As we already know all firms have an objective like profitability, profit maximisation or satisfactory level of profit. But profitability in any industry does not depend only upon the performance of the firm. It also depends upon monopolist power, product diversity, or inefficient use of resources etc. Economists have used the hypothesis of normal profit. It is the rate of profit which makes the firm not to leave the industry. The performance level affects the quantity of profit significantly.

2. Productivity. It is an index of production of per unit input used, if more production is possible by the same units then there is growth in productivity. Growth in production is an indicator of efficient performance of an industry. But this index is also not without practical shortcomings. Till we can not keep the other factors stable, it is difficult to measure productivity of certain means/ inputs, like labour on capital. Besides this the units of labour, capital, or land are heterogeneous, so when a change occurs in the quantity of an input, there is also a change in its quality. For example when we recruit more workers, first we recruit more skilled ones and then the less skilled.

3. Growth. Information about the performance of an industry can be derived from its growth rate also. The measure of growth rate of an industry can be known from the product, employment and wealth creation. But every index creates problems in measuring the performance. For example, it is possible that in an industry more and more people get employment, or there is a rapid rate of wealth accumulation. But it is also possible that the resources are not efficiently used. Likewise when the growth rate is high we do not have information of production cost, whether it is more or less.

4. Effect on Index. Now the question arises whether the market structure affects the indexes of market performance. Profitability is one of the many indicators of performance. For example in perfect competition, a firm earns normal profit in long term while in monopoly or market having monopolist power, the firm earns extra-normal profit in long term also. Excessive seller concentration, barriers in entry and product difference can make firm earn more profit in long term also. Likewise we take growth index. Both in monopoly and oligopoly markets firm produces less than its capacity or there is a position of extra capacity.

5. Ill Effect on Firm's Growth. Thus, the growth of the firm is affected adversely. Productivity and efficiency are associated with each other. In the position of monopoly and oligopoly a firm has extra capacity which means inefficient use of resources and low level of productivity. Lastly, the social performance of a firm is also affected by market structure. In monopoly and perfect competition, consumer and labour, both are exploited. Growth in competition decreases the power of exploitation of the producers.

6. Social Performance. The performance level of an industry can be evaluated in the item of many social bases. These social bases can be income redistribution or other indicators of social welfare. For example the social performance of the medicine industry can be measured by the decrease in the illness period or death rate. If the expansion/growth of any industry results in decrease of present inequalities of income in society, or it helps in reducing poverty or unemployment then the performance level of the industry can be called high.

PRICE DETERMINED UNDER PERFECT COMPETITION

As is popularly known, prices under perfect competition are determined by the forces of supply and demand.

Responses to a change in demand or to a change in supply may be primarily either in price on in quality. If the demand is highly elastic, consumers will respond readily to price changes by dropping out of the market when prices are raised a little and by coming in and increasing purchases when prices are lowered a little. As a result, most of the adjustments to changes in supply (an increase leading to reduction in price and a decrease leading to an increase in price) will be adjustments in quantity purchased if the demand is highly elastic. If the demand is inelastic the adjustments will take place primarily in prices. Similarly, if sellers respond readily by greatly increasing their offerings on slight increase in price, or by heavy withdrawals on slight price drop, the adjustments to changes in demand will be large

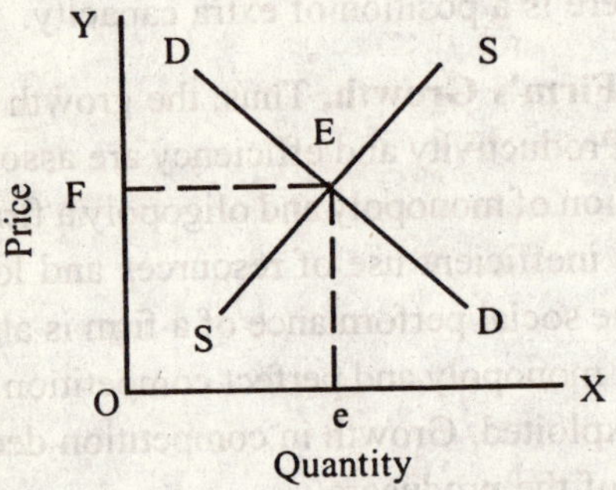

in quantity exhchanged. If sellers are quite unresponsive to price in their offerings (if supply is very inelastic) the adjustments to changes in demand will take place largely through shift in price. In view of the above, we may state the following rules and illustrate them:

1. If demand rises, price goes up and vice versa.

2. If supply rises, price goes down and vice versa.

3. Given a shift in the demand curve, price will rise less or fall less if the supply curve is elastic (flat);

4. Given a shift in the supply curve, price will rise less or fall less if demand curve is elastic;

5. If both the demand and supply increase, sales are bound to increase but price may or may not rise.

6. An increase in demand with a simultaneous decrease in supply will raise price and increase sales if the new demand price for the old equilibrium amount is higher than its new supply price.

Effect of Time in Determination of Price

In a dynamic economy the study pertaining to the role of time element in the determination of price is of great significance. Prof. Thomas writes "Time plays an important part in economic theories. It is of special importance in relation to the problem of value. If society were static, that of production, but society is dynamic. Habits, tastes and fashions are continually changing, while methods and volumes of production vary frequently.

Prof. Marshal was the first to explore the role of time element in price determination. He believed that unstable equilibrium is attained by the demand and supply forces in the short-run. As the time elapses equilibrium becomes stable. Pr·ce during the short period can be higher or lower than the cost of production, but the longer the period, the more will be the tendency for price being equal to the cost of production.

It is difficult to draw a correct line of demarcation between the short and long period. Prof. Marshall states, "Just as we contrast civilized with uncivilized races, and establish many general prepositions about either group, though no hard and fast division can be drawn between the two, so we contrast long and short periods without attempting any rigid demarcation between them."

From the point of view of price determination, Marshall has divided time element into four periods:

(i) Very short period. A very short period is a market condition where the supply remains perfectly inelastic. Time is so short that where the supply remains perfectly inelastic. Time is so short that additional units of a commodity cannot be produced. What will be the time limit is a very short period depends upon the nature of an occupation. In an automatic plant it can be a few hours and in agriculture it may be of a few months. Supply being static, the price is governed solely by the changes in demand. Larger the demand higher the price, and smaller the demand lower the price. It can be explained by means of a diagram as shown is Fig.

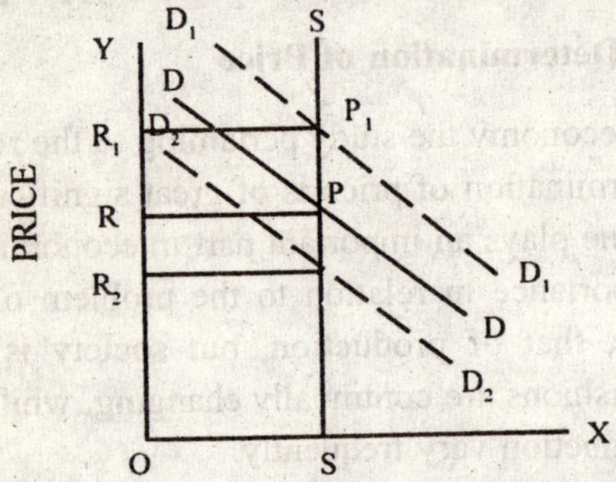

Fig. 4

In Fig. DD is the original demand curve and SS the supply curve which shows a perfectly inelastic curve. At OR price, OS units can be sold and purchased. Increase in demand shifts the demand curve to D_1D_1 and the price also increases to OR_1. Fall in the demand shifts the demand curve to the left to D_2D_2 and the price also falls to OR_2.

(ii) Short period. In a short period time is limited. New firms cannot be set up and the techniques of production cannot be altered. By making intensive use of existing resources, and increasing the number of working hours supply can be increased to some extent. According to Stigler, "Economists generally defined the short run as the period within which the rate of supply from given plants is variable but the number and size of plants is fixed."

The supply curve of individual firms is perfectly inelastic but that of the whole industry is elastic. In short period demand plays much greater role than the supply in price determination. This can be explained by means of a diagram as follows:

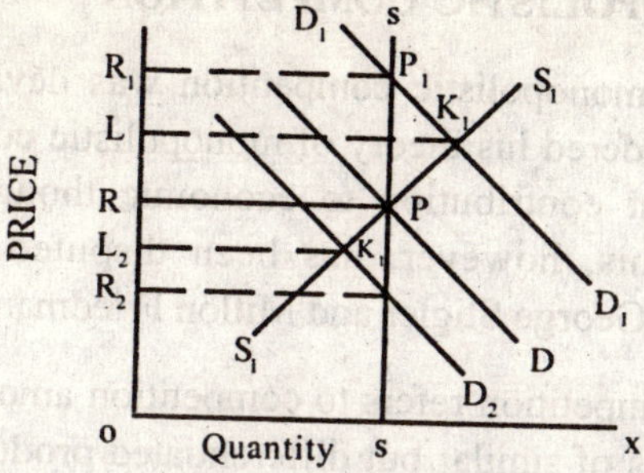

Fig. 5

In Fig., P is the original equilibrium point and OR the equilibrium price. Increase in demand shifts the demand curve to D_1D_1 and the price also increases to OR_1. High price induces the sellers to increase supply. Supply curve shifts to S_1S_1. As a result of this, the price comes down to OL. It is clear that the increase in demand is more than the increase in supply.

(iii) Long period. Long period is a situation in which supply can adjust itself to the changing demand. The number and size of firms can vary in response to the change in demand. If demand for a particular commodity is increasing, many new firms will be induced to enter the market. Likewise the existing firms may raise there scale of production. Conversely, if demand is decreasing, supply can also contract to adjust itself to demand. Possibility of change in supply in response to a change in demand makes supply the dominant factor in price determination. According to Prof. Marshall. "As a general rule, the shorter the period which we are considering, the greater must be the share of our attention which is given to the influence of demand on value, and the longer the period the more important will be the influence of cost of production on value." Long period price is also known as the normal price.

(iv) Very long period. The time is so long that a full account can be taken of the changes in income, taste, fashion and even technology etc. Supply can be fully adjusted to the changing demand. Supply can be increased by changing the techniques of production, making use of new inventions etc. The price in the very long period is governed by the cost of production. Price under this period is called secular price.

MONOPOLISTIC COMPETITION

The concept of monopolistic competition was developed by Chamberlin who considered his theory of monopolistic competition as the most important contribution to economic thought in the twentieth century. This, however, has been disputed by some economists, including George Stigler and Mitlon Friedman.

> Monopolistic competition refers to competition among a large number of sellers of similar but differentiated products which means that the products sold by different firms are close, but not perfect, substitutes for one other.

According to Chamberlin, neither model of perfect competition nor of monopoly could explain market behaviour of such business firms. He argued, "Monopolistic competition is a challenge to the traditional view point of economics that competition and monopoly are alternatives and that individual prices are to be explained in terms of neither the one or the other. By contrast, it is held that most economic situations are composites of both competition and monopoly, and that, wherever this is the case, a false view is given by neglecting either one of the forces and regarding the situation as made up entirely (even though "imperfect") of the other."

Characteristics of Monopolistic Competition

There are three main characteristcs of monopolistic competition : First, the number of business firms under monopolistic competition is so large that no firm is dependent on other firms. This implies that each firm can take decisions more or less independently and need not worry much about the reactions of other firms producing similar products. Second, the products of the various firms in a monopolistically competitive market are similar but differentiated which means that they are close but not perfect substitutes. According to Chamberlin, product differentiation is the basic characteristic of monopolisitc competition and, in fact, it is this characteristic which distinguishes monopolistic competition from perfect competition. Product differentiation does not mean that there are necessarily real differences in the products of different firms. Quite often the differences are imaginary. Consider some of the popular soft drinks presently available in the country. Coca Cola, Pepsi Cola, Campa Cola and Thums up are similar but differentiated products.

According to Chamberlin, different firms producing similar but not homogeneous products constitute a 'group'. He defines the group thus: "The group contemplated is one which has ordinarily been regarded as composing one imperfectly competitive market : A number of automobile manufacturers, of producers of pots and pans, of magazine publishers, or of retail shoe dealers. From our point of view, each producer within the group is a monopolist, yet his market is interwoven with those of his competitors, and he is no longer to be isolated from them." The concept of group is thus different from that of an industry which is a collection of firms producing a homogeneous good."

Third, under monopolistic competition, there is freedom of entry in the sense of a freedom to produce substitutes. Chamberlin has argued that since "free entry" in its fullest sense implies that every producer could if he wanted to produce commodities completely identical to those of any other producer, it is quite incompatible with monopolistic competition.

Basic Assumptions

Chamberlin's theory of monopolistic competition accepts practically all the assumptions of perfect competition. There is only one difference between the two. Whereas perfect competition assumes that all firms produce homogeneous products, there is product differentiation under monopolistic competition. In brief, the assumptions of monopolistic competition are as under:

(1) The number of buyers and sellers in the 'group' is sufficiently large.

(2) The goods offered by different producers though different are close substitutes.

(3) The firm operates with the belief that it definitely processes information regarding the demand curve of its product and the cost curve.

(4) There is freedom of entry (freedom to produce substitutes) and exit of firms in the group.

(5) The sole object of the firm is to maximise profits in the short-run and the long-run.

(6) The long-run is constituted of several short periods which are free from one another. The implication of this statement is that the decisions of some particular short period neither affect the decisions of the future periods nor are, in turn, affected by the decision of any previous period. However, the optimum decisions of any period are valid for the other periods as well. Thus, if the firm maximises its profits in the short-run, its profits in the long-run will also be maximum.

(7) The most heroic assumption made by Chamberlin is that the demand and cost curves of all goods produced by the firms constituting the 'group' are identical or uniform. Chamberlin admits that this assumption is unreal but considers it useful from the point of view of simplifying the analysis of group equilibrium. However, his 'heroic' assumption leads "to a model which is very restrictive, since it precludes the inclusion in the 'group' of similar products which have different costs of production."

SHORT-RUN EQUILIBRIUM IN MONOPOLISTIC COMPETITION

As discussed above, there are a number of firms operating under monopolistic competition. The goods produced by them are different but substitutes. Therefore, though all these goods will fall under one 'product group', their cost and demand curves will be different from one another. This is a complex situation and Chamberlin has made a simplifying assumption that all firms have identical demand and cost functions. We shall first follow Chamberlin and analyse the monopolistically competitive market behaviour in terms of a firm which is similar to other firms belonging to 'a product group'.

Short-Run Equilibrium with Chamberlin's Heroic Assumptions

Chamberlin has used average cost curve and two different demand curves in his model. The first demand curve designated as DD is based on the assumption that the prices of competing firms in the group are always the same as the price of the firm being analysed. It is called the pro-rata (share-of-the-market) demand curve because it shows that the demand for the firm's product at each price is a fractional part of the demand for the general class of the product. If there are 100 sellers, it will show a demand at each price which will be exactly 1/100 of the total demand at that price. The second demand curve designated as dd is based on the assumption that the prices of the competitors remain fixed. It is thus called the perceived demand curve. Chamberlin has not used marginal cost and marginal revenue curves, but they are implicit in his analysis. Following Joan Robinson who has used both marginal cost and marginal revenue curves explicity, we shall include these curves in our exposition.

In Figure 6, we have drawn DD and dd demand curves of the representative or "typical" firm. The pro-rata demand curve, DD shows the quantity that will be purchased at each price from this firm

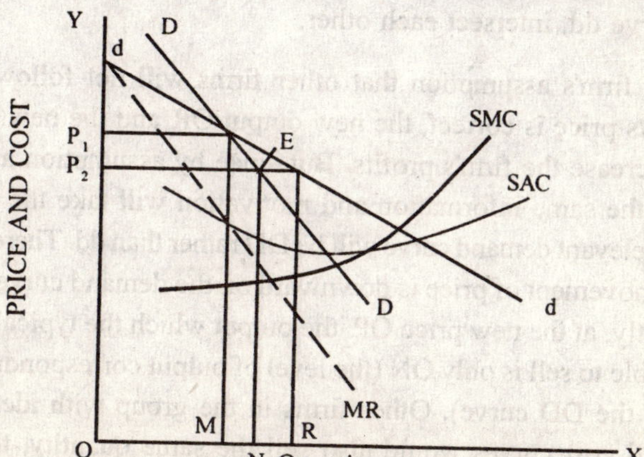

Fig. 6 Initial price and output decisions

when its price remains always the same as the prices of its competitors. The perceived demand curve, dd shows the amount that will be purchased at each price from the typical firm when its price is either higher or lower than the prices of its competitors. Only at the point of intersection of the two demand curves the price of the typical firm will be the same as that of the competitors. Using these two demand curves, it is possible to analyse the determination of the short-run equilibrium position of the representative firm under monopolistic competition. The two other curves relevant for the analysis are short-run marginal cost (SMC) and marginal revenue (MR) curves. The short-run average cost (SAC) curve is not relevant to determine short-run equilibrium of the firm. However, it is relevant to show whether at the equilibrium price firm makes profits or not.

In Figure (6), the initial market price is OP_1 at which the firm is selling OM quantity of the product. Now if the firm assumes that other firms will not react to any change in its price, the dd curve will become the relevant demand curve for the decision making and the firm's attempt will be to operate as a monopolist given this demand curve. Since the objective of the firm is to maximise its profits, it will produce OR quantity of the product to sell it at OP_2 price, because at this output level the short-run marginal cost curve, SMC and the marginal revenue curve (MR) which has been derived from the demand curve dd, intersect each other.

If the firm's assumption that other firms will not follow any change in its price is correct, the new output OR and the new price OP_2 will increase the firm's profits. But since by assumption all the firms with the same information and motivation will take the same action, the relevant demand curve will be DD rather than dd. Therefore, the actual movement of price is downward on the demand curve DD. Consequently, at the new price OP_2 the output which the typical firm would be able to sell is only ON (the level of output corresponding to point E on the DD curve). Other firms in the group with identical demand and cost curves would also sell the same quantity, that is ON. At price OP_2 all the firms in the product group earn economic profits (profits over and above normal profits) because price OP_2 is higher than the average cost of producing the output ON.

Figure 7 shows the situation that results from the determination of price at the level OP_2 in Figure 6. Since at this price all firms in the group are selling their products, the demand curve dd slips downward along the demand curve DD until it intersects the latter at the price OP_2. The reasoning followed earlier can now be repeated. Again the typical firm making assumption that other firms in the group will not follow any change in its price, behaves like a monopolist with the demand curve dd and attempts to sell an output OR_1 at the price OP_3. It may be noted that OR_1 is the output level at which the firm's short-run marginal cost is equal to its marginal revenue derived from demand curve dd. However, under monopolistic competition no firm can behave like a monopolist. Any change in the price by a firm will surely be followed by other firms. Therefore, other firms also cut their price to OP_3, which means that it is the demand curve DD, rather than the demand curve dd which is relevant. Each firm in the group thus sells only ON_1 output at the price OP_3 (point corresponding to OP_3 price on DD curve is E). Since this price is higher than the average cost of producing ON_1 quantity of the product, each firm earns economic profits.

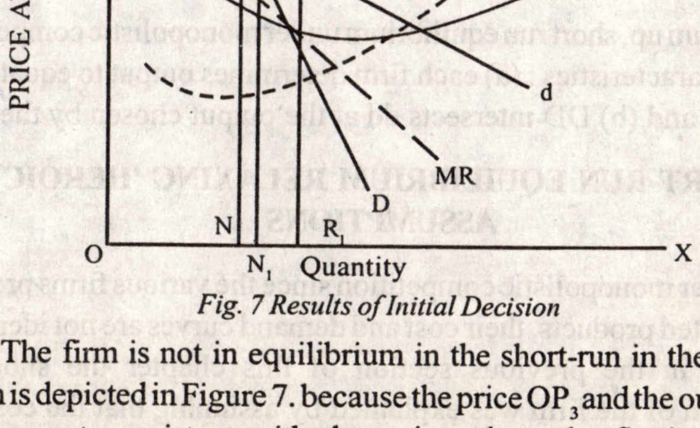

Fig. 7 Results of Initial Decision

The firm is not in equilibrium in the short-run in the situation which is depicted in Figure 7. because the price OP_3 and the output level ON_1 are not consistent with the point where the firm's perceived marginal revenue is equal to its short-run marginal cost. Therefore, the typical firm once again has the incentive to alter its selling price and other firms will have the motivation to follow it. This process will continue until the conditions shown in Figure 8, are realised. In Figure 8, the typical firm produces OA quantity of the product and

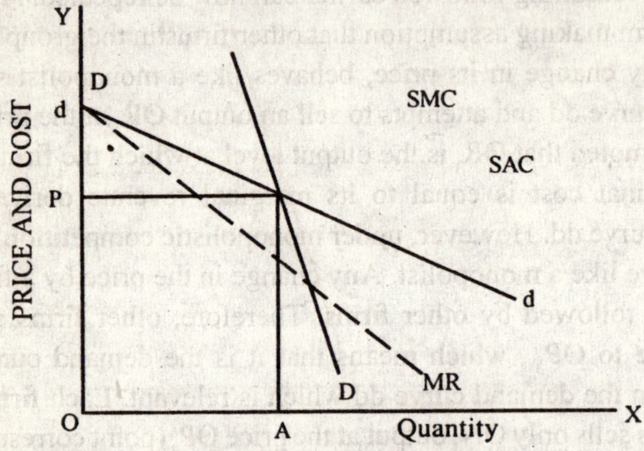

Fig. 8 : Short-run equilibirum

sells it at the price OP. This represents the short-run equilibrium position for the typical firm and also for each firm in the product group because at the output level OA the perceived marginal revenue MR equals the short-run marginal cost SMC and the curve DD intersects *dd* at this output level. Figure 8 shows that in the short-run equilibrium position, the typical firm is earning economic profits. However, this is not necessary.

To sum up, short run equilibrium under monopolistic competition has two characteristics : (a) each firm determines output to equate MR and SMC, and (b) DD intersects dd at the output chosen by the firm.

SHORT-RUN EQUILIBRIUM RELAXING 'HEROIC' ASSUMPTIONS

Under monopolistic competition since the various firms produce differentiated products, their cost and demand curves are not identical. However, in the previous section of this chapter the short-run equilibrium of the firm was explained by assuming that the cost and demand curves of all the firms belonging to a product group are identical. Now we relax this assumption which means that we regard that cost and demand curves of different firms under monopolistic competition are not identical and as a result each firm will determine a price for its product which will be different from the prices of the differentiated products of other firms but difference in these prices may not be large.

Of the many firms constituting a product group we shall now concentrate our attention on the equilibrium of only two of them in the discussion that will follow.

Like other firms, the two firms selected by us will also try to maximise their profits or minimise their losses. Therefore, they will fix

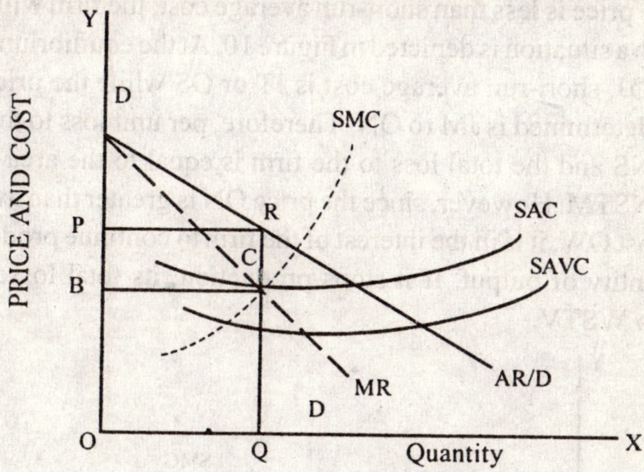

Fig. 9 : Short-run equilibrium of a profit earning firm under monopolistic competition.

the output and price at that level which maximises their profits or minimises their losses. As we know, maximisation of profit requires that the level of production should be pushed to the point where the short-run marginal cost (SMC) becomes equal to the marginal revenue (MR). It is important to remember in this context that in the short-run, price should be greater than average variable cost. This is due to the reason that if price is less than the average variable cost, the firm will stop production. Equilibrium of a firm under monopolistic competition in the short-run can be understood with the help of Figure 9. In this figure, the short-run average cost (SAC), average variable cost

(SAVC) and marginal cost (SMC) curves are all 'U' shaped. The slope of the demand curve (AR/D) is negative, and accordingly, the marginal revenue (MR) curve also slopes downward from left to right.

Since short-run marginal cost and marginal revenue are equal at output OQ, this is the equilibrium level of output. In this situation the price to be determined will be QR or OP. The short-run average cost at this output level is QC or OB. Therefore, per unit economic (supernormal) profit is OP–OB =BP and the total economic profit that the firm earns over and above the normal profit is BP × OQ which is equal to the area of the rectangle BPRC.

If the price is less than short-run average cost, the firm will incur a loss. Such a situation is depicted in Figure 10. At the equilibrium level of output OJ, short-run average cost is JT or OS while the price that would be determined is JM ro ON. Therefore, per unit loss to the firm is MT or NS and the total loss to the firm is equal to the area of the rectangle NSTM. However, since the price ON is greater than average variable cost OW, it is in the interest of the firm to continue production of OJ quantity of output. If it stops production, its total losses will increase to WSTV.

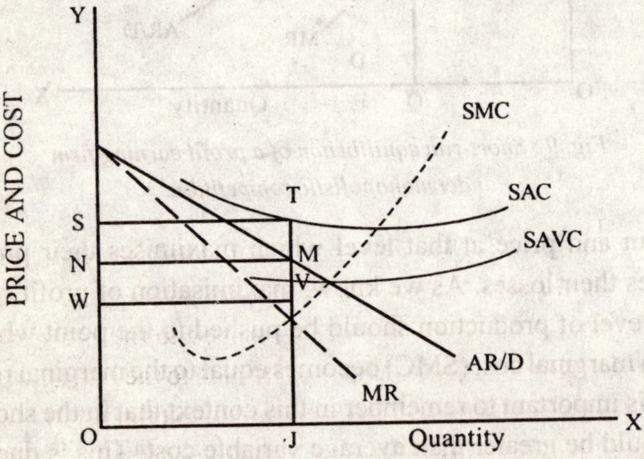

Fig. 10 : Short-run equilibrium of a firm incurring a loss under monopolistic competition

All other firms in the product-group will determine their prices like these two firms. Since each firm in the group seeks its own profit maximising position, it equates it own short-run marginal cost to its own marginal revenue. Yet the prices charged by different firms will not be substantially different.

LONG-RUN EQUILIBRIUM IN MONOPOLISTIC COMPETITION

As already stated earlier in this chapter, firms under monopolistic competition do not produce perfectly homogenerous goods. Therefore, Chamberlin perfers to call them as constituting a 'group' rather than an 'industry'. The task of deciding the equilibrium of a group is more difficult and complex than that of deciding the equilibrium of an industry. Firms falling in a group indulge in product differentiation. As a result, the consumers purchase goods produced by different producers according to their own preferences. Therefore, demand for goods produced by different producers has to be different as regards quantity and elasticity. Thus, their demand curves are different. Their cost curves also differ from one another due to their different levels of efficiency. This shows that determining the equilibrium of the group is a complex task. To simplify matters, Chamberlin makes the following 'heroic' assumptions:

(1) Firms falling under the group produce very close substitutes.

(2) Demand curves of all the firms have the same nature and elasticity. This implies that all firms have an equal share in the market.

(3) The number of firms in the group is so large that each firm regards itself as independent from the behaviour of other firms. The implication of this assumption is that the price and output decisions of a particular firm affect other firms in an insignificant manner and thus it pays no attention to them.

(4) All firms possess the same level of skill and efficiency, and therefore, their cost curves are similar in nature.

Of these heroic four assumptions, the first three are known as uniformity assumptions, while the last one is known as the symmetry assumption. All these four assumptions are cruical in Chamberlin's analysis.

Long-Run Equilibrium with Heroic Assumptions

If the firms under monopolistic competition are able to earn some economic profits (in addition to the normal profits) in the short run and it is hoped that these profits will accrue in the future as well, new firms will be attracted to this field of production. These new firms will produce some other (new) substitutes of the existing products. As a result, the demand for the products of the existing firms will decline on the one hand, and on the other the prices of resources (raw material, labour, etc.,) will increase due to their increased demand. The operation of these two forces will wipe away the economic (monopolistic) profits and all the firms constituting the group will earn only normal profits.

Firms of the group can also incur losses in the short-run. If there are certain firms which do not hope to improve their performance in the long-run they will close down their business. The buyers of the products of these firms will shift over to other producers. As a result, the price of the good in question will increase. The exit of some firms will also force down the prices of resources required for production. Due to the operation of these two factors—increase in the price of the good and fall in the prices of resources required for production—the price will become equal to the average cost in the long-run and all firms will get only normal profits.

Long-run equilibrium of firms constituting the group is exhibited in Figure. On the basis of Chamberlin's heroic assumptions all these firms have identical demand and cost curves. Therefore, their equilibrium positions will be same. Figure (11) shows both dd and DD demand curves of the typical firm. The demand curve dd is the firm's perceived demand curve which implies that the firm looks at demand with an assumption that any change in the price of its product will not be followed by competing firms. Demand curve DD assumes that prices of the competing firms will be the same as that of the typical firm. In the long-run the typical firm and also the competing firms will earn only normal profits because under monopolistic competition entry of new firms to the product group is uninhibited. As new firms enter, the demand curve DD will move to the left until economic profits are reduced to zero.

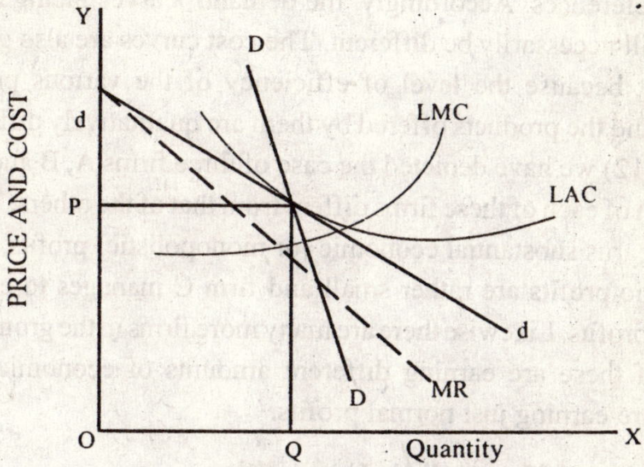

Fig. 11 : Long-run equilibrium

Shifting of demand curve DD to the left requires an explanation. The demand curve DD, in fact, indicates the proportional demand for the firm's product which means that if in a product group there are 100 firms, then the demand for the product of each firm will be 1/100 of the total demand for the products of all the firms belonging to the product group. Assuming that total demand remains constant, entry of new firms to the product group will reduce the demand for the product of each firm. Let us now assume that 20 new firms have joined the product group and as a result the demand for the product of each firm would be reduced to 1/120 of the total demand. This will cause a leftward shift in the demand curve DD.

The long-run equilibrium is thus obtained when each firm in the product group receives only normal profits. This condition is satisfied when *(a)* the demand curve dd is tangent to the long-run average cost curve, and *(b)* the demand curve DD intersects both dd and the long-run average cost curve at the point of tangency.

Diversities of Demand and Costs

Now let us abandon the assumption that demand and cost curves of different firms constituting the group are identical. The fact is that the buyers are never neutral between different producers. They have clear preferences. Accordingly, the demand curves facing different firms will necessarily be different. The cost curves are also generally different because the level of efficiency of the various producers differs and the products offered by them are qualitatively different. In Figure (12) we have depicted the case of three firms A, B and C. The situation of each of these firms differs from that of the others. Whereas firm A earns substantial economic (or monopolistic) profits, firm B's economic profits are rather small and firm C manages to earn only normal profits. Likewise there are many more firms in the group. While some of these are earning different amounts of economic profits, others are earning just normal profits.

Evaluation of Monopolistic Competition

Chamberlin's theory of monopolistic competition is highly controversial and even more than sixty years after the publication of the Theory of Monopolistic Competition economists are unable to agree on the significance of Chamberlin's theory. We shall now briefly discuss the major criticisms of the theory of monopolistic competition.

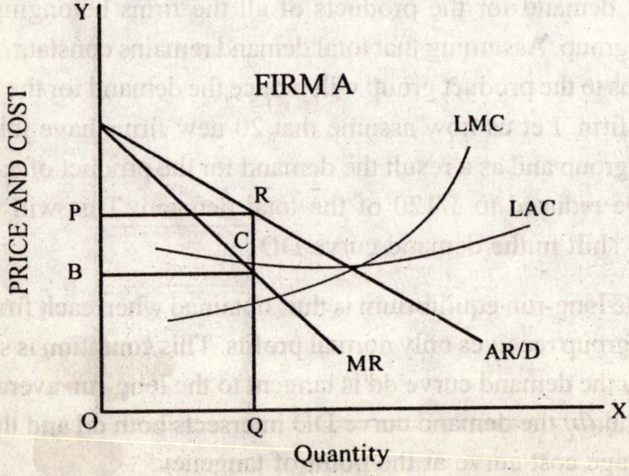

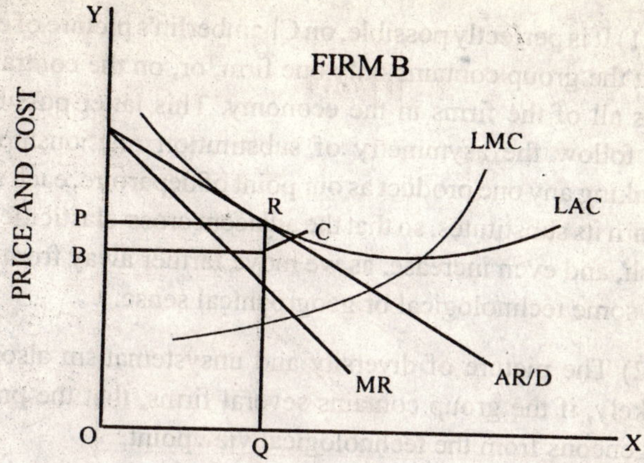

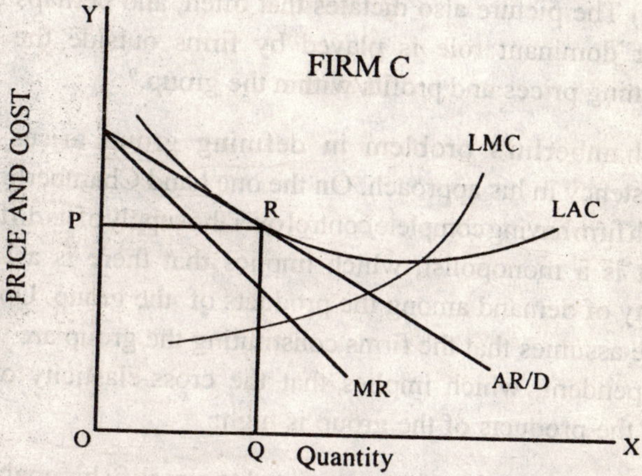

Fig. 12. Long-run equilibrium—diversities of demand and costs

The most severe critic of Chamberlin's theory is George Stigler. According to him, the concept of 'group' in Chamberlin's theory is ambiguous. In defining the perfectly competitive model we assume that all firms selling a homogeneous product constitute an industry. In monopolistic competition, the precise boundaries of an industry cannot be determined because of the lack of homogeneity in the product. Chamberlin has used the term "group" as a broad equivalent to an industry. Stigler focusses on three implications of Chamberlin's definition of the group:

"(1) It is perfectly possible, on Chamberlin's picture of economic life, that the group contains only one firm, or, on the contrary, that it includes all of the firms in the economy. This latter possibility can readily follow the asymmetry of substitution relationships among firms; taking any one product as our point of departure, each substitute has in turn its substitutes, so that the adjacent cross-elasticities may not diminish, and even increase, as we move farther away from the 'base' firm in some technological or geogrpahical sense.

(2) The picture of diversity and unsystematism also makes it very likely, if the group contains several firms, that the products be heterogeneous from the technological viewpoint.

(3) The picture also dictates that often, and perhaps usually, a large or dominant role is played by firms outside the group in determining prices and profits within the group."

Chamberlin's problem in defining group arises from an inconsistency in his approach. On the one hand Chamberlin assumes that each firm having complete control over the supply of its differentiated product is a monopolist, which implies that there is a low cross-elasticity of demand among the products of the group. On the other hand he assumes that the firms constituting the group are very much interdependent, which implies that the cross-elasticity of demand among the products of the group is high.

Chamberlin, therefore, attempted to simplify his analysis which he thought was possible by assuming that both demand and cost curves for all the products are identical throughout the group. This is known as the uniformity assumption. A second simplifiying assumption known as the symmetry assumption is that the impact of changes by any firm in any of the decision variables affects so many firms that non of them reacts.

PRICE DISCRIMINATION UNDER MONOPOLY

In case of simple monopoly, the monopolist charges a single price from all buyers in all markets. But a monopolist does not always charge the same prices from all the purchasers of his commodity or service. He charges different prices from different classes of people. He may divide his sale among a number of markets and charge a different price in each market. This peculiar feature of monopoly is known as price discrimination or differential pricing. In the words of **Beneham.** "Monopolist may be able, however, to divide his sales among a number of different markets and to charge a different price in each market."

Forms of Price Discrimination

There are three forms of price discrimination :

(a) Personal discrimination;

(b) Local or geographical discrimination; and

(c) Trade or purpose discrimination.

(a) Personal Discrimination. When a monopolist charges different prices from different classes of people for same type of services it is personal discrimination. Railways charging different fares from different classes of ticket-holders or a monopolist doctor charging more consultation fee from rich people and less consultation fee from poor people are examples of personal price discrimination.

(b) Local or Geographical Discrimination. Discrimination is local when for the same commodity a monopolist charges a higher price at one place and a lower price at the other place. For example, a monopolist may sell his goods in another country at a price much lower than that he charges from the buyers in his own country. This practice, on the part of the monopolist is known as dumping. Dumping may be practised for several motives, viz., *(a)* to dispose of surplus stocks; *(b)* to capture new markets; and *(c)* to develop new trade relation with other countries.

(c) Trade or Purpose Discrimination. Discrimination is according to trade or purpose when a monopolist charges different price for his commodity according to the uses to which the commodity is put. For example, the monopolist sells electricity at different prices according to its uses. He charges more per unit of consumption for domestic purposes than for industrial purposes.

Price discrimination may also be adopted on other basis such as income, tastes, age group etc.

Objectives of Price Discrimination

(1) Through the device of price discrimination, the monopolist aims at maximising his monopoly revenue. He divides his sale in different markets and charges as high a price from each market as he can possibly charge taking other relevant factors into account. Thus from market he gets the maximum monopoly revenue. He charges higher prices from those who can afford to pay high prices and lower from those who can not pay high prices. Thus he squeezes out the maximum from the society. The monopolist charges on 'what the traffic can bear' principle.

(2) Another objective of price discrimination may be to dispose off his surplus stock in foreign markets at lower prices.

(3) He may want to drive his rivals out of the market by offering commodities and services at very low prices or at dumping prices. (*i.e.*, at a price much below the cost) and may charge higher prices in other markets to make up the losses. The main purpose behind this type of behaviour is to capture the market for himself.

(4) The object of price discrimination may be to develop a new market. The monopolists charge rather lower prices in order to establish in the new market and may charge somewhat higher price in already established markets.

(5) Where monopolist could not utilise the plant to its full capacity, he can increase the production of the commodity by utilising the unutilised capacity and offer the commodity at lower prices in some new-national or international-market.

Conditions for Price Discrimination

The fundamental condition for success of price discrimination is the assumption of monopoly. Therefore, the price discrimination is impossible under perfect competition:

(a) Market Segmentation. The first condition is that it should not be possible for the buyer in one market to transfer themselves to the other market. For example, the doctor is successful in his policy of charging higher prices from the rich because the rich cannot become poor to avail of the concession given to the poor patients.

(b) Markets Sealing. The second condition is that it should not be possible to transfer a unit of commodity from low priced market to high priced market otherwise the purchaser shall not buy from the monopolist *i.e.*, from the dear market but purchase in the cheap market.

(c) Multiple Demand Elasticities. The other necessary condition is that the consumer's elasticities of demand for the commodity should not be equal. The monopolist can charge different prices for the same commodity in different market on the assumption that there is variation in elasticity of demand for the commodity in different market. He can charge higher price in the market where demand is inelastic and lower price in the markets where demand is elastic.

Determination of Price and Output Under Discriminating Monopoly

In monopoly the problem of a producer is to maximise his total profits in different market. A monopolist will maximise his profits when the marginal revenues in each of the two markets are equal and at the same time they are also equal to the marginal costs of the monopolists entire output.

Let us suppose, the monopolist has two markets I and II. The average revenue curves or demand curves in the two markets are AR_1 and AR_2 respectively. The corresponding marginal revenue curves in two markets are MR_1 and MR_2 respectively. These markets have different elasticities of demand at each price. The marginal cost curve is same for both the market. Now the monopolist has to determine his entire output regardless of how it is distributed. For this he has to follow the profit maximizing rule MR = MC. The total (combined) marginal revenue curve (ΣMR) and marginal cost curve are shown in Panel (c) of the diagram given below.

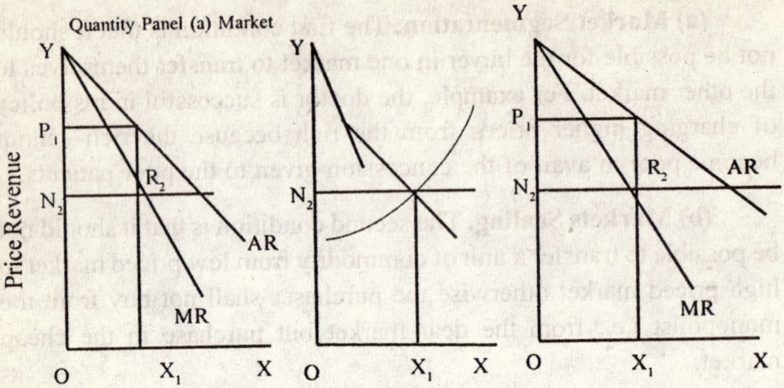

Fig. 13.

In the diagram the monopolist is in equilibrium at point 'R' where MC = ΣMR and equilibrium level of output is OX. Now the problem before the monopolist is how to distribute the output OX between the two markets I and II. For this he will follow the rule $MR_1 = MR_2 = MC = \Sigma MR$. Following this principle, the discriminating monopolist will sell OX_1 output in market I and OX_2 output in market II. With this distribution of total output marginal revenue in market I (OM_1) is equal to marginal revenue in market II (ON_2). The equilibrium points of market I and market II are E_1 and E_2 respectively. The prices charged by the monopolist from market I and marekt II are OP_1 and OP_2 respectively.

OLIGOPOLY

Oligopoly refers to a market situation with a few (but more than two) sellers. Under oligopoly, the industry is dominated by a few firms who are producing an identical product or producing close substitutes but not perfect substitutes. Oligopoly has been variously called as limited competition, incomplete monopoly or multiple monopoly etc. But these days the term oligopoly is used popularly to refer competition among the few. An oligopoly situation may emerge in any industry when :

(a) Economies of scale or advantages of large scale production exit-as a result, a few firms are able to supply all or much of the total industry output (steel industry, automobiles, cement, petroleum industries in India are good examples).

(b) Superior entrepreneurs reduce the large number of firms into a few, through mergers and holding companies.

(c) The exclusive ownership of patents and other rights by a few firms or exploitation of the advantages of product differentiation creates oligopoly market.

(d) The controlling power of a few firms over the available national resources reduces competition only to a few firms.

(e) The need for heavy investment of capital in some industries prevents the entry of larger number of firms.

Generally in an oligopoly market, there are a few well established firms with products well-known in the market. It might be really different for a new entrant to popularise its new product against the already established product.

Classification of Oligopolies

Oligopolies have been classified into various types:

(a) On the basis of competitors into the industry oligopoly may be closed or open one. Open oligopoly permits free and easy entry of new firms while closed oligopoly does not allow entry of new firms and the industry is closely controlled by a few well entrenched firms.

(b) On the basis of the nature of the product produced and marketed, oligopolies are distinguished between pure and differentiated. Pure oligopoly refers to the situation where all the rival firms are producing an identical or homogeneous product, while differentiated oligopoly refers to market situation in which each rival is producing a different variety of a product. Petroleum industry is an example of the former and the soap industry is an example of the latter.

(c) Partial and Full Oligopoly. Depending upon the dominance by a few or a large number of firms.

(d) Collusive and non-collusive Oligopolies. Depending upon whether the competing firms are combining through some agreement or collusion between them or not.

(e) Organised and Unorganised Oligopolies. On the basis of whether they work on the basis of some agreement on prices, output quotas, sharing of the markets etc.

Features of Oligopoly

The following prominent features of oligopoly will enable us to distinguish oligopoly easily from other market situations such as perfect competitions, monopoly etc.

(i) First, every firm under oligopoly has to be conscious of the reactions of the rivals. After all there are only a few firms and what one firm does will definitely influence the others.

As the number of firms is few, any change in output produced by one firm will have a direct effect on the other who naturally, retaliate by changing their own prices, output, products etc. Each firm will have to estimate, as best as it can, the nature of its rival's reactions to its product, price and output policies. This is not so under perfect competition and monopoly.

(ii) Secondly, the oligopoly is characterised by indeterminateness. A firm does not know for certain whether its decisions regarding price and output will affect its competitors favourably or adversely. It does not know whether its competitors will approve or disapprove of its decisions and in what way, their reactions will be known. Hence the oligopoly firm's demand curve for the product is clearly indeterminate since the traditional assumption of "other things being equal" does not apply here.

(iii) Oligopoly firms may show conflicting attitudes to one another. On the one side, they may appear to realise the disadvantages of competition and rivalry and may work out some policy of collusion or they may continuously come in conflict with one another as each is interested in maximising its share of profits. One results of this conflict is the uncertainty in the minds of sellers.

(iv) Oligopoly firms resort to various aggressive or defensive marketing methods to increase their share of the market or to prevent a decline in their share of market. They resort to extensive advertisement and sales promotion. In fact there is competitive advertisement and sales promotion between them. Aggressive sales promotion by some provokes others to do the same.

(v) An oligopoly seller has some monopoly power over the product it produces (brand, name patent etc.) but it does not acquire monopoly control of the market. This is the basic difference between oligopoly and monopoly. At the same time, oligopoly restricts competitions, as there are only a few sellers, under perfect competition, the number of sellers is too many. Besides, the oligopoly producer has to be fully conscious of the reactions of his rivals. But the firm under perfect competition receives the price from the market and does not bother what the rivals think or act.

Price Determination Under Oligopoly

Generally, models of oligopoly and duopoly are based on the usual assumption of profit maximisation. In practice, however, oligopoly firms may have difficulties in attaining maximum profits. It may be remembered that maximum profit is related to the concepts of demand and cost. But under oligopoly conditions, firms lack information about the market prices and costs. Further an oligopoly firms may have consideration such as not disturbing the market conditions through constant adjustment of price and output with the idea of maximising profits or invite government interference and regulation of potential competition. Finally, the oligopoly itself may place certain restraints on firms maximising profits. These restraints may be considerations of safety, desire for stable profits and the conservative policy of large corporation which follow the principle of "live and let live".

There is no system of pricing in an oligopoly market. We have already referred to indeterminancy of oligopoly demand and the uncertainty about the reaction patterns of rivals. Naturally, it is not easy to analysis the price system under oligopoly. Economists distinguish between these different kinds of pricing under oligopoly viz., independent pricing, pricing under collusion, and pricing under price leadership.

Kinds of Pricing Under Oligopoly

1. Independent Pricing. Every firm under oligopoly may estimate the reaction and calculations of its rivals and then fix its own price and output. On the one extreme, each firm may fix a price-a monopoly price-assuming its product to be completely different from the products of all its rivals. On the other hand, if all firms are producing more or less identical products, they will fix a common or identical price for the product. In practice, however, this may not be so, as firms produce different varieties of product, have different costs of production and enjoy different shares of the market. Independent pricing, under these conditions, will lead to price wars between rivals; the ultimate result may be either price instability and continuous price wars or price stability when a satisfactory price has been found. There is bound to be antagonism, uncertainly and insecurity among the rivals and therefore, a constant tendency to come together. But in general, belief among economists is that independent pricing cannot last long and it is bound to lead to either price leadership by the leading firm or some type of collusion between the rival firms.

Generally business firms follow the "cost plus pricing" system of fixing the selling price of products. For instance, a firm may calculate its average cost of production and then add say 20 or 30 per cent when a firm produces multiple products, it may calculate only the AVC and add say 50 or 60 per cent to take care of overhead costs (AFC) and profits.

2. Pricing under Collusion. Collusion implies "to pay together." When competing firms cooperate in pricing they are said to collude. Collusion may be of various types. Open or explicit collusion is generally sanctioned by the government or tacit or implicit collusion is normally secret. Collusion may be based on agreements either oral or written. Collusion may be based on written agreements between rival producers on prices, output, divisions of sales territories etc. and creates what is known as cartels.

The cartel agreement may estimate the price to be fixed, the quantity to be produced, the allocation of markets and the sharing of markets. In case there are too many units in the industry, cartel agreement may specify the closing down of inefficient plants temporarily or permanently. In precise perfect cartel may not be practicable because:

(a) It is possible that some of the firms in the industry may not join the cartel organization.

(b) Even if all the firms are members of the cartel agreements it is possible that new rivals may not become a party to such an agreement.

(c) The distribution of profits among members may be source of dissatisfaction and may result in the dissolution of the cartel.

(d) The collusive price may be secretly under-cut by members through special concessions, discounts and rebates.

Thus perfect collusion may not be possible in practice. Instead some form of imperfect collusion between rival oligopoly firms may be agreed upon. Most theories of oligopoly are relevant only for short period. In the long-run, industries grow or decline; economic and human resources move from one industry to another. Besides industries come under the impact of technological changes and change in consmers' tastes and preferences, the result is that there are pressures working towards the reduction of cost and prices.

❐

10

Macro Economics Concepts

The term macro economics applies to the study of relations between broad economic aggregates. It is the study of economic system as a whole. Macro economics is that branch of economic analysis which studies the behaviour of not one particular unit, but of all the units taken together, like total national income, output and employment, total consumption, saving and investment, aggregate demand and supply and general price level. A few important definitions of macro economics are given below:

Culberston, J.M., "Macro economics theory is the theory of income, employment, prices and money."

Gardner Ackley, "Macro economics deals with economic affairs in the large. It concerns the overall dimensions of economic life to use a metaphor, it studies the character of the forest independently of the trees which compose it."

Boulding, K.B., "Macro economics is that part of economics which deals with great aggregates and averages of the system rather than with particular items in it attempts to define these aggregates in a useful manner and to examine how they are related and determined."

Thus the study which analysis the determination and fluctuation of various aggregates and averages in the economy as a whole is called macro economics.

SCOPE OF MACRO ECONOMICS

The macro economics attempts to answer the truly big questions of economic life-full employment or unemployment, capacity or undercapacity production, a satisfactory or unsatisfactory rate of growth, inflation or price level stability.

The questions which provide the basis of macro economics are:

(a) What determines the rate at which the output grows?

(b) What provides employment to nation's work force?

(c) What determines the levels of a country's exports and imports?

(d) What determines the direction and the rate of change of prices?

(e) What determine the magnitude of the total output of a country during some given period of time?

(f) What determine the level of prices?

All these questions regarding the level and rate employment, income and prices indicate about the subject matter of macro economics. The answer for these questions can be given by considering the theory of income and employment, the theory of price level and the theory of economic growth. In other words, we shall be examing such aggregates as employment, output, income, consumption, investment, supply of money, general price level, exports and imports. All these areas of study are the subject matter of macro economics. The macro economics given an answer to the question how the level of employment, price and growth are determined?

Besides, macro economics study the role of government in determining the levels of employment, prices, exports, imports etc. and uses policy instruments for achieving the macro objectives.

IMPORTANCE OF MACRO ECONOMICS

According to J.K. Mehta as long as men live in a society, the economist cannot afford to neglect the study of macro economy.

The theoretical, and the practical importance of macro economics is given below:

1. Helps in the Formulation of Economic Policies. Macro economics helps in the formulation of economic policies. The days of 'laissez faire' are over and government interven in economic activities. For example, during depression level of employment and output declines continuously. Macro economics can help in finding the causes for unemployment and depression and can suggest for the adoption of suitable policies to cope with these situation.

2. Helps in Understanding and Controlling Trade Cycle. Trade cycles is feature of the capitalist form of economy. The theory of trade cycle can be understood and built up only with the help of macro economics. The understanding of this theory helps us in analysis the causes of fluctuations in income, output, and employment and suggesting remedies to control them.

3. Helps in Functioning of an Economy. The functioning of modern economy is very complex and complicated. Macro economics helps in understanding its functioning. The knowledge of the behaviour pattern ofthe aggregative variables such as consumption, saving, investment, output and national is very essential to understand the functioning of a complex economic system.

4. Helps in Understanding Micro Economics. The study of macro economics is essential for the proper understanding of micro economics. For example the demand for industry could not have been formulated with reference to the behaviour pattern of one individual's demand. The demand curve for industry was possible only after the behaviour our pattern of several individual consumers had been examined and analysed. Only then we reach at the aggregate values. Thus we can say that the knowledge of macro economics is not possible without understanding micro economics.

5. Helps in Study of Economic Development. The major problem of most of the developing countries is to accelerate the rate of economic development. Study of macro economics has shown the path of the high rate of growth. For example, it has been formed that rate of capital formation is very high in the developed countries. Therefore the developing countries should increase the rate of capital formation to accelerate the rate of growth.

6. Helps in Study of National Income. National income an aggregate concept has the importance in macro economics. National income presents the overall picture and performance of the economy within a given period. The study national income helps in comparing the performance of different regions or sectors of the economy over a period of time. It tells us the state of the people living in the economy. Without a study of national income, as a result of development in macro economics, it was not possible to formulate correct economic policies.

7. Inflation & Deflation. Most of the developing and developed worlds are facing the problem of price rise. A substantial and substained increase in the general price level is known as inflation. On the other hand, a substantial and sustained decline in the prices is known as deflation. Both these situations are associated with the general price level and this general price level is the subject matter of macro economics. Macro economics approach is of utmost importance to analyse and understand the effects of inflations and deflation. Different sections of society are affected differently as a result of changes in the value of money. Macro economic analysis enables us to take certain steps to counteract to adverse influences of inflation and deflation.

8. Helps in Nature of Material Welfare. Macro economics enables us to study the nature and size of the material welfare of the nations. The problem of measuring social welfare is not easy; even welfare economics does not help us. Those who are interested in the material and social welfare of all must study problems in their macro economics setting. This adds to the importance of macro economics because when the chief objective of the studies of economics is the welfare of entire society, economics become the study of macro economics.

LIMITATIONS OF MACRO ECONOMICS

1. False Generalisation. Despite the immense importance of macro economics, there is the danger of excessive generalisation from individual experience to the system as a whole. For example saving is a virtue for an individual but it becomes evil when all families undertake savings. Similarly, the withdrawal, by an individual from a bank do not create any harm. But if all the persons rushed to withdraw the bank would perhaps collapse.

2. Heterogeneous Elements. It may, however, be remembered that macro economics deals with such aggregates as aggregate consumption, saving, investment and income, all composed of heterogeneous quantities. Money is the only measuring rod. But the value of money itself keeps on changing rendering economic aggregates immeasurable and incomparable in real terms. As such, the sum or average of heterogeneous individual quantities lose their significance for accurate economic analysis and economic policy.

3. Excessive Aggregative Thinking. Macro economics suffers from excessive thinking in terms of aggregates, as it may not be always possible to have the homogeneous constituents. Prof. Boulding has pointed out that 12 oranges + 13 oranges = 25 oranges is a meaningful aggregate; but 12 oranges + 13 shoes constitute a meaningless aggregate; it is the last aggregate which brings forth the fallacy of excessive aggregative thinking.

4. Limited Application. Macro economics deals with positive economics in the sense of an analysis or how the aggregate theoretical models work—these are far removed from policy applications. These models explain the functioning of an economy and working of things in abstract and precise terms. Their abstraction and precision make such models unsuitable for use due to changes in significant veriables from time to time and from one situation to another.

The limitations discussed above are in the nature of practical difficulties. With the evolution of Keynes' General Theory of Income and Employment and his basic equation, $Y = C + I$; interest in the study of macro economics has depend. Significant breakthroughs in the computation of national income accounts prove it beyond doubt that the limitations of macro economic studies are not insurmountable.

BASIC CONCEPTS USED IN MACRO ECONOMIC ANALYSIS

(1) Stock and Flow Variables

The economic variables may be grouped as stock variables and flow variable. A flow variables refers to a quantity measured between two points of time. In other words, the flow variable is the rate at which production, consumption, sales, income, inflation, etc. take place between two points in time. Flow variables always require time dimension like per month, per hour, per day, per year etc. For example, Net National Product at Factor Cost *i.e.* National income is a flow variable and must represent a period of time *i.e.* year to which it belongs. We may say that the national income for the year 1994-95 is Rs. 2,82,000 crores. It means that final goods and services worth Rs. 2,82,000 crores were produced during the year 1994-95. One important point here is that flow variable is related to a specific period of time. The measurement of flow variable without specific period of time is meaning less. For example it is worthless to say that national income is Rs. 2,82,000 crores without making reference to the period of time it belongs. All the flow variables are rate of flow over some specified period of time and have time dimension.

The stock variable, on the other hand has no time dimension. A stock variables refers to a quantity measured at any given point in time. For example, the Balance-Sheet or Stock Statement shows the assets and liabilities of a business firm at a point in time. It means it is on a particular day *i.e.* on 31.3.1995. Similarly total money supply, total bank deposits, wealth, inventories, capital stock, debts etc. stock variables, are measured a particular point in time.

The main distinction between the stock and flow variables depends on the time dimensions to which the two relate. Stock variables have a time reference associated with them; while flow variables have a time dimension. Although both stock and flow variables are dated, a stock variables is different from a flow variable because a point in time is different from a period of time.

(2) Functional Relationship

The variables can be classified as dependent and independent variables. A dependent variable means a variable, the value of which depends on the value of other variables *i.e.* it varies in some unique way with the variation in some other independent variables. For example a change in price cause a change in the demand for the commodity. Hence demand is a dependent variable. On the other hand a variable is independent, the value of which influences the value of other variables. In above example price is a independent variable because it influences the value of other variables *i.e.* demand.

A functional relationship exists between two variables when they are related in such a way that the value of one depends uniquely upon the value of the other. For example,

$$D_x = f(P_x, p_1 \ldots\ldots P_{x-1}, y)$$

i.e. demand for commodity *x* is the function of price for commodity x (P_x), prices of related goods ($p_1 \ldots p_{x-1}$) and the income of the consumer (y). Here demand is the dependent variable and P_x, $p_1 \ldots p_{x-1}$ and *y* are the independent variables. Similarly,

$$C = f(y)$$

where *C* is consumption and *y* stands for income. Here consumption varies with the variation in income in some unique way. In above equation *C* is a dependent variable and *y* is an independent variable. The relationship between two variables (*C* and *Y*) and more variables (D_x and (P_x, $P_1 \ldots P_{x-1}$, y) *i.e.* between dependent and independent variables is known as functional relationship.

(3) Economic Model

Economic model is a set of equations or relationship among a group variables. The economic model is used to summarise the working of the national economy or of a business firm or some other economic unit. The range of economic model begins from the very simple to the very complex. According to Macdongall, "an economic model is a simplification of reality." Gardner Ackley, "An economic model consists simply of a group or set of economic relationships, each one of which involves, at least one variable also appears in at least one other relationship which is a part of the model—Economic model, then, are succinet model is a simplification of reality." Thus an economic model has a number of equations, each one explaining the behaviour of one of the variables. The relationship between variables is expressed relationship either in functional form or in any other form like words, tables, graphs to. In this way, each variable is mutually related to or linked with each other. For example the 'Marshallian Demand Curve' is a simple model which deals with a single relation between two variables. Similarly 'The Marshallian Cross' consisting of two relationships, a demand curve and a supply curve, is another valuable model. Thus an economic model is a set of relationship among a number variables is a series.

(4) Equilibrium

Equilibrium is usually defined in economics as a position of rest, or as a set of balance between opposing forces. In simple words equilibrium may be referred to as a situation when the two oppositing forces like demand and supply forces tend to balance or changes in two opposite variables offset each other. The equilibrium is a situation that is characterised by a lack of tendency to change. In other words, it can be referred as a state requiring no change over time. In the state of equilibrium, the opposite forces acting on the system are in a continuious state of change. As long as the opposite forces of the variables offset the net effect of initial changes, the initial position of equilibrium does not get disturb. The economists feel that the state of equilibrium is considered best because it does not make any change in the existing situation.

(5) Ex-ante and Ex-post

Ex-ante and ex-post are the latin words. These words are being used of 'beforehand' and afterward respectively. The word ex-ante stands for anything planned, anticipated or intended. For example, ex-ante saving is the amount that people wish to save out of their incomes in a particular period. Ex-post on the other hand, refers to the quantities of saving, consumption or investment made at the end of the period in the questions. Thus it is popularly known as realised saving, consumption or investment.

It is not necessary that ex-ante and ex-posts results will be the same. These may differ in-value and thus can affect the future plans.

The understanding of the above concepts helps us to study macro economic analysis in right perspective.

11

Inflation

The term 'inflation' is used in many senses and it is difficult to give a generally accepted precise and scientific definition of the term. Popularly, inflation refers to a rise in price level or fall in the value of money. Kemmerer states, "Inflation is too much money and deposit currency—that is too much currency in relation to the physical volume of business being done." This is what Coulburn also means when he defines inflation as : "Too much money chasing to few goods." That volume of money is responsible for the fall in the value of money or rise in prices is given expression to by several writers—"abnormal increase in the quantity of money" (T.E. Gregory), "the issue of too much money" (Hawtrey), etc. The implication in these definitions is that prices rise due to an increase in the volume of money as compared to the supply of goods. This is the quantity approach to the rise in the price level. But it should not be forgotten that the prices may rise due to other factors also—such as rise in wages and profits. Besides, there can be an inflationary pressure on prices without the prices actually rising.

Keynes mentions the following four related terms while discussing the concept of inflation:

(1) Reflations, (2) Inflation, (3) Disinflation and (4) Deflation.

Using a trade cycle model, we may clarify these terms as under:

(1) Reflation. It is a situation of rising prices, deliberately undertaken to relieve depression. With rising prices, employment, output and income also increase till the economy reaches the full employment ceiling.

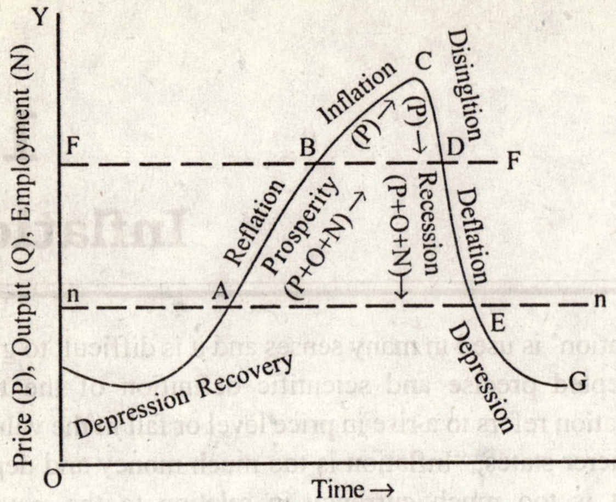

Fig. 1 The Model of a Trade Cycle

In the above diagram, FF line represents the full employment ceiling and represents the normal path. In the beginning when the economy is at a point of below full employment equilibrium, an increase in money supply leads the economy to move on the path of AB. However, till the economy of employment and output. The situation is, thus, described as "semi-inflation" or "Reflation".

(2) Inflation. It occurs when prices rise after the stage of full employment in the economy, with no corresponding rise in employment and output.

The following are the main characteristics of inflation:

(a) Inflation is a long-term operating dynamic process.

(b) Inflation is a process of persistently rising price level.

(c) Inflation is fostered by the interaction of a multitude of economic factors.

(d) Inflation, in a real sense, is a post-full-employment phenomenon.

(e) A cyclical movement is not inflation. Inflation is rising trend in the price level.

(d) Inflation price rise is persistent and is irreversible within a short time; thus, it should be distinguished from a price rise which may occur temporarily, due to short-term scarcity or during a cyclical upswing.

(g) Inflation is indigenous to the economic system.

(h) By and large, inflation is also a monetary phenomenon. It is usually characterised by an overflow of money and credit. In fact, the root cause of inflation is the expansion of money supply beyond the normal absorbing capacity of the economy.

In Fig, 1, the economy's path up to BC is inflationary.

(3) Disinflation. When prices are falling due to anti-inflationary measures adopted by the authorities, with no corresponding decline in the existing level of employment, output and income, the result is "disinflation'.

When acute inflation afflicts the community, disinflation is adopted as a curve. Disinflation is said to take place when deliberate attempts are made to curtail expenditure of all sorts to lower prices and money incomes for the benefit of the community.

In Fig. 1, the path CD represents disinflation.

(4) Deflation. It is a condition of falling prices accompanied by a decreasing level of employment, output and income. Deflation is just the opposite of inflation. Deflation occurs when the total expenditure of the community is not equal to the existing prices. Consequently, the value of money goes up and prices fall. However, each and every fall in price cannot be called deflation. For instance, when the inflationary spiral is controlled by an effective monetary and fiscal policy, along with increase output and employment, and prices begin to fall, it is not called deflation. The process of reversing inflation without either creating unemployment or reducing output is called "disinflation" and "deflation".

Deflation is an under-employment phenomenon.

In Fig. 1, the path DEG shows deflation.

Characteristics of Inflation

(1) It is a continuous rise in prices.

(2) Inflation is a long term operating dynamic process.

(3) Inflation is purely a monetory phenomena.

(4) It is not a high price but a rising price.

(5) Inflation is endogeneous to economic-System.

(6) A cyclical movement not inflation but continuity in price rise must be there.

(7) In real sense true inflation occures after full, employment.

Types of Inflation

On different grounds, economists have classified inflation into various types. Some of the major categories are discussed here.

(I) Creeping, Walking, Running and Galloping Inflation

According to the rapidity with which prices increase, we have:

(i) **Galloping Inflation.** In case of hyperinflation, prices rise every moment, and there is no limit to the height to which prices might rise. Therefore, it is difficult to measure its magnitude, as prices rise by fits and starts. If, within a year, the prices rise by 100 per cent, it is a case of hyperinflation of galloping inflation.

(ii) **Running Inflation.** When the movement of price accelerates rapidly, running inflation emerges. Running inflation may record more than 100 per cent rise in prices over a decade. Thus, when prices rise by more than 10 per cent a year, running inflation occurs.

(iii) **Walking Inflation.** When the rise in prices becomes more pronounced as compared to a creeping inflation, there exists walking inflation in the economy. Roughly, when prices rise by more than ten per cent and within a range of 30 per cent to 40 per cent over a decade, or by 3 to 4 per cent a year, walking inflation is the outcome. Walking inflation presents a warning signal for the occurrence of running and galloping inflation.

(iv) Creeping Inflation. It is the mildest form of inflation. Keynesian economists do not consider this kind of inflation dangerous at all for the economy. When prices rise within a range to ten per cent over a decade or around about one per cent per annum, there occurs creeping inflation in the economy. Kent, for instance, opines that when prices rise by not more than three per cent a year, there is creeping inflation which does not disrupt the economic balance.

(II) Excessive, Cost Deficit and Flight Inflation

Discerning inflation, according to the factors which influence money supply and demand for goods and services, we have :

(i) Cost Inflation. When inflation emerges on account of a rise in factor cost, it is called cost inflation. It occurs when money incomes (wage rate, particularly) expand more than real productivity. Cost inflation has its course through the level of money cost of the factors of production and in particular through the level of wages rates. Due to a rising cost of living index, workers demand higher wages, and higher wages in their turn increase the cost of production, which a producer generally meets by raising prices. This process of spiraling may reach higher and higher levels, in this case, however, cyclical anti-inflation remedies of monetary controls are not relatively effective.

(ii) Excessive money supply inflation. This is classical types of inflation, where there is an excess of money supply in relation to the availability of real goods and services. This type of inflation is usually conceived with reference to the cyclical fluctuations in the economy, and measures of monetary controls to check inflationary or deflationary trends.

(iii) **Deficit Inflation.** When the government budgets contain heavy deficit financing, though creating new money; the purchasing power in the community increases and prices rise. This may be referred to as deficit-induced inflation. During a planning era, when government launches upon investment, it usually resorts to deficit financing, when adequate resources are not found. An inflationary spiral develops due to deficit financing, the production of consumption goods fails to keep pace with the increased money expenditure.

(iv) **Flight Inflation.** This types of inflation refers to the relationship between money supply and goods, where there is a flight from the currency, reflecting increased velocity of spending. This is the result of peoples' psychological reactions when they find an intolerable decline in the value of money. It has been said that this stage is always reached by recurring budget deficits, and then the creation of new money under deficit financing.

(III) War, Post-war and Peace-time Inflation

Under the criterion of time, we have:

(i) **Peace-time Inflation.** By this is meant the rise in prices during the normal period of peace. Peace-time inflation is often a result of increased government outlays on capital projects having a long gestation period; so a gap between money income and real wage goods develops. In a planning era, thus, when government's expenditure increases, prices may rise.

(ii) **War-time Inflation.** It is the outcome of certain exigencies of war, on account of increased government expenditure, which is of an unproductive nature. By such public expenditure, the government apportions a substantial production of goods and services out of total availability which causes a downward shift in the supply; as a result, an inflationary gap may develop.

(iii) **Post-war Inflation.** It is a legacy of war. In the immediate post-war period it is usually experienced. This may happen when the disposable income of the community increases when war-time taxation is withdrawn, or public debt is repaid in the post-war period.

(IV) Comprehensive and Sporadic Inflation

From the coverage or scope point of view, we have:

(i) **Comprehensive Inflation.** When prices of every commodity throughout the economy rise, it is called economy-wide or comprehensive inflation. It is a normal inflationary phenomenon and refers to the rising prices of the general price level.

(ii) **Sporadic Inflation.** This is a kind of sectional inflation. It consists of cases in which the averages of a group of prices rise because of increases in individual prices due to abnormal shortage of specific goods. When the supply of some goods becomes inelastic, at least temporarily, due to the physical or structural constraints, the sporadic inflation has its way. For instance, during drought conditions where there is failure of crops, foodgrain prices shoot up.

Sporadic inflation is a situation in which direct price control, if skilfully used, is most likely to be beneficial to the community at large.

(V) Open and Repressed Inflation

An inflation is open or repressed according to government's reaction to the prevalence of inflationary forces in the economy:

(i) **Repressed Inflation.** When the government interrupts a price rise, there is repressed or suppressed inflation. Thus, suppressed inflation refers to those conditions in which price increases are prevented at the present time through adoption of certain measures like price controls and rationing by the government, but they rise in future on the removal of such controls and rationing. The essential characteristic of repressed inflation, in contrast to open inflation, is that it seeks to prevent distribution through price rise under free market mechanism and substitutes instead a distribution system based on controls. Thus, the administration of controls is an important feature of suppressed inflation.

(ii) **Open Inflation.** When the government does not attempt to prevent a price rise, inflation is said to be open. Thus, inflation is open when prices rise without any interruption. In open inflation, free market mechanism is permitted to fulfil its historic function of rationing the short supply of goods and distributes them according to consumer's ability to pay. Therefore, the essential characteristics of an open inflation lies in the operation of the price mechanism as the sole distributing agent. The post-war hyper-inflation during the nineteenth twenties in Germany is a living example of open inflation.

However, many economists like Milton Friedman and G.N. Halm opine that if there has to be any inflation, it is better open than suppressed. Suppressed inflation is condemned as it breeds a number of evils like the phenomenon of black market, hierarchy of price controllers and rationing officers, and uneconomic diversion of productive resources from the essential industries to the non-essentials or less essential goods industries since there is free price movement in the latter and hence more profitable to investors.

We may add to the above list, the following different kinds of inflation, based on various other causes.

(VI) Profit Inflation

In his recent book, Growthless Inflation by Means of Stockless Money, Professor Brahmananda mentions profit inflation as a unique category of inflation. The concept of profit inflation was originated by Keynes in his Treatise on Money. According to Keynes, the price level of consumption goods is a function of the investment exceeding savings. He considered the investment boom as a reflection of profit boom. Inflation is unjust in its distribution effect. It redistributes income in favour of profiteers and against the wage-earning class. During inflation, thus, the entrepreneur class may tend to expect an upward shifting of the marginal efficiency of capital (MEC); hence, entrepreneurs are induced to invest more even by borrowing at higher interest rates. Eventually, investment exceeds savings and economy tends to reach a higher level of money income equilibrium. In economy it is operating at full employment level or if there are bottlenecks of market imperfections, real output will not rise proportionately, so the imbalance between money income and real income is corrected through rising prices.

(VII) Foreign-Trade Induced Inflation

For an international economy, Prof. Brahmananda has categorised the following three types of inflation as being caused by factors pertaining to the balance of payments:

(1) Key-currency Inflation;

(2) Export-Boom Inflation; and

(3) Import Price-like Inflation.

When a country having a sizable export component in its foreign trade experiences a sudden rise in the demand for its exportables against the inelastic supply of exportables in the domestic market, it obviously implies an excessive pressure of demand which is revealed in terms of persistent inflation at home.

Again, trade gains and sudden influx of exchange remittances may lead to an increase in monetary liabilities which is further reflected in the rising pressure of demand for domestic output causing an inflationary spiral to get further momentum. Such a permanent case for an export-boom inflation is, however, ruled out in the Indian economy, because neither export trade is a significant portion of Domestic National Product nor is there a continuous boom of export demand, causing terms of trade to move up favourable all the time.

CAUSES OF INFLATION

The general price theory states that a price rise may occur due to either of the following two situations:

(a) when the aggregate demand increases, and/or

(b) when the aggregate supply falls.

If there is an increase in aggregate demand, without any corresponding increase in supply or if there is a fall in supply without any fall in aggregate demand, the prices will go up. Thus, price-rise or inflation is caused by the two sets of causes *viz*:

(a) Causes which induce an increase in demand, and

(b) Causes which produce a fall in supply due to increase in costs.

Inflation caused by the first set of causes is called 'demand-pull inflation' while that caused by the second set of causes is known as 'cost-push inflation'

(A) Demand-Pull Inflation

Demand pull inflation occurs when the aggregate demand increases without any increase in output. It means the prices will not go up if output increases along with the demand. If production is not increasing with the increase in demand, it is a state of full employment and therefore, demand inflation occurs only when the production reaches at full employment level. Here, demand is in excess of the available supply at the existing prices.

The following are some inflationary factors that induce demand of goods and services:

(1) Money Supply. Increase in money supply is the major factor that induces demand for goods and services. Increase in money supply increases, on the one hand, money income of the people that can be spent in purchasing the goods on the other hand, increases bank deposits which are the basis of the expansion of credit. The policies of central and commercial banks are also responsible for expansion of credit money. For example, a slash in the bank rate makes the credit cheaper. Expansion of actual money and credit money increases the demand for loans for production purposes Increased supply of money and bank credit adds something to the demand of goods and services, on the one hand, and to the cost due to interest element on the other hand. These factors push up the prices.

(2) Raising the Velocity of Money. Velocity of money pertinently goes up during boom period. It happens when people stop preferring liquid money and their consumption function dominates the saving attitude. People prefer to spending on consumption which brings an increase in the velocity of money and thus gives a spurt to prices.

(3) Disposable Income. Disposable income refers to the income payments to various production factors after personal taxes have been paid. An increase in the disposable income results in an increase in the absolute amount of consumption expenditure in the economy that boosts up prices.

(4) Deficit Financing. Deficit financing is a technique through which the government covers the budgetary gap. When the government spends more than what it expects to collect as revenue, the deficit is met by issuing more currency in the market or by borrowing the funds from foreign governments or international agencies. It will result in more money in the market and will increase in the price level because the disposable income of countrymen increases.

(5) Increased Foreign Demand. Increased foriegn demand will naturally push the prices of the domestic goods and services because it increases the overall demand. This factor is particularly significant if country's balance of trade is favourable or exports are higher than imports.

(6) Increase in Business Outlays. Increase in business outlays, or capital expansion, takes on a speculative characters during an inflationary boom. Most of the new equipment and plants are financed by speculative borrowing, not to mention an increase in their replacement demand. Most of the expenditure of the business find way into income stream *via* dividend wages, interest and other income payments. These income payment are also inflationary in character.

(7) Increase in Population. If the population of a country rises rapidly, it will pressurise the demand of goods and services. If money supply does not increase, the velocity of money will consequently increase the prices provided the increase in output is less than proportionate to increase in demand due to increased population. In this regard Prof. Coulborn says, "If population increases rapidly, while the aggregate of money remains stable, the consequent rise in the velocity of circulation is likely to outweigh the countervailling decrease in the volume of money per head; further a rapid increase of population may increase output less than proportinately, another factor tending to raise prices."

The cumulative effect of all these factors is that the aggregate demand function in an economy shifts upward, resulting in an inflationary rise in prices.

(B) Cost-Push Inflation

The second major cause of inflation is the increase in the cost of production. When cost of production increases, the supply curve will go downward, provided there is no increase in demand at the prevailing prices. Thus increase in cost of production, decreases the supply resulting in upward trend in price level.

The following factors responsible for the increase in cost and consequently resulting in higher prices are:

(1) Higher Wage Rates. Strong trade unions, very often demand for higher wages for their members and successfully manage to get it because the enterpreneurs have no other choice. This increase in wages is not linked with the increased productivity and hence the cost of production goes up. The producers shift this increased burden on the consumers by charging higher prices for their commodities. This is a never ending wage price spiral. Higher prices of goods amounts to higher cost of living and a fall in real wages. To neutralise the fall in real wages, again higher wages are demanded and granted which again are passed on to the consumers and thus inflationary trend continues.

(2) Fall in the Supply of Basic Inputs. Whenever basic and strategic raw materials and other input like iron and steel, cement, cotton etc. go in short supply, their prices will tend to move upward. The cost of production of finished goods in which such raw materials are used, increases thereby and consequently their selling prices, thus, would be a sources of cost push inflation.

(3) Higher Profit Marginals. Another factor causing cost push inflation is higher profit margins fixed by the producers. It is especially possible in monopolistic or near-monopolistic market situations where the producers (or heading producers) fix up higher profit margins arbitrarily without any increase in other elements of cost. If some powerful producers succeed in revising their profit margins upward, the other followers-producers also increase their profit margins and this phenomenon would push up the prices because profit becomes the part of selling price. Thus higher profit margins inflate the price level.

(4) Higher Taxes. Another source of cost-push inflation is higher tax especially indirect tax like sales tax, excise duties etc. imposed by the government. Such taxes increase the selling prices of the commodities because producers generally shift the burden of such taxes to consumers. Thus higher indirect taxes push the commodity prices in the market.

(5) Administered Higher Prices of Inputs. Sometimes, the prices of a number of important inputs are administered by the government or by supplying agency or organisation. Such administrators of prices keep on revising the prices of controlled inputs at regular or irregular intervals. The revised prices are generally fixed upward. Higher prices of inputs raise not only the prices of outputs in which they are used but they raise the general price level as basic inputs are used as basic raw materials in a number of industries. For example, prices of crude oil are administered by the Organisation of Petroleum Exporting Countries (OPEC) which keeps on revising the prices of crude oil upward from time to time. As oil is a basic input for a number of industries, it raises the general price level and therefore establishes a powerful cost push inflationary forces in the economy.

(6) Natural Factors. Fall in agricultural production owing to insufficient or excessive rainfall, and other natural calamities like earthquakes, floods, drought conditions, famine and other destructive mishappenings moves the prices of agricultural consumer goods upward. In addition to that, industrial production is also affected as the supply of inputs falls short. Both these factors exert inflationary pressures.

(7) Low Industrial Production. Various causes tend to affect the industrial production negatively resulting in the short supply of consumer goods. Such factors are strikes and lock outs, non-availability of factors of production, break down of power supply, operation of law of diminishing return, etc. Fall in supply will naturally increase the prices.

(8) Government Policies. Various policies of the government also help raising the general price level in the country. For example wage policy fixing the wages of workers working in specified industries; industrial policy, not allowing certain industries to be in operation without license or providing excessive protection to industries; export policy, making export of certain commodities obligatory, thus leaving the domestic demand unsatisfied etc., affect the supply position of industrial production unfavourably and price trend shows an upward move.

The cumulative effect of all the above factors sets in cost-push inflation in the economy.

Demand pull and cost push inflation in an economy go together and no demarcation line can be drawn between the two. Both affects each other. In both the cases demand exceeds supply and prices of factor inputs rise.

EFFECTS OR CONSEQUENCES OF INFLATION

Inflation has its multifold effects on different sections of the society and on the economic activities. Some effects are good and some others are quite undesirable for the economic development of the country and to different sections of the society. Modern economists are of the view that a mild degree of inflation is not only desirable but also a necessary condition for growth specially in developing countries where manpower and natural resources are underutilised. A slow rise in prices may induce the investors to undertake innovations and expand the level and scale of production. But, it is desirable only as long as it is kept within control table limits and is not allowed to gallop further. Galloping inflation, certainly, has same serious consequences. The Consequences of inflation can be discussed under two sub-heads:

(A) Effects on Production or on Economic Activities

As we explained in the above lines that a mild inflation serves as a tonic for the economy of the country and therefore, is a necessary condition for the growth of the economy. A mild degree of inflation has some good effects:

With an increase in the price level, the profit margins of producers lead to widen. Rise in price level also increases, the costs of inputs but the prices of inputs move slowly, as compared to the prices of the final products. The producers thus, have a wider profit margins. It encourages more investments in industries because investments in industries shall be more attractive due to greater profit margins. It will lead to industrial progress of the country as new and new industrial units will be promoted by the industrialists to earn more profits. The industrial expansion boosts up the employment level. Expansion of industrial base requires the employment of more and more labour and thus unemployed manpower and resources are utilised.

But this favourable trend continues so long as the prices are rising at a slow speed and the state of full employment is not achieved. But as soon as the full employment point is achieved, it becomes self-generating and creates uncertainty in the economic system. It degenerates into runway inflation or hyper inflation. This situation is not desirable for investment and production activity and has the following adverse effects on the productive activities of the economy:

(i) The hyper inflation results in the fall of money value that discourages savings on the part of general public. With the reduced savings, capital accumulation suffers a serious set back, because of the increasing propensity to consume, rather than to save something for future.

(ii) Reduced capital accumulation shall effect the investment in productive activities adversely that will consequently hamper the industrial production in the country.

(iii) As inflation creates uncertainty in the economic activities, the production will be affected adversely on this account. The enterpreneurs will be discouraged from taking business risks in production.

(iv) Runaway inflation also affects the pattern of production as the rise in general price level distrubs the price relationship. The prices of some commodities go up rapidly, while of some others; move rather slowly and of some, remain stationary or may even fall. There is, therefore, a diversion of resources from production of some to others mainly from the essential goods industries (which are low profit generation) to luxury goods industries (which are more profit-prone industries). This results in further shortage of essential consumer goods to the common man, pushing the prices upward.

(v) Inflation gives stimulus to speculative activities on account of the uncertainty generated by continually rising price level. In order to earn more profits, businessmen prefer to engage in speculative activities rather than to invest money in productive activities.

(vi) Inflation disrupts the smooth functioning of the price mechanism, thereby creating allround confusion in the economy. Artificial demands and supplies take place, disturbing the forces of demand and supply.

(vii) The worst effect of hyper-inflation is that, in course of time, it results in a flight from domestic currency on account of its constant diminishing value. The people lose confidence in their home currency and rush to buy foreign currencies of stabler value to safeguard their interest.

Thus, on production side, mild degree of inflation, gives encouragement to produce more till the stage of full employment but later on, production activites are discouraged.

(B) Effect on Society or on Distribution

A prolonged period of persistent inflation results in redistribution of income and wealth. Inflation does not effect all sections of society alike. Some gain from inflation while some others lose. These 'gains' and 'losses' results in redistributing the income and wealth within the society. The effects of inflation on different sections of society may be discussed as under:

(i) Debtors and Creditors. When inflation sets in debtors as an economic group tends to Again. During inflation, the value of money falls sharply but the debtor has to repay the same amount of money he had borrowed few years hence. In this way, he returns less purchasing power to the creditor than what he actually borrowed. Creditors, on the other hand, are losers during inflation because they receive lesser purchasing power than what they had actually lent.

(ii) Wage and Salary Earners. Wage and salary earners generally lose during inflation. Although their wages and salaries also go up in the wake of rising prices but wages and salaries generally do not rise in the same proportion in which the price level or their cost of living rises. Thus the real value of their fixed income falls and they are badly hit during inflation.

(iii) Producers or Businessmen. Producers or businessmen gain during inflation as the prices of their stock suddenly go up. It is a tonic for the businessmen and producers. Though, the cost of production also goes up but prices rise at a faster rate than the cost of production and thus, it results in higher profits.

(iv) Investors. We can distinguish two types of investors:

(a) investors in equities (equity shares), and

(b) investors in fixed interest-yielding securities like bonds and debentures. Inflation bestows favours on the former and is rather harsh on the latter. In case of former type of investors, equity dividends increase as a result of increasing corporate profit during inflation. On the other hand latter types of investors get fixed dividend (on preference shares) or interest on bonds and debentures. Inflation erodes the value of such dividend and interest with the rising prices. Therefore, their interests are adversely affected.

The small middle class investors generally keep their savings in fixed deposits in commercial banks or in their provident fund accounts maintained by their employers through insurance covers. The value of their savings fall sharply on maturity and therefore, household savings during inflation get discouraged. People prefer to spend more of its income in purchasing consumption goods and therefore, their will and ability to save are affected seriously. It badly hit the process of capital formulation, in the absence of which rapid industrial development cannot be expected.

(v) Farmers. Farmers gain during inflation. Like other producers, farmers gain because of the time lag involved in the purchase of inputs and sale of output. Moreover, the prices of farm products go up while the costs incurred by them do not go up to the same extent. Again, farmers are generally debtors and as debtor, they are to pay less purchasing power during inflation.

To conclude, we say that inflation redistributes income and wealth but it increases disparity of income and wealth in the society.

It penalises consumers, labours, creditors, small investors, and fixed income group while it rewards businessmen, debtors and farmers.

CONTROL OF INFLATION

Inflation is harmful to the economic development and to the various sections of society and, therefore, should be contained. There are three lines of action that can be adopted to check inflation namely:

(1) Monetary measures,

(2) Fiscal measures, and

(3) Other measures,

(1) Monetary Measures. Monetary measures are those measures of the government which aim at regulating the money supply in an economy. Such measures directly hit the inflationary boom. As Central Bank is the sole authority to control the money supply, this step is, therefore, taken by the Central Bank of the country. Money supply, at any time, consists of currency and bank-credit. Bank credit creates a proportinately larger share of money supply in an economy. Therefore, the bent of monetary authority is to regulate the flow of bank credit. The following monetary measures are popular curbing inflationary pressures:

(a) Bank-Rate Policy. Bank rate is a rate at which Central Bank of the country accepts and lends money to the commercial banks. This rate affects the bank-credit issued by the commercial banks to businessmen. An increase in bank rate, certainly, makes the bank-credit dearer because lending rate of interest is increased accordingly. It will discourage borrowing by businessmen from banks, resulting in a fall in the intensity of inflationary measures in the the economy.

Again, increased interest rate, consequent upon the increase in bank rate, will attract savings and induce people to save more rather than to spend money on consumer goods.

The measure will, reduce the supply of bank-credit and currency.

(b) Increased Re-discount Rates. To curb inflation, the Central Bank generally increases the re-discount rates. An increase in the rediscount rates leads to an increase in bank rates, because there is definite relationship between the two. An increase in bank rates tends to discourage borrowing by businessmen from banks, resulting in a fall in the intensity of inflationary pressures in the economy. An increase in interest-rates consequent upon the increase in the bank rate will make savings attractive than before and induce people to spend less on consumer goods. But the increase in re-discount rates as a weapon to check an inflationary boom has its limitations too. Firstly, if the bank rates do not rise *pari passu* with the rise in rediscount rates, there will be no decline in business borrowings, and hence, the inflationary pressures will continue, even though the rediscount rates have been raised. Secondly, the effectiveness of higher re-discount rates as an anti-inflationary weapon shall be considerably undermined if the commercial banks have an easy access to additional reserves.

(c) Sale of Government Securities in the Open Market. Another method to check the inflationary boom is to resort to sale off government securities to the public by the Central Bank. As the buying public purchase and pay for those government securities, the commercial banks, reserves with the Central Bank are correspondingly reduced and they are obliged to adopt a restrictionist credit policy in relation to business requirements. But the sale of government securities as an anti-inflationary weapon is also subject to limitations. Firstly, this policy may be rendered ineffective if the commercial banks are able to increase their reserves by selling their stocks of government securities to the Central Bank. Secondly, this policy may also be offset by increased borrowing from or by increased sales of treasury bills to the Central Bank of the commercial banks.

(d) Higher Reserve Requirements. An increase in reserve requirements of the member banks also serves as an anti-inflationary weapon during inflation. It absorbs the excess reserves of the banking system and, thus, prevents them from forming a basis for further credit expansion. But this method is also subject to limitations.

Firstly, if the commercial banks happen to have very large excess reserves, even the raising of the reserve requirements may not significantly curtail their power to create credit. Secondly, the ability of commercial banks to increase the reserves through sale of government securities may render higher reserve requirements ineffective to check credit expansion.

(e) Higher Margin Requirements. It is a method of selective credit control. The Central Bank in its pursuance of an anti-inflationary policy may raise the margin requirements of loans to higher levels. The higher the margin requirements, the lower the amount of loan that the borrower can obtain from the bank. Thus, higher margin requirements have the effect of checking undue monetary expansion.

(f) Consumer Credit Control. During an inflationary boom, facilities for instalment buying are reduced to the minimum to curtail excessive spending on the part of the consumers. This is done *(i)* by raising the minimum initial payments on specified goods, *(ii)* by extending the application of consumer credit control to a large number of consumer goods, and *(iii)* by reducing the length of the payment period, etc.

(2) Fiscal Measures. The major anti-inflationary fiscal measures are the following:

(a) Government Expenditure. To counteract increased private spending at a time of inflation, the government should, at such a time, reduce its own expenditure to the minimum extent possible to help limit the aggregate demand. As against this, it may, however, be said that it is not so easy to reduce government expenditure particularly during the war period. Secondly, any drastic cut in government expenditure to cure inflation may actually land the economy in a slump.

(b) Public Borrowing. The object of public borrowing is to take away from the public excess purchasing power which, if left free, would surely exert an upward pressure on the price-level in view of the limited supplies of goods and services in the economy. If voluntary borrowing does not yield adequate results, it may become necessary to resort to compulsory borrowing from the public.

(c) Debt Management. The existing public debt should be managed in such a manner as to reduce the existing money supply and prevent further credit expansion. Anti-inflationary debt management usually requires the repayments of bank held debt out of a budgetary surplus. The idea is that the government securities held by commercial banks should be retired by the government out of the budgetary surplus. This would check the power of commercial banks to encash their securities and add to the reserve for the purpose of credit expansion.

(d) Taxation. The problem during inflation is to reduce the size of disposable income in the hands of the general public in view of the limited supply of goods and services in the market. It is, therefore, necessary to take away the excess purchasing power from the public in the form of taxes. The rates of existing taxes should be steeply increased, while new taxes should be imposed on commodities so as to leave less money supply with the public to spend.

(e) A Suitable Income Policy. At a time of inflation, the government must also adopt a suitable price-income policy. It should strictly control wages, salaries and profits to keep spending at a low level to fight inflation.

(f) Over-valuation. An over-valuation of domestic currency in terms of foreign currencies will also serve as an anti-inflationary measures. Firstly, it will discourage exports and thereby increase the availability of goods in the domestic market. Secondly, by encouraging imports from abroad, it will add to the domestic supply of goods in the economy. But over-valuation as an anti-inflationary weapon suffers from several limitations.

(3) Other Measures. These measures can be used to supplement monetary and fiscal measures undertaken to contain inflationary pressures:

(a) Expansion of Output. Increased production is the best antidote to inflation because inflation arises partly due to inadequacy of output. But it becomes rather difficult to increase output at a time of inflation because of the full utilization of resources. It is suggested that if it is not possible to increase output as a whole, steps should be taken to increase the ouput of those goods which seem to be extremely sensitive to inflationary pressures by shifting productive resources from the less inflation-sensitive goods. In other words, a re-allocation of productive resources is suggested to step up the output of inflation-sensitive goods, such as, food, clothing, housing, etc. Steps may also be taken to increase supply of consumer goods through large-scale imports from other countries to absorb excess money supply.

(b) Price Control and Rationing. The object of price control is to lay down the upper limit beyond which the price of a particular commodity would not be allowed to rise. To ensure the successful functioning of price control two condtions will have to be satisfied. Firstly, the government should have under its control adequate stocks of the commodities concerned. Secondly, the demand for the concerned commodites should be controlled through rationing, failing which the richer sections shall be able to buy a major portion of the available stocks.

(c) Wage Policy. During an inflationary boom, the wages have to be controlled so as to curb the inflationary pressures in the economy. Wage increases may be allowed to workers only if their productivity increases. If this principle is observed, higher wages shall not lead to higher unit costs and, hence, to higher units prices.

Thus, the above steps taken simultaneously, may improve the situation a lot.

DEMAND PULL INFLATION

The most common cause for inflation is the pressure of ever rising demand on a stagnant or less rapidily increasing supply of goods and services. The expansion in aggregate demand may be the result of rapidly increasing private investment and/or expanding government expenditure for war or for economic development. At a time when demand is expanding, and is exerting pressure on prices, attempt may also be made to expand production. But this may not be possible either because unemployed resources are not available or because shortages of transport, power, capital and equipment, etc., may prevent output from increasing in proportion to expanding demand and inflationary situation in the country. Expansion in aggregate demand, after the level of full employment, will push up only the short period, resources are used for growth and for creating fixed assets and for the production of consumer goods. Necessarily, large expenditure will create large money income and large demand but without a corresponding increase in supply of real output.

According to the demand-pull theory, prices rise in response to an excess of aggregate demand over existing supply of goods and services. The demand-pull theorists point out that inflation might be caused, in the first place, by an increase in the quantity of money, when the economy is operating at full employment level. As the quantity of money increases, the rate of inflation will fall and, consequently investment will increase. This increased investment expenditure will soon increase the income of the various factors of production. As a result, aggregate consumption expenditure will increase leading to an effective increase in the effective demand. With the economy already operating at the level of full employment, this will immediately raise prices, and inflationary forces may emerge. Thus, when the general monetary demand rises faster than the general supply, it pulls up prices. Demand pull inflation, therefore, manifests itself when there is active cooperation, or passive collusion, or a failure to take counteracting measures by monetary authorities.

Demand-pull or just demand inflation may be defined as a situation where the total monetary demand persistently exceeds total supply of real goods and services at current prices so that prices are pulled upwards by the continuous upward shift of the aggregate demand function. By using the aggregate demand and supply curves, in Fig. 2, the demand-pull process can be graphically illustrated.

In Fig. 2, the X-axis measures real output, and the Y-axis measures the price level. Curves D, D_1 and D_2 represent the aggregate supply function, which slopes upward from left to right and, at point F it becomes a vertical straight line. The point F suggests that the economy has reached a level of full employment. Hence, the real output tends to be fixed or inelastic at this point. Assuming that the D cruve interseets the S curve at point F, the real output or income is at full employment and the price level is OP. When there are increase in the aggregate demand function beyond D, either due to an increase in autonomous investment (I), or because of an increase in the propensity to consume (C) or government spending (G), represented by a shift in the aggregate demand curve, such as D_1, D_2, the supply to total real output being inelastic, the price level tends to rise from P to P_1 and then to P_2.

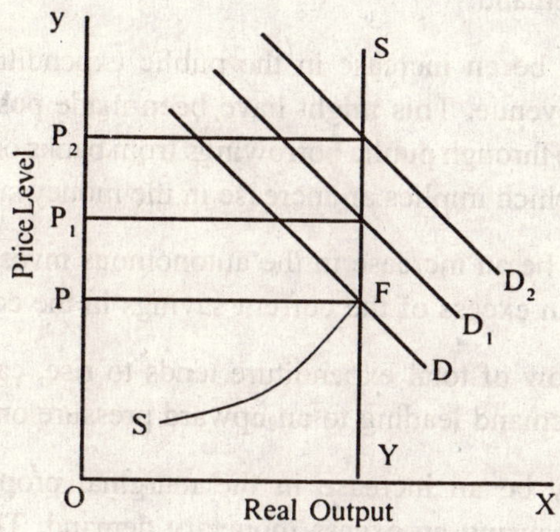

Fig. 2 Demand-Pull Inflation

However, demand-pull inflation can also occur without an increase in the money supply. This can happen when either the marginal efficiency of capital increases or the marginal propensity to consume rises, so that investment expenditures may rise, thereby leading to a rise in the aggregate demand which will exert its influence in raising prices beyond the level of full employment already attained in the economy.

According to the demand-pull theorists, during the process of demand inflation, rise in wages accompanied or follows the price rise as a natural consquence. Under the condition of rising prices, when the rate of profit is increasing, investment and employment, in that they bid against each other for labour, so that labour-prices (*i.e.* wages) may rise.

In short, the inflationary process, described by the demand-inflation theory, implies the following sequences : Increasing demand increasing prices-increasing costs-increasing income-increasing demand-increasing prices and so on.

It should be noted that the concept of demand-pull inflation is associated with a situation of full employment where increase in aggregate demand cannot be catered to by a corresponding expansion in the supply of real output. There can be many reasons for such excess monetary demand:

1. There may be an increase in the public expenditre (G) in excess of public revenue. This might have been made possible (or rendered necessary) through public borrowings from banks or through deficit financing, which implies an increase in the money supply.

2. There may be an increase in the autonomous investment (I) in firms, which is in excess of the current savings in the economy.

Hence, the flow of total expenditure tends to rise, causing an excess monetary demand leading to an upward pressure on prices.

3. There may be an increase in the marginal propensity to consume (MPC), causing an excess monetary demand. This could be due to the operation of demonstration effect and such other reasons.

4. In an open economy, an increasing surplus in balance of payments also leads to an excess demand. Increasing exports also have an inflationary impact because there a generation of money income in the home economy due to export earnings but simultaneously, there is reduction in the domestic supply of goods because products are exported. If an export surplus is not balanced by increased savings, or through taxation, domestic spending will be in excess of the value of domestic output, marketed at current prices.

5. A diversion of resources from the consumption goods sector either to the capital goods sector or the military sector (for producing war goods) will lead to an inflationary pressure because while the generation of income and expenditure continue, the current flow of real output decreases on account of high gestation period involved in these sectors. Again, the opportunity cost of goods is quite high in terms of the consumption goods meant for the civilian sector. This leads to an excessive monetary demand for the goods and services against the real supply, causing the prices to move up.

Therefore, it is said that the demand-pull inflation can be averted through deflationary measures adopted by the monetary and fiscal authorities. Thus, passive polices are responsibile for demand-pull inflation.

COST PUSH INFLATION

The cost-push inflation is caused by an increase in production costs. It is generally caused by two factors: *(a)* an increase in wages, and *(b)* an increase in the profit-margins of the entrepreneurs. The increase in wages may be caused by a monopolistic labour union through pressure tactics. This attempt on the part of the trade unions to push up wages invariably causes cost inflation in the economy.

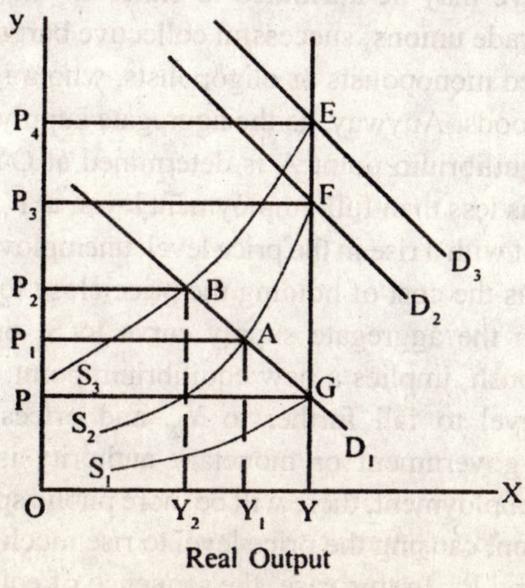

Fig. 3 Cost-push Inflation

Cost inflation is also caused by an organized attempt on the part of the industrialists to push up their profit margins. But the profits-push elements are not so important in causing inflation as the wage-push elements are. Powerful trade unions get the wages pushed up even without an equivalent increase in the productivity of the workers. Under these circumstances, the increase in wages cannot but result in an increase in prices. When cost inflation arises in one particular industry, it soon spreads to the other factors of economy as well. The reason being that the various sectors of the economy are closely linked with each other.

The phenomenon of cost-push inflation is graphically illustrated in Fig. 3. the figure, In the D curves represent the aggregate demand function, and the S curves, the aggregate supply function. The full employment level of income is OY which can be maintained only at rising prices levels, P, P_1, P_2 and P_3.

Now, if we begin with price level P, G is the point of intersection of the aggregate supply curve; D and S. Let us assume that the aggregate supply function shifts upward as S_2, which becomes a vertical straight line at point A, and merges with the S, G line the previous supply curve at full-employment level. The upward shift in the supply curve may be attributed to either an increase in money wages due to trade unions' successful collective bargaining, or to the profit-motivated monopolists or oligopolists, who might have raised the prices of goods. Anyway, as the aggregate supply curve shifts to S_1, the new equilibrium point A is determined at OY_1 level of real output, which is less than full-employment level, at P_1 level of prices. This means that with a rise in the price level, unemployment increases. It is regarded as the cost of holding the price close to P. Similarly, a further shift in the aggregate supply curve to S_3 on account of a further wage-push, implies a new equilibrium point, B. This causes the income level to fall further to Y_2. and prices to rise to P_2. however, the government or monetary authority is committed to maintain full employment, there will be more public spending or more credit expansion, causing the price level to rise much more—such as from P to P_3 and P_4. In this case, the sequence of equilibrium points become A-B-F-E.

Cost-push inflation may occur either due to wage-push or profit-push. Cost-push analysis assumes monopoly elements either in the labour market or the product market. When there are monopolistic labour organisations, prices may rise due to wage push. And, when there are monopolies in the product market, the monopolists may be induced to raise the prices in order to fetch high profits. Then, there is profit-push in raising the prices.

However, the cost-push hypothesis rarely considers autonomous attempts to increase profits as an important inflationary element. Firstly, because profits are generally a small fraction of the total price, a rise in profits would have only a slight impact on prices. Secondly, the monopolists generally hesitate to raise prices in absence of obvious demand-pull elements. Finally, the motivation for profit-push is weak since at least in corporations, those who make the decision to raise prices are not the direct beneficiaries of the price increase.

Hence, cost-push is generally conceived as a synonymous with wage-push. When wages are pushed up, cost of production increases to a considerable extent so that prices may rise. Since wages are pushed up by the demand for high wages by the labour unions, wage-push may be equated with union-push.

❐

12

Balance of Payments

Kindleberger defines balance of payments as "a systematic record of all economic transactions between the residents of the reporting country and residents of foreign countries during a given period of time," It thus follows that:

(i) Balance of payments is a statement of systematic record of all economic transactions between one country and the rest of the world.

(ii) It includes all transactions, current as well as capital.

(iii) It is a record pertaining to a period of time. Usually it is an annual statement.

(iv) It is a way of listing receipts and payments in international transactions of a country.

(v) It adopts a double-entry book-keeping system. It has two sides: debit and credit. Payments are recorded on the debit side and receipts on the credit side.

(vi) In accounting sense, debit and credit will always balance each other. In other words, balance of payments is always in balance.

That is to say, debit or payment side of the balance of payments account of a country represents the total of all the uses made out of the total foreign exchange required by the country during a given period, while the credit or receipts side represents the sources from which this foreign exchange was acquired by this country in the same period. The two sides of such must necessarily balance. If, in the actual balance of payments account the credits and debits do not balance, the balance is usually achieved by adding an item called errors and omissions.

(vii) It contains two sets of account: *(a)* current account and *(b)* capital account. Real and short-term transactions are recorded under current account. Capital account records all financial and long term transactions.

STRUCTURE OF BALANCE OF PAYMENTS

A balance of payments statement is a summary of a nation's total economic transactions undertaken on international trade account. It is usually composed of two sections: *(i)* the current account, and *(ii)* the capital account.

CURRENT ACCOUNT

Current account mainly consists of two sub-groups: *(i)* merchandise or the trade account, and *(ii)* invisible account.

In the trade or merchandise account, only transactions relating to goods are entered. That is, all goods exported and imported are recorded in the trade account.

The invisible account usually comprises the services account and gifts or charities account. The services account records all the services rendered and received by the resident of the nation. It consists of such items as banking and insurance charges, interest on loans, tourist expenditure, transport charges etc. Similarly, the gifts or charities account consists of all those items which are received or given away free by residents of the nation. It may be in kind or in cash. It goes without saying that these are all referred to as invisible transactions in the balance of payments theory and, therefore, recorded in the invisible account. It is interesting to note that the International Monetary Fund (IMF) includes the following items as invisible transactions:

(i) International transportation of goods, including warehousing, while in transit, and other transit expenses.

(ii) Travel for reasons of business, education, health, international conventions or pleasure.

(iii) Donations, migrant remittances, legacies.

(iv) Repayment of commercial credits.

(v) Insurance premiums and payments of claims.

(vi) Investment income, including interest, rents, dividends and profits.

(vii) Miscellaneous service items such as advertising, commissions, film rental, pensions, patent fees, royalties, subscriptions to periodicals and membership fees.

(viii) Contractual amortization and depreciation of direct investment.

From the following table, we can get a good idea of the items which enter the balance of payments.

Table 1 : Balance of Payments - Current Account

(Rs. crores)

	Credits	*Debits*	*Net*
1. Merchandise	54,340	55,420	–1,080
2. Travel	5,300	440	+ 4,860
3. Transportation	2,810	2,160	+ 650
4. Insurance	340	310	+ 30
5. Investment Income	2,660	3,610	– 90
6. Government, not included elsewhere	780	440	+ 340

Contd.

	Credits	*Debits*	*Net*
7. Miscellaneous	3,150	2,580	-- 570
8. Transfer payments	1,020	90	+ 12,920
Total, Current Transactions	82,400	6505	+ 17,340
Errors and Omissions			– 150
Total Deficit, current account			+ 17,190

1. This represent amounts received or paid by the government as, for example, for the upkeep of its organisations abroad.

2. Covers receipts and payments mainly for services, such as film rentals, technicians and agency services.

3. These include gifts, receipts by missionaries, etc. They also include transfers by Governments, receipts of cash grants, etc. Donations and gifts are known as "unrequired payments" as nothing is given in return.

In the balance of payments in Table 1 there are visible and invisible items of trade. The visible item is merchandise; and the invisible items of trade are tourist traffic, transportation, banking and insurance and investment income. Both visible and invisible items together make up the Trade Account, or what is commonly known as current account. Interest on loans, tourist expenditure, banking and insurance charges, etc., are similar to visible trade since receipts from selling such services to foreigners are very similar in their effects to receipts from sales of goods; they provide income to the people who produce the goods or services concerned.

It will be noted from the above table that the most important item in the balance of payments—current account is merchandise which refers to imports and exports of goods. Balance of trade refers to merchandise. In the above table, balance of trade does not balance, and shows a deficit of Rs. 1080 crores. Another important deficit item is investment income; India receives Rs. 2660 crores from her investments abroad but she has to pay Rs. 3610 crores to foreigners for their investments in India. When all current items are taken together, India has a surplus of Rs. 17,380 crores; including "errors and omissions, the total overall surplus comes to Rs. 17,190 crores.

Balance of Payments - Capital Account

There are certain capital transactions which include such items as borrowing and lending of capital, repayments of capital and sale and purchase of assets to and from foreigners. The following table gives an example overall balance of payments - capital account.

Table 2 : Balance of Payments: Capital Account

(Rs. Crores)

Items	*Credits*	*Debits*	*Net*
1. Private Loans	1,770	1,010	+ 760
2. Banking	3,920	3,240	+ 680
3. Official Loans etc.	13,940	32,570	– 18,60
Total : Capital and Monetary Gold	19,630	36,820	– 17, 190

The above table gives the capital account of India's balance of payments. The capital account deals with loans from or to foreigners, capital repayments from or to foreigners and purchase of assets by or from foreigners.

The three items mentioned in Table 2 are as follows:

(a) "Private Loans" includes foreign official bonus received and repaid by the private sector.

(b) "Banking" represents movement in banking capital excluding R.B.I.

(c) "Official Loans" etc. relate to:

(i) Loans-credits represent utilisation of various foreign loans and credits received by the official sector including the drawings from the I.M.F., debits cover loans extended by India to other countries as well as any repurchases of the drawings from the I.M.F.

(ii) Amortisation in credits cover repayments by other countries of official loans extended to them, while debits show repayments of loan on official account.

(iii) Miscellaneous covers other official capital receipts and payments including those of R.B.I.; and

(iv) Resources represent changes in official foreign exchange holdings, gold holdings of R.B.I. and S.D.R. holdings of Government.

The distinction between the current account and capital account should be noted. The current account deals with payments for currently produced goods and services; it includes also interest earned or paid on claims and also gifts and donations. The capital account, on the other hand, deals with payments of debts and claims of a country. The current account of the balance of payments affects the level of national income directly. For instance, when India sells its currently produced goods and services to foreign countries the producers of those goods get income; in other words, current account receipts (credit items) have the effect of increasing the flow of income into the country. On the other hand, when India imports goods and services from foreign countries and pays for them, money which would have been used to demand goods and services within the country, flows out to foreign countries; current payments (debits) to foreigners involve reduction uf the flow of income within the country and constitutes a leakage. Thus the current or trade account of the balance of payments has a direct influence of the level of income in a country. The capital account, however, does not have such a direct effect on the level of income: it influences the volume of assets which a country holds. The capital account deals only with the externat assets and reserves of a country. But, then, the two accounts taken to gether should necessarily balance. The surplus on the trade account must be equal to the deflcit on the capital account; likewise the deficit in the trade account will be equal to the surplus on the capital account.

BALANCE OF TRADE AND BALANCE OF PAYMENTS

There is a marked distinction between the concepts of balance of trade and balance of payments.

Balance of trade refers to the merchandise account of exports and imports only. Balance of payment is a broader term and it includes balance of trade. It is more comprehensive than the balance of trade. It includes all international economic transactions and items such as merchandise trade, services, banking, insurance, capital flows, gold buying and selling, etc.

As we know, a country may export and import many items, both visible and invisible. Balance of trade refers to the visible items only. Import or export of goods is a visible items because it is an open trade between the countries and can be easily certified by the customs officials. On the other hand, balance of trade is more comprehensive in scope and covers the total debits and credits of all items, visible as well as invisible. Thus, the balance of trade is only a partial study ofthe balance of payments. It simply refers to the difference between the value of exports and visible imports. This is what is represented in the trade or merchandise account section of the current, account in the balance of payments statement. Thus, balance of trade is nothing but a major component of the balance of payments. However, balance of payments includes apart from balance of trade or merchandise account, the invisible account which is again composed of the services sector and gifts and charities account comprising a variety of invisible items, plus a record of capital account.

In short, balance of trade is a partial picture, while balance of trade is a complete picture of country's international economic relations.

Further, in the accounting sense, balance of trade may be deficit or surplus. It may, thus, be imbalanced. But, balance of payment as a whole must always balance. For that reason, there is an item like "Errors and Omissions" in its structure.

Balance of Payments Always Balances

Since the balance of payments statement is drawn up in terms of debits and credits based on a system of double-entry book-keeping, if all entries are made correctly, the total debits must equal total credits. This is because two aspects (debits and credits) of each transaction recorded are equal in amount and appear on the opposite sides of the balance of payments account. In the accounting sense, balance of payments of a country must always balance.

In other words, debit or payment side of the balance of payments accounts of a country represents the total of all the uses made out of the total foreign exchange acquired by a country during the given period, while the credit or the receipt side represents the sources from which this foreign exchange was acquired by this country in the same period. The sides as such necessarily balance.

To illustrate the point, a simple hypothetical account of a country's balance of payments is represented in Table 3.

TABLE 3

Country's Balance of Payment Account

Cash (Receipts)		*Deposits (Payments)*	
	I. Current Transactions		
Item	*Rs. Crores*	*Item*	*Rs. Crores*
(1)	*(2)*	*(3)*	*(4)*
1. Merchandise Trade (Goods exported)	2,000	8. Merchandise trade (goods imported)	3,000
2. Services exported	1,000	9. Services imported	2,000
3. Income from foreign investment	2,000	10. Foreign income from investment at home	2,000
4. Unilateral Receipts	2,000	11. Unilateral payments	1,000
Sub-total	6,000	Sub-total	8,0000

Contd.

(1)	(2)	(3)	(4)
II. Capital Transactions			
5. Long-term borrowings	2,000	12. Long-term lendings	800
6. Short-term borrowings	1,000	13. Short-term lendings	600
7. Sale of Gold/Assets	1000	14. Purchase of gold/ assets	500
Sub-total	4000	Sub-total	1900
		15. Errors & Omission	100
Grand Total	10,000	Grand Total	10,000

In Table 3, rows 1 and 8 show the country's visible exports and imports. Rows 2 and 9 refer to items of invisible trade. Rows 3 and 10 pertain to investment income. Rows 4 and 11 denote unilateral transfers like donations and gifts (private as well as official). Rows 5, 6,12 and 13 show capital movement. Rows 7 and 14 reveal gold out flow and gold inflow. Further, items 1 to 7 enumerate receipts and items 8 to 14 show payments. Item 15 refers to the act of errors and omissions as a balancing factor. Thus, total value of both credit and debit sides is the same (Rs. 10,000 crores in our example).

It should be noted that the two accounts—current and capital-in the balance of payments should necessarily balance. The surplus of the trade or current account must be equal to the deficit in the capital account, or the deficit in the current account must be equal to the surplus in the capital account. Thus, the balance of current account need not be equal but can show a surplus or a deficit. In our example, the balance of current account shows a deficit (—) of Rs. 2000 crores. There is, however, a corresponding surplus of Rs. 2000 crores in the balance of capital account. As a result, the credit and debit sides of the balance of payments are exactly balanced.

The balance of payments, in the accounting sense, must always balance. Debits must always equal credits if the entries are correctly made. Thus, there can be no disequilibrium in the balance of payments as a whole.

However, while a nation's international accounts must always balance, its accounts need not be in equilibrium. Say, if a country's balance of payments shows a debit balance in merchandise and services accounts (on current account side), its credit balance in the other accounts (on the capital account side) must be sufficiently large so that total debits equal total credits. That is to say, when a country has debit balance on current account, it is either importing capital on a long or short-term or it is exporting gold, or it is receiving donations from foreigners and thereby its credit in the current account is extended to the extent of debit in the current account.

In a functional sense, thus, there may be a disequilibrium in the balance of payments of a country. Operationally, a country at a time may be receiving more payments from abroad than what it has to make. Thus, when total receipts exceed total payments, there is a surplus balance of payments. It is regarded as "a favourable balance." Sometimes a country has to make more payments abroad than what it receives. Then, there is a deficit in its balance of payments. It is regarded as an "unfavourable balance."

Hence the usual analytical approach to the balance of payments is to consider it as the difference between receipts from and payments to foreigners by the residents of the country. Symbolically, thus, the balance of payments may be defmed as:

$$B = R - P$$

where,

B stands for balance of payments.

R denotes receipts from foreigners, and

P stands for payments made to foreigners.

Clearly, thus, when B is zero, the balance of payments can be regarded as equilibrium balance of payments. That is to say, a country's balance of payments may be said to be in equilibrium when its receipts are equal to its payments on account of its transactions with other countries of the world. Such a country with equilibrium balance of payments is often called a country in "external balance". However, a country's balance of payments is said to be "favourable" or in "surplus" when the total receipts from the rest of the world exceed the total payments to the rest of the world. Symbolically, when the B is positive, it is called a favourable balance of payments. On the other hand, if a country's receipts froIn foreigners fall short of its payments to foreigners, its balance of payments is said to be unfavourable or in deficit. Symbolically, when B is negative, it is called an "unfavourable" or "adverse", balance of payments. A country whose balance of payments is in surplus is often referred to as a "surplus" country. Similarly, when its balance of payments is in deficit or adverse, it is called a "deficit" country.

Briefly, thus the phenomenon of disequilibrium in the balance of payments is viewed from the balance of transactions on current account as such. A disequilibrium—surplus or deficit—in this sense shows strengthening or weakening of a country's external capital position which is measured by the balance of its external assets to liabilities.

TYPES OF DISEQUILIBRIUM IN THE BALANCE OF PAYMENTS

The following are the main types of disequilibrium in the balance of payments:

(i) Secular disequilibrium;

(ii) Cyclical disequilibrium;

(iii) Structural disequilibrium;

(iv) Fundamental disequilibrium; and

(v) Temporary disequilibrium.

Secular Disequilibrium

When an economy moves from one stage to another of development, a deep-rooted, long-seated disequilibrium takes place. It is due to the excessive investments and technological changes. Population growth also affects it.

Cyclical Disequilibrium

It occurs on account of business cycles. Depending upon the phases of trade cycles like prosperity and depression, demand and other forces vary, causing change in the terms of trade as well as growth of trade and accordingly a surplus or deficit will result in the balance of payments. Cyclical fluctuations cause disequilibrium in the balance of payments because of cyclical changes in income and income elasticities. When prices rise during prosperity and fall during depression, a country which has a highly elastic demand for imports experiences a decline in the value of imports and if it continues its exports further, it will show a surplus in the balance of payments.

Structural Disequilibrium

It emerges on account of structural changes occurring in some sectors of the economy at home or abroad which may alter the demand or supply relations of export or imports or both. Suppose, if foreign demand for India's jute products decline because of some substitutes then the resources employed by India in the production of jute goods will have to be shifted to some other commodities of export. If this is not easily possible, India's exports may decline, whereas with import remaining the same, a disequilibrium in the balance of payments will arise. Similarly, if the supply condition of export items is changed, *i.e.*, supply is reduced due to crop failure in prime commodities or shortage of raw materials or labour strike, etc., in case of manufactured goods, then also exports may decline, to that extent and structural disequilibrium in the balance of payments will arise.

Moreover, a shift in demand occurs with the changes in tastes, fashions, habits, income, economic progress, etc. Propensity to import may change as a result. Demand for some imported goods may increase, while that for certain goods may decline leading to a structural change.

Furthermore, structural changes are also produced by variations in the rate of international capital movements. A rise in the inflow of international capital tends to have a direct impact on a country's balance of payments.

As Kindleberger observes, "structural disequilibrium at the goods level occurs when a change in demand or supply of exports or imports alters a previously existing equilibrium or when a change occurs in the basic circumstances under which income is earned or spent abroad, in both cases without the requisite parallel changes elsewhere in the economy." Similarly, strikes, political disturbances, etc. which affect supply of exports also create a structural disequilibrium.

In fine, structural disequilibrium at the factor level takes place when a country's factor prices deviate disproportionately to its factor endowment.

Fundamental Disequilibrium

I.M.F. Uses the term 'fundamental disequilibrium' to describe a persistent, long-run disequilibrium, especially, deficits which exist continuously for long period of time in a country's balance of payments. Unchecked series of short-run disequilibrium in a country's balance of payments ultimately lead to the 'fundamental disequilibrium' in the long run. There are deep-rooted causes and factors in the country's economy which are responsible for the emergence of a fundamental disequilibrium in its balance of payments.

It is also referred to as long-term disequilibrium caused by dynamic forces and long-term factors. A persistent disequilibrium over a long period may cause chronic and serious disequilibrium in the balance of payments position of a country. The main object of micro economic policy of a country is to correct this fundamental disequilibrium. It is functional in nature. To correct this, various measures are required to be undertaken.

Temporary Disequilibrium

Random or temporary type of factors may lead to a temporary disequilibrium in the balance of payments, *e.g.* outbreak of war, etc.

CAUSES OF DISEQUILIBRIUM

A disequilibrium in a country's balance of payments position may arise either for a short period or for along period. Any disequilibrium in the balance of payments arises owing to a large number of causes or factors operating stmultaneously. Types of disequilibrium differ from country to country, while the different kinds of disequilibrium and their causes in the same country will differ at different times. However, following are the important causes producing adisequilibrium in the balance of payments of a country:

(1) Cyclical fluctuations, their phases and amplitudes, differences in different countries, generally produce cyclical disequilibrium.

(2) Huge development and investment programmes in the developing economies are the root causes of the disequilibrium in the balance of payments of these countries. Their propensity to import goes on increasing for want of capital for rapid industrialisation, while exports may not be boosted up to that extent as these are the primary producing countries. Moreover, their exports quantum of primary commodities may decline as newly created domestic industries may require them. Thus, there will be structural changes in the balance of payments and structural disequilibrium will result.

(3) A vast increase in the domestic production of foodstuffs, raw materials, substitute goods, etc. in advanced countries has decreased their need for import from the agrarian underdeveloped countries. Thus, export demand has considerably changed, resulting in structural disequilibrium in these countries. Similarly, advanced countries also will suffer in their exports as a result of loss of their colonial markets, the tendency of the poor nations for self-reliance and their ways and means of curtailing their imports. But disequilibrium (deficit) in balance of payments seems to be more persistent in the underdeveloped or developing nations than in the advanced rich nations.

(4) High population growth in poor countries also has adversely affected their balance of payments position. It is easy to see that

increase in population increases the needs of these countries for imports and decreases the capacity to export.

(5) Another reason for a surplus of deficit in the balance of payments arise out of international borrowing and investment. A country may tend to have an adverse balance of payments when it borrows heavily from another country, while the lending country will tend to have a favourable balance and a deficit balance of payments.

METHODS OF CORRECTING AN ADVERSE BALANCE OF PAYMENTS

If a country experiences an adverse balance for a short period or once in a way, it may easily correct by a favourable balance later. But when an adverse balance becomes chronic, appearing year after year, the government will have to take drastic steps to correct it, lest the country loses all its foreign exchange and gold reserves and is also unable to raise any more loans outside. There are five methods by which a country can try to correct an adverse balance of payments, *viz.*, deflation, exchange depreciation, devaluation, exchange control and restriction of imports and promotion of exports. We shall describe each one of these methods now.

(i) Deflation and Adverse Balance. An adverse balance of payments is only a symptom, the fundamental cause being excessive demand for foreign goods (either for investment or for consumption). The basic solution to correct an adverse balance, therefore, is to curtail demand for foreign goods by restricting consumption. Deflation, meaning fall in prices and in incomes, attempts to restrict demand for foreign goods. Suppose that India experiences an adverse balance of payments and is losing its past accumulated sterling balances and other foreign currency reserves. The Reserve Bank of India may adopt a policy of deflation by raising the bank rate; this will result in fall in prices and in incomes. Reduction of money incomes will be followed by reduction in demand and imports. Besides, exports may be stimulated since money costs may be expected to decline along with the decline in money incomes. Moreover, Indians will attempt to buy goods within India rather than from abroad as internal prices are lower than prices elsewhere. Thus, imports are checked and exports are stimulated and adverse balance is corrected by the use of a deflationary policy adopted by the monetary authorities in the country. Further, a higher rate of interest within the country will attract foreign funds which can be used to correct adverse balance of payments.

Deflation is generally followed when countries are on gold standard or on fixed exchange rates (*i.e.*, under conditions in which there is no possibility of changing the exchange rates). But deflation is disliked for two important reasons: First, reduction in money incomes implies reduction in wages which is strongly opposed by the trade unions. Secondly, deflation implies unemployment and suffering to different groups of people, particularly to the working classes. Accordingly, deflation is not regarded as a suitable method for correcting an adverse balance of payments.

(ii) Exchange Depreciation and Adverse Balance. By exchange depreciation, we mean a decline in the rate of exchange of one currency in terms of another. If India experiences an adverse balance of payments with regard to the United States, the Indian demand for American currency—the dollar—will rise, and the price of dollar in terms of the rupee will go up. The dollar, therefore, will appreciate in value while the rupee will depreciate in value.

The appreciation in the value of the dollar will raise the price of American goods and thus will reduce India's demand for American goods. Thus India's imports will decline. At the same time, depreciation in the value of the rupee will stimulate exports from India for two reasons. In the first place, the Americans will find the Indian currency cheap and, therefore, the Indian commodities also cheap. Hence, they will buy more from India. Secondly, the Indian exporters will be interested in exporting more for every dollar earned abroad will get a larger amount of rupees than before.

Thus imports will be checked and exports stimulated. A favourable balance may, thus, come into existence to pay off the earlier deficit. Exchange depreciation is automatic and will correct a mild adverse balance of payments. But exchange depreciation is defective in many respects. First, it is not suitable to a country which wants to keep its exchange rate fixed and does not want to change it. Secondly, exchange depreciation makes international trade risky and hence it reduces volume of trade. Thirdly, the terms of trade—*i.e.*, the rate at which exports exchange for imports—will go against the country whose currency depreciates in value. This is so because, as we have seen, foreign goods have higher prices and local gods have lower prices. The country with depreciating currency will have to export more to pay for the same volume of imports. Lastly, experience in certain countries has shown that exchange depreciation may result in inflationary situations by making goods more expensive.

(iii) Devaluation and Adverse Balance. Devaluation of a currency means lowering of the value of a currency in terms of gold or in terms of other currencies. The difference between devaluation and depreciation is that while devaluation is the reduction of the value of a currency by the government, depreciation stands for automatic reduction in the valus of a currency by market forces. But, in substance, both mean the same thing lower value for a currency in terms of foreign currencies and both have similar effects. When the local currency depreciates in value and the foreign currency appreciates in value, the foreign commodities are made costly and hence imports are checked while the local commodities are made cheap and hence exports are promoted. Thus, a tendency towards a favourable balance of payments is created.

A chronic adverse balance of payments implies one of two things—either *(a)* the country has been depending upon imports to a large extent and for various reasons, is not in a position to pay for them by a corresponding amount of exports or *(b)* the currency of the country is overvalued in terms of the foreign currency and, therefore, at the present exchange rate the foreign currency is cheap and consequently the foreign commodities are also cheap, resulting ultimately in larger imports and lesser exports.

Devaluation is the proper method of correcting an adverse balance of payments which is due to overvaluation of a currency. It may also be resorted to by a country if it is interested in making its commodities cheap in foreign markets so' as to get a competitive advantage over other countries in the international markets and thus push up its exports.

Conditions for the Success of Devaluation. The immediate effect of devaluation of a currency will be reflected in the increase in exports and decrease in imports. This is to be expected since, by devaluation, the domestic currency will become cheap and, therefore, the domestic goods will also become cheap to foreigners, while the foreign currency will become costly and, therefore, foreign goods will become costly to consumers of the devalued currency. By curtailing imports and by expanding exports, devaluation creates favourable balance of payments and removes the chronic adverse balance of payments which had existed earlier. It will, however, be successful only under the following favourable circumstances:

(a) Cost-price Structure. There should be no change in the cost-price structure in the devaluing country. Only the external value of the currency-unit has been reduced through devaluation. But it is possible for costs and prices within a country to change for two reasons: First, the merchants and speculators may raise the prices of those goods whose imports have been cut off or reduced owing to devaluation. Secondly, imports which have now become costly because of devaluation may form a significant part of the consumption of the working and middle classes, in which case, the cost of living will rise, necessitating higher wages and higher prices. As a result of these reasons, the costprice structure in the devaluing country may change and thus may prevent the favourable effects of devaluation to come into existence.

(b) Elasticity of Demand. The demand for imports and exports should be elastic. If Indian demand for foreign goods is inelastic, that is, whatever be the price of the foreign commodities, India will buy more or less the same amount; the total value of imports will increase as a result of devaluation. At the same time, if foreign demand for Indian goods is inelastic, India will not gain anything by lowering its price level through devaluation, for the same amount will be sold whatever be the price and, therefore, as a result of devaluation the total value of exports will fall. Thus, if the demand for imports and

exports is inelastic, devaluation will worsen the balance of payments situation by increasing the total value of imports but at the same time reducing the total value of exports. It can be successful only if demand is elastic on both sides-that is, demand for imports is elastic, and as a result when the prices of foreign goods are high due to devaluation, imports will be curtailed; likewise, dem and for exports by the foreigners is also elastic and as a result, when the local goods are cheap, exports will be stimulated.

(c) Co-operation of Other Countries. The efficacy of devaluation of a currency by a country will depend upon the co-operation of foreign country or countries whose currencies have appreciated as a result of devaluation. Foreign countries will experience contraction of demand for their exports from the devaluing country, while their own demand for the goods of the devaluing country will expand due to lower exchange rate of the latter's currency. The natural tendency under the circumstances is to retaliate. This may take the form of high tariffs to prevent imports from the devaluing country or grant of subsidies to push up exports or devaluation of their currencies too.

To conclude, devaluation, as a method of correcting an adverse balance of payments, has much to commend itself. It combines the advantages of both exchange depreciation and stable exchange rates. However, it expects many favourable factors to exist for its success. In the past, particularly in the 1930's, devaluation by one country had always been followed by similar devaluation by other countries also. If devaluation has to succeed and competitive exchange depreciations to be avoided, international co-operation and agreement will be essential.

(iv) Exchange Control and Adverse Balance. Exchange controls relate to government regulation of exchange rates as well as restriction on conversion of the local currency against foreign currency. Exchange controls may be adopted by a country under many circumstances:

First, exchange control may be introduced if the monetary authorities feel that the normal mechanism of the free exchange market may not be desirable or effective.

Secondly, exchange control may be necessary when there is a heavy run on a country's foreign reserves either as a result of the heavy adverse balance of payments or as a result of movement of capital out ofthe country. Such a flight of capital out of the country may arise because of a suspected depreciation of the currency or because of safer investment elsewhere.

Thirdly, exchange control may be introduced by a country to prevent the import offoreign goods into the country and thus encourage local industries and bring about increased level of economic activity and employment.

Fourthly, exchange control may be adopted by a country to secure an adequate amount of foreign currency to buy essential foreign goods. During World War II, belligerent countries adopted exchange control to enable them to conserve their foreign currency reserves which could be used to import only the most essential war materials.

Fifthly, exchange control may be adopted by a country to freeze the assets of foreign nationals so that they might not be able to use them to help their own countries; this type of exchange control was extremely common during World War II.

Sixthly, exchange control may be adopted by a country in order to over value or under value its exchange rate or to avoid fluctuation in the exchange rate. A country may fix higher exchange rate and maintain it at that level, if it, has to import foreign goods cheaply or if it has to make payments to others in foreign currency. A country may undervalue its currency if its intention is to export more and curtail its imports. Exchange control may also be used to avoid fluctuations in the exchange rates due to speculative forces or erratic movements of short-term capital.

Lastly, exchange control is a necessity in planned economy, since the Government which aims at controlling different aspects of economic activity in the country should also be in a position to control and influence the foreign exchange market. Foreign exchange control is an essential and one of the vital control mechanisms in the hands of the Government.

(a) Intervention. For an effective control of foreign exchange rates and foreign exchange market the government should have a central authority-*viz.*, the central bank which should have complete power to control and regulate the foreign exchange market. Anyone wanting foreign exchange should purchase it only from the central bank and from no other source. Likewise, anyone wanting to sell foreign exchange should sell it only to the central bank. The buying and selling of foreign exchange by a single authority enables the latter to adjust the demand and supply of foreign exchange according to the needs of the country.

Pegging Operations. Government intervention in the foreign exchange market takes the form of "pegging up" or "pegging down" the currency of the country to a chosen rate of exchange. The pegging operations take the shape of buying and selling of the home currency either by the government or by the central bank of the country in exchange for the foreign currency in the foreign exchange market. Let us illustrate the pegging operations with an example.

Suppose that the Government of India has fixed the exchange rate of the rupee at 5 pence per rupee. In a free exchange market, this exchange rate will fluctuate depending upon demand and supply ofthe rupee in terms of the pound-sterling. If the British demand for the rupee is far greater than Indian demand for the pound-sterling, the exchange rate of the rupee will go up-say to 6 or 7 pence. If the Government of India is interested in fixing or pegging down the exchange rate at 5 pence per rupee, it would offer to sell rupees to any amount at the official rate. So long as the Government is prepared to sell rupees at 5 pence per rupee, the market rate of exchange cannot go beyond this rate. In a similar manner, if the foreign demand for the rupee is less and Indian demand for the pound-sterling is more, the rate of exchange will go against India say 4 or 3 pence per rupee. To prevent this fluctuation, the Indian Government should be prepared to sell foreign currency against the rupee at the fixed exchange rate. So long as the Government is prepared to do so, the market rate of exchange cannot fall below the official exchange rate.

Thus, buying and selling of foreign currency against the local currency with the defmite objective of maintaining a fixed exchange rate is known as pegging operations. If pegging operations are carried on to maintain the exchange rate at a higher level, they are then known as "pegging up" operations. If they are done to keep the exchange rate at a lower level, they are termed as "pegging down" operations.

Effects of Intervention. Intervention of the Government in the foreign exchange market has the effect of neutralising the forces of demand and supply of foreign exchange. But the buying and selling operations would have to be continued indefinitely so long as the market forces of demand and supply persist against the exchange rate fIxed and maintained by the Government. If the Government cannot do so, either because of shortage of foreign reserves or because of any other reason, the Government will either have to resort to the alternative method of direct exchange control, *viz.*, restriction, or the Government will fail in their purpose of controlling the rate of exchange.

In the inter-war period, Exchange Equalisation Funds were established in England, France and the U.S.A. with the definite purpose of maintaining the rate of exchange of their respective currencies at a fixed level. Experience of these Stabilisation Funds showed clearly that their success would depend upon the amount of foreign exchange reserves they possessed (not the local currency reserves because they could be easily increased through printing of more currency notes in an emergency). It was, therefore, found that selling of foreign currency was limited by the amount of foreign reserves held by the Stabilisation Funds and hence it was difficult to peg up a currency if the market forces of demand and supply were working toward a lowering of the exchange rate. It is generally felt that Government intervention—or pegging up and pegging down operations—can at best be a temporary expedient to remove fluctuations in the exchange rate.

(b) Restriction. As Government intervention in the foreign exchange market has been found a weak weapon of exchange control, a more powerful weapon has been devised in exchange restriction. Exchange restriction refers to the policy by which the Government restricts the supply of its currency coming into the exchange market. Exchange restrictions may be of three types:

(a) Centralise all trading in foreign exchange with one central authority normally, the central bank of the country.

(b) Prevent the exchange of national currency against foreign currencies without the permission of the Government.

(c) Make all foreign exchange transactions through the agency of the Government.

All those who have to make payments to any foreign country will have to make the payment not to the foreign creditor directly but to the central bank of the country which will keep the amount in the name of the foreign creditor. The amount will not be available to the foreigner in his own currency but can be used by him for purchases in the country practising exchange restriction. This system is known as "blocked account." It is so called because the amount credited to that account cannot be converted into the creditor-country's currency.

The system of blocked accounts was originally introduced by Nazi Germany in 1933 and was later adopted by Great Britain, France and others. The system of blocked accounts led to two difficulties. First, foreigners who had exported goods to Nazi Germany and who found their accounts blocked by the German central bank refused to export again to Germany. As a result the volume of imports and exports of Germany dwindled to the minimum. Secondly, blocked accounts led to black-marketing in foreign exchange. A person who found his foreign reserves blocked would like to dispose it of somehow and convert it into his own currency. Consequently, people with blocked accounts disposed of their reserves at lower rates than the official rates.

The system of multiple exchange rates is a form of exchange restriction, first practised by Germany and later followed by Argentian, Brazil and many other countries. The system of multiple exchange rates implies fixing different exchange rates for imports and different types of commodities. The objective generally is to secure as good a price as possible for exports and reduce imports to the minimum. The advantage of this system is that the Government can increase or reduce the import or export of any commodity by simply fixing a particular exchange rate for that commodity only. But it puts too much arbitrary power into the hands of the Government to influence trade. The system of multiple exchanges is, therefore, condemned by the International Monetary Fund.

(c) Exchange Clearing Agreements. Exchange clearing is a method of exchange control which was practised during the Depression of 1930's. Under it, two countries engaged in trade pay their respective central banks the amounts payable to their respective foreign creditors. The central banks then use the money in offsetting the corresponding claims. Let us illustrate this with an example. Suppose India has exchange clearing agreement with the U.S.A. The Reserve Bank of India will open an account, with itself, in the name of the Federal Research Banks of America which, in its own, will open an account, with itself, in the name of the Research Bank of India. All Indians who have imported goods from America will pay in rupees to the credit of the Federal Reserve Banks in the Research Bank of India. All Indian exporters of goods to the U.S.A. will receive payments from the Reserve Bank of India out of the account in the name of the Federal Reserve Banks. In the same manner, the Federal Reserve Banks of America will provide similar services to American imports and exporters out of the account keep in the name of the Reserve Bank of India. All that happens is a notification by one central bank ofthe other that a certain payment has been made or received. This system is essentially one of offsetting each other's payments, and the basic assumption is that the countries entering into such an agreement will see that imports and exports are more or less equal and that there is no necessity for either making payments to or receiving payment from the other country.

Exchange clearing agreements were first entered into by Germany with Switzerland in the 1930's. Two clear advantages arise out of exchange clearing agreements. First, imports and exports between two countries can take place without their being unduly worried about the problem of fmding scarce foreign exchange. For, as pointed out above, the importers pay the price of their imports into a central account out of which payment is made to domestic exports. Secondly, under this system, transactions do not pass through foreign exchange market and even a country without any reserve of foreign currency can import goods from foreign countries.

Exchange clearing agreements thus have favourable effects on international trade as compared to exchange restrictions which tend to restrict the volume of trade between countries.

However, the system of exchange clearing agreement has many disadvantages. In the first place, there is a possibility of the exploitation of an economically weaker nation by a stronger nation. While Nazi Germany imported important raw materials to build her economy for war, Hungary, Rumania and other weaker nations which entered into exchange clearing agreements with Germany were often forced to import unwanted goods. In many cases, Germany imported goods from other countries for which it could not pay in the currencies of foreign countries. Foreigners were paid in German currency at the Reisch Bank (the German central bank) which blocked its conversion to foreign currency. Foreign governments were forced to enter into exchange clearing agreements with German and buy whatever goods Germany was able to offer in order to liquidate their blocked accounts.

Secondly, exchange clearing agreements lead to bilateral trade at the expense of multilateral trade, since they attempt to equalise trade between respective countries. Bilateral trade may have the tendency to divert trade from normal trade chartnels into abnormal channels.

Finally, exchange clearing agreements have the effect of reducing the volume of international trade: Besides, they attempt to do away with the foreign exchange market. In fact, if these agreements become common, the customary free foreign exchange markets will be completely eliminated.

Indirect Methods of Exchange Control. We have described above the direct methods of controlling and regulating the foreign exchange rates and the foreign exchange market. But there are several indirect methods also for regulating the rates of exchange. The most important indirect method is the use of tariff duties and quotas and other quantitative restrictions on the volume of international trade. Restriction of imports by the use of tariffs leads to the decline of the demand for foreign currency and if exports are maintained at the usual level, or are increased, the rate of exchange will go up in favour of the country imposing import restrictions. In this sense, import duties and other quantitative restrictions may have an effect on the rate of exchange but an import duty imposed specifically to protect local industries against foreign competition cannot be properly called a method of exchange control since the main objective is to restrict imports.

Another indirect method of exchange control is the rate of interest. A high rate of interest in a country, say England, will attract short-term capital from other countries like the U.S.A., Germany, etc. (to earn a higher interest rate); this will lead to a greater demand for the pound-sterling and a higher exchange rate for the pound in terms of other currencies. A lowering of the rate of interest will have the opposite effect.

These methods of exchange control are known as indirect methods because, properly speaking, they do not control the exchange rate but only influence it. On the other hand, the direct methods of intervention, restriction, and exchange clearing agreements have the effect of directly controlling the exchange rate of the foreign exchange market.

(v) Import Duties and Quotas and Adverse Balances. The most usual device to restrict foreign trade is to impose taxes known as duties or tariffs on some or all imports. Import duties are better than all other methods, for they cut down the demand for imports and thereby reduce or eliminate the adverse balance of payments. Tariffs have other advantages also by protecting certain home industries, they may remove unemployment, stimulate investment and promote recovery if the economy is suffering from depression.

Import quotas, the other direct method of controlling imports, implies the fixing up by the Government of maximum quantity of a commodity to be imported during a given period. Import quotas may be of different types. Either the Government may fix the quantity of a commodity but may not prescribe the country or countries from which it should be imported or the Government may fix the quantity had also prescribe different quantities to be imported from various countries.

Import quotas are said to be more advantageous as compared to import duties. For one thing, home producers know exactly what quantities of imports will come in. For another, import quotas are easily adjusted by the Government without resort to legislation and, therefore, are more flexible. Moreover, they are more suitable for purposes of negotiating trade concessions with other countries. But import quotas have certain drawbacks too. There is always the possibility of corruption and discrimination in fixing import quotas. Besides, they do not bring in revenue as customs duties do.

Besides the use of import duties and quotas to curtail imports, the Government may follow policies designed to promote exports such as by reduction of export duties, use of export bounties and subsidies, and so on. Ultimately, these measures of checking imports and promoting exports are of far greater importance in correcting adverse balance of payments that the first four methods.

To conclude, equilibrium in the balance of payments is a desirable objective, particularly, when the country has achieved full employment. Any tendency towards adverse balance of payments should be corrected with the least amount of delay. Five methods are available to a government towards this end. All of them aim at curtailing imports and stimulating exports: Of these methods, the direct method of restricting imports through import duties and import quotas on the one side, and export promotion, on the other, is possibly the best. In fact, this method is always used even when other methods had been adopted by the Government.

❐

13

Money Supply

Money is a complex phenomenon in a modern economy. Money, by and large, may be regarded as something which is generally used as a means of payments and accepted for the settlement of debts. By the term "supply of money" is meant the total stock of domestic means of payments which is held by the public. Here, public refers to individuals, business firms, state and local government bodies, etc., all categories of holders of money other than the Central Government of treasury, central bank and commercial banks, all these being money-creating agencies.

The cash balances held by the central and State Governments in the central bank and in treasuries are not to be considered as part of money supply, since they arise out of the non-commercial and administrative operations of the government. Again, money supply refers to the stock of money held by the public in disposable form only. Thus, money supply is the quantity or stock of money in circulation.

Money supply is a stock as well as a flow concept. When money supply is viewed at a point of time, it is a stock of money held by the public on a particular date. It refers to the total of currency notes, coins and demand deposits with banks that is held by the public. When viewed over a period of time, money supply becomes a flow concept. A unit of money is spendable as well as respendable. Thus, it may be spent several times during a given peirod, passing from one hand to another. The average number of times a unit of money circulating from one hand to another in the spending process during a given year is referred to as the "velocity of circulation of money." The flow of money is measured by multiplying a given stock of money held by the public with the velocity of circulation of money. According to Fisher, the flow the money supply over a period of time is : MV where,

M = Stock of money held by the public.

V = Velocity of circulation.

In view of the complexities of money in a modern economy, there are different views held by monetary analysts regarding the composition of money supply. These views may be broadly classified into: *(i)* the traditional or narrow sense and *(ii)* the modern or expanded sense.

TRADITIONAL VIEW

According to the traditional view, the money supply is composed of: *(i)* currency money and legal tenders, *i.e.,* coins and currency notes, and *(ii)* Bank money, *i.e.,* chequable demand deposits with commercial banks.

Currency money is regarded as high-powered money because it is a legal tender.

The backbone of a currency system is the central bank notes and coins. This is because, generally, the central bank possesses the monopoly of notes issue. In certain countries, the treasury also issues notes or coins along with the central bank. In India, for instance, one rupee notes are issued and managed in circulation by the Government of India. The rest of the notes and coins are issued and managed by the Reserve Bank of India.

However, the particular denominations of currency in circulation as well as the proportion of the total money supply which is held in the form of currency are governed by the sections of the public. The treasury, the central bank and the commercial bank are merely agents through which the preference of the public is expressed.

The actions of the public in choosing the hold more or less currency or more or less of particular denominations are normally influenced by any, or all, of the following factors: *(i)* the physical volume of trade and transactions and the nature of the trade, whether wholesale or retail. Retail trade would normally require a large amount of coins and notes of small denomination; *(ii)* the price level; *(iii)* the methods of payment, that is, payment by cheque or by cash; *(iv)* the volume of demand deposits; *(v)* the banking habit of people; *(vi)* the distribution of national income among different groups of people; and *(vii)* the methods of taxation, public loans, deficit financing, etc.

Bank Money. The commercial banks' demand deposits are generally referred to as a constituent of money supply, because they are transferable by cheques in the settlement of debts. It is through payments made by cheques that the volume of demand deposits undergoes constant change.

The creation of bank money or demand deposits depends on the credit creation activities of the banks, which is based on the cash volume the high-powered money held by them. The bank money as such, is regarded as secondary money.

Conventionally, therefore, the total money supply is composed of high-powered money and secondary money.

The relative amounts of the two constituents of money supply namely, currency money and demand deposits, depend upon the degree of monetization of the economy and the banking habit and banking development in the country. In economically advanced countries such as the U.S.A., it is demand deposits which form the bulk of the total supply of money. For instance, almost 80 per cent of the money supply of the U.S.A. is made up of demand deposit accounts of the public in commercial banks. Thus, most of the payments are cheque payments in that country. It is estimated that over 90 per cent of the total volume of money payments are made with deposit money as the medium of exchange. In underdeveloped countries, such as India, on the other hand, the proportion of currency money to the total money supply with the public is considerably large because a very high percentage of transactions are performed through cash payments, rather than through cheques.

MODERN VIEW

According to the modern or expanded approach, money supply includes: *(i)* Coins, *(ii)* Currency notes, *(iii)* Banks' demand deposits, *(iv)* Time deposits with banks, *(v)* Financial assets, such as deposits with non-banking financial intermediaries like the Unit Trust, building societies, post-office savings banks, etc., *(vi)* Bills-Treasury and exchange bills, *(vii)* Bonds and equities.

In short, the modern view extends the phenomenon of money to the whole spectrum of liquidity in the asset portfolio of the individuals in a modern economy.

This controversy about the components of money supply has arisen on account of the difference of opinion regarding the significance and relationship between money supply and price level and the efficacy of monetary policy in a modern economy.

As pointed out by the RBI's Second Working Group on Money Supply in India, the basic reason for the said dispute "can be found in the basic difference implicit in the approaches of the Quantity theorists and the "Keynesians" to the most distinguishing characteristics of money, that is, the concept of money as a medium of exchange and as a store of value. The general recognition of the store of value function of money has given rise to the fairly widely accepted phenomenon of substitutability between money traditionally defined as a medium of exchange and the whole spectrum of financial assets obtaining in an economy. The liquidity approach stresses the store of value function of money.

Hence, in the modern concept of money supply, all those assets which remain abundantly liquid while performing store of value function are considered as money along with currency and demand deposits. These assets are easily convertiole into money if that is required for payments purposes. In modern approach the four different concepts of money supply are being used namely M_1, M_2' M_3 and M_4

M_1 = currency held by public + Net demand deposits of banks+other deposits of the RBI (C+DD+OD)

M_2 = M_1 + Post Office savings deposits

M_3 = M_1 + Net time deposits of banks

M_4 = M_3 + Total deposits with the post office Savings organisation (excluding National Savings Certificates)

DIFFERENT APPROACHES REGARDING MEASURE OF MONEY SUPPLY

Based on different notions of defining money in a modern economy there are four major approaches regarding the appropriate measure of money stock, namely:

1. Traditional approach,
2. Chicago School's or Monetarist Approach,
3. Gurley-Shaw Approach; and
4. Radcliffe or Liquidity Approach.

Traditional Approach. The traditional approach emphasises the significance of money as a medium of exchange and holds that money supply is constituted by currency money plus chequable demand deposits of banks held by the public. Conventionally, thus, the stock of money at a point of time is measured by aggregating the issue of currency notes and the amount of demand deposits with banks.

Monetarist Approach. The Chicago school is led by Milton Friedman, however, on empirical consideration, holds that money includes all those things which are perfect substitutes for one another. Thus, according to their view, money supply constitutes currency plus demand deposits plus time deposits.

Gurley-Shaw Approach. The Gurley-Shaw approach, on the other hand, visualises that totality of financial liabilities of monetary and non-monetary financial intermediaries as a whole and not the quantity of money alone determines the spending decisions of the public-households and the firms-in a modern economy. Thus, their concept of money supply includes all alternatives, liquid stores of value such as currency, demand deposits, time deposits, equity share, units of Unit Trust, etc.

Liquidity Approach. The Radcliffe or Liquidity Approach, however, offers a completely new line of thinking and a much wider concept of money supply. The Radcliffe Committee holds that money supply is just a part of the wider structure of liquidity that is relevant to the spending decisions of the commodity. Prices are affected by the spending decisions of the people which in turn is determined by the general liquidity of the economy. Hence, the concept of money supply should be viewed in terms of general liquidity which includes cash, all kinds of bank deposits, deposits with other institutions, near-money assets, and the borrowing facilities available.

The Radcliffe Committee, however, observes that money supply in a modern economy, cannot be successfully measured empirically, as the degrees of liquidity of different constituents of money supply (money, near-money and real assets) are varying in nature and are relative in time variation.

MEASUREMENT OF MONEY STOCK

Following liquidity approach to money, RBI sums up the following assets as aggregate monetary resources:

(1) Currency (C);

(2) Demand Deposits of Banks (DO);

(3) Other deposits of the RBI (OD);

(4) Post Office savings deposits;

(5) Time deposits of banks; and

(6) Time deposits of post offices.

According to the second working group on money supply, money supply is both an economic and a policy-controlled variable. The group observes that for monetary analysis and policy, a single measure of money stock cannot be used, as it would be not only inadequate but misleading, too. In fact, from the standpoint of money as a medium of exchange, in a modern economy, the monetary aggregates are fundamentally composed of those assets possessing the attribute of "superior liquidity". In recent years, this, Reserve Bank of India has adopted four measures of money stock in a descending order of liquidity criteria as follows :

(i) M_1,

(ii) M_2,

(iii) M_3, and

(iv) M_4

where :

M, = (i) currency notes and coins with the public (cash on hand of all banks is excluded, + (ii) Demand deposits with all commercial and co-operative banks (inter-bank deposits are excluded) + (iii) Other deposits held with the Reserve Bank of India. (Balance in account No.1 of the International Monetary Fund, the Reserve Bank of India Employees' Pension, Provident and Guarantee Funds and adhoc liability items are excluded.)

Conceptually, the category M_1 is the same as traditional sense of money supply with the public.

M_2 = (i) M_1 + (ii) Savings deposits with Post Office Savings Banks.

The category M_2 is prescribed as a compromise between the need for conceptual neatness and operational feasibility. This is on account of the fact that Post Office savings bank deposits are relatively less liquid than demand deposits with banks, but more liquid than time deposits.

M_3 = (i) M_1 + (ii) Time deposits of all commercial and cooperative banks (inter-bank time deposis are excluded).

The category M_3 represents aggregate monetary resources (AMR) as has been conceived by the first working group of the R.B.I. on the concept of money.

M_4 = (1) M_3 + (ii) Total deposits with the post office Savings Organisation. (National Savings Certificates are excluded.)

The category M_4 is an extension of M_3 as aggregate monetary resources (AMR), aggregated by the second working group. From the viewpoint of monetary management, M_1 signifies a flow, whereas M_3, refers to stock and both should be tackled with due care.

The second working group claims that these new categories of measuring money stock in the Indian economy have a much wider spectrum of monetary aggregates, in view of their varying degree of liquidity and, thus, may bring the money supply data of the R.B.I. more close to reality.

DETERMINANTS OF MONEY SUPPLY

Cash in circulation and demand deposits are the basic components of money supply. Cash money is issued by the Central Bank and demand deposits are created by the commercial banks. In this regard, Chandler states that the major determinants of the quantity of money in an economy are:

(i) The size of the monetary base;

(ii) Community's choice regarding cash and credit proportions in holding money; and

(iii) The cash reserve ratio.

Monetary Base. An important determinant of the extent of the money supply in a modern economy is the magnitude of the monetary base. The term "monetary base" refers to the supply of funds available for use either as cash or as central bank's reserves. Money. supply varies directly in relation to the changes in this base.

The monetary base, in general is composed of the following:

(i) monetary gold stock;

(ii) reserve assets, such as government securities, bonds and bullion, etc. with the central bank, and

(iii) amount of central bank credit out standings.

Generally, the amount of monetary gold stock—whether coined or used, as backing for gold certificates is being used either as cash or as bank reserves. As Chandler points out, the amount of monetary gold stock in an economy is determined by *(a)* the stock of gold accumulated in the past; *(b)* the net addition made to monetary gold stock from the current domestic production of gold. (To derive the net addition to stock, we have to deduct the real cost of production of gold as well as the amount of consumption of gold for non-monetary purposes); and *(c)* the imports and exports of gold.

Second, the monetary base is also formed by the reserve assets of the central bank, on the basis of which it can issue notes.

Lastly, the central bank credit is a major element of the monetary base today. When a central bank increases its loans and investments, it makes payments to borrowers or sellers of securities (other than commercial banks), either by paying cash or by giving a deposit credit with itself. In any case, this tends to uplift the reserve funds of the commercial banks.

The relative importance of these three components of monetary base, however, varies with different monetary systems. Under the pure gold standard, the monetary gold stock assumes significance, whereas, under the convertible paper standard, as is commonly adopted today, the stock of monetary gold has no importance in the monetary base as such. The present-day monetary base is, by and large, determined by the currency money and the central bank credit.

Community's Choice. The size of the monetary base is an important determinant of the money supply. However, there is no constant relationship between the two. The monetary superstructure, supported by each rupee of that base, may very greatly in size. The relative amounts of cash and demand deposits which the community wishes to hold has great significance in this regard. If the community chooses to make payments by cheques rather than by cash in a greater proportion, then larger will be the total volume of money that will be maintained by a given monetary base. This is because, one rupee in the hands of the public supports only itself, that is, one rupee of money; while one rupee with a commercial bank, in its reserves, can support several rupees of money in the form of derivative demand deposits (due to the multiple extension of credit in the banking system). Thus, the samę amount of monetary base can support a larger stock of aggregate money supply in an economy with banking development than in the economy without adequate banking facilities or with least banking habit among the people.

Further, the community's preference for money as a liquid asset also depends on the extent of monetization. In an economy with high degree of monetization, people would demand more money, so there will be a pressure on the government to create more supply of money to cater to the growing needs of the economy. In those areas of the country where barter is prevalent, money supply cannot be extended so rapidly.

Cash Reserve Ratio. The cash reserve ratio is also an important determinant of the quantity of money in a modern economy because it determines the multiplier co-efficient of credit creation by banks. The money multiplier is larger the smaller the reserve raito r. The money multiplier is also larger the smaller the currency deposit ratio c. When the currency deposit ratio is smaller the smaller proportion of high-powered money is being used as currency and the larger the proportion that is available to be reserves.

Supply behaviour in the money market can be specified by the money supply function. A money supply function expresses the functional relationship between the quantity of money supplies and its determinan t variables. A commonly adopted money supply function is that money supply is a function of the rate of interest, that is,

Ms = f (i), where $\frac{\Delta Ms}{\Delta i}$ >0 (which implies that there is a positive relationship between the rate of interest and money supply).

Here, Δ Ms denotes a marginal change in money supply; Δi implies a marginal change in interest rate *i*; while >0 implies a positive change or an increase.

In reality, however, money supply is a function of many variables. The actual factors influencing money supply are :

(i) The quantity of total legal tenders (1) possessed by the banks.

(ii) The cash reserve ratios for demand deposits and time deposits (dr and tr, respectively).

(iii) The rate of interest (i), and

(iv) The national income Y, because it determines the currency required by the public.

Thus,

Ms = f(l, dr, tr, i Y)

where,

$$\frac{\Delta Ms}{\Delta i} > 0; \quad \frac{\Delta Ms}{\Delta\, dr} > 0; \quad \frac{\Delta Ms}{\Delta\, tr} > 0;$$

$$\frac{\Delta Ms}{\Delta 1} > 0; \text{ and } \frac{\Delta Ms}{\Delta Y} > 0;$$

Here, the factors I, dr, and tr are under the control of the central bank, while factors such as i and Y are determined by the market forces.

It, Therefore, follows that money supply is determined jointly by the action of the central bank, the commercial banking system, and the general public. In this regard, the traditional view holds that the central bank dominates the behaviour of the public and the banking system in affecting money supply. Thus, the central banking policy, by and large, influences the quantity of money in an economy. To the traditionalists, variables such as income, rate of interest, and other money market conditions are determined by the money supply rather than they being determinants of money supply.

Empirical studies, however, support the traditional view that money supply is determined primarily by factors controlled by the central bank. However, the view has not been completely discarded by the empirical evidence. It is, however, believed that factors governed by public action and commercial banks, activities influenced by the market forces, such as the rate of interest, etc. play a subordinate role in the whole picture.

❐

14

Theories of Demand for Money

Money is not demanded because it satisfy the needs of people but it is demanded for its functions it performs. The two functions of money are very important. Firstly, money makes exchange of goods convenient and secondly, it is used for the hoarding of purchasing power. In brief, the demand for money is the derived demand. The economists generally do not agree on the cause of demand for money. In this context, two approaches prevalent—*(I)* classical approach—This approach is further sub-divided into cash transaction approach and cash balance approach; and *(II)* Keynesian Approach.

(I) The Classical Approach

Broadly speaking, the classical approach of demand for money has been interpreted in two different ways, depending upon the two notions relating to the nature and functions of money. As we know, there are two fundamental functions of money, that of a medium of exchange and that of a store of value. Accordingly, there is the medium of exchange concept of demand for money, and the store of value concept of the demand for money. The former is the cash transaction view and the latter, the cash balance view of demand for money.

(a) The Cash Transaction View. To the classical economists, money is demanded by the people only as a medium of exchange and, therefore, implies that it is not demanded for its own sake. Thus, the classicists believed that the demand for money is essentially for money to spend, or for the performance of transactions. This means that the demand for money emerges from the volume of transactions of goods and services to be carried on, during a given period. Thus, they thought that the demand for money was determined by the total quantity of goods and services that had to be paid for, during a given period. Further, the quantity of money people would require to hold (*i.e.* their demand for money) for these transactions depends on the velocity of circulation of money. This view is also designated as the transactions approach to the demand for money.

According to quantity theory of money, demand for money is always equal to the supply of money. In other words, the money, market always remains in equilibrium. This equilibrium can be explained with the help of following equation:

Supply of Money = Demand for money.

$$MV = PT$$

Here M stand for stock of money, V for velocity of money, P for price per transaction and T for number of transactions. The demand for money (Md) is equal to the price per transaction and the number of transactions. Symbolically.

$$Md = PT$$

If, in a year, T is 2000 units and P is Rs. 20 per unit, then

$$Md = Rs.\ 20 \times 2{,}000 = 40{,}000$$

In this approach, the demand for money is defined objectively, in a mechanical sense only, and no attention is paid to the motives belind the demand for money.

(b) The Cash Balance View. The alternative approach of classical theory of demand for money was developed by Cambridge economists namely Marshall, Pigou and Robertson. This approach is therefore known as Cambridge approach.

Cambridge approach was the first such effort which realised that like any other commodity money can be demanded for its own and money has utility. According to this approach money is not just for spending. It can be held as a form of wealth or asset which commands other forms of wealth in exchange, all the time. Thus, money being the most liquid asset, can serve as an efficient store of value, so it is demanded for its own sake. In this sense the demand for money is the inverse of the velocity of circulation; we can say either that the demand for money has increased or that the velocity of circulation, the rate of spending, has diminished, or conversely.

In short, this approach to the demand for money stresses to the public's needs for money balances, as a store of value at a particular point of time. In this context, it involves evidently, the reason for the people's preference to hold liquid cash or money rather than other assets, as a store of value.

The asset demand for money at a particular time refers to the demand of households, firms and the government for money to be kept as cash balance as distinct from other assets. Money can be stored as a form, of wealth and it can be conveniently converted into other forms of wealth. Being the most liquid asset, money serves as a store of value and, therefore, it is demanded for its own sake. This demand for money to be kept as cash balance depends on various subjective motives, *viz.*, transactions motive, precautionary motive, speculative motive and deflationary motive. It is to this asset demand for money that Keynes gives the name liquidity preference. While the transaction demand for money is demand over a period of time, the asset demand for money is demand at a point of time. The transactions demand for money is based on the assumption of static conditions, since it relates to a period of time. The asset demand is demand for money at a point of time (which may differ from one point of time another) and, therefore, relates to dynamic conditions. In dynamic conditions, the demand for money is influenced by such factors as the pattern of income payments, the nature and pattern of expenditure, the organisation of credit, etc. These factors change from time to time affecting the demand for money in a country. The equation for Cambridge demand for money is given below:

$$M = f(W, P, y, r_i, r_k, r_e, V, X) \qquad ...(i)$$

Here M stands for nominal demand for money, Py for money income, r for nominal rate of interest, r_k for rate of return on real capital, r_c for rate of return on goods associated with expected prices, V for utility of money and X for institutional factors. We can see here that this Cambridge demand function is similar to Friedmen's demand function.

The above mentioned Cambridge demand function could not become popular. It was Pigou's equation of demand function which gained popularity. This demand function, based on Pigovian analysis and assumptions is given below:

$$M = KPy \qquad ...(ii)$$

In mathematical sense Fisher's cash transaction approach and Cambridge's cash balance approach produces the same conclusion that demand for money is directly and proportionately related to the money income (PY). The part of money kept in form of nominal cash balances is known as K. This is nothing but the reciprocal of income velocity of money. Both approaches of demand for money gives us the same result.

$$M = kPY = \frac{PY}{V} \qquad \left(\text{Here } k = \frac{1}{V}\right)$$

There two approaches also have some differences. Fisher approach on the one hand, emphasis exchange demand for money, the Cambridge approach, on the other hand, emphasise the asset demand for money.

(II) The Keynesian Approach

In 'The General Theory of Employment, Interest and Money' Keynes has emphasised the function of asset demand for money. In the Keynesian sense, the demand for money is the demand for liquidity. Hence the Keynesian approach to the demand for money has been designated as the cash balance or liquidity preference approach.

Now one question may be asked: Why should there be demand for money to hold? Keynes has given three important reasons for holding money (or demanding money)—*viz.* transaction motive, precautionary motive and speculative motive. To Keynes, the total demand for money implies total cash balances. Analytically, total cash balances may be classified into two parts:

(i) Active Cash Balance; and

(ii) Idle Cash Balances.

(1) ACTIVE CASH BALANCES

Active cash balances relate to the demand for money hold under transactions and precautionary motives. In other words, transactions demand for money and precautionary demand for money together constitute active cash balances hold by the people.

(a) Transaction Demand for Money. Money being a medium of exchange, the primary demand for money balances arises directly out of its use for carrying on ordinary trade and business affairs of the economy. The transactions-prompted, demand for money arises on account of the lack of synchronisation between receipts and payments. Individuals in general, do not receive money income as frequently as they make payments. Thus, when income is received at discrete intervals of time, but is paid out more or less continuously against the exchange of goods and services, it is inevitable that people should need a certain stock of money all the time in order to carry out their transactions.

Briefly, thus, the transactions motive concerns the demand for money balances as a medium of exchange—as a means of bridging the gap between periodic receipts and payments.

Keynes, in dealing with the transactions motive, recognised both an income and a business motive.

The Income Motive. This refers to the transaction motive of the households, *i.e.* consumers' class. From the consumer's point of view, the amount of money which he will hold to satisfy the transactions motive will depend both on the size of his income and on the intervals of time between receipt of the various instalments and then, its disbursement. As income increases, there is the income motive for increasing transactionary demand for money. Obviously, a rich man will hold more money to satisfy his income motive than a poor man will.

The Business Motive. This refers to the transactions motive of the entrepreneur class or business community. Businessmen require money balances in order to meet business expenses, like payment for new materials and transport, payment of wages and salaries and allied current expenditure. Money balances held under this motive will depend on the turnover of the firm.

It follows, therefore, that the amount of money balances held under the transactions motive will depend: *(i)* on the time and size of firms' incomes, and *(ii)* on the turnover of business. As income rises, and the business becomes more prosperous, the amount of money demanded for the transactions motive will rise.

It is commonly stated that the transactions motive for holding money fluctuates with the level of money income. This is justified by the assumption that transactions and hence, transactionary demand for money, fluctuate in proportion to changes in money income.

It should be noted, then, that the transactions demand for money is income-determined and is relatively stable because income does not change all of a sudden. Moreover, changes in the rate of interest have no such influence in changing the transactions demand which is determined by the level of income. Thus, the transactions demand for money is interest-inelastic.

Nevertheless, the trend of a community's aggregate demand for money, under the transactions motive, depicts a high degree of correlation of proportionality to the size of money of national income. In symbolic terms, if *Lt* represents the transactions demand for money, the money demand function may be stated thus:

$$Lt = f(Y),$$

Where, Y stands for the level of national income.

(b) Precautionary Motive. In addition to the amount needed for meeting normal and foreseen expenditures, individuals and business firms will keep additional sums of money on hand to provide protection in the event of emergency—this is the precautionary motive for holding money. Failure to have sufficient amount of money might force an individual or firm into liquidation at certain times. One misfortune may lead to another. For instance, illness reduces income on the one hand and increase expenditure on the other; it will necessitate emergency borrowing and thus impair a person's credit standing as well as his ability to meet other emergencies. The volume of money required to satisfy precautionary motive will differ widely with individuals and business firms, according to the nature of their business, their access to the credit market, the ease with which their other securities can be converted into money when emergency arises, and so on.

The precautionary motive is similar to the transactions motive for holding money, for in both cases money is demanded to meet transactions. But in the case of transactions motive, money is held for ordinary transations, while in the case of precautionary motive, transactions are unforseen and unexpected. While transactions motive is based on the fact that holding of money is very convenient and that the value of money in terms of other goods is relatively certain, precautionary motive of holding money depends upon the degree of uncertainty in personal and other conditions. In the event of a war or rumour of a war, or in times of financial crisis, people like to hold more money to meet unforseen contingencies. In general, the cash balances held for the transactions and precautionary motives are directly dependent on the level of national income and are a stable function of the latter.

We can, therefore, state that

$L_t =$ K (Y), in which

$L_t =$ transaction demand for money (here transactions include precautionary purposes also)

Y = level of national income

K = fraction of national income which is to be kept for transactions purposes.

Suppose that the community wants to hold 25 per cent of the national income for transations purposes, then k is 1/4. Suppose further, that national income of India is Rs. 60,000 crores; k(Y) would be Rs. 15,000 crores. It is assumed that k is a constant positive fraction. According to Keynes, the transactions demand for cash balances is income-elastic but interest-inelastic—whatever be the rate of interest, the same amount of money will be demanded for transactions putposes. In Fig. 1 (a) the transactions demand for money (L_t) is a vertical line; it is interest-inelastic. But some economists would not agree with this view. According to them, if the rate of interest is very high, there can be a shift from transactions demand for money to demand for interest-bearing assets.

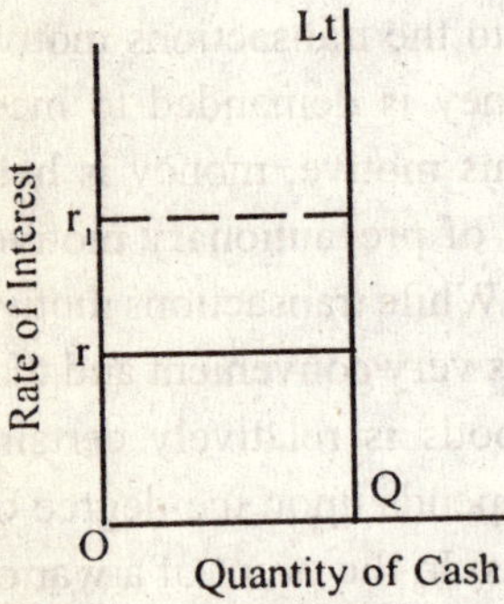

Fig. 1 (a)

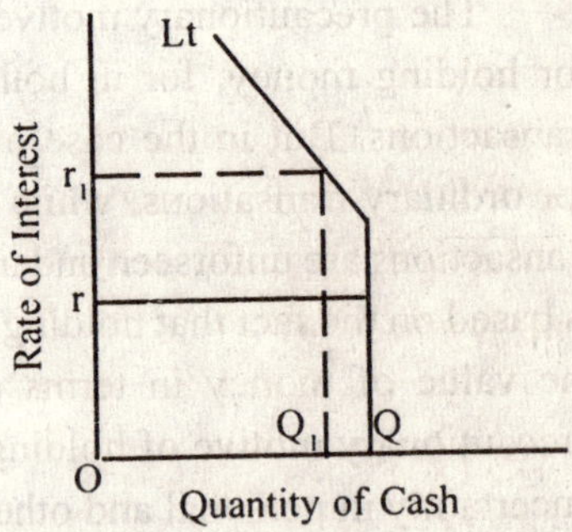

Fig. 1 (b)

In Fig. 1 (b) L_t is vertical up to a point after which it has a backward slope-for exapmle, at r_1 rate of interest, the cash balances for transactions declines. But for the sake of simplicity and convenience, we assume that Lt is a fraction of income [L_t = k(y)] and that it is interest-inelastic-in terms of a figure, it is a vertical line, as in Fig. l(a).

Keynes lumps together the transactions and precautionary motives on the ground that they are fairly stable and constant over time and exert no influence on the rate of interest. Both are determined by income.

(2) IDLE CASH BALANCES (SPECULATIVE DEMAND FOR MONEY)

All people speculate about the future level of prices of all types of assets and securities. They will like to hold those securities whose prices they anticipate to rise and they will hesitate to hold those securities whose prices they fear wll decline. Here is the speculative motive for holding money or securities. Keynes defines the speculative motive as "the desire of earning profit by knowing better than the market what the future will bring forth." The speculative motive for holding money can be illustrated with a simple but highly imaginary example. Suppose that the long-term rate of interest is expected to decline in the near future. Asa result, securities bearing fixed interest can be expected to rise in value. Suppose a bond with the face value of Rs. 100, carries a fixed interest rate of 5%. Suppose further, the market rate of interest is 4%. Then the market value of the bond will be Rs. 100 × 5/4 = Rs. 125. Accordingly, those who have such securities would wish to hold on to these securities so as to secure capital appreciation in the value of the securities in the future. Or, those who have funds may convert them into fixed interest-bearing securities now so as to dispose them of later. Thus, if people anticipate rise in the price of securities (*i.e.*, fall in the rate of interest), they would hold less money with them but would hold more securities. On the other hand, if people anticipate a fall in the price of securities (*i.e.*, a rise in the rate of interest) they would dispose of their securities now at higher prices, hold inoney to buy securities when their prices would have fallen.

Thus, people and institutions who have the option to hold their wealth in the form of money or in securities will be influenced by the rate of interest and their anticipation regarding the future. How much money people would hold for speculative purposes would depend upon such factors as the present rate of interest, the rate of interest they expect in the future when the change in the rate of interest will occur, and so on. The professional speculators will bother more the capital gain and less for actual interest income. But the ordinary wealth-holders consider the flow of regular income as more important than capital appreciation or depreciation due to a change in the rate of interest.

In practice, a very low rate of interest will induce people to keep their wealth in the form of money rather than in the form of bonds. This is partly explained by the fact that the income from securities will be low and hence it will be necessary to keep large amounts of cash for transactions and precautionary purposes. Again, at low interest rates (*i.e.*, at high prices of securities) the desire to hold cash will be strengthened by the belief that interest rates will rise rather than fall further; in such a case the price of securities will decline and would be advantageous to buy them at that time.

We can also show the relation between the speculative motive and the other motives for holding money. The speculative motive for holding cash depends upon the psychology of the speculators and their anticipation regarding the future. The amount of money held for speculative purposes will be varying according to circumstances. On the other hand, transactions and precautionary motives for holding money are held constant at any time. Further, speculative motive depends upon the rate of interest-interest-elastic—while the other motives being constant are not dependent upon the rate of interest; at the same time speculative holding of money influences the rate of interest too. Finally, there may be circumstances when it will be difficult to distinguish between speculative and precautionary motives. For instance, a fall in the prices of all types of securities may result in a stock market crash. People will like to hold more money by disposing of their securities. This can be explained in terms of precautionary motive or in terms of speculative motive.

Thus the speculative demand for cash balances is a negative function of the rate of interest and we can write it as :

$L_s = l(r)$, in which

L_s = speculative demand for money, and

r = rate of iterest.

The speculative demand for money is illustrated in Fig. 2.

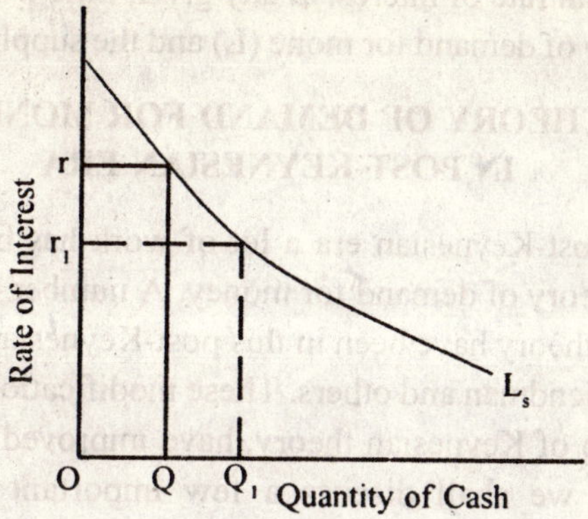

Fig. 2

At a lower rate of interest, the quantity of cash demanded for speculative purpose expands. The aggregate demand for cash is the sum of transations demand and speculative demand for cash. In other words,

$$L = L_t + L_s$$

$$= k(Y) + l(r)$$

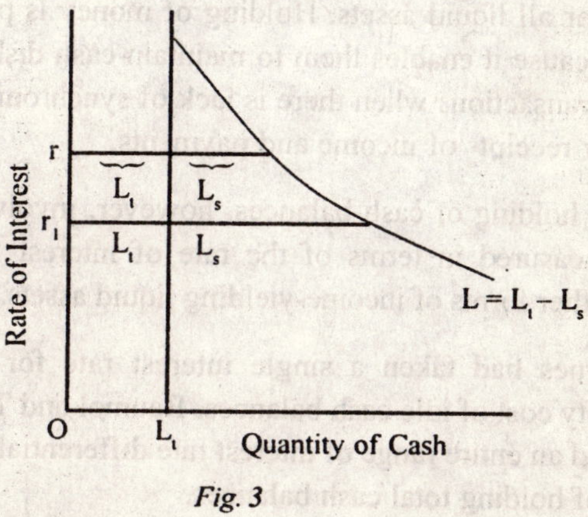

Fig. 3

It will be clear from Fig. 3, that Lt is fixed for every state of interest; but L_s expands for a lower rate of interest.

The actual rate of interest at any given time will be determined by the equality of demand for mone (L) and the supply of money (M).

THEORY OF DEMAND FOR MONEY IN POST-KEYNESIAN ERA

In the post-Keynesian eıa a lot of work has been done in the field of the theory of demand for money. A number of modifications in Keynesian theory have been in this post-Keynesian era by Baumol and Tobin, Friendman and others. These modifications which tried to fill up the gap of Keynesian theory, have improved and refined this theory. Now we shall discuss a few important post-Keynesian developments.

(I) Portfolio Balance Approach to Demand for Money

Based on Keynes' liquidity preferene theory, Baumol and Tobin have developed an alternative approach to transactions demand for money called, "Portfolio Balance Approach" in which the portfolio behaviour of individuals and institutions has been stressed in the process of monetary management.

In this approach, the demand for money is viewed as a joint demand for all liquid assets. Holding of money is preferred by the people because it enables them to maintain cash disbursements and carry on transactions when there is lack of synchronization between timings or receipts of income and payments.

The holding of cash balances, however, involves costs which can be measured in terms of the rate of interest forgone by not holding other forms of income-yielding liquid assets.

Keynes had taken a single interest rate for measuring the opportunity cost of idle cash balances. Baumol and Tobin, however, considered an entire range of interest rate differentials for measuring the cost of holding total cash balances.

In the asset portfolio, different types of assets have different degrees of cost, liquidity, money value certainty, income certainty and real value certainty.

Cash balances have little cost of acquisition. But, holding of cash does not yield any income. Further, cash has money-value certainty but is unstable in real value, *i.e.* its purchasing power. Cash is the most liquid asset.

On the other hand, bonds and other long-term securities have no easy liquidity but they are income-yielding assets and their real value is more certain.

For balancing the different degrees of different characteristics of these different assets, the portfolio assets will be so maintained by prudent people that funds will be distributed in such proportions of the given assets that their marginal yields become equal. Thus, the choice between money and near-money assets is primarily decided on the basis of the average rate of returns and the relative variance in certainty of income yields.

James Tobin states that the optimal inventory holdings of cash balances is determined by many related factors, such as:

(i) Rate of returns on alternative liquid assets available;

(ii) Cost of exchanging assets;

(iii) Volume of non-financial transactions;

(iv) Transaction and delivery costs which are to be balanced against interest and carrying costs;

(v) Pattern or risk aversion or minimisation in combination with different assets in the portfolio.

Baumol assets that firms and individuals would usually keep the value of their income in certain money balances for the exchange utility function and the rest in the form of income-yielding assets. The following formula is suggested by him for measuring the transaction demand for money holding:

$$Md / p = \sqrt{(2bT) / i}$$

where, Md/p = demand for cash balance in real terms.

T = volume of transactions.

i = the rate of interest.

b = brokerage fee and/or all other charges meant for borrowing or converting a bond or other assets into cash.

It shows that the demand for money is stable and negatively related to the rate of interest. David Laidler's empirical tests based on the U.S. data confirm this.

(II) Wealth Theory of Demand for Money

Milton Friedman propounded the wealth theory of demand for money. In his view, money is "a durable consumer goods held for the services it renders, and yielding a flow of services proportional to the stock". Money is demanded as an asset or capital; as such the theory of demand for money is a part of the theory of capital.

In examining the demand for money, Friedman presumes that people do hold money and rather than investigating the motives behind liquidity preference, he sought to find out how much they would seek to hold under different conditions.

Considering money like a durable goods Friedman stated that it is also subject to the law of Diminishing Marginal Rate of Substitution, *i.e.*, with an increase in the stock of money held, its values tend to diminish relative to the services other assets are rendering.

According to Friedman money is a form of asset for holding wealth. Here, he agrees with Pigou that money is one asset among many others that is held by people not as it store of value but just as a claim over wealth, because it renders extra services. To the productive enterprise, for instance, money is a capital goods, being a source of productive resources and other services.

Thus, Friedman holds that the theory of demand for money becomes as special topic in the theory of capital.

Friedman identifies the demand for money on the part of the ultimate wealth-owning units in the society with that of the demand for consumption service. As such, the demand for money is assumed to depend on three major factors: *(i)* total wealth to be held in various forms of assets—the analogue of budget constraints; *(ii)* relative price of and return on one form of wealth as compared to alternative form; and *(iii)* tastes and preferences of the wealth owning units.

Hence, Friedman goes beyond the traditional quantity theory approach by stressing that money demand is determined not only by price and income levels, but also by an important factor, *i.e.*, the cost of holding money or cash balances.

According to him, the cost of holding cash balances can be measured in terms of *(i)* the rate of interest that can be earned on alternative assets, say, bonds or equities, etc.; *(ii)* the expected rate of change in the price level. Any increase in the rate of interest or an increase in the price level leads to a decrease in the cash balances, the people wish to hold. For instance, let us consider a government bond yielding 10 per cent interest. It costs an individual Rs. 10 a year to hold Rs. 100 in cash instead of holding it in the form of a bond, an income-yielding asset. Similarly, if prices in general are rising at the rate of 10 per cent per year, it will need Rs. 110 in cash to buy at the end of the year as much as Rs. 100 at the beginning, so that it costs an individual Rs. 10 a year to hold Rs. 100 in cash in place of real goods worth Rs. 100. Consequently, at higher holding costs, that is, when interest rates are higher and/or there is large rise in the price level, people will tend to economise on cash balances; they will thus try to spend more on goods and meet their obligations with less cash on hand and with less demand deposits in the banks. Conversely, a decrease in the interest rate or in the rate of increase in the price level reduces the cost of holding money, which in effect leads to increase in the liquidity preference.

In short, there is an inverse relationship between the demand for money and the cost of holding money.

Friedman, thus, asserts that money is one of the major alternative forms of holding wealth; *(i)* money-cash balances; *(ii)* bonds; *(iii)* equities; *(iv)* physical non-human goods; and *(v)* human capital.

Friedman further points out that money yields real returns in the form of convenience, security and perfect liquidity. Money may also yield a money return, say interest earned on saving deposits with a bank. The magnitude of real return, however, varies inversely with the price level. With a fall in prices, when the value of money improves, cash balances yield a sort of capital gain. Anyway, basically money balances provide security and liquidity, while other assets yield income.

Bonds and equities, for instances, are claims to perpetual income streams of constant nominal value. Returns on bonds are influenced by *(i)* changes in the interest rates and *(ii)* changes in their market prices.

Real goods held by ultimate wealth-owning units yield income in kind utility, which cannot be measured by an explicit rate of interest. However, their real return tends to be affected by the changes in the price level.

Human capital is the discounted value of the expected income yield. It has, however, a limited degree of substitutability with other forms of asset holding. For instance, people may sell their assets in order to spend for training by which they can improve upon their abilities to earn more in future.

Hence, a distinction between human and non-human wealth in the demand function becomes necessary ort account of the former's limited degree of substitutability. To this, Friedman adds "utility" determining variables which affect tastes and preferences of wealth-owing units which take the form of demand function.

In his analysis of demand function, thus, Friedman remarks that money-holding is a necessity, and other assets are like "comforts" or "luxuries". With an increase in income, thus the holding of other assets in proportion increases.

To Friedman the demand for money is a problem of capital theory. Thus, with simplified economic assumptions, estimating non-observable variables and forming a sequence of mathematical simplifications, he resolves a formalistic demand function as under:

$$M = f\left(P, Y, \frac{1}{P}.\frac{dp}{dt}, rb, re, w, u\right)$$

Where,

M = aggregate demand for money

P = general price level.

Y = total flow of income.

$\frac{1}{P}.\frac{dp}{dt}$ = size of a nominal return in the form of appreciation or depreciation in money value, per rupee of real assets—physical goods—which together with P implies the rate of real return on these as sets.

rb = bond yields, the market bond interest rate.

re = equity yields, the market interest rate of equities.

w = ratio of non-human to human wealth. It is closely linked to the ratio of wealth to income.

u = utility-determining variables which tend to influence tastes and preferences.

Friedman, however, mentions that this demand equation is independent of the nominal units used for measuring money variables. Further, the amount of money demand changes proportionately to the changes in the unit in which prices and money income are expressed. Hence, the equation expresses the first degree homogeneous function of P and Y.

Thus,

$$\lambda M = f\left(\lambda P, \lambda Y, \frac{1}{P}.\frac{dp}{dt}, rb, re, w, u\right)$$

$$\text{If, } \lambda = \frac{1}{p}, \text{ then}$$

$$\frac{M}{P} = f\left(\frac{y}{p}, \frac{1}{p}.\frac{dp}{dt}, rb, re, w, u\right)$$

Thus, the equation represents demand for money as a demand for real balances, as a function of "real" variables, independent of monetary values.

With a change in per capita income, people's standard of living changes. With such a change in the standard of living, people may desire to hold cash balances more or less according to the change. In Friedman's view, thus, money is a luxury like durable consumer goods. Hence, an increase in real income is linked to a more than proportionate increase in the real cash balances. Therefore, the income elasticity of demand for money is greater than unity: $\left(\frac{\%\Delta M}{\%\Delta Y}\right) > 1$ (where, M stands for demand for money and Y represents real income).

Friedman asserts, however, that the income to which cash balances are adjusted is over a long period of time, *i.e.*, permanent income rather than current income.

❐

15

Monetary Policy

Monetary policy is basically concerned with the monetary system of the country. It deals with monetary decisions and measures and such non-monetary decisions and measures as have monetary effects.

Monetary policy is usually defined as the central bank's policy pertaining to the control of the availability, cost and use of money and credit with the help of monetary measures in order to achieve specific goals.

The central bank of a country is the traditional agent which formulates and operates monetary policy.

A monetary policy is regarded as passive when the central bank's decision to abstain deliberately from applying monetary measures and active when it seeks to achieve, certain ends through the enforcement of positive monetary measures.

Monetary policy is only a means to an end, not an end in itself. The aims, objects and scope of monetary policy are conditioned both severally and collectively by the economic environment and philosophy of time. In a broad sense, however, monetary policy itself cannot be ordained to operate, on its own, as a foolproof controlling measure but rather in conjunction with the fiscal policy and debt management. In fact, monetary/policy, fiscal policy and debt management may be lumped together as a national financial policy.

Traditionally, credit control measures and decisions are she instituting elements of a monetary policy. Monetary and credit policies operate on the following interrelated factors:

(i) the availability of credit and its flow.

(ii) the cost of borrowing, that is, the rate of interest;

(iii) the general liquidity of the economy; and

(iv) the volume of money.

A sound monetary policy is the main prerequisite of a successful and comprehensive programme of development planning. A proper monetary policy is, however, not a sufficient condition but a necessary one for economic growth, because economic growth is basically a real phenomenon and not a monetary phenomenon. Indeed, Money has a dynamic role to play, because it activises idle resources and the spending of money leads to its allocation. A well-structured monetary policy can direct its efficient allocation.

In the economically advanced countries, the monetary authority concentrates on the regulatory aspect of monetary measures in order to achieve the goal of economic stabilization, while in a developing economy like India, monetary policy tends to be typical in nature cilming at controlled expansion. The policy of controlled expansion contains the attempt at reconciliation of two contradictory motives: *(i)* to facilitage economic growth; and *(ii)* to restrain inflationary pressures:

OBJECTIVE OF MONETARY POLICY

Monetary policy, in essence is the economic policy of the gover:nment in the monetary field. Thus, the objectives of monetary policy must be regarded as being part of the overall economic objectives to be pursued by the government. Indeed, the objectives of a monetary policy can be manifold in the context of the general economic policy of a country. But the various objectives of monetary policy are not always mutually consistent. The monetary authority of a country has to select, on the basis of priority assigned alternative ends, when they are incompatible with, or conflict with, one another. Thus, the monetary authority should possess a clear idea of the range of choice among its various ends in the prevailing economic condition and the general economic aims of the country. The traditional objectives of monetary policy prior to World War II were commonly considered to be the maintenance of price stability and exchange stability. The Radcliffe Committee, however, suggested the following objectives of monetary policy to be followed by a modem government of a developed country which are ident,ical with those of the general economic policy:

1. A high and stable level of employment.
2. Steady economic growth and a high and growing level of income and the improvement in the nation's standards of living.
3. A margin in the balance of payments in order to contribute something to the economic development of the outside world.
4. Reasonable price stability to maintain the internal value of money intact.
5. A stable exchange rate and strengthening of foreign exchange reserves.

The prime objectives of monetary policy, however, changed from time to time in relation to exigencies of circumstances and economic consideration. The generally accepted important goals of monetary policy can be enumerated as : *(1)* neutrality of money; *(2)* exchange stability and equilibrium in the balance of payments; *(3)* price stability and control of business cycles; *(4)* full employment; and *(5)* economic growth.

(1) Neutrality of Money

The neutral monetary policy was expounded by Prof. Hayek. According to him, the monetary authority shculd aim at the complete neutraility of money. He holds that money should be a passive factor. It should not be allowed to interfere with the economic forces like productives efficiency, real cost of production and consumer preferences. The purpose of money is just to facilitate exchange transactions without creating any disturbances in the functioning of economy. Hence, the quantity of money should be so controlled as to result in the total output, total transactions and prices of goods and services being exactly what they would be in an efficient barter economy.

The policy of neutral money seeks to do away with the disturbing effects of the changes in the quantity of money on important economic entities such as prices, output, employment and income.

Thus, under the policy of neutral money, the monetary authority has to keep the quantity of money perfectly stable. It should be noted, however, that the perfect stability of money for the neutrality goal implies that the quantity of money is to be kept constant at all items and in all circumstances, for cyclical fluctuations in an economy are primarily caused by changes in the supply of money.

Firstly, it is pointed out that the concept, which is based on the quantity theory of money according to which changes in the money supply cause corresponding changes in the price level, is an outmoded concept, and, therefore, has been discarded by economists.

Secondly, a neutral money policy will not ensure stability in the price level, for in a modern economy, technological and scientific developments play a vital role in increasing production and if, under such conditions, quantity of money is kept fIxed, it would only lead to deflationary conditions, and hence to a fall in prices.

Thirdly, some critics point out that the concept of neutral money and the purpose for which it is aimed at are not only contradictory to each other but impracticable as well. In fact, the concept, being based on the laissez faire philosophy in which perfect competition in a really free economy is assumed, has long been considered obsolete in a modern dynamic economy. Further, to ensure stability in a modern economy, it is essential for the monetary authority to maintain an effective supply of money. Apparently effective monetary control by the central bank and the laissez faire policy can never go together.

Finally, the above concept does not apply to cases of depression when prices are falling even though money supply remains unchanged and volume of goods and services decline. In a depressionary period, even when the quantity of money is increased in the economy, it cannot revive the price levels.

In conclusion, it may be affirmed that a neutral money policy cannot check the occurrence of business fluctuations in an economy and that money has come to stay as an active element in a modern economy.

(2) Exchange Rate Stability

Maintenance of stable exchange rates is an essential condition for the creation of international confIdence and promotion of smooth international trade on the largest scale possible. Instability in exchange rates might lead to undesirable effects such as weakening of the value of currency in the world market, speculation and even flight of capital abroad.

The objectives of exchange stability of a monetary policy could easily achieve an equilibrium in the balance of payments of a country under the gold standard. Traditionally, countries faced with balance of payments problems have used monetary policy as a means of eliminating their deficits.

A restrictive monetary policy tends to reduce a country's balance of payments deficit in the following ways:

(i) Under dear money policy, higher interest rates make it less attractive for foreign countries to borrow from the deficit country and induce them to invest there.

(ii) It tends to reduce demand in the country, which in turn tends to reduce the demand for imports as well as for domestic goods.

(iii) Reduction in domestic demands holds down the rate of inflation or reduces prices which makes imported articles less attractive and makes the deficit country's exports more attractive to foreigners. Thus, import is curtailed and export expanded.

Though a policy of stabilisation of exchange rates was justified in the interest of maintaining stable international economic relations, the exchange stability goal of monetary policy has been criticised in the following grounds:

(i) Exchange stability can be achieved only at the cost internal price stability. But fluctuations in the domestic price level or changes in the purchasing power of money causes severe disturbances in the economy of a country. This may call for internal prices stability which is of prime importance for the smooth functioning and progress of the domestic economy.

(ii) Since inflationary or deflationary movements in some countries are passed on to some others through fixed exchange rates, it puts the affected country at the mercy of other countries. This may serious affect the economy of the country whose prosperity does not depend upon foreign trade.

(3) Price Stabilisation

Fluctuations in prices and cyclical variations are the chief among other disadvantages of a monetary system under capitalism. The object of monetary policy apparently to reduce these disadvantages to a minimum. Thus, in the view of economists like Cassel and Keynes, a more important aim of monetary policy is to achieve and maintain price stabilisation and normal course of business activity through appropriate credit regulation measures adopted by the central bank.

A price stabilisation policy is advocated on the following grounds;

(1) Inflation is unjust and ruins the general economic welfare of the community.

(2) Price stability creates difficult problems of production and distribution, affecting differently different sections of the

community. In short, there are innumerable evil aspects of inflation (rising prices) or deflation (falling prices).

(3) Deflationary price level breeds increasing unemployment and falling level of output and income. It ultimately leads to depression, and is, therefore, inexpedient.

(4) Briefly, the changes in the price level cause disturbances in economic relationships within a country as well as among countries. This may produce dire economic and social consequences to all concerned. Only a policy of price stabilisation will eliminate such disturbances.

(5) A fine stabilisation of internal prices is essential to augment community's economic welfare.

(6) The policy of stabilisation will eliminate cyclic fluctuations, since for the purpose of maintaining price stability, undue credit expansion or contraction (which are generally supposed to accentuate a boom or slump) will have to be controlled.

(7) Active and stable prosperity is possible only during periods of relatively stable prices. When the value of money is reasonably stable, there will be greater confidence in the forward contracts and credit transactions and this promotes business activity. Money as a store of value and a standard of deferred payments can function very well only in periods of price stability.

(8) Equitable distribution of national income is ensured by price stability.

Apparently, the goal of price stabilisation implies that in general the average price level as measured by the wholesale price index or consumers' price index should not be allowed to vary beyond narrow margins.

Generally, a policy of price stabilisation is objectional on a number of grounds as listed below:

(1) The concept of price stabilisation being vague, it is difficult to determine the price level to be selected for stabilisation.

(2) Price changes are a symptom rather than a cause of cyclical fluctuations. The price level itself does not offer any preventive or remedial measure and, therefore, price stability as the criterion of monetary policy cannot be accepted as a suitable aim.

(3) Price stabilisation may hinder economic progress, as it will remove much of the price incentives to the business community and as such productive activity will suffer from stagnation.

(4) A policy of price stabilisation ignores the dispersion of individual/prices which together constitute the "average price level" The structure of prices in general and individual prices in particular rather than the general price level as such are important in triggering economic activity in the system.

Variations in prices are useful for the successful working of the price mechanism for economic adjustments in a free enterprise economy.

(5) Stability of prices in the face of declining costs adversely affects economic relations and functioning:

(a) It may prove to be inflationary and encourage over-investment and over-expansion that must lead to their subsequent collapse.

(b) It permits debtors to appropriate the benefits of gain in economic efficiency at the expense of creditors;

(c) It prevents the sharing in the benefits of economic improvements by people of fixed income groups like salaries employees and pensioners.

(6) Price stabilisation policy is not a very feasible phenomenon. A central bank cannot effectively control the volume of credit in the economy as a whole, because a large chunk of financial activities is carried out through non-banking financial intermediaries and thus,

outside the control of the central bank. Moreover, during a deflationary period, expansion of money supply may fail to bring prices to the original level.

(7) Economic history reveals that economic stabilisation can never be guaranteed by mere price stabilisation, as there can be disharmonies and dislocations in the economic system even though prices are stable in a free economy.

Alternatively, there may be the policy of rising price level or falling price level.

The Policy of Slowly Rising Prices or Mild Inflation

Against rigid price stabilisation, some economists have advocated a policy of gently rising prices on the following counts:

(1) It may safeguard against the risk of deflation, when a rising price level is favoured by the monetary authority by adopting cheap money policy as an anti-deflationary measure and a policy of economic development *via* inflation.

(2) It will prevent under-employment and depression. It gives continuous'stimulation to the business community to invest and expand which will assure continuous economic progress with a high level of employment and prosperity.

(3) Rising prices distribute income in favour of profiteer's class whose marginal propensity to save is very high and thereby the rate of saving can be enhanced for capital formation and other productive activity. This is especially advocated for an under-developed country with a capital deficiency.

(4) It has been argued by some economists that rising prices stimulate not only production, but consumption also. The policy of rising price level is regarded as a policy of stimulating consumption and raising the level of effective demand by inducing consumers, producers, wholesalers and retailers to buy the stock of goods in anticipation of further rises in prices. Thus, a rising prices policy, it is assumed, not only ensures an increase of output but secures a market

for the larger output, without which over-production is liable to occur.

(5) To most economists, however, the most important motive of the policy of rising prices is the desire to stimulate production. Thus, prosperous periods are usually assumed to be accompanied by rising prices, while depressions are accompanied by falling prices. Prosperity can be achieved; it is assumed, through the stimulating effect of the rise in prices caused by monetary expansion. Thus, rising prices are favoured because they mean the prospect of higher turnover, higher profits and lower risks. A rising price level is indeed a very powerful stimulus to trade.

The above mentioned points can well be summarised by quoting Prof. Samuelson, thus: "In mild inflation the wheels of industry are initially well lubricated, and output in near capacity. Private investment is brisk, jobs plentiful. Such has been the historical pattern."

Drawbacks of a Slowly Rising Prices Policy

The rising prices policy is subject to the following disadvantages:

(1) It tends to discourage aggregate saving and encourage extravagance on the part of both consumers and producers.

(2) It may lead to an over-expansion which may ultimately lead to crisis and collapse. In view of rising prices, the producers are not very much induced to bring down their costs of production. When there is a seller's market during inflation, producers are able to sell almost anything they produce. Under such circumstances, quality may become a Secondary consideration. However, producers are liable to make mistakes in their judgment of the market demand, but amidst rising prices, such mistakes may only mean a slower turnover and smaller profits.

(3) In spite of its business stimulating effect, a policy of rising prices could hardly be expected to provide the economic millennium. Inflation, however good it may look in the beginning, ultimately brings chaos and distractions in the economy. It encourages

speculation and easy money-making activities through hoarding, black-marketing, etc. Inflation may also displace rational judgement of the entrepreneur by provoking speculation which may lead to over-expansion in investment followed by an inevitable collapse."

Policy of Slowly Falling Prices

Some economists, however, have advocated a policy of slowly falling prices for the following reasons:

(1) In contrast to rising prices, which reward speculative businessmen and protect the inefficient from the penalties of their errors, falling prices require high grade managerial performance and efficiency for business survival. This, is a very desirable result from the point of view of public welfare.

(2) Falling prices policy is better than a stable price policy in an advancing economy in the sense that it saves the society from the inflationary effect which would have been caused under price stability. It is a policy which allows a lower cost of production caused by technological progress to produce its effect on prices and avoid an inflationary bias.

(3) When prices do not fall so very rapidly, as to unduly depress business activity, the distribution of income will be improved under such a policy because of the increased share being enjoyed by the wage-earning and consumer classes.

(4) A falling prices policy is very desirable to check a speculative boom and to enforce the liquidation of unsound ventures that had developed under the influence of prolonged inflation.

(5) A great merit of a falling prices policy is that it complies with consumers' clamour for returning to the 'good old days' of low prices.

(6) From the standpoint of foreign trade, falling prices policy will stimulate exports and discourage imports and make the balance of payments position favourable.

Stabilisation of prices has its merits and drawbacks, whereas inflation and deflation are not unmixed blessings. In a dynamic world, it is impracticable to strike a happy medium between inflation and deflation. Thus, the best solution seems to be that a changing trend in prices from time to time as the circum stances call for with a reasonable level of stability should be the aim of monetary policy. In other words, under undesirable galloping inflationary conditions, a falling prices policy may be adopted as an anti-inflationary measure, while in an inexpedient deflationary situation, a rising prices policy may be followed with the aim of restoring prices to their previous level. This is how a reasonable (but not absolute) degree of price stability may be attained.

(4) Full Employment

Since the publication of Keynes's General Theory, most economists considered full employment as the foremost and ideal objectives of monetass policy. Thus, the use of monetary policy for promoting full employment is of recent origin. According to many modern economists, economic stabilisation can be conbined with the objective of having a high or full level of employment.

According to Growther that the obvious objective of a monetary policy of a country should be the attain equilibrium between saving and investment at the point of full employment. According to Dueserberry, however, monetary policy is one of a set of instruments

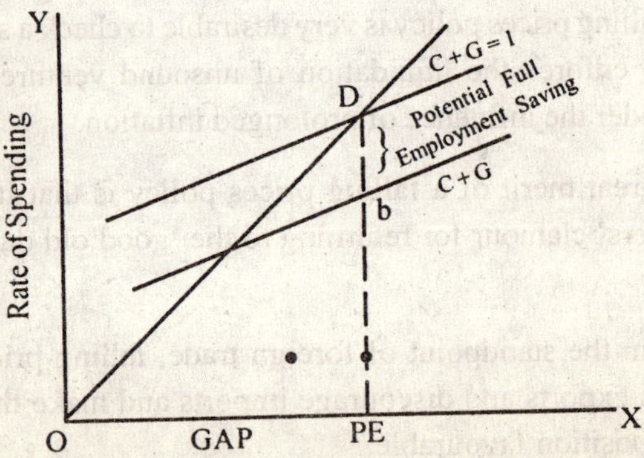

Fig. 1: Rate of Investment required for full employment

which can be used in achieving the full employment goal. The appropriate use of anyone instrument of policy depends on the manner in which the other polices are followed. To him, the main task of monetary policy is to find a level of interest rates which exactly equates investment demand with full employment saving. As a matter of fact, some particular rate of investment is required to achieve full employment. This can be illustrated diagrammatically as in Fig. 1.

In the above diagram, the line C + G shows the consumption plus government expenditure at any level of income resulting from a particular combination of government expenditure and taxes under a given fiscal policy. Thus, the task of monetary polky is to produce an investment demand which makes the C + G + 1 line pass through a point a above FE, *i.e.*, full employment point. The distance bd is the potential full employment saving of the economy. Hence, monetary policy is to put that amount of money supply in circulation which may produce a level of interest rates which exactly equates investment demand with full employment saving. This can be sho'wn diagrammatically as in Fig. 2.

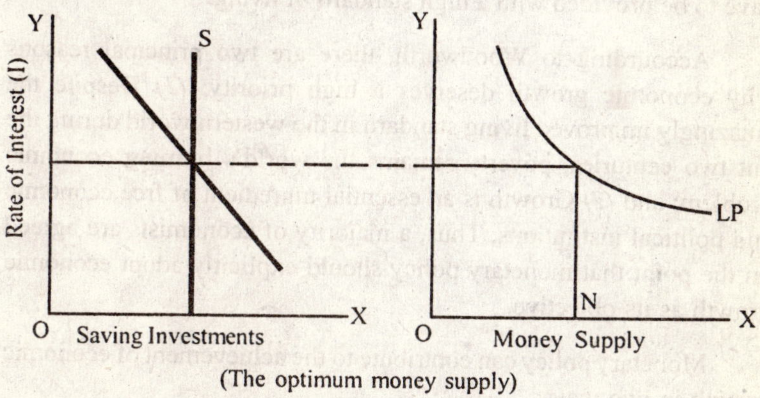

Fig. 2: Determination of money supply required for a full employment rate of investment.

In Fig. 2 the vertical line S shows, full employment savings in (a) shows the level of invtstment associated with differen clevels of interest rates out of full employment increases.

OR is the ideal interest rate at which investment becomes equal to saving at full employment equilibrium level of income. In panef (b) the LP curve represents liquidity preference at the demand for money at this full employment level of income. In relation to this demand for money, OM amount of money supply is necessary to achieve the OR rate of interest, which is suitable to induce investment required for full employment, and the full employment saving and investment level will be equated at such a rate. Thus, ON, the optimum money supply is to be released by the monetary authority for the sake of full employment.

(5) Economic Growth

While economic growth is unquestionably a primary goal of any economy, there is heated controversy in regard to qualifications as an objective of monetary policy. Till now amajority of economists considered monetary policy asa short-run policy primarily aimed at full employment and mitigating cyclical fluctuations and not concerned with economic growth as such. Recently, however, it has been realised by many that it is not enough to achieve full employment but that the economy should develop at an ever-growing pace if people have to be provided with a high standard of living.

Accourding to Woodworth, there are two principal reasons why economic growth deserves a high priority: *(1)* Despite the amazingly im proved living standard in the western world during the put two centuries, poverty remains the world's burning economic problem; and *(2)* Growth is an essential ingredient of free economic and political institutions. Thus, a majority of economists are agreed on the point that monetary policy should explicitly adopt economic growth as its objective.

Monetary policy can contribute to the achievement of economic growth in qvo ways:

(1) The monetary authority can help economic development by creating a favourable environment for saving and investment which greatly influences economic growth. For this, the monetary policy's aim of price stabilisation is very important. Reasonable price stability

encourages both saving and investment. As saving is the main source of capital formation, when saving increases under favourable circumstances, capital formation can also be accelerated which in turn accelerates economic growth.

(2) It is sometimes argued that a tight or restrictive money policy impedes while an expansionist or easy money policy promotes economic growth. But as a matter of fact, neither view is true, since the truth lies somewhere midway. A tight money policy is not conducive to growth only when it is applied at a wrong time, say when there is deficient demand. In a situation with deficient demand and unemployed resources to a large extent, an easy money policy is most suitable, but if it is carried far beyond the stage of full employment, it will generate an inflationary impact, and to control a speculative boom in such a situation, a tight money policy will be appropriate. Thus, the important thing is that they should be applied at the appropriate time; otherwise, they do more harm than good to economic growth. Therefore, a flexible monetary policy has been advocated to achieve economic growth with price stability. Briefly, thus, monetary policy can assist in promoting economic growth by maintaining reasonable price stability and optimum use of economic resources in an economy.

In brief, monetary policy is necessarily concerned with all the major objectives of economic policy, namely, price stability, exchange and economic stability, full employment, economic growth etc. Since these objectives to some extent are in conflict, therefore monetary authorities are always confronted with the problem of priorities.

ROLE AND OBJECTIVES OF MONETARY POLICY

The various objectives of monetary policy are interrelated. They also usually conflict with one another. Thus the objective of price stability may conflict with the objective of exchange rate stability. Also the attainment of full employment may conflict with the goal of price stability and so on. Now we shall discuss two following sets of conflicting objectives.

(1) Exchange Stability *vs* Price Stability. These are the two contradictory goals of monetary policy. It is difficult to pursue together. Some economists favour exchange stability at the cost of price stability and others favour price stability. The best course is that a mid-way solution harmonising both objectives should be aimed at. Then, the question may arise whether it is possible to do so, or whether the two objectives, price stability and exchange stability, are really compatible with each other.

Of course, the above two objectives are contradictory under the gold standard. According to the rule of the gold standard, stability of exchange rates alone should be aimed at and no parallel efforts be made to stabilise the domestic price level. A monetary policy aiming at both will miserably fail in its mission and would achieve nothing. However, under certain conditions, these two objectives may be found quite consistent and compatible. For instance, the monetary authority can work for both if its gold reserves are sufficiently large to maintain exchange stability, continuing to export gold and not to have a resource to credit contractions consequent upon such outflow of gold. In such cases, domestic price and economic stability as well as exchange stability can be ensured.

Secondly, it may be pointed out that both the objectives can be harmonised when the policy adopted by the monetary authority for maintaining stable exchange rates also coincides with the policy of price stabilisation. For instance, if there is an outflow of gold, a contraction of credit is to be initiated according to the rules of the gold standard, which may however also become necessary, at the same time, if the economy has been operating at full employment level and internal prices have been rising. Similarly, an expansionist money policy may be conducive to both exchange stability and price stability when there is an influx of gold in the country and there is need of credit expansion to stimulate investment, employment and prices in the economy. Such a coincidence, however, is rarely observed.

In reality, the interpretation of the broad principles and objectives of monetary policy varies from country to country and the result is a disequilibrium which calls for a disharmony between the two accepted objectives, *viz.* price stability and exchange stability. In the present era, however, exchange stability is assigned secondary importance as compared to internal price stability because modern states have accepted the prime duty of welfare maximisation and a reasonable exchange flexibility is permissible under the ambit of control of the International Monetary Fund of which most of the countries are members. In fine, today, the goals of full employment and economic growth have assumed superiority over the stability goal and hence, the object of a monetary policy is to follow a price policy corresponding to the needs of the country concerned in view of its growth and employment policy.

(2) Full Employment and Economic Growth. The objectives of full employment and economic growth should be distinguished from each other. The following are the important points of distinction between the two objectives:

(i) Full employment is a static notion. It refers to the full utilisation of existing capacity of the economy with given productive resources, technology and production methods. Economic growth, on the other hand, is a dynamic concept. It implies an enhancement of productive resources through technological advancement, exploitation of new fields, new territories, new methods etc. It involves uplifting the country's production-possibility frontier as a whole.

(ii) Full employment implies exploitation of job opportunities by lifting the actual production frontier up to its maximum limits under the constraint of available resources. While economic growth means creation of more employment opportunities by raising the potentialities of production frontier by developing additional resources.

(iii) In technical jargon, the full employment objective implies raising the actual output schedule of a country to its production possibility frontier with a reasonable degree of economic stability. The economic growth objective, however, implies raising the production possibility frontier itself, together with the actual output schedule. It involves structural changes. This is what Whittlesey wants to convey when he says that "the ideal output under full employment objective is the country's economic potential at the prevailing level of technology, while under the economic growth objective, it is the countries" economic potential at a progressive level of technology and specially at a level which progresses in an ideal manner.

(iv) Full employment objective is relatively a short span phenomenon. It aims at economic stabilisation through the elimination of cyclical fluctuations that are faced by an advanced capitalist economy. Economic growth, on the other hand, is a long-term objective of monetary policy. Its aim is to improve the standard of living of the people, to remove poverty by increasing the level of income, output and employment in the economy. This objective is largely adopted by governments of underdeveloped countries. However, there is no reason why an advanced economy should not adopt it.

(v) Full employment objective puts stress on the maintenance of effective demand; thus, during a depression it implies correcting the deficiency of demand and when there is inflation due to excess demand, it implies curbing it.. The objective of economic growth, however, stresses on increasing the volume of the complementary resources essential for securing the productive employment of available labour rather than on the maintenance of effective demand as such.

Sometimes, rising prices of inflation, it is suggested, serves the goals of both full employment and economic growth. However, inflation may tend to hinder economic growth if the to capacity. This is because:

(a) It encourages the production of consumption goods rather than capital goods, as prices of consumption goods rise faster than those of capital goods during an inflationary period. However, economic growth is pre-conditioned by the increase in capital goods as such.

(b) Inflation makes for inefficiency and reduces the incentive to make the best possible use of available productiye resources.

(c) Moreover, when deflationary measures are taken to curb excessive inflation during the course of full employment, it tends to discourage long-range planning in industry which is again detrimental to economic growth.

(d) If may cause industrial disharmony and indiscipline which gives rise to frequent strikes and lockouts that may hinder growth considerably.

In short, the policy of price stability at full employment level pursued by the monetary authority is not conductive to the growth objective as such. Thus, a monetary policy serving wholeheartedly the immediate ends of full employment is liable to become entirely unsuitable from the standpoint of growth objective. However, to the extent that a reasonable price and economic stability of full employment objective is conducive to growth, it can easily be regarded as a part of the growth objective, and there can be no conflict between the two objectives and their measures. In fact, the adoption of the growth objective does not mean that monetary policy should disregard reasonable price and economic stabilisation as such.

To sum up, the concepts of full employment and economic growth are all together different and the former is more suitable to the advanced countries at underemployment equilibrium while the latter is most suited to the newly developing nations and countries suffering from long-run stagnation.

SCOPE OF MONETARY POLICY IN UNDERDEVELOPED COUNTRIES

The scope of monetary policy in underdeveloped countries is extremely limited, compared to that in advanced countries for the following reasons:

(1) The money market is unorganised in an underdeveloped country, and therefore the monetary management of the central bank cannot be perfect.

(2) Changes in bank rate or other monetary instruments are proved to be ineffective in underdeveloped countries also on account of the existence of a vast non-monetised sector in their economies.

(3) In most of the underdeveloped nations, money supply-primarily consists of currency in circulation while bank deposits form relatively a small proportion of it. Lack of banking habits on the part of the people in poor countries makes it difficult for the monetary authority to influence the economy by controlling the banking system.

The above stated factors impose a limit on the scope of monetary policy in underdeveloped countries. However, this does not mean that monetary policy has no role to play at all. Despite its various limitations, the monetary policy in an underdeveloped country can greatly assist economic growth "by influencing the supply and use of credit, combating inflation and maintaining the balance of payments of equilibrium."

Monetary policy and management have an active role to play in a scheme of planning for economic development in an underdeveloped country. It would have to take on a direct and active role firstly, in increasing or helping to create the machinery needed for financing developmental activities allover the country, and secondly, in ensuring that the finance available flows in the direction intended. Briefly, thus, the monetary policy in an underdeveloped economy has to be used to activises the growth process and to create favourable conditions for fostering economic development with reasonable stability.

EFFICACY OF MONETARY POLICY

It is generally conceived that monetary policy is more effective in checking economic activity than in stimulating it. In other words, monetary policy is more effective in checking boom conditions than in generating recovery from recession or depression. In times of depression or stagnation, the monetary authority can do very little. It cannot enforce investment merely by following an easy money policy or credit expansion as such. It can control the money rate of interest to some extent but not the rate of profit which may be a very low or even in a negative quantity during a depression. Investment generally seems to be interest inelastic. The interest-inelasticity of investment can be explained on two counts: *(1)* interest represents a minor element of total costs in short-term investments, and *(2)* in making long-term investments, business expectations and other economic variables are far more important than the influence of interest rates. Thus, when there is overall pessimism prevailing in the economy and the marginal efficiency of capital is very low, mere monetary expansion by the monetary authority cannot do anything substantial. Moreover, there is no direct relationship between the quantity of money and the price level as was traditionally assumed. There are many other factors affecting prices and business activity as powerfully as the money supply. Most of them being non-monetary in nature, cannot be controlled by monetary action alone. Depression needs action to revive effective demand by raising the consumption and marginal efficiency of capital through public investment programs and such other measures. Hence, fiscal policy was advocated as a powerful weapon for offsetting and checking depression and unemployment. Only in times of prosperity can monetary policy be used effectively, as it can control speculative boom and inflation by regulating undue credit expansion. Thus, it seems that monetary policy is admirably suited to situations requiring the restraint of inflationary pressures of requiring high short-term interest rates to lessen the flow of capital for reducing a deficit in the balance of payments.

In formulating an effective monetary policy, the following two points should be borne in mind:

(i) the magnitudinal dimension, and

(ii) the time dimension.

The strength of the effectiveness of the monetary policy is measured by its magnitudinal dimension; while the lag involved in its effectiveness is measured by the time dimension of the policy.

Again, the strength of monetary policy is determined by the elasticity as well as the degree of stability of functional relations-monetary and real-in the economy. It has been observed that the strength of the monetary policy is inversely related to the interest rate elasticity of demand for money assets. But, it is directly related to the interest rate elasticity of demand for real assets. Thus, when low elasticity of demand for money is combined with high elasticity of demand for real assets, the monetary policy will have a stronger effect. In such cases, a large percentage change in the interest rates is needed to induce the people to adjust their money balances, and this large percentage change will induce a larger change in the demand for real assets; that there will be a larger change effected in output of goods and services in order to correct the resulting sizable discrepancy between the desired and actual holdings of real assets. Contrarily, if a highly elastic demand for money is combined with a highly inelastic demand for real assets, the monetary policy will operate with a weaker effect on the economy. For, only then a small percentage in interest rates will be necessary to induce the people to adjust to a large percentage change in the monetary supply, which again will induce even a lesser percentage change in the demand for real assets so that the output of goods and services will not change much in the process of adjustment. In actual practice, however, the interest rate elasticity of demand for money is found to be generally low, varying within the range of -0.1 to -0.9 so that moderate doses of monetary policy are supposed to have considerably strong effects.

Further, any destabilisation in these functions evidently tends to reduce the effect of monetary policy designed. And in practice, no asset demand function is perfectly stable, but there is less evidence to show that a shift in demand functions has produced a significantly weakening effect on the monetary policy.

The monetary authority however has to learn from its past experience to judge the size of the magnitudinal effect of its operations. Nowadays, econometric models are also being constructed to estimate the effectiveness of a monetary policy. A correct knowledge of magnitudinal effect is, however, very much helpful in prescribing the correct dosage off monetary policy according to the requirement of the prevailing circumstances.

Similarly, the knowledge of time dimension of a monetary policy is of great help in prescribing the appropriate timing of the policy action. The time dimension factor measures the lags involved in the working of monetary policy. There are a number of such lags: *(i)* the action lag-a-lag between the time when a need for a policy change is recognised and the actual change effected; *(ii)* the credit market lag-a-lag between the time when monetary policy is changed and the time when such change leads to changes in important monetary variables like interest rates, the supply of money (credit, especially) and other financial assets; *(iii)* recognition lag-a-lag between the time when a change in policy is required and the time when this essentiality is recognised; *(iv)* the output lag-the-lag between the time when the monetary and financial market conditions change and the time when these changes bring about changes in the real income and output. The first two types of lags are described as "inside lag", and the last two are called "the outside lag" of monetary policy.

The outside lag in the effect of monetary policy is a distributed lag. The effect of monetary policy on prices, income, employment, etc., cannot be perceived at a moment of time; it is, however, distributed over a span of time. Whenever a monetary policy is changed its effect may be generated immediately but it ends only aftet a sufficiently long period of time. However, a longer lag is not good as it impairs the effectiveness of monetary policy. Under a longer lag, the effect of a change in monetary pol.cy cannot be set according to need, as the effect will not be predictable with certainty. Thus, under a long and variable time lag, a discretionary monetaıy policy's efficacy is very much doubted. Therefore, some economists like Milton Friedman advocate for replacing discretionary policy with a monetary rule of increasing the stock of money at a constant rate of growth. Friedman argues that a constant rate of growth in the money supply would facilitate steady economic growth, so that the growth with stabilisation objective of monetary policy will materials. He firmly holds that economic instability is due to variations in the growth of money supply under the discretionary monetary policy.

Most of the economists, today, however, feel that the central bank's management of stock of money alone is totally inadequate in pursuing goals like curbing of inflation through effective checks on spendings. In a modern economy, the capacity to spend and propensity to consume are basically determined by the liquidity position rather than just quantity of money. Thus, what is wanted is to influence the general liquidity structure of the economy as a whole. Unless general liquidity is controlled, there is no hope for a real control on spending activities in a modern economy. The liquidity of an economy is constituted by the quantity of money (the amount of cash and demand deposits) and the stock of financial wealth and its components. Thus, the flow of liquid assets in an economy is the result of debt-creation activities of the various agencies of money and capital market of the country. Apart from the central bank's issue of currency money from time to time, commercial bank's credit creation activities reflected in the multiple expansion of their derivative deposits generate a flow of first-grade liquid assets in the economy.

The banking sector also provides second-grade liquid assets like time and savings deposits. Again, a good deal of liquid assets are created in the non-banking sector of the modern economy. The state treasury, for instance, issues treasury bills on a large scale. Further, whenever public debt is extended by the government, other forms of assets like gilt-edged securities, bonds, etc., are created. Moreover, there is a variety of non-bank financial intermediaries such as insurance companies, savings banks, hire-purchase finance companies, discount houses, acceptance houses, building societies, unit trusts, investment trusts, etc., where dealings in the money and capital market tend to generate a flow of various kinds of financial assets having different degrees of liquidity. The main functions of the institutions of financial intermediaries is to act as intermediary between savers' class and the investors' class in the community. By issuing primary securities, these institutions tap the saved resources of individuals and re-lend or provide assistance to the business corporations and industries by buying their shares, securities, etc. or by issuing direct loans and thereby tend to provide indirect securities to the ultimate lenders. Moreover, financial intermediaries increase the liquidity of securities by lending on them. In fact, "financial intermediaries manufacture liquidity; they create claims which are more liquid than the securities they buy and issue them to savers. Thus, more savings are canalised into investment activity."

In short, the role of financial intermediaries in a modern economy is significant as they induce savings through the convenience, security and interest earnings which they furnish to savers.

Again, their activities also help in tapping the resources of potential savings, as by providing attractive means of savings, they discourage people to hoard savings in the form of cash. The types of near-money assets created by the financial intermediaries, thus, tend to reduce the demand for money to hold cash-balances as an asset. The assets created by fmancial intermediaries serve as a close substitute for money, thus releasing the flow of money in current transactions from the precautionary holding of money in balances which help in reducing the pressure on the monetary authority and to create additional money supply for catering to the needs of growing transactionary demand for money in a dynamic economy.

The income yield of the assets of these financial intermediaries implies an increase in the purchasing power of the asset holders which in turn improves their spending and consuming capacity. Again, the velocity of money spending tends to increase on account of the increased liquidity position of the financial sector by the activities of these intermediaries. The rate and magnitude of spending in an economy determines the flow of total expenditure which bears influence on the economic activities and the flow of income and output. As such, in a modern economy, the liquidity position created by the activities of financial intermediaries is significant, as it influences the total expenditure of the community.

In order to produce desired changes in the economic activity, the central bank pursues a monetary policy to bring about changes in the quantity of money and credit thereby to cause changes in the flow of spending which influences the level and mode of economic activity. The central bank in this regard usually adopts monetary measures of credit control such as bank rate policy, etc., which affect the flow of bank credit in the economy. Modern monetarists, however, feel that this is not enough. The central bank must aim at influencing the total volume of liquidity rather than the quantity of money alone to bring forth effective results. It has been contended that the fundamental object of monetary action of the central bank is to change the level of aggregate demand by influencing the community's rate and volume of spending.

However, the crucial factor determining the people's spending is the general liquidity of the entire economy rather than the cash and credit balances possessed by them. Cash and credit balances constitute a part of the wider structure of liquidity in an economy. In reality, the financial assets created by the financial intermediaries and other agencies of the money market constitute the rest (the large part) of the general liquidity in a modern economy. In a modern community, thus, the decision to spend does not depend simply on the cash and credit balances held by the people, but to a large extent on the potential liquidity constituted by the possible alternative of raising funds either by selling an asset held or by borrowing.

❐

16

Fiscal Policy

The term, fiscal policy, embraces the tax and expenditure policies of the government. According to Arthus Smithies, Fiscal policy is a "policy under which the government uses its expenditure and revenue programmes to produce desirable effects and avoid undesirable. effects on the national income, production and employment." Fiscal policy in short refers to the budgetary policy.

Broadly speaking, the taxation policy of the government relates to the programme of curbing private spending. Expenditure policy deals with the channels by which government resources are pumped into the private economy. Government spending on new goods and services directly adds to aggregate demand and indirectly increases income through secondary spending which takes place on account of the multiplier effect. Taxation, on the other hand, operates in reducing the level of private spending by reducing the disposable income and the resulting savings in the community. Hence, under the budgetary, phenomenon, public expenditure and revenue can be combined in various ways to achieve a desired stimulating or deflationary effect on aggregate demand.

Fiscal policy has a quantitative as well as a qualitative as well as a qualitative aspect. Changes in tax rates, the structure of taxation, and its incidence, influence the volume and direction of private spending in the economy. Similary, changes in government's expenditure and its structure of allocation will also have quantitative and redistributive effects on income, consumption and aggregate demand of the community. As a matter of fact, all government spending is an inducement to increase the aggregate demand and has an inflationary bias in the sense that it releases funds for the private economy which are then available for use in the course of trade and business. Similarly, a reduction in government spending has a deflationary bias and it reduces the aggregate demand. Thus, the composition of public expenditure and composition of public revenue not only help to mould the economic structure of the country, but may also be expected to exert certain effects on the economy at certain times and a quite different impact at other times.

It was Keynes who popularised the interest in fiscal policy as a measure attaining macro economic goals like increasing the level of employment and income in an economy. Prior to Keynes, the classical economists believed in the principle of sound finance in which small and balanced budget was considered to be the ideal one. Keynes, for the first time, stressed the need to of State intervention in the economic field and advocated for an unbalanced budget. In fact, modern fiscal policy is by and large an application of the principles of functional finance. It has been recognised that budgetary measures carry significant influences on the functioning of the economy and therefore, modern public finance is regarded as functional finance.

BALANCED BUDGET APPROACH

According to the classical economists, however, fiscal policy should have the minimum range of operations and the budget should be balanced annually. They firmly stuck to the doctrine of lassez faire and Say's law of markets. According to Adam Smith, economic equilibrium and progress are attained through inherent and self-oriented endogenous forces of the economic system. In classical opinion, thus, when full employment is supposed to reach automatically, productivity of government services in the economic field is nil. And since government services are rendered at the cost of the national product, it amounts to a cut in the aggregate national product. Thus, when government's productivity is zero in a free enterprise economy, it is desirable that government confines itself only to its primary functions of protection and security of life and property and does not interfere with the free working of the economic system. Even if government efforts are productive, it cannot increase national income and level of economic activity above the level reached without its intervention. Thus, when full employment, optimal allocation of resources and equitable distribution can be achieved automatically through the operation of free economic forces, fiscal operations have to be of a non-regulatory, non-interfering nature. As such, the smallest budget was considered to be the best in the classical era. As such, classicists firmly advocated a balanced budget, in the sense that current annual revenue and expenses of the government must be equal. It, thus, does not provide for borrowings. The balanced budget principle was thus recognised as a principle of sound finance in orthodox economics.

Under the theory of sound finance, classicists favoured a balanced budget criterion for the following reasons:

(i) Unbalanced budgets may generate inflation on account of large and unproductive public expenditure.

(ii) If the budget is unbalanced, the government has to borrow. The government's market borrowings cause reduction in loanable funds available to private productive employment and investment activities.

(iii) Unbalanced budgets imply a wide extension of state functions beyond the capacity of the government, which may invite irresponsible governmental action.

(iv) A balanced budget, on the other hand, is a limited budget designed in a rational way.

(v) A series of unbalanced budgets imply an increase in the burden of public debt.

(vi) Economic stability is secyired by the adoption of a balanced budget policy. Unbalanced budgets, on the other hand, cause economic uncertainty and promote instability.

Furthermore, when the public debts mature, the government will have to impose additional taxes to obtain resources for their repayment. Thus, additional taxation would again tend to have an adverse effect on the incentive to work and save. It would also cause the accentuation of income distribution. Moreover, government borrowings cause the rate of interest in the money market to rise, as the demand for loanable funds rises. A rise in the rate of interest adversely affects investment activity in the private sector.

In short, according to the principles of sound finance, a budget must be balanced annually and the gap between revenue and expenditure should be minimum. Thus, classical economists firmly advocated a laisser-faire policy and were confident of the unhampered optimum operations of the free enterprise economic system. Neo-classical economists, however realised the socially undesirable effects of unregulated free enterprise on the economic system. It was argued by them that careful state action for raising income and public spending was essential to attain maximum social welfare under the concept to welfare state developed in the neo-classical era.

UNBALANCED BUDGET APPROACH

Keynesian revolution in economic thinking reconstituted the whole basis of public finance and affirmed functional finance as a fiscal norm in modern times. Though the lead in the development of "functional finance" concept was taken by Keynes, credit goes to Prof. A.P. Lerner for coining this concept. Lerner puts that: ''The principle of judging fiscal measures by the way they work or function in the economy, we may call "functional finance". He contends that the fiscal operation of the government—taxing, borrowing, public spending, management of public debt, etc., deficit financing, etc.—should be designed with the objective of fulfilling certain functions which have an immediate bearing and far-reaching effects on the economic system as a whole. In economic philosophy, the term "functional finance" embraces public expenditure, public revenue and debt management which are regarded as fiscal instruments effectively used to achieve objectives like attainment and maintenance of full employment with economic stability.

As Prof. Chelliah points out, the functional concept of fiscal policy, thus, implies that: *(i)* the fiscal operations of government should be conducted on a functional basis, and public finance should not be considered as being induced solely by the need for securing social goods meant for collective consumption, and *(ii)* the budget need not always be balanced. As a matter of fact, the fiscal norm of functional finance is the complete antithesis of the orthodox rule of balanced budget. The functional finance norm suggests the formation of large budgets with a wider functional coverage of government spending to promote basic economic goals, *e.g.* *(a)* to obtain optimal allocation and efficient use of scarce resources at full-employment level, *(b)* to achieve economic stability and bring about an equitable distribution of income and wealth in the best possible manner.

Quite contrary to the classical notion, the concept of functional fiscal policy suggest that the state need not and should not assume a passive role in the economic affairs of the country. It implies that public spending may be incurred not merely for the sake of its direct benefits, but for the sake of indirect effect it produces in raising the level of income, output employment; and the public revenue may be raised not to meet an anticipated expenditure, but to curtail excessive demand and curb inflationary potentials in the economy. Taxation is, thus, regarded as an important and effective weapon in the hands of government to promote economic progress with stability.

Lerner suggest the following rules for government's responsibility and activity under functional finance:

(i) The government should incur public debt by borrowing money from the private sector only during inflation when it is absolutely essential to mop up the excessive purchasing power from the public, thereby reducing the pressure of excess monetary demand.

(ii) The government budget should be directed towards the achievement of full employment and price stability. For this purpose, the government budget need not necessarily be balanced.

(iii) During depression only, public expenditure in excess of current public revenue may be met by deficit financing, *i.e.* printing additisnal currency notes.

In short the main tenet of functional finance is the formation of unbalanced budget from time to time for perfecting the countercyclical goal of fiscal policy. A surplus budget is recommended during inflation and a deficit budget for recovery through excessive public spending during a deflation or depression.

Functional finance, thus, deliberately aims at unbalancing the budgets with a view to attaining and maintaining full employment level in a developed economy. In an underdeveloped economy, however, the main problem is not one of full employment but that of rapid economic growth. In a developing economy, thus, the functional aspect of fiscal policy is to be conceived in the context of a planned process of economic development.

OBJECTIVES OF FISCAL POLICY

Fiscal policy, in modern era, subscribes to the following major macro economic goals:

(a) Full employment.

(b) Economic stabilisation.

(c) Economic growth.

(d) Social justice or equality in the distribution of income and wealth.

(a) Fiscal Policy for Full Employment. Keynes regarded public finance as compensatory finance ordained to attain and maintain full employment in the economy. To pursue this goal, Keynes suggested that:

(i) Taxation should be devised to promote and sustain consumption and investment.

(ii) Public expenditure has to be compensatory one. It has to be in a planned way to finance public works programmes and provide social security measures.

(iii) Public borrowings should be on a large scale to finance productive public expenditure.

(iv) To raise the level of effective demand and to overcome depressionary forces, budget should be in deficit and it should have deficit financing.

(v) Direct taxes should be lowered to encourage savings and investments directed towards creation of more employment opportunities.

(vi) Public expenditure should be meant for uplifting the level of aggregate demand, investment and employment.

Once full employment level is reached, it has to be constantly maintained by adopting appropriate fiscal measures from time to time.

(b) Fiscal Policy and Economic Stabilisation. Economic stability is another prime aim of a sound fiscal policy. This goal implies maintenance of full employment with relative price stabilisation. Price stability hence means relative price stability. Inflation should be curbed and deflation should be avoided. In short, economic growth and stability are the twin objectives jointly pursued by a developing country's fiscal policy. The forces stimulating growth process should be given a boost at a time while inflationary pressures are to be curbed.

(c) Fiscal Policy and Economic Growth. Poor countries are entangled in the vicious circle of poverty. It should be broken. Thus, rapid economic growth is the fundamental objectives of fiscal policy in a developing economy.

Fiscal policy as a means of encouraging growth process has the following objectives:

1. To realise and mobilise potential resources into the productive channels. For this fiscal policy should aim at improving marginal propensity to save and the consequent increment saving ratio. The following methods have been suggested by Prof. Tripathy for raising the incremental saving ratio:

   (i) Increase in the rates of taxation.

   (ii) Public debt.

(iii) Imposition of additional taxes.

(iv) Direct physical control.

(v) Revenue of public enterprises.

(vi) Deficit financing.

2. To induce and stimulate private sector investment.
3. To promote investment into socially desirable channels.
4. To accelerate the rate of economic growth. In this regard, fiscal measure must be conducive to growth process. In no way should fiscal means adversely affect the ability and willingness to work hard, save more and invest.
5. To alter the pattern of investment and production in such a way as to improve the general economic welfare and sustain egalitarian goals like equity in distribution and eradication of poverty.

(d) Fiscal Policy and Social Justice. A welfare state should provide social justice by giving equitable distribution of income and wealth. Fiscal policy can serve as an effective means of achieving this much desired goal of socialism in developed as well as developing countries. Progressive tax system can be of much use in realising this objective. Moreover, public expenditure helps in redistributing income from the rich to the poor section of the society.

Thus, fiscal policy insists that in a budget, growing allocation should be made for programmes like free medical care, free education, subsidised housing, subsidised essential commodities like milk, etc.

FISCAL POLICY AND UNDERDEVELOPED ECONOMY

The nature of fiscal policy in an underdeveloped economy is bound to be different from that of a devloped country. In a developed economy, the problem is not so much that of achieving economic stability on account of business fluctuations caused by the trade cycle. The compensatory fiscal policy is eminently suited to achieve a high degree of economic stabilization in a developed economy. But the problem in an underdeveloped economy is not so much that of economic instability as that of promoting rapid economic growth in the country. The fiscal policy, as such, must not only be that of compensatory spending as in a developed economy, but also one capable of promoting rapid economic growth in the country. The following could be the major objectives of fiscal policy in an underdeveloped country:

(i) The first objective of fiscal policy in an underdevelped country should be to maximize the level of aggregate saving by applying a cut to the actual and potential consumption of the public at large.

(ii) The second objective of fiscal policy should be to divert capital resources from less productive to more productive, and from socially less desirable to socially more desirable uses. This objective is implicit in planned economic development.

(iii) The third objective should be to maximize the rate of capital formation to break down economic stagnation and to lead the country on the path of rapid economic progress.

(iv) The forth objective of fiscal policy should be to protect the economy of an underdeveloped country from the demon of inflation. It can undermine the very process of economic growth. As such, the fiscal policy of an underdeveloped country should be designed in such a manner as to curb inflationary forces arising during the process of economic growth.

(v) The fifth objective of fiscal policy should be to eliminate, as far as possible, the glaring economy inequalities bedevilling the economy and to bring about an equitable distribution of income and wealth in society. The objective, however, clashes with the first objective, namely, that of rapid economic growth through maximization of the rate of capital formation. Rapid economic growth is not possible without maximization of aggregate saving in the economy. And aggregate savings cannot be increased unless there are wide disparities in income and wealth distribution. A wise, prudent government should attempt through appropriate measures to reconcile the two conflicting objectives of rapid growth and social justice in a judicious manner.

(vi) The sixth objective of fiscal policy should be to eliminate, as far as possible, sectoral imbalances arising in the economy from time to time. Though the fiscal policy as visualized above, will help to maintain price-stability in the economy as a whole by curbing inflationary forces, there may arise sectoral price fluctuations in certain sectors of the economy on accout of the existence of certain bottlenecks. To ward off that possibility, fiscal policy must be attuned to correct such imbalances in time before they could inflict any damage on the economy.

FISCAL POLLCY IN DEVELOPED COUNTRIES

The role of fiscal policy in a developed economies to function as an anti-cyclical measure. It assumes a balanced position only in a normal price stability period. During recession, however, the government must adopte a deficit budget policy while a surplus budget policy is to be followed to combat inflation. During a depression, a deficit budget can be created in the following ways:

(i) Taxation rates are kept unchanged but public expenditure is increased.

(ii) The level of public expenditure is kept unchanged but the taxation rates are reduced.

The second method is regarded as more significant as an anti-depressionary measure. This excess of expenditure may be financed through public borrowings plus deficit financing, *i.e.* creation of new money.

Keynes contends that increase in public expenditure or investment in public works will lift the economy out of a depression. The merit of public works programmes is that they increase personal incomes and consumption by a multiple of the initial expenditure without adversely affecting the marginal efficiency of investment in the private sector. In other words, an increase in government spending will increase national income. Though the idea of public works programmes as a remedy for unemployment is very old, Keynes's multiplier aspect of it is a modern innovation.

The public works expenditure (or public ex-investment) has two variants: *(i)* Public spending and *(ii)* Pump-priming

Public spending or compensatory spending, on the other hand, refers to government expenditure which is undertaken with the idea of compensating the decline in private investment. During depression, private investment declines due to the low marginal efficiency of capital, whose automatic revival is not possible. In this situation there is no alternative for the government but the resort to public investment to fill the gap in private investment. Thus, compensatory public spending must necessarily be on a very large scale and must be continued till private investment becomes normal.

Pump-priming refers to that initial public expenditure which helps to inistiate and revive economic activity in a depressed economy. The idea is to increase private investment through public expenditure. Pump-priming is not intended to replace private investment. Its objects is only to stimulate private investment, and not to supplement it.

Of the two forms of public expenditure, the multiplier theory is not related to pum-priming. Pum-priming process presumes that a temporary new expenditure incurred by the government will have a lasting tendency to raise the level of economic activity. Whereas the multiplier theory assumes that the income generating effects of additional expenditure will continue only till the expenditure is present, with some time lag.

Further, the theory of pump-priming implies that the economic system has been in an unstable equilibrium; hence the injection of additional public spending to put it back on the track from which it was derailed by some fortuitous event. Keynes's multiplier theory goes beyond the pum-priming theory. Keynes's theory is that the economic system is characteristically in stable underemployment equilibrium from which there is not tendency to deviate. Therefore, repeated pushes and not just a single push, are required to put the economy on the high gear. Furthermore, the multiplier theory does not imply that public spending will stimulate private investment due to the stimulus it gives to private consumption. This may happen but not as a part of the multiplier doctrine.

Compensatory spending, thus, refers to that public investment which is autonomous in nature and which leads to a rise in the country's investment function by compensating for the deficiency in the private sector investment.

Keynes considered that there is always a multiplier effect of compensatory public spending in generating national income. The process of income propagation, however, depends on the marginal propensity to consume. Thus, the multiplier co-efficient (k) is measured as the reciprocal of marginal propensity to save. That is:

$$k = \frac{1}{MPS}$$

Further, increase in income is k times increase in public investment.

Hence, on account of multiplier effect, revival process due to compensatory public spending becomes cumulative. However, if public expenditure has to be income-propagating, it must represent a new expenditure and not a substitution of one expenditure for another. In order to have significant expansionary effects, a programme of public investment should be financed by borrowing further rather than by taxation. The expenditure of funds raised by taxation represents mainly a substitution of one form of expenditure by another, that is, a reduction in private spending and an increase in government spending.

Keynes further advocates deficit financing to realise the multiplier effect of public expenditure. The term "deficit financing" means that the government spends more than it collects in taxes, leaving the budget unbalanced. When the government spends more money than it takes away from the public in the form of taxes, there must be a net addition to the money-income available for spending by the public.

This represents a net addition to the effective demand. When there is unemployment, this increase in effective demand results in more employment and the creation of a larger real national income. The amount of increase in effective demand will be at least equal to the amount of the new or additional spending, which is further equal to the excess of money the government spends over the amount which it takes away from the tax-payers in the form of taxes.

Deficit financing takes place when the government borrows from the public or when the government prints new money to spend. Hence, deficit financing is a particular manner of financing income creating expenditure. The important point is that the spending should represent new expenditure. New expenditure will increase the national income and out of the enlarged income, savings will increase by an amount equal to deficit. Thus, Keynes advocates monetary expansion through income-creating expenditure, which is designed to increase both investment and consumption, as the appropriate policy in depression years. According to Keynes, however, once private investment becomes normal, expenditure on public works should be stopped because public investment does not complete with or supplant private investment but only helps in its revival and normalisation. If expenditure on public works is not slackened even after the normalisation of private investment, it may lead to inflation.

In adopting compensatory financing public programmes as an anti-depression measure, however, the following difficulties may be encountered:

(1) The required magnitude of public investment is to be determined in relation to the duration and amplitude of the depression, along with the multiplier effect causing income propagation. It is, however, difficult to measure the amplitude of the contractionary phase and the severity of the depression at the time of recession.

(2) There has to be a proper timing of public investment. But it is difficult to forecast the advent of depression.

(3) The advent of depression cannot be checked so soon by the immediate enforcement of compensatory public spending.

(4) Any public work project when undertaken has to be completed. And, if it does not coincide with the contraction phase and if it is prolonged further even when depression is overcome, it will generate inflation. Avoidance of inflation is again an avowed objective of modern fiscal policy.

(5) When compensatory public spending is financed through public loans, it adds to the burden of public debt.

ROLE OF FISCAL POLICY IN DEVELOPING COUNTRIES

The fiscal policy in developing countries should apparently be conducive to rapid economic development. In a poor country, fiscal policy can no longer remain a compensatory fiscal policy. It has a tough role to play in a developing economy and has to face the problem of growth-cum-stability.

The main goal of fiscal policy in a newly developing economy is the promotion of the highest possible rate of capital formation. Under-developed countries are encompassed by vicious circle of poverty on account of capital deficiency; in order to break this vicious circle, a balanced growth is needed. It needs accelerated rate of capital formation. Since private capital is generally shy in these countries, the government has to fill up the lacuna. A mounting public expenditure is also required in building social overhead capital. To accelerate the rate of capital formation, the fiscal policy has to be designed to raise the level of aggregate savings and to reduce the actual and potential consumption of the people.

An important aim of fiscal policy in a developing economy is to create an equitable distribution of income and wealth in the society. Here, however, a difficulty arises. The aims of rapid growth and attainment of equality in income are two paradoxical goals, because growth needs more savings and equitable distribution causes reduction of aggregate savings as the propensity to save of the richer section is always high and that of the poor income group low. As such, if high economic growth is the objective, the question arises as to what extent inequalities should be reduced. Of course, many a time, under the goal of socialism, the government unduly resorts to reduction of inequalities at the cost of growth which may lead to the distribution of poverty rather than prosperity. A reconciliation of these two contradictory goals of grwoth and reduction of inequalities can definitely bring forth better results.

Another objective of fiscal policy, in a poor country is to divert existing resources from unproductive to productive and socially more desirable uses. Hence fiscal policy must be blended with planning for development.

Relative prices stability constitutes an important objective. Furthermore, fiscal policy in a poor country has an additional role of protecting the economy from high inflation domestically and unhealthy developments abroad. Through inflation to some extent is inevitable in the process of growth, fiscal measures must be designed to curb inflationary forces.

The approach to fiscal policy in an economy which is developing must be aggregative as well as segmental. The former may lead to overall economic expansion and reduce the general pressure of unemployment; but due to the existence of bottlenecks, though general price stability may be maintained, sectoral price rise may inevitably be found. These sectoral imbalances are to be corrected by appropriate, segmental fiscal measures which would remove frictions and immobilities, turn demands into proper directions, seek to eliminate bottlenecks and other obstacles to growth.

For less developed countries such as India the following main objectives of fiscal policy may be restated as:

(i) To increase the rate of savings and discourage actual and potential consumption.

(ii) To increase the rate of investment and capital formation, so as to accelerate the rate of economic growth.

(iii) To imporve the standard of living of the masses by providing social goods on a large scale.

(iv) To diversity the flow of investments and spendings from unproductive uses to socially most desirable channels.

(v) To check sectoral imbalances.

(vi) To reduce widespread inequalities of income and wealth.

For the purpose of development, not only an expansionary budget but a deficit is desirable too in a developing country. The government expenditure on developmental planning projects must be increased. It may be financed even by means of deficit financing. Deficit financing, here, refers to the creation of new money by printing additional notes by the government or by borrowing from the central bank which ultimately means creation of additional money supply. However, the government must use the technique of deficit financing cautiously. An excessive dose of deficit financing may lead to inflation which may endanger economic growth.

Public borrowing also is an important means of getting resources for development of the public sector. External loans are useful to some extent when the country has to import machines, capital goods, etc., from a foreign country and the country has a scarcity of foreign exchange.

Further, fiscal policy in a poor country may be used to reduce inequalities in income and wealth distribution by means of taxes and government expenditure. Taxation has to be progressive and government spending must be welfare oriented.

Anyway the effectiveness of fiscal measures in promoting development in a poor country depends on the incentive administered to the strategic points in the productive set-up by virtue of the consequences of taxation and public spending.

It must be noted that fiscal policy in a development economy has to operate within a framework influenced by social, cultural and political conditions and institution, which may inhibit the formulation and implementation of goods economic policies.

It short, for promoting economic growth, the fiscal policy must be first formulated in such a way that it will increase the rate of volume of investment in the public and private sectors. The tax policies must discourage unproductive and speculative investment. Second, fiscal policy must mobilise more and more resources for capital formation. Hence, taxation must be used to curb excessive consumption. Third, it must encourage an inflow of foreign capital.

Fiscal policy, however, cannot be effective when there are loopholes in the taxation laws and the tax administration is corrupt so that there is large-scale tax evasion. Again, if the government is extravagant in spending on non-developmental items, then a technique such as deficit financing may prove to be inflationary. Again, market imperfections, bottlenecks, shortages of raw materials, and lack of entrepreneurial skills, do not allow fiscal policy to be effective.

Nonetheless, of all the economic policies, fiscal policy today assumes unique importance in realising general economic goals, depending on the size of the fiscal measure adopted and their timing. The exact change effected in the national income will depend on the form and the magnitude of public revenue, especially, the rates and structure of taxation and the mode of public spending by the government. Further, when prices are rising, government has to adopt a surplus budget at an appropriate time in order to avoid secular inflation. But, there is practical difficulty in knowing the changing conditions or appearance of price stability; hence it is very difficult to forecast perfect timing. Political and administrative delays tends to aggravate the problem and the desired effect of fiscal programme may not be realized. Sometimes, even if the fiscal action is taken at a right time, in quantitative or qualitative terms, it may not be adequate or appropriate.

There are three important fiscal means taxation, public borrowings and deficit financing which must be used in a harmonious combination so as to produce the best over all effect in realising the macro economic goals.

However, taxation measures in particular may be used to accomplish the following objectives:

(i) Curtailing consumption and thus garnering resources for public sector investment;

(ii) Reshaping the pattern of investment in a socially desirable manner;

(iii) Inducing the people to work hard, save and invest in production;

(iv) Curbing the use of scarce resources in unproductive private investment and then diverting them to the productive public sector; and

(v) Reducing inequalities in income and wealth through progressive taxation.

Since voluntary savings are insufficient in poor countries, the total volume of savings is compulsorily raised through taxation and such resources are transferred from private hands to the government for its most efficient use. Of course, the success is very much conditioned by the productivity, efficiency and honesty of public sector. Government can very well use taxed revenue for capital formation. And taxes are generally non-inflationary in character. It is their unique merit. Lewuis, in the context of economic growth, suggests that the marginal rate of taxation should exceed the average rate, so that tax receipts would grow faster than national income and thus the government will automatically get more resources for implementing further development programmes. It would also tend to reduce the inflationary pressure in a growing economy.

But taxation has its limits in a poor country where the taxable limit is relatively low on account of general poverty and low per capital income. Excessive taxation may have a disincentive effect on savings and investment. Further, indirect taxation is not only regressive in effect, but may also tend to have an inflationary pressure. Nevertheless, a properly devised tax policy can certainly help in achieving the growth-stability objective of fiscal policy.

Besides taxation, public borrowing also a seem to be an important means of mobilising savings in government hands. It is also a sort of non-inflationary method of financing government programmes, as public debts divert money savings of the people to government securities—less liquid assets. This tends to curb consumption and relieves inflationary pressure. Moreover, the resources so realised by the government can be productively invested for the creation of economic and social overhead capital.

But, growth needs huge investments which cannot be fully met by taxation and borrowings alone so that government in a poor country has to resort to deficit financing.

Fiscal policy has the following limitations:

(1) It is inappropriate to deal with problems that requires structural adjustment.

(2) It cannot adjust the distribution of money flows.

(3) Theory of fiscal policy assumes operation of the multiplier effect. But, reality, it cannot be easily estimated on account of many leakages involved.

(4) It has operational limitation due to the involvement of time lags. There may be delays in diagnosing recessions and inflation and then devising and pursuing appropriate fiscal measure.

(5) Its efficiency depends on strict financial descipline on the part of government and its correct value judgement.

(6) It is also difficult to decide the magnitude of fiscal action and the optimum size of budget.

❒

17

Measurement of National Income

National income is the aggregate money-value of all goods and services produced in a country during one year, account being taken of the deductions made due to wear and tear and depreciation of plants and machinery used in the production of goods and services. It is distributed among the factors of production in the form of rent, interest, wages and profits. There are two main defmitions of national income by Marshall, Pigou and Fisher.

Marshall has defined national income as follows: "The labour and capital of a country acting upon its natural resources, produced annually a certain net aggregate of commodities, material and immaterial, including services of all kinds. The limiting word 'net' is needed to provide for using up raw and half finished commodities and for the wearing out and depreciation of machinery and plant....And net income due on account of foreign investments must be added in. This is the true net annual income or revenue of the country or the national dividend." Marshall's definition has been criticized on the following grounds:

Firstly, the goods and services produced in a country are so many and of so many varieties that it is very difficult, though not impossible, to measure accurately the national output or income of a country. *Secondly,* there are some commodities, quite a substantial part of which does not become available for sale in the market. How to evaluate such commodities has not been explained by Marshall. *Thirdly,* the danger of double counting is implicit in Marshall's definition. There is every possibility of certain items being counted twice, if we take census of the total production of a country as suggested by Marshall. Despite these criticisms; it cannot be denied that Marshall's definition possesses the twin advantages of simplicity and comprehensiveness in an adequate measure.

While Marshall has approached national income from the production end, Fisher approaches it from the consumption end. According to him, "The national dividend or income consists solely of services as received by ultimate consumers, whether from their material or from their human environments. Thus, a piano or an overcoat made for me this year is not apart of this year's income, but an addition to the capital. Only the services rendered to me during this year by these things are income." Thus, according to Fisher, the national income of a country is determined not by its annual production, but by its annual consumption.

Fisher's definition appears to be better and more scientific than that of Marshall because he includes in the national income of the country only the money-value of the actual consumption of goods and services during the year. But Fisher's definition has little practical value, the reason being that in actual life it is exceedingly difficult to calculate the money-value of the annual consumption of goods and services in a country. There may be several difficulties in estimating the money-value of the consumption of goods and services. Thus, the consumption-oriented measurement of national income is not a practical possibility. We are then left with the second possibility, namely, the measurement of national income from the production end. Marshall has attempted to measure national income from this end.

METHODS OF MEASUREMENT OF NATIONAL INCOME

There are three methods of measuring national income, namely, *(i)* Census of Production Method, *(ii)* Census of Expenditure Method, and *(iii)* Census of Income Method.

(i) Census of Production Method. According to this method, we find out the monetary value of the entire national output of a country in a year. This includes all sorts of outputs, agricultural, industrial, mineral and forest outputs. We evaluate the entire national output of a country in a year and that constitutes the gross national product (G.N.P.) of the country concerned. From this, we have to deduct the total depreciation undergone by the machinery and plant in the entire economy during one year. Since this constitutes an item of cost, the total depreciation has to be deducted from the gross national product to arrive at the net domestic product (N.D.P.) at factor cost of the country concerned. If to this net domestic product we add net income accruing to the country from abroad, that constitutes the net national product or net national income at factor cost.

While evaluating the national output of the country concerned, care has to be taken to see that only final goods and services are to be included in the national output of the country, failing that there is a possibility of double counting or certain items of output being counted more than once in the national income.

This method is also known as national income by industrial origin. The main advantage of this method is that it indicates clearly the relative importance of the different sectors of the national economy by revealing their respective contributions to the national income of the country concerned. But this method can be used only when correct and up-to-date statistical data are available.

(ii) Census of Expenditure Method. The gross national product can be viewed as the nation's total expenditure on goods and services produced during the year. Each unit of goods and services produced is matched by an expenditure on that unit. Most of the goods and services produced in the country are bought by the consumers. But the unsold goods and services are regarded as having been bought by the producers who hold them as stocks or inventories. The monetary value of the total national production is equal to the total national expenditure. The total national expenditure can be split up into the following four categories.

(a) ***Gross Domestic Private Investment.*** This item includes private investment in capital or producer goods, such as, buildings, machinery, plant, equipment, etc. Such goods are primarily purchased by business firms. Houses are also

included in this category of expenditure because they are so durable that they represent, in fact, capital goods.

(b) ***Personal Consumption Expenditure.*** It includes the consumption expenditure made for both durable goods and non-durable goods in the country during the year. This also includes expenditure on services, such as, transport, education and post and telegraph services.

(c) ***Net Foreign Investment.*** As is well known, the entire production of a country is not sold within the country. A part of it is exported to other countries. This part of the production should be included in the G.N.P. of the country. At the same time, the country imports some finished goods from abroad. The value of imports should be deducted from the value of exports. If the balance is positive, it should be added to the other items of expenditure. If it is negative, it should be subtracted from the sum of the other expenditure terms. It is, thus, clear that if the entire production of a country is produced at market prices, the amount so spent will represent the G.N.P. of the country. Therefore, we have to add the above four categories of expenditure to estimate the G.N.P.

(d) ***Government's Purchases of Goods and Services.*** The Government also purchases from the market consumer goods, such as, paper, stationery, etc., as well as investment goods, such as, machinery and equipment for their own enterprises. In addition, the government also purchases a number of different services, such as, military, police and secretarial services.

(iii) Census of Income Method. The expenditure incurred on purchasing goods and services produced in a country during the year also becomes the income of the various factors which collaborated in the production of those goods and services. We can group these factor-incomes in the following categories: *(a)* Wages and salaries of the employees, *(b)* Rental incomes of persons, *(c)* Incomes of non-company business, *(d)* Corporate profits, and *(e)* Income from interest. The first category includes the wages and salaries received by the employees during the year plus certain supplements. These supplements are the contributions which the employers make to social security and other provident and pension funds of the workers. The second category includes the incomes earned by individual proprietors, partners, and self-employed persons. The third category comprises rental incomes earned by individuals on agricultural and non-agricultural properties. The fourth category includes corporate profits earned by the business corporation before the payment of corporate profit taxes or the payment of dividends to the shareholders. Thus, the corporate profits used in calculating the G.N.P. are equal to the sum of corporate profit taxes plus dividends paid to the shareholders plus undistributed corporate profits.

An aggregate of the above five categories of incomes will not be equal to the G.N.P. as estimated by the census of expenditure method. There are two such leakages. Firstly indirect taxes levied by the government on goods and services and, secondly, depreciation of machinery, plants and buildings. The expenditure incurred by the households (or, factors) on goods and services includes the indirect taxes levied by the government. The income from these indirect taxes goes to the government, and is not available to the factors concerned. The payment on account of depreciation also does not become available to the factors in the form of income. Therefore, while estimating the G.N.P. by the income.method, we have to add indirect taxes and depreciation charges to the factor-incomes.

CONCEPTS ASSOCIATED WITH NATIONAL INCOME

Gross National Product. In calculating national income, we add up all the goods and services produced in a counlry. Such a total represents the gross value of final products turned out by the whole economy in a year, which is technically called Gross National Product. GNP, thus, may be defined as the aggregate market value of all tinal goods and services produced during a given year. The concept of final goods and services stands for tinished goods and services, ready for consumption of households and tinns, and exclude raw materials, semi-finished goods and, such other intermediary products. More specifically, all sales to houseliolds, business investment expenditures, and all government expenditures are treated as final products. But, intermediary goods purchased by business firms are obviously regarded as final goods.

In an open economy GNP may be obtained by adding up:

(1) The value of all capital goods produced which is defined as Gross Investment. Gross investment, in the real sense, here implies the increase in inventories plus gross products of buildings and equipments. It, thus, includes the provision for the consumption of capital assets, *i.e.*, depreciation, or replacement allowances.

(2) The value of all consumption goods which are currently produced.

(3) The value of government services which are measured in terms of government expenditure on various goods and services for rendering certain to the benefit of the entire community.

(4) The value of net products, *viz.* the difference between total exports and total imports of the nation. This value may be positive or negative.

(5) The net amount earned abroad. This represents the difference between the income received by the nationals from abroad on their foreign investment, minus the income paid by them abroad on the foreigner's investment.

In an open economy GNP at market price, thus, represents:

$$GNP = C + I + G + (X - M) + (R - P)$$

where,

C stands for consumption goods,

I stands for capital goods/or gross investment,

G stands for government services,

X stands for exports,

M stands for imports,

R stands for income receipts from abroad, and

P stands for income paid abroad.

In a closed isolated economy, however, GNP = C + I + G.

Gross Domestic Product (GDP). When we take the sum total of values of output of goods and services in the country, without adding net factor incomes received from abroad, the figure so obtained is called Gross Domestic Product (GDP).

$$GDP = C + I + G + (X - M).$$

This is measured at market prices.

A measurement of GNP has been illustrated below in the Table 1 below.

Table 1

Final Output (GNP)

Item	*Value of Current Market Price (Rs. Crores)*
Consumption (C)	6540
Investment (I)	3340
Government Purchases (G)	1230
Net Exports (X – M)	+ 150
Net Income from the rest of world (R – P)	+ 20
Total	11280

In measuring GNP, each finished product is multiplied by its price. Thus, the relative importance of particular goods is expressed by its relative price. Further, with changes in prices the GNP also changes. During inflation, thus, GNP appreciates simply on account of rising prices. To know the real GNP, therefore, we must deflate a given GNP total from the market price to the constant price.

GNP represents the measure of the economic output in an economic system. The final output included in the GNP is composed of the followed uses: *1*. Consumption, *2*. Investment, *3*. Government spendings, and *4*. Net exports. As Schultze points out, all output flows to one of these four uses.

The consumption expenditure component of national product constitutes the expenditure on durable goods, perishable goods, and services which are marketed during the year.

The investment component implies that part of the current product which is not consumed but used for adding further or replacing the real capital assets. It refers to gross investment. Gross investment minus depreciation (for replacement requirement) is equal to net investment.

Net National Product (NNP). It refers to the value of the net output of the economy during one year. NNP is obtained by deducting the value of depreciation or replacement allowance of the capital assets from the GNP. To put it symbolically: NNP = GNP – D, where D = depreciation allowances. This value is measured at current prices, while GNP is expressed at current market prices. Net National Product, infact, is the value of total consumption plus the value of the net investment of the community.

National income, in its technical sense, is obtained by deducting indirect taxes from the net product measured at current market prices. Such a figure is also called NNP at factor cost, as it represents payments made to the factors of production during the process of production.

NATIONAL INCOME AT MARKET PRICE AND FACTOR COSTS

In the national income analysis, usually a distinction is made between national income at market price and national income at factor costs. National income at market price means the money value of goods and services produced. It is the price of the aggregate output and services at current market prices. This price also includes some element of taxes and subsidies.

Let us suppose that the price of a bottle of beer is Rs. 60. In this case, the national income at market price is Rs. 60. But there is some element of tax in the above price. Let us suppose, the tax is Rs. 20. Then, the national income at factor cost is Rs. 40, because the factor of production which have contributed to the production of one bottle of beer will get only Rs. 40 and the balance of Rs. 20 will go to the government as tax.

Let us now analyse the implications of the elements of subsidy. Let us suppose the fair price of a bottle of whiskey is Rs. 40 but its actual cost of production is Rs. 50. The difference of Rs. 10 between the actual cost of production (Rs. 50) and the fair price shop price (Rs. 40) is borne by the State. In this case, the national income at market price is Rs. 40 but it is Rs. 50 at factor cost because the factors of production would receive Rs. 50 for the production of one bottle of whiskey.

Thus, gross domestic product at factor cost = Income earned by the factor of production + Depreciation.

Net Domestic Product at factor cost = Income earned by the factor of production-Depreciation+Taxes-Subsidy.

National Income at market price+National Income at factor cost + Taxes – Subsidies–Depreciation.

We are now in a position to examine the interrelationship between the three definitions of national income given above. These is close relation between national income as a flow of goods, as a flow of expenditure, and as a flow of income. In fact, they are so interrelated that total production total income and total expenditure are described as a circular flow of income, activities. The firms hire the factors of production to produce goods and services. The factors of production create real income. The factors of production are paid out of this real income, in terms of money as a reward for their services. They, in turn, spend this income. Thus, income leads to expenditure, *i.e.*, expenditure creates demand for goods. This demand, in turn, leads to production. The flow is from production to income generation to expenditure, and from expenditure to production. National income is, therefore, the total flow of wealth produced, distributed and consumed by the economy as a whole during the course of a year. These three things—total production, total income and total expenditure are really one and the same thing when reviewed from different angles. Each approach, with suitable adjustment, will give exactly the same GNP or NNP.

DIFFICULTIES IN THE MEASUREMENT OF NATIONAL INCOME

In measuring national income, we are confronted with certain conceptual difficulties which may be set forth below:

(i) It has not been found possible to include certain categories of services performed by the citizens in the national income. For example, there is no method available to us for computing the value of the services rendered by a mother for her children.

(ii) The calculation of the total value of depreciation and replacement poses yet another difficult problem. At what rates should the depreciation be calculated for different types of machinery, plants and buildings? These cannot be a uniform rate for calculating the depriciation on all these fixed assets.

(iii) There is no fool-proof method evolved yet to evaluate the raw materials, unfinished, semi-finished and finished goods found lying in the godowns of the business firms. Without a correct evaluation of these goods, we cannot arrive at reliable estimates of the national income of a country.

(iv) Another problem which confronts us relates to the income earned by foreign firms operating in the country. Should that income be added to the country's G.N.P. or should it be treated as the income of the foreign country to which the firms belong? There is no unanimity among the economists on this important issue. In addition to the above conceptual difficulties, there are certain special difficulties arising in the underdeveloped countries while estimating national income. These difficulties are set forth below:

(a) The available statistics in these countries are not only inadequate but also unreliable. For example, statistics pertaining to agriculture in India are not complete. We have no reliable estimates of production costs in Indian agriculture. There are no statistics worth the name for small-scale and medium industries.

(b) The overwhelming majority of the small producers in the underdeveloped countries are illiterate and ignorant and are not in a position to keep any account of their productive activities. So they cannot give to the investigator information about the quantity or value of their output.

(c) The existence of a large non-monetized sector in under-developed countries also makes the computation of national income difficult. As is well known, quite a substantial part of the agricultural output in these countries does not reach the market at all. Either it is consumed at home by the agriculturists themselves or is exchanged for other goods and services in the village. This presents several difficulties in the calculation of income.

(d) There is little of occupational specialization on the part of the people in underdeveloped countries. Many persons take up more than one activity to earn their livelihood. It becomes difficult to collect information about their incomes etc.

IMPORTANCE OF NATIONAL INCOME ESTIMATES

The following points indicate the great importance of accurate national income estimates in the economy of a country:

(1) An increasing national income is a symptom of growing economic progress. A decreasing national income, on the contrary is a symptom of economic deterioration in the country concerned.

(2) Since the national income estimates represent the monetary measure of the volume of production in a country in a year, they give us an idea of the aggregate production in the country concerned.

(3) The economic welfare of a country, as we know, is closely connected with the magnitude of its national income. An increase in the national income of a country, other things remaining the same, also implies an increase in the economic welfare of the community.

(4) The national income estimates give an idea of the rate of national income growth in a country. The rate of national income growth also represents, it should be remembered, the rate of growth of the economy concerned. Hence, from this point of view, the national income estimates are of great importance for the economy of a country.

(5) The national income estimates throw light on the contributions of the various sectors of the economy to the gross national product of the country concerned. These estimates also reveal the comparative importance of the various sectors in the national economy.

(6) The national income estimates also throw light on the volume of consumption, saving and investment in the economy. The level of consumption shows the level of economic welfare in society, while saving and investment determine the economic growth of a country.

(7) By comparing national income estimates of different countries, we can compare their standards of living and the levels of economic welfare achieved by them.

(8) The national income estimates also show how the national income of a country is distributed among the various sections of the population. An increase in the share of labour (*i.e.*, wages) out of the national income is a clear indication that the economic inequalities are lessening in the country concerned.

(9) Economic planning is the order of the day. All countries whether socialist or capitalist or mixed are increasingly resorting to planned economic development through five year plans. Now this formulation of economic plans is

simply not possible without reliable estimates of national consumption, national saving and national investment. No economic plan can, indeed, be formulated without adequate national income statistics. Further, the evaluation of the working of the economic plans is also not possible without reliable national income etimates.

(10) It needs hardly be said that national income estimates are indispensable for the formulation of economic policy of government. No government can formulate a correct, realistic and well balanced economic policy without having at its disposal correct and realiable estimates about the volume and distribution of national income in the country concerned.

CHANGES IN THE SIZE AND DISTRIBUTION OF NATIONAL INCOME

National income is sometimes looked upon as a measure and index of economic welfare of a country. An improvement in the per capita income of the country is treated as proof of the increased economic welfare of the people of that country. Likewise, a country with a higher per capita income is supposed to enjoy greater economic welfare (or, a higher standard of living) than a country with a lower per capita income. Let us now examine the question: How far is national income a reliable index of economic welfare?

Let us see what economic welfare is and how does it differ from non-economic welfare. Total welfare is genraly divided into two parts: *(i)* economic welfare, and *(ii)* non-economic welfare. Proof. Pigou has distinguished economic welfare (from non-economic welfare) as "that part of social welfare that can be brought directly or indirectly into relation with the measuring rod of money." Thus, according to Pigou, economic welfare is that part of total welfare, which can be expressed in monetary terms directly or indirectly. Non-economic welfare, on the contrary, is that part of total welfare which is not amenable to money measurement.

Let us now revert to the question with which we started this section: How far is national income, a reliable index of economic

welfare. The answer to this question is not so easy because several factors have to be taken into account before we arrive at any positive conclusion. The following points have to be borne in mind before arriving at any positive conclusion.

(1) Since the national income is generally measured in terms of current monetary values, a rise or fall in the general price-level will cause the national income to rise or fall even though there is no change in the actual production of goods and services in the economy.

(2) As already emphasized earlier, the national income estimates take into account only those transactions which are carried through the medium of money. The nominal value of the national income of a country may increase in one year simply because some activity which was previously carried on without the use of money is now being conducted with the help of money, even though there has been no change in the real supply of goods and services being produced in the economy. For example, if the farmers in a country decide to keep a smaller proportion of their food-output at home for self-consumption (or, decide to bring a larger proportion of it in the market for sale), the nominal value of the national income of the country will increase, though there is no increase in rhe total output of food in the economy.

(3) Even the per capita income is not a fool-proof index of economic welfare An increase in per capita income may not necessarily be accompanied by an increase in the economic welfare of the community. Suppose, the national income of a country increases and the per capita income also increases. But the increase in the national income may be due more to the production of capital goods than to the output of consumer goods. Though the national income (and also the per capita income) has increased due to the faster output of capital goods, it indicates little or no improvement in the economic welfare of the people.

(4) The national income total may not reveal the true picture of an economy. A rise in national income does not necessarily mean a rise in the living standard (or, the economic welfare) of the people. If the national income of a country increases, but its population increases at a faster rate, to per capita income will certainly decline, and along

with it, the economic welfare of the people will also go down. Per capita income is, therefore, a better index than the national income total of the economic welfare of a community.

(5) An increase in per capita income may not indicate an improvement in the economic welfare of the community for another reason. The national output, no doubt, increases (and consequently, the income per capita also increases), but there may be a change in the composition of national output in favour of war-goods. An increase in the production of war-goods though it may increase the national income (and also per capita income), will not increase the economic welfare of the people. War-goods like arms and ammunitions may increase the fighting capacity of the nation, but they do not increase the economic welfare of the community.

(6) To enquire whether the increased national income has increased economic welfare, we have also to take into account the distribution of the increased income. A rise in the national income does not necessarily imply a rise in everyone's income. If the increased national income goes into the pockets of the richer sections, it is possible that the other sections may even be poorer than before. Some people, no doubt, will be better off than before, but the decline in the welfare of the poor may be greater than the increase in the welfare of the rich. Hence, economic welfare as a whole may be reduced.

(7) An increase in the total of the national income (or, per capita income) should also be interpreted with reference to the general economic environments in which it has been brought about. Higher national income may have been brought about by employing women and children or by forcing the workers to work for long hours (without holidays) under extremely insanitary conditions, or by resorting to industrial conscription and forced direction of labour. In all such cases, the rise in the national income will not indicate a rise in the economic welfare of the people.

8. Finally, if an increase in the national income is accompanied by a deterioration in the tastes of the people or a decline in public morality, the economic welfare of the people may actually be reduced consequent upon the increase in national income. For example, as the

national income increases beyond a point, the people of the country may spend their increased incomes on drinking, gambling and other evil things, which by reducing the non-economic welfare, will ultimately reduce the economic welfare of the people also.

We, thus, arrive at the conclusion that neither national income nor per capita income can be a true index of economic welfare. If the national income or income per capita of a country rises, we should not straightway jump to the conclusion that the economic welfare of the people of that country has increased. We should pronoune our judgment only after taking into account the above-mentioned points.

CONTRIBUTION OF KEYNES TO NATIONAL INCOME ANALYSIS

Keynes' contributions to national income analysis are of a revolutionary nature. According to Prof. K. Kurihara, "Largely as a result of Keynes analytical contribution, we non have national income analysis which consists in *(a)* analysis of income formation and propagation, *(b)* analysis of the relevant factors affecting the behaviour of the components of national income, and *(c)* analysis of the effects of the change in any particular element of national income on general activity and particularly on the level of employment." Prior to the appearance of the General Theory, national income data were not collected officially. Keynes put life into dead national income figures, by demonstrating how consumption and investment expenditures can affect the income stream and lead to booms and busts, inflation and deflation. By advocating the policy of public works, Keynes created awareness amongst governments about the speedy collection of national income data, with a view to timing the execution of policies at the first sign of depression or inflation. The government budgets have been a revolutionary change. We owe the ideas of inflationary and deflationary gaps to Keynes, which have been so useful in a voiding wartime inflation and post war recessions. The main contributions of Keynes to national income analysis are as follows:

(1) Keynesian income analysis has enabled us to classify all spending into spending on consumption goods (C) and spending on

investment goods (I) reducing the complex elements of spending into simple variables, thereby making the process of income generation understandable (Y = C + I).

(2) The basic income equation Y = C + I, of Keynes, has all the variables in monetary terms. We have already read that every monetary transaction has two aspects—as one man's income is another man's expenditure. It has, therefore, become possible to carry on dynamic income-expenditure analysis.

(3) Keynesian income analysis has further facilitated the determination and verification of the quantitative relations of macro-units such as income, consumption, saving and investment.

(4) The classical belief in the tacit assumption of full employment (*i.e.*, constant aggregate output) has given place to the determination of the level of aggregate output and employment *i.e.*, the determination of factors which affect the level of employment at any particular time, may be full employment, under employment or overfull employment.

(5) National income data as obtained through the Keynesian income—expenditure approach forms the basis of public policy, monetary as well as fiscal, both with respect to inflation and deflation.

(6) Keynesian national income studies enables us to give more attention to the neglected problem of income distribution, thereby establishing a relationship of inadequate output with unequal distribution of wealth—which are the two basic evils of our society according to D.H. Robertson.

With the appearance of General Theory a new lease has been given to the national income 'analysis. So large has been the impact of Keynes on national income accounting that there is now no country. however backward, which does not have an organisation for collection of data. Advanced countries have gone a step further to prepare 'flow of funds' accounts which will help in having a still clearer picture of the economy, which forms the basis of Keynesian employment theory.

CAUSES OF INCOME INEQUALITIES

Following are the main causes which lead to the emergence of income inequalities in capitalist economy.

(1) Heredity. All persons are not born alike. Some are endowed with intelligence while others are not. Some have better physique, while others are sickly. This makes all the difference in life. The physically and mentally better-endowed persons get a better start in life and are more successful than their less-endowed fellowmen. Heredity, thus, is an important cause of income inequalities.

(2) Differences in Jobs. Income inequalities arise mainly from differences in jobs. Some jobs carry fat salaries while others fetch grossly inadequate earnings to the holders. Persons engaged in trade and industry earn fabulous income particularly during times of inflation and all-round shortages. This creates an enduring basis for income inequalities in a country.

(3) Environment. All children are not brought up in the same environment. Those born in rich, affluent, and influential families have a better start in life through better education, better training and social influence. Those born in poor families residing in slums, are denied the opportunity to receive adequate nutrition, proper education and effective training to qualify for better and more lucrative jobs. This results in inequality of opportunity which is the basic cause of income inequality.

(4) Private Property. Private property which is a sacred institution in a capitalist economy is, indeed, the root cause of income inequality. Under capitalism, a person is free to hold any property he likes. He Can own a farm or a firm or a house or a coal mine. Property once acquired by a person continues multiplying and enlarging itself with the passage of time. Those owning properties derive large incomes which are the major causes of income inequalities in a capitalist economy. The propertied class is a rich, influential and resourceful class under capitalism. Differences in property thus constitute fruitful cause of income inequality.

(5) Social Background. The job that a person is able to secure is determined today more by his social background and social contacts than by his own ability and competence. The result is that men of even ordinary intelligence succeed in getting lucrative posts in the private or the public sector institutions through family influence. Brilliant young men, or the contrary, with no social contacts have to remain contented with ordinary jobs, carrying meagre salaries.

(6) Inheritance. Inheritance is another importance feature of a capitalist society. Under this, the wealth is transmitted from one generation to another without any restrictions. It is true that inheritance is not an original cause of economic inequalities, but it does perpetuate income inequalities by transmitting property from the father to the son. The inequalities of today are thus transformed into the inequalities of tomorrow.

MEASURE TO REDUCE INCOME INEQUALITIES

The socialist countries have tried to abolish income inequalities through the abolition of private property and the socialization of the means of production, like farms, factories, mines, etc. But they have not succeeded in abolishing income inequalities altogether. Income inequalities continue to persist even now in these countries though not on as large a scale as in capitalist countries. We can suggest the following measures to reduce income inequalities in a capitalist country:

(1) Steeply Graded Wealth Tax. A steeply graded wealth-tax will also have the effect of lessening economic inequalities in a capitalist country. By reducing glaring disparities in the distribution of wealth, this tax will certainly take away the basis of income disparities.

(2) Highly Progressive Income-tax. The imposition of a highly progressive income-tax can go a long way in reducing income inequalities in a capitalist country. This will prevent the rich from becoming richer. High income-taxation will have to be supplemented by other direct taxes like capital gains tax, excess profits tax, expenditure tax, etc.

(3) Death Duty or Estate Duty. The imposition of highly progressive death duty will help to prevent the perpetuation of economic inequalities from generation to generation.

(4) Equality of Opportunity. To have relative income equality, it is essential to ensure equality of opportunity to all the citizens residing in the country. This implies that all children, whether born in rich or poor families, should have equal chances to develop their genius. They should have equal opportunities of getting education, training and jobs or of getting a start in private trade and industry. The State may give special stipends or scholarships to the children of the poor and backward classes so that they could also have equal chances of acquiring the highest educational and technical qualification. Recruitment to government jobs be made through impartial agencies, like the Public Service Commissions, strictly on the basis of merit. The State may also extend loans on easy terms to persons of backward classes desirous of entering private trade and industry.

(5) Taxes on Luxuries. Heavy taxes on luxury items consumed by the rich like motor cars, T.V. sets, refrigerators, etc., will certainly curb the consumption of these commodities and help to promote in the country an atmosphere of social equality.

(6) Extension of Social Security Services. Extension of social security services like subsidized food, cheap housing, free medical aid, sickness allowances, unemployment benefit, provident fund, gratuity, social insurance and old age pensions will promote income inequalities in two ways. On the other hand, the expenditure on these schemes will be financed through taxation of the richer classes; and on the other, the benefits of these services will flow to the poorer classes. This then involves both levelling down and levelling up processes simultaneously.

(7) Fixation of Minimum Wage. To reduce income inequalities and to stop exploitation of the working class, the government may fix minimum wages for certain occupations and industries where the workers are being paid unduly low wages. Governments in several countries have already taken steps in this direction.

❑

18

Consumption Function

This law states that there is a common tendency for people to spend more on consumption when income increases, but not to the same extent as the rise in income, because a part of the income is also saved. The community as a rule, consumes as well as saves a larger amount with a rise in income. To quote Keynes in this context. "The fundamental psychological law upon which we are entitled to depend with great confidence, both a priori from our knowledge of human nature and from the detailed facts of experience, is that men are disposed, as a rule and on the average, to increase their consumption as their income increase, but not by as much as the increase in their income."

This Law is a statement of a tendency about which there can be little doubt in actual practice. The law is generally considered to be consisting of three related propositions:

(i) Then when the aggregate income increases, aggregate consumption expenditure also increases, but by a somewhat smaller amount. The reason is that as income increases, consumers wants get more and more satisfied with the result that it is no longer necessary to spend the additional increase in income on consumption. The expenditure on consumption is definitely increased but not in the same proportion in which the income increases.

(ii) That an increase of income will be divided in some proportion between saving and spending, although that proportion can be worked out in practice only after comprehensive empirical study. This proposition follows from the first proposition. It is evident that when the entire increase in income is not spent on consumption, a part of that increased income is saved. It is possible that, to start with, a person may not save because his income is too small, but as his income increases, he does like to save some portion of his increased income for the rainy day.

(iii) That an increase of income is unlikely to lead either to less spending or less saving than before. In other words, as the income of a person increases, his spending and saving both go up. It is not possible for a person to spend less when his income goes up, unless the happens to be a confirmed miser. A normal person will certainly increase his consumption expenditure when his income goes up. The reason is that he would like to enjoy greater amenities and comforts of life when his income increases. Consequently his spending and saving both go up when his income increases.

The first proposition is the most important and may be considered to be the core of Keynes' Psychological Law of Consumption. What the Law stresses is the tendency of people to fail to spend on consumption items the full amount of an increment of income. An illustration of this Law may be given in the Table below:

Table

(In crores of Rupees)

Income (Y)	*Consumption (C)*
1000	800
2000	1500
3000	2000
4000	2400
5000	2750
6000	3000

Looking at the above Table, it becomes evident that consumption expenditure does not increase in the same proportion in which the income increases. To start with, the income increases by Rs. 1,000 crore, but the consumption expenditure increases only by Rs. 700 crore. Again, when the income increases from Rs. 4,000 crore to Rs. 5,000 crore (*i.e.*, by Rs. 1000 crore) the consumption expenditure increases only from Rs. 2400 crore to Rs. 2750 crore (*i.e.*, only by Rs. 350 crore). Thus, the increase in consumption expenditure fails to keep pace with increase in aggregate income. This tendency is so deep-rooted in people's habits, customs, traditions and the psychological set-up that it is difficult to change it without effecting structural changes in society.

Assumptions of the Law

The operation of the Law depends upon three assumptions. If these assumptions are not realized, the Law shall fail to work. These assumptions may also be referred to as the limitations of the law. These are as follows:

(i) Propensity to consume will remain stable owing to the constancy of the existing psychological and institutional complexities influencing consumption expenditure.

(ii) It is assumed that there exists a wealthy capitalistic economy, in which there is no government restriction on consumption when income increases.

(iii) General economic conditions are normal and there are no abnormal and extraordinary circumstances such as war, revolution, inflation, etc.

Kurihara suggests that Keynes's Law, based on these assumptions, may be regarded as a rough approximation the actual macro-behaviour of free consumers in the normal short period.

IMPLICATIONS OF THE PSYCHOLOGICAL LAW OF CONSUMPTION

A more detailed analysis of Keynes's law shows that it has the following important implications:

(1) The vital point in the law is the tendency of people not to spend on consumption the full amount of an increase in their income. There is thus a "gap" between aggregate income and aggregate consumption. Assuming the consumption function to the stable during a short-run period, the "gap" will widen with an increase in income. This gives rise to the problem of investment. Investment should be increased to fill the gap between income and consumption. Keynes, therefore, stresses that investment is the crucial and initiating determinant of levels of income and employment. If investment fails to increase in a situation of increased incomes, output and employment will inevitably fall, unless, indeed, the consumption function rises to wipe out the gap between income and consumption. But, the short-run consumption function being stable, the investment function has to play a crucial role. Thus, for Keynes, it is the inadequacy of investment which accounts for the existence of unemployment. Evidently, it is intenaed to increase employment and income, one has to tackle the investment function, the second component of effective demand. Keynes's psychological law of consumption, thus, emphasises the crucial importance of investment in any programme of full or a high level of employment.

(2) This law also explains the unique nature of income generated in a community. Whenever the supply of money is increased in a community, the income does not increase in the same proportion in which the supply of money is increased. The people do not increase their consumption expenditure in the same proportion in which the income increases.

(3) An explanation of the turning points of a business cycle is also provided by this law. The upper turning point from a boom is caused by a collapse of the marginal efficiency of capital owing to the fact that consumption expenditure does not keep pace with increase in income during the prosperity phase. Similarly, the law explains the revival of the marginal efficiency of capital and the down turning point of recovery from a depression, on the basis of the fact that when income is reduced, a consumption expenditure does not decrease in the same proportion.

(4) Since the increase in consumption expenditure does not keep pace with the increase in income, there arises the danger of an over saving gap in the community. Rich and prosperous communites are exposed more to the danger of this over saving than poor backward communities.

THE CONSUMPTION FUNCTION

The consumption function or the propensity to consume is nothing but an expression of an empirical income-consumption relationship. In technical terms, Keynes postulates that cetries paribus consumption is a function of income. Algebraically, the relationship between consumption, as a dependent variable and total real income as the independent variable may be expressed as:

$$c = f(y)$$

where, *c* is the real aggregate consumption expenditure, y is the total real income and *f a* function of or depends upon. It must be noted here that Keynes mentions certain subjective and objective factors of co-determinants of consumption, but he considers real income as the principle variable upon which consumption depends.

In dealing with consumption function or the propensity to consume, Keynes considered its two technical attributes: *(i)* the average propensity to consume and *(ii)* the marginal propensity to consume, both having substantial economic significance.

(i) The concept of the average propensity to consume or APC indicates the ratio of aggregate consumption expenditure to aggregate income, *i.e.*, it is the ratio of *c* to *y* and is expected to c/y. If *y* and *c* are Rs. 1000 and Rs. 800 respectively then, APC is 800/1000 or 8/10 or 80 percent.

(ii) The marginal propensity to consume or MPC, on the other hand indicates low an additional increment of income will be divided between spending and saving. It may be defined as the rate of the change in the consumption upon the change. In Income, or as the rate of change in the average propensity as Income changes. The

MPC can be found by dividing an Increment (or decrement) in consumption by an increment (or, decrement) in income. Thus, the formula is $\frac{\Delta c}{\Delta y}$. The symbol D indicates the change in income or consumption. For example if Dc and Dy are 800 and 1000 respectively then the value of MPC is 800/1000 or 8/10 or 80 percent.

Table

Income (y)	*Consumption* (c)	*APC* $\left(\frac{c}{y}\right)$	*MPC* $\left(\frac{\Delta c}{\Delta y}\right)$
1000	800	.8	.8
2000	1600	.8	.8
3000	2400	.8	.8
4000	3200	.8	.8
5000	4000	.8	.8
6000	4800	.8	.8

The distinction between APC and MPC can be illustrated diagrametically. The income (y) and consumption (c) are on x and y axis respectively. The curve *cc* represents the propensity to consume or consumption function. When the level of income is Rs. 4,000 and 3200 consumption is 3,200 then APC is therefore $\frac{3200}{4000}$ = 80 per cent or .8. The MPC can also be illustrated diagrammatically. In the diagram when the level of income rises from Rs. 4000 to Rs. 5000 then the level of consumption increase from Rs. 4000 to Rs. 4800.

Hence MPC is $\frac{\Delta c}{\Delta y} = \frac{800}{1000} = \frac{8}{10}$ or 0.8.

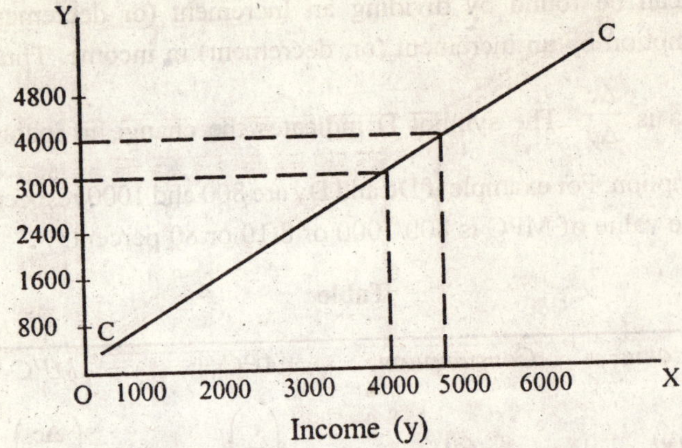

The concept of MPC is of vital importance in employment theory. It throws light on the possible division of additional income between consumption and saving. It also tells us how the extra income will be divided between consumption and investment because in the Keynesian system saving is, in the ultimate analysis, equal to investment.

If the MPC (marginal propensity to consume) is known, the MPS (marginal propensity to save) can be easily derived. The formula is 1-MPC or $1-\frac{\Delta c}{\Delta y}$. In the above example, if the MPC is 0.6 then the MPS must be 0.4. The MPC + MPS are equal to one. If one quantity is known, the other quantity can be easily derived, the reason being that the income of the community is divided between saving and spending. If spending is a known quantity, then saving can be easily derived by deducting spending from income. It should be noted that MPC must always be positive and less than 1.

The MPC is higher in the case of poor than in the case of rich people. The greater is any man's income, the more of his basic human needs will have already been satisfied and greater will be the tendency for him to save in order to provide for the future. The MPS (Marginal Propensity to Save) of the richer classes is greater than that of poorer classes. If, at any time, it is desired to increase aggregate consumption then the purchasing power should be transferred from the richer (with a lower propensity to consume) to the poorer classes (with a higher propensity to consume). Likewise, if it is desired to reduce community consumption, the purchasing power must be taken away from the poorer classes by taxing consumption.

EMPIRICAL RELATIONSHIP BETWEEN APC AND MPC

The two consumption propensities are closely interrelated.

(i) When the MPC is constant, the consumption function is linear, *i.e.* a straight line curve. The APC will also be constant only if the consumption function passes through the origin. When it does not pass through the origin, the APC will not be constant.

(ii) As income rises, the MPC also falls, but it falls to a greater extent than the APC.

(iii) As income falls, the MPC rises, The APC will also rise but at a slower rate.

FACTORS DETERMINING PROPENSITY TO CONSUME

According to Keynes, two types of factors influence the consumption function: subjective and objective. The subjective factors and endogenous or internal to the economic system itself. The subjective factors relate to psychological characteristics of human nature, social structure, social institutions and social practices.

The objective factors affecting the consumption function are exogenous, or external to the economy itself. These factors may at times undergo rapid changes. Thus, objective factors may cause in the consumption function.

Subjective Factors

Subjective factors basically underlie and determine the form of the consumption function (*i.e.* its slope and position).

The subjective factors concerned are: *(i)* behaviour patterns fixed by the psychology of human nature, and *(ii)* institutional arrangements of the modern social order, and social pactices relating to the behaviour patterns of business firms with respect to wage and dividend payments and retained earnings, and the institution controlling the distribution of income.

Human behaviour regarding consumption and savings out of increased income depends on psychological motives. First, there are motives which "lead individuals to refrain from spending out of their incomes." Keynes enlists eight such motives:

(1) The Motive of Foresight. The desire to provide for anticipated future needs, *e.g.* in relation to old age, family education, etc.

(2) The Motive of Precaution. The desire to build up a reserve against unforeseen contingencies.

(3) The Motive of Improvement. The desire to enjoy a gradually increasing expenditure since it gratifies the common, instinct to look forward to a gradually improving standard of life rather than the contrary.

(4) The Motive of Calculation. The desire to enjoy interest and appreciation, because a larger real consumption, at a later date, is preferred to a smaller immediate consumption.

(5) The Motive of Avarice. The desire to satisfy pure miserliness, *i.e.* unreasonable, but insistent abstinence from expenditure as such.

(6) The Motive of Independence. The desire to enjoy a sense of independence and the power to do things.

(7) The Motive of Enterprise. The desire to secure a masse demanoeuvre to carry on speculation or establish business projects.

(8) The Motive of Pride. The desire to possess or to bequeath a fortune.

To this, Keynes adds a corresponding list of motives on consumption such as enjoyment, short-sightedness, generosity, miscalculation, ostentation and extravagance.

Subjective motivations also apply to the behaviour patterns of business corporations and governmental bodies. In this respect, Keynes listed the following motives for accumulation:

(1) The Motive of Enterprise. The desire to do big things, to expand, to secure resources to carry out further capital investment.

(2) The Motive of Financial Prudence. The desire to ensure adequate financial provision against depreciation and obsolescence and to discharge debt.

(3) The Motive of Liquidity. The desire to face emergencies and difficulties successfully.

(4) The Motive of Improvement. The desire to secure a rising income and to demonstrate successful management.

Keynes maintains that the strength of all these motives may very considerably according'to the institutions and the organisation of the economic society. Since economic and social institutions and organisations are formed by habits, race, education, morals, present hopes and past experiences, techniques of capital equipment and the prevailing distribution of wealth and established standards of life, all these factors are unlikely to vary in the short run. They therefore affect secular progress only very gradually. In other words, these factors, subject to slow change and over a long period, may be considered as given or stable.

Objective Factors

Objective factors, subject to rapid changes and causing violent shifts in the consumption function are considered below:

(1) Money Income. It is an important factor affecting a community's propensity to consume. As community increases, conumption also increases; and as community income falls, consum ption also decreases.

(2) Financial Policies of Corporations. The policies of joint stock companies and corporations with respect to dividend payments and investment also affect consumption in various ways. If corporations and companies keep more reserves and distribute less of their profits as dividends, it will lower the disposable income with consumers. On the other hand, if more income is distributed in the form of dividends, more will be spent on consumption.

(3) Distribution of Income. Another factor determining how much will be spent for consumption out of a given income of the community is the way in which income is distributed. There is great inequality in the distribution of income in the modern capitalist societies with the result that the rich find it easy to save. This widespread inequality of income lowers the overall propensity to consume as the rich have already fulfilled most of their basic wants. A more equal distribution of wealth will go to raise the propensity to consume.

(4) Windfall Gains or Losses. Sudden and unexpected gains and losses in income affect consumption accordingly. It is believed that the well-to-do increase their consumption well above the normal level as a result of windfall gains. In the late twenties, there were huge windfall gains on account of the boom conditions in the American economy and the consumption function shifted upwards. Keynes gave specific recognition to the possibility that consumtion spending might be influenced not only by income but by capital gains.

(5) Changes in Expectations. The expectations of the people regarding the future events also affect the propensity to consume. Individuals may rush to purchase goods much in excess of current needs, if they expect a war or fear a shortage on account of any other reason. Thus, the amount of consumption as a ratio of current income will rise and consumption function will shift upwards (without any rise in income).

(6) Fiscal Policy. The fiscal policy of the Government relating to taxation, expenditure and public debt, and the changes therein have significant effect on the consumption function. The Government's fiscal policy resulting in highly progressive tax system brings about more equitable distribution of income, thereby shifting the consumption function upwards, as more equal distribution of wealth increases the propensity to consume. On the other hand, a regressive tax structure (involving heavy indirect taxes) will reduce total consumption in the economy.

(7) Terms of Credit and Consumer Durables. Terms of credit specially relating to consumer durables like electric gadgets, machines, radios, television-sets, cars, scooters etc., constitute an important influence on consumption expenditure. Recenitly, not to speak of advanced economies but even in developing economies like India there has been a considerable increase in the volume of purchases of consumer durables financed by consumer credit; as such its cost and availability have assumed great importance. Besides, the rate of interest, the size of down payments, length of the periods during which balances must be paid are important considerations affecting consumer expenditures.

(8) Demographic Factors. Even at a given level of income, the expenditure of consumer may vary widely from one family to another. These variations in expenditure are due to demographic factor which include factors like thc size of the family, stage in the family 'life cycle', place of residence, occupation etc. Large families spend more than small families-families with children of college-going age have different pattern of expenditure than of school-going age. Usually urban families spend more than rural families. Demographic factors like age, sex composition of families occur over a long period and may, therefore, be ignored in short-run analysis.

(9) Wages and Propensity to Consume. Classical economists laid stress on the stimulating effects of wage-cuts on the propensity to consume. Their argument was that a general reduction in wages will result in a general reduction in prices (because marginal costs fall on account of the pressure of lower wage rates). The lower prices will increase consumption. But such an approach represent a vague attempt to apply certain principles relating to the price and demand for a particular product to the problem of total consumption. Actually, the effects of wage-cuts are likely to be more un favourable on the propensity to consume. It has been found that wage-cuts may result in more unequal distribution of income as it may be shifted from high consuming groups (the poor) to the high saving groups (the rich) and thus, may lower rather than raise the consumption function. When the wages are cut while the incomes of other groups, like rentiers and businessmen remain the same, the wage-profit relationship will be upset. While wages fall, profit and rent continue to increase. As a result, the propensity to consume of the workers is adversely affected because their purchasing power is reduced as a result of wage-cuts. Further, if the general cut in money-wages is expected to be repeated over and over again, consumers will tend to withhold their demand in anticipation of a further fall in prices, thereby shifting the saving function upwards and depressing the consumption function. It is, therefore, clear wage-cuts, by redistributing the income in favour of the groups with lower marginal propensity to consume (and high MPS), will cause income and output, as also the employment, to decline.

(10) Rate of Interest. If the rate of interest rises, people will consumes less and save more in order to take advantage of the higher rate of interest. On the other hand, if the rate of interest falls, people will consume more and save less.

SIGNIFICANCE OF THE CONCEPT OF CONSUMPTION FUNCTION

It has been widely agreed that the Keynes concept of the consumption function is an outstanding contribution of economic thought. Hansen aptly remarked that "Keynes's analysis of the consumption function is a major landmark in the history of economic doctrines." In fact, this concept has revolutionised the entire economic thinking in modern times. Briefly, we may mention the points of its significance as under:

(1) In the short-run, since the consumption function is assumed to be a stable phenomenon, it stresses the importance of investment in the theory of employment and income. From the stability principle

of the propensity to consume. Keynes draws the conclusion that "employment can only increase pari-passu with an increase in the investment." Thus, investment is regarded as a crucial factor, determining employment in the short-run. It, then, inevitably follows that in order to increase the level of employment, investment should be increased.

(2) The concept of the consumption function provided, for the first time, a satisfactory explanation of the up and down in the trade cycle. According to the Keynesian theory, the upper-turning point (or the down-turn from prosperity), is due to the marginal propensity to consume being less than unity. The tendency to save more and more and consume less and less (in terms of percentage) as income increases during a prosperity phase, tends to undermine the strength of a boom, which ultimately gives way to a slump. Thus, Keynes directly explains in terms of a sudden collapse of the marginal efficiency of capital, which is primarily due to decline in the demand for consumption goods as a result of less and less aggregate consumption expenditures from arising income. Similarly, Keynes's doctrine of the consumption function indicates that a severe depression is arrested by the fact that consumption does not decrease as rapidly as income decreases. Thus, the concept of consumption function throws a spotlight on the theory of trade cycle too.

(3) On the basis of the principles of consumption function, Keynes was able to prove the validity of Say's Law of Markets, which was a fundamental postulate of the classical theory. By showing that consumption expenditure rises proportionately less than an increase in income, Keynes ruled out the poss:bility of supply always creating its own demand—the dictum of Say's Law. The nature of the propensity to consume, as described by Keynes, easily proved not only the possibility but also the probability of supply exceeding demand leaving to over production and large-scale unemployment. As a matter of fact, Keynesian hypothesis, of the marginal propensIty to consume being less than unity, implies that all that taken off the market (spent) as income increases. In other words, all that is produced is not demanded. Thus, supply exceeds

demand which ultimately results in general oveproduction and mass unemployment, because the entrepreneurs will fail to get back in sales receipts an amount equal to that which must justify current output. Thus, the refutation of Say's Law implies that the economy is not self-adjusting and that there is a necessity of conscious public control to avert general overproduction and unemployment.

(4) Finally, the concept, especially the term "marginal propensity to consume," is very useful in explaining the multiplier theory and process of income propagation in the Keynesian theory of income and employment. The MPC being less than unity serves as a major leakage from the generation of income stream, through consumption expenditure flow turn by turn-which reduces the magnifying effect of the multiplier to a considerable extent.

We may, thus, conclude that the Keynes's' formulation of the consumption function is an epoch-making contribution to the tools of economic analysis.

MEASURES TO INCREASE CONSUMPTION SPENDING

Keynes rightly pointed out that it is difficult to affect people's consumption behaviour in the short period. In the long run, however, propensity to consume can be raised by certain measures. These are:

(1) Wage and Income Policy. A long-run increasing wage rate policy can help in raising the consumption schedule of the wages earners and salaried people.

(2) Redistribution of Income. By taxing the rich class progressively, and by providing subsidies to the poor people, and egalitarian redistribution of income is made which can favourably affect the consumption function.

(3) Consumer's Credit. Liberal consumption loans and the development of hire-purchase schemes in the sale of durable consumer goods can also stimulate the propensity to consume of average families.

(4) Social Security. A well-devised scheme of social security measures, such as old-age pension, unemployment relief, employment insurance, etc. can give security to the working class, which would definitely create a favourable effect in raising their propensity to consume. Economists like Kurihara have recommended an extensive system of social security for achieving a high consumption economy, in order to solve the problem of "paradox of thrift", in wealthy nations.

(5) Urbanisation Trend. With economic progress because of widespread urbanisation in the economy, peoples' habit may change and their propensity to consume improve. The demonstration effect of the urban living in rural areas too help in this matter to some extent.

(6) Tax Reduction. A reduction in direct taxes would increase a disposable income of the people so that they may become inclined to consume more. Again, a reduction in commodity taxation such as sales tax, excise duties, etc. will also improve the purchasing power of the people while the relative cheapness of the goods will induce them to consume more.

(7) Advertisement and Sales Propaganda. A constant publicity drive through advertisement and sales propaganda influences the psychology of the consumers and they may be induced to spend more.

□

19

Investment Function

The term "investment" is applied to the production of goods not meant for immediate consumption but to be used in further production. The investment includes the purchase of stocks and shares, government bonds, equities etc. on the stock exchange. The meaning of investment in the Keynesian sense is a little different from its ordinary sense. In Keynesian sense, merely buying existing stocks and shares or bounds or equities would not constitute investment. It may be required as financial investment, but certainly not real investment. In Keynesian sense investment means real investment *i.e.*, the purchase of securities, bonds or equities of the new companies. In other words it means addition to the existing stocks of real capital stocks." When we buy existing securities or bonds, it does not mean addition to the real capital assets. It simply means transfer of rights from one party to another. While one party has made the investment, another party has made disinvestment. The investment of one party is cancelled against the disinvestment of the other party. There has been no not addition to employment. The investment in Keynesian sense imply the increase in the plant and equipment, stock of finished goods and inventories. In other words, Keynesian investment implies the creation of new capital goods such as machinery, factory buildings and stores and it directly create additional job and new output.

TYPES OF INVESTMENT

Investment may be private investment or public investment; it may be induced or autonomous, it may be gross investment or net investment; it may be financial investment or real investment; it may be planned or unplanned investment. According to Hicks, investment is of two types, induced as described above, and autonomous it is independent of variations.

(1) Induced and Autonomous Investment—Induced investment is that investment which changes with a change in income, that is why it is called income elastic. In a free enterprise capitalist economy, investments are induced by profit-motive. Such investment is very responsive to changes in income *i.e.*, induced investment increases as income increases. The shape of the induced investment curve, therefore, is upward sloping, indicating a rise in investment as a result of a rise in income.

Induced Investment in income. The autonomous investment is independent of variations in output. Explaining autonomous investment, Hicks remarks; "Public investment, investment which occurs in direct response to inventions and much of the long range investment (as Mr. Harrod calls it) which is only expected to pay for itself over a long period, all of these can be regarded as autonomous investments." Autonomous investment is not sensitive to changes in income. In other words, it is independent of income changes and is not guided or induced by profit-motive only. Autonomous investments are made primarily by the Government and are not based on considerations of profit. Autonomous investments are a peculiar feature of a war or a planned economy, for example, expenditures on arms and equipment to strengthen the defence of India may be called autonomous investment as it is incurred irrespective of the level of income or profits. The curve of autonomous investment is represented by a stratight line running from left to right and parallel to the horizontal income axis. The distinction between induced and autonomous investment it is shown in the diagrams below:

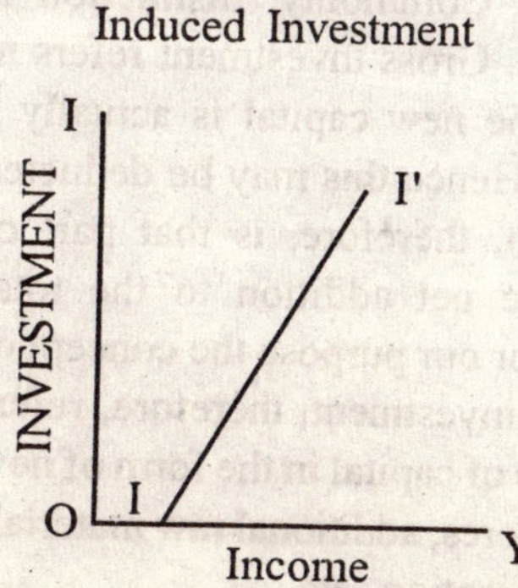

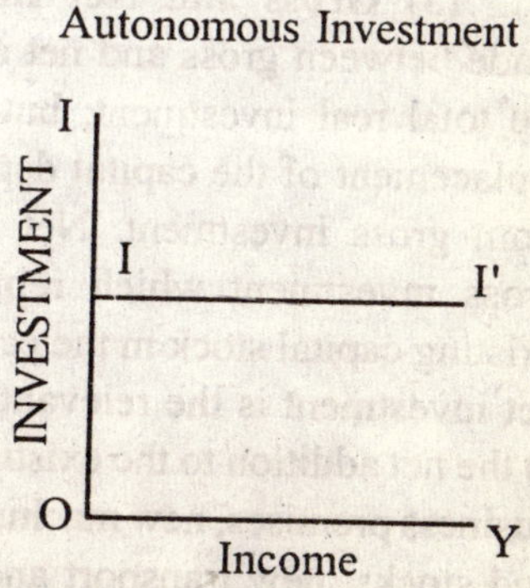

(2) Financial and Real Investment. When a peson makes a deposit in a bank, it is an investment from his point of view as he will be getting an interest income out of it; but nothing new has been created and there is no increase in the volume of capital for the economy. Again, when a person buys shares from someone, he is investing but then the seller of the shares has actually disinvested. Likewise, when a person buys a house from another, the former has invested, while the latter has disinvested. In all these examples, the total volume of real capital remains the same. These are examples of financial investments which are investments from the point of view of individuals but are of no significance from the point of view of the economy as a whole.

On the other hand, when a person puts up factory or a workshop, he has invested and no one has disinvested. The new factory or workshop represents net addition to the existing total productive capacity of the economy. His act of investment is important not only for him, but also for the economy. From the point of view of the economy, it is the real investment which is important. At the same time, it is not always correct to assert that financial and real investments are two separate things. In fact, except in those situations where financial investment relates to the purchase of old shares or old assets by someone from someone else, it leads to a simultaneous increase in the real investment. Thus, when an individual purchases shares of a new company, the financial investment will really represent real investment.

(3) Gross and Net Investment. Commonly, distinction is made between gross and net investment. Gross investment refers to the total real investment; but part of the new capital is actually a replacement of the capital depreciated. Hence this may be deducted from gross investment. Net investment, therefore, is that part of gross investment which represents the net addition to the total existing capital stock in the economy. For our purpose the concept of net investment is the relevant one. Net investment, therefore, refers to the net addition to the existing volume of capital in the form of new business premises, new machinery and stores, additional raw materials and stocks, new transport and communication, etc.

(4) Planned and Unplanned Investment. Net investment may be planned or unplanned (*i.e.*, unintended. Planned investment implies a deliberate addition to the existing volume of capital through addition to inventory stock or installation of an additional machine. It is motivated by larger sales or by anticipation regarding favourable price changes, profit margins,etc. Unplanned or unintended investment takes place when unsold finished goods accumulate on account of poor sales. Keynes did not attach much importance to this classification of investment.

(5) Induced and Autonomous Investment. Investment is also sometimes classified as induced investment and autonomous investment. Induced investment is induced by the profit-motive. It is also referred to as profit-motivated investment. It occurs in response to actual or anticipated increases in outlays for specific existing projects. Among the important causes of induced investment are income-gains and population growth which lead to a greater demand for goods and services. In general, therefore, induced investment is a expenditure for additional equipment in order to produce greater quantities of a given commodity or service. The induced investment curve is an upward sloping curve indicating an increase in investment as the result of an increase in income or price-level or population growth. Induced investment is invariable made by private entrepreneurs.

Autonomous investment, in contrast, is independent of economic activity. It occurs independently of rising economic activity as a result, for example, of the introduction of new products or processes. This type of investment is not responsive to changes in income, prices, or population growth. It is autonomous of these economic changes. That is why it is said to be income-inelastic. The autonomous investment curve is represented by a straight line running from left to right and parallel to the X-axis or income-axis. This type of investment is also autonomous of the profit-motive. Such a type of investment is often undertaken by the State in a war or a planned economy.

MEASURES TO STIMULATE INVESTMENT

The various fiscal, monetary and other measures to stimulate investment are enumerated below. We have already seen the various measures which stimulate consumption, it is therefore, natural and, useful to examine the measures that stimulate investment:

(1) Government Spending. The level of investment can also be stimulated by Government investment. There are many socially useful investments like construction of dams, roads, low-cost housing, slum clearance, recreation houses etc., which are essential from the point of view of the community but which are not undertaken by private businessmen because they do not ensure quick profits. Direct investment by Government in the United States in these socially desirable projects ensured full employment and led to favourable multiplier effects. This type of government spending may assume the nature of compensatory public spending which is incurred on the assumption that private investment, left to itself, is no longer capable of maintaining full employment either in the short-run or in the long. run. Keynes, therefore, stressed the need for public investment as a balancing factors, when the economy happens to pass through a period of depression.

(2) Tax Concessions. It is argued that tax concessions allowed on company and corporation profits would stimulate investment during depression period and will work as a great incentive for new entrepreneurs. Many economists like Hansen, Lerner and Klein have supported this view. Doubts have, however, been expressed as to the efficacy of tax reductions to stimulate investment. Tax reductions on incomes lead to a loss in government revenues, which may be made up by indirect taxation on commodities thereby depressing the marginal propensity to consume and hence effective demand. Thus, whatever is gained on the one hand is lost on the other. Despite, it cannot, be denied that unduly heavy taxation does act as a great disincentive on new investment, as is perhaps the case in India.

(3) Pump Priming. Tax reductions may not encourage private investment. In order to cope with the deficiency of private investment, a programme of Pump Priming is necessary. Under it, public investment is undertaken not only to meet the deficiency of private spending but also to take the economy out ofthe depths of depression. The idea is to 'prime' the 'pump' of private spending. Once the economy starts working towards full employment, public investment is given up. Pump priming is a helpful policy not only as a method of financing but also as a method of spending. As a method of financing, it not only facilites investment but also stimulates credit expansion. Pump priming stimulates private investment through its magnifying effects on income *via* the multiplier.

(4) Wage Level. Sometimes, reduction in the wage level is suggested to increase the level of investment activity on the ground that reduction in wages will reduce the total wage bill and hence the cost of production thereby leading to a rise in the expected rate of profitability (MEC). Under such circumstances businessmen will be encouraged. But such an argument ignores the dual nature of wages. Wages are not only costs to employers but also incomes to workers, and if reduced considerably, may adversely affect the purchasing power of the workers and hence effective demand. Thus, the stimulating effects of wage reductions on investment are of doubtful validity.

(5) Rate of Interest. Keynes favoured for a long time in his earlier books a low rate of interest to stimulate private investment. Such a policy is based on the assumption that investment is sensitive to changes in the rate of interest. Monetary authorities, by increasing the quantity of money (other things remaining the same) can lower the rate of interest to give a fillip to investment activity. Low interest-rates especially give stimulus to investment in some sectors of the economy. For example, provision of low interest government loans has raised the activity in the construction of residential houses, establishment of co-operatives and transport facilities, etc., But in his 'General Theory' Keynes did not have much faith in the ability of the interest rate to stimulate investment. According to him, recent studies have shown that interest rate is more or less an insignificant factor affecting investment activity.

(6) Price Policy. Frequent fluctuations in prices have been found to be one of the important causes of the instability of private investment. Certain amount of stability in the price level, it is felt, will surely stimulate private investment. To achieve the objective of stability in prices, a price-support policy has been suggested. Such a policy implies open market operations in commodities, that is,

Government purchases and sales of certain storable commodities with a view to adjusting their supply to demand. When prices decline and the symptoms of overproduction appear the Government would make bulk purchases to prevent further fall in price. Similarly when prices rise, the Govt. would release the stock to prevent further rise in prices. In this way the Govt. attempts to sense some stability in prices which, in turn, will promote private investment.

(7) Abolition of Monopoly Privileges and Encouragement of Competition. Prof. Klein suggests that the abolition of certain monopoly privileges can serve as a stimulus to investment. He writes, "It is said that the patent system which grants at least 17 years monopolies on new inventions serves to decrease the volume of investment by holding innovations which would otherwise call for increase investment. The innovations are suppressed because they conflict with certain vested interests."

Similarly, when conditions are developed to encourage competition in the market by permitting easy entry of new firms, the volume of investment in the economy would definitely rise. In a country like India, relaxing the licensing system, development related to new firms, special priorities to the new sector, etc., can help in stimulating the rate of investment.

(8) Economic Planning. By an appropriate economic planning, creation of a suitable industrial base and the construction of social overhead capital, the volume of investment can be increased in an economy. In India, the volume of investment has increased considerably over a period of time due to the planning efforts.

(9) Technological Change and Innovation. When technological improvement takes place and the capital-output ratio tends to rise, the demand for capital increases which induces more investment in the capital goods sector. Again, there may be innovations like the introduction of the new products, new methods of production, new markets, etc., on account of which investment is likely to increase in the economy.

❑